STOCK
TRADER'S
ALMANAC
2 O 2 2

Jeffrey A. Hirsch & Christopher Mistal

WILEY

www.stocktradersalmanac.com

Editor in Chief	Jeffrey A. Hirsch
Editor Emeritus	Yale Hirsch
Director of Research	Christopher Mistal

For general information about our other products and services, please contact our Customer Care Department within the United States at 800-762-2974, outside the United States at 317-572-3993, or fax at 317-572-4002. For bulk or custom orders, please contact Special Sales at specialsales@wiley.com.

Wiley publishes in a variety of print and electronic formats and by print-on-demand. Some material included with standard print versions of this book may not be included in e-books or in print-on-demand. If this book refers to media such as a CD or DVD that is not included in the version you purchased, you may download this material at http://booksupport.wiley.com. For more information about Wiley products, visit our website at www.wiley.com.

ISBN: 978-1-119-84591-1 (paper)
ISBN: 978-1-119-84593-5 (ePDF)
ISBN: 978-1-119-84592-8 (ePub)
SKY10030555_101421

THE 2022 STOCK TRADER'S ALMANAC

CONTENTS

DIRECTORY OF TRADING PATTERNS & DATABANK

STRATEGY PLANNING AND RECORD SECTION

INTRODUCTION TO THE FIFTY-FIFTH EDITION

Once again, we have the honor of introducing the new edition of the *Stock Trader's Almanac*. The *Almanac* provides you with the necessary tools to invest successfully in the twenty-first century.

J.P. Morgan's classic retort "Stocks will fluctuate" is often quoted with a wink-of-the-eye implication that the only prediction one can make about the stock market is that it will go up, down, or sideways. Many investors agree that no one ever really knows which way the market will move. Nothing could be further from the truth.

We discovered that while stocks do indeed fluctuate, they do so in well-defined, often predictable patterns. These patterns recur too frequently to be the result of chance or coincidence. How else do we explain that since 1950 the Dow has gained 27726.69 points during November through April compared to just 6588.43 May through October? (See page 54.)

The *Almanac* is a practical investment tool. It alerts you to those little-known market patterns and tendencies on which shrewd professionals enhance profit potential. You will be able to forecast market trends with accuracy and confidence when you use the *Almanac* to help you understand:

■ How our presidential elections affect the economy and the stock market— just as the moon affects the tides. Many investors have made fortunes following the political cycle. You can be sure that money managers who control billions of dollars are also political cycle watchers. Astute people do not ignore a pattern that has been working effectively throughout most of our economic history.

■ How the passage of the Twentieth Amendment to the Constitution fathered the January Barometer. This barometer has an outstanding record for predicting the general course of the stock market each year, with only 11 major errors since 1950, for an 84.5% accuracy ratio. (See page 18.)

■ Why there is a significant market bias at certain times of the day, week, month and year.

Even if you are an investor who pays scant attention to cycles, indicators and patterns, your investment survival could hinge on your interpretation of one of the recurring patterns found within these pages. One of the most intriguing and important patterns is the symbiotic relationship between Washington and Wall Street. Aside from the potential profitability in seasonal patterns, there's the pure joy of seeing the market very often do just what you expected.

The *Stock Trader's Almanac* is also an organizer. Its wealth of information is presented on a calendar basis. The *Almanac* puts investing in a business framework and makes investing easier because it:

■ Updates investment knowledge and informs you of new techniques and tools.

■ Is a monthly reminder and refresher course.

■ Alerts you to both seasonal opportunities and dangers.

■ Furnishes a historical viewpoint by providing pertinent statistics on past market performance.

■ Supplies forms necessary for portfolio planning, record keeping and tax preparation.

 The WITCH icon signifies THIRD FRIDAY OF THE MONTH on calendar pages and alerts you to extraordinary volatility due to expiration of equity and index options and index futures contracts. Triple-witching days appear during March, June, September and December. Some readers have questioned why we do not use the term "quadruple witching," as some in the business do. As we point out on page 106 the market for single-stock and ETF futures remains small and their impact is virtually nonexistent. If and when single-stock futures trading volume expands and exerts influence on the market, we will reconsider. Until such time, we do not believe the term "quadruple witching" is applicable.

 The BULL icon on calendar pages signifies favorable trading days based on the S&P 500 rising 60% or more of the time on a particular trading day during the 21-year period January 2000 to December 2020.

 The BEAR icon on calendar pages signifies unfavorable trading days based on the S&P falling 60% or more of the time for the same 21-year period.

Also, to give you even greater perspective, we have listed next to the date every day that the market is open the Market Probability numbers for the same 21-year period for the Dow (D), S&P 500 (S) and NASDAQ (N). You will see a "D," "S" and "N" followed by a number signifying the actual Market Probability number for that trading day based on the recent 21-year period. On pages 123–130 you will find complete Market Probability Calendars, both long term and 21-year for the Dow, S&P and NASDAQ, as well as for the Russell 1000 and Russell 2000 indices.

Other seasonalities near the ends, beginnings and middles of months; options expirations, around holidays and other times are noted for *Almanac* investors' convenience on the weekly planner pages. All other important economic releases are provided in the Strategy Calendar every month in our e-newsletter, *Almanac Investor*, available at our website *www.stocktradersalmanac.com*.

One-year seasonal pattern charts for the Dow, S&P 500, NASDAQ, Russell 1000, and Russell 2000 appear on pages 42, 44 and 46. There are three charts each for the Dow and S&P 500 spanning our entire database starting in 1901 and one each for the younger indices. As 2022 is a midterm election year, each chart contains typical midterm election year performance compared to all years.

The Russell 2000 is an excellent proxy for small- and mid-caps, and the Russell 1000 provides a broader view of large caps. Annual highs and lows for all five indices covered in the *Almanac* appear on pages 151–155. Top 10 best and worst days, weeks, months, quarters and years for all five indices are listed on pages 172–181.

We have converted many of the paper forms in our "Strategy and Record" section into computer spreadsheets for our own internal use. As a service to our faithful readers, we are making these forms available at our website *www.stocktradersalmanac.com*.

Midterm election years have historically been the second worst year of the four-year cycle over multiple time frames. And they have been atrocious for first year democrats with an average loss of –0.2% for DJIA (see our 2022 Outlook on pages 8–9 for more). You can find all the market charts of midterm election years since the Depression on page 26, "Midterm Election Years: Where Bottom Pickers Find Paradise" on page 28, "Prosperity More Than Peace Determines the Outcome of Midterm Congressional Races" on page 30, "Why A 50% Gain in the Dow Is Possible From Its 2022 Low to Its 2023 High" on page 34, and "Midterm Election Time Unusually Bullish" on page 104.

Our 2022 Outlook on pages 10–11 projects a more cautious position than last year. "How to Trade Best Months Switching Strategies" appears on page 38. "Summer Market Volume Doldrums Drives Worst Six Months" is updated on page 50. Sector seasonalities, including several consistent shorting opportunities, appear on pages 94–98. On page 80 we have included some sage advice from an old friend and market legend in "Marty Zweig's Investing Rules."

We are constantly searching for new insights and nuances about the stock market and welcome any suggestions from our readers.

Have a healthy and prosperous 2022!

2022 OUTLOOK

From mid-March 2020 when Wall Street went into lockdown to late May 2020 when the new bull market was declared, the market flipped from near-unbridled optimism to deep despair and then back to hopefulness in about ten short weeks. By this time last year markets had rebounded like it was 1933 or 2009, but had paused below the old 2020 highs temporarily.

A combination of human resiliency, perseverance and ingenuity with monetary and fiscal support from the Feds fueled the steepest rebound on record since the 1932–1933 bull market that lead us out of the depths of the secular bear market low in the Great Depression. From the March 23, 2020, closing lows to the closing highs at the time of this writing DJIA is up 87%, S&P 500 is up 90% and NASDAQ is up 106%. The Federal Reserve and the federal government have done a commendable job keeping the spigots open and the economy flush with cash and supporting the immunologists, but our hats are off to the drug makers that developed safe and effective vaccines in record time.

Perhaps happy days are here again. But there is a relevant parallel to that past. While the 1930–1932 bear market was twenty times longer than the 40-day long shortest bear on record in 2020 and more than twice as deep, like 2020 it was an election year that was marked by a change in political party power in the White House with a one-term republican president being ousted by a democrat.

Like 1933 the current rally has gone strong into the middle of post-election year 2021. Markets gained little ground in the latter half of 1933 with an October low and a year-end rally, but no new high for the Dow. Our current outlook is for the market to bounce around in a mostly sideways trading range until Q4 2021 when we expect the yearend rally to push us to new highs this time around based on fundamentals, technicals, monetary policy and fiscal stimulus.

Next year is likely to be a different story for the market. Keeping with our comparison to President Franklin Delano Roosevelt's first term, after the Dow gained 66.7% (the second best yearly gain on record) in 1933 his first year in office, 1934 his second year, a midterm year, had a measly 4.1% DJIA gain.

Now that the market has soared past the 2020 highs, it's almost as if the shortest bear on record didn't even happen. But it did and this red-hot economy will likely slowdown and the snapback market rally will likely pause next year, opening up the potential for a garden-variety midterm-year correction or mild bear. Pent-up demand and free money have driven stocks to new heights with some help from innovative business people, both large and small, and some stellar science that created the vaccines.

But like the old Blood, Sweat & Tears classic track "Spinning Wheel" taught us: "What goes up must come down." So our outlook for midterm election year 2022 is less than sanguine. Midterm election years continue to be a volatile year for stocks as Republicans and Democrats vie for control for Congress, especially under new presidents. Incumbent presidents usually lose seats in the House of Representatives (see page 28) and with the razor-thin margins Dems have in both the House and Senate they could easily give up control of Congress in the midterms.

Post-election years have been improving and election years have been getting worse since way before Covid-19. But pre-election years continue to remain robust while midterm years have been persistently lackluster. The chart here of the "S&P 500 Midterm Election Year Seasonal Pattern 1946–2020" does not paint a rosy picture for 2022. Along with the pattern for all midterm years since WWII, we have overlaid the patterns for first-term midterm years, all democratic presidents midterm years as well as the second year of new democratic presidents.

All midterm years average an S&P 500 gain of about 6%, Democratic president midterm years average about 4%, but first-term midterm years average a loss of

–0.6% and the second year of new Democratic presidents have been down –2.3% on average. All four tend to hit an early year high in April at the end of the Best Six Months with a low point during the Worst Six Months May-October.

Inflation has reared its ugly head but we are in the transitory camp. Sure it will likely be higher than the recent past. The recent uptick of 5% CPI growth is more a product of the historic reopening. The job market, especially in the service industry, remains tight. The service industry was clearly hit the hardest. Soaring demand as the economy reopened quickly caught a lot of businesses flat-footed. Price gains also reflect temporary supply bottlenecks and sharp price drops in 2020 make inflation comparisons to 2021 look larger. When the dust settles the rate of inflation is likely to cool down later this year, if the bond market is any indication.

Seasonality and cycles have been back on track since September 2020 and that sets 2022 up for muted market gains. Covid-19 changed modern life and the market irreversibly. Jackets are no longer required and work from home is workable for many still. Crowds are less prevalent but traffic is arguably worse as less are comfortable on mass transit. Technology and commodities flourished as did all forms of innovation. Restaurants almost have to have a robust take-out option and outdoor seating. Is masked air travel here to stay and will we need a Covid-19 booster annually like we do for the flu? But all in all it looks like we made it to the other side of the pandemic and the market and economy have returned to their normal cycles and seasonal patterns.

After the summer doldrums and year-end 2021 rally we expect the market to stall in early 2022 at modest new highs toward the end of the Best Six Months (page 54). Then the usual disappointment with unmet promises from the incumbent administration will hold the market back through Q2–Q3 2022. This of course would create the next great buying opportunity. The perennial sweet spot of the 4-Year Cycle (page 82) is from Q4 midterm year to Q2 pre-election year where a "50% Gain in the Dow is Possible from Its 2022 Low to Its 2023 High" (page 34). NASDAQ averages a 70% gain from its midterm low to its pre-election year high.

So unless the market crumbles this year under non-transitory inflation or some exogenous event, enjoy the post-pandemic rally, but be prepared for gains to be harder to come by in 2022 and be ready to pounce on the usual midterm bottom. Longer term our May 2010 Super Boom Forecast when the Dow was around 10,000 for the Dow to reach 38,820 by the year 2025 may still be ahead of schedule. (Check out the update of the Super Boom Forecast in the April 11, 2019, subscriber alert on our website.)

Jeffrey A. Hirsch, June 22, 2021

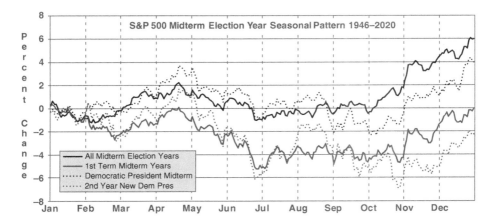

2022 STRATEGY CALENDAR

(Option expiration dates circled)

	MONDAY	TUESDAY	WEDNESDAY	THURSDAY	FRIDAY	SATURDAY	SUNDAY
JANUARY	27	28	29	30	31	1 JANUARY New Year's Day	2
	3	4	5	6	7	8	9
	10	11	12	13	14	15	16
	17 Martin Luther King Day	18	19	20	(21)	22	23
	24	25	26	27	28	29	30
FEBRUARY	31	1 FEBRUARY	2	3	4	5	6
	7	8	9	10	11	12	13
	14 ♥	15	16	17	(18)	19	20
	21 Presidents' Day	22	23	24	25	26	27
MARCH	28	1 MARCH	2 Ash Wednesday	3	4	5	6
	7	8	9	10	11	12	13 Daylight Saving Time Begins
	14	15	16	17 ♣ St. Patrick's Day	(18)	19	20
	21	22	23	24	25	26	27
APRIL	28	29	30	31	1 APRIL	2	3
	4	5	6	7	8	9	10
	11	12	13	(14)	15 Good Friday	16 Passover	17 Easter
	18 Tax Deadline	19	20	21	22	23	24
MAY	25	26	27	28	29	30	1 MAY
	2	3	4	5	6	7	8 Mother's Day
	9	10	11	12	13	14	15
	16	17	18	19	(20)	21	22
	23	24	25	26	27	28	29
JUNE	30 Memorial Day	31	1 JUNE	2	3	4	5
	6	7	8	9	10	11	12
	13	14	15	16	(17)	18	19 Father's Day
	20	21	22	23	24	25	26

Market closed on shaded weekdays; closes early when half-shaded.

2022 STRATEGY CALENDAR

(Option expiration dates circled)

MONDAY	TUESDAY	WEDNESDAY	THURSDAY	FRIDAY	SATURDAY	SUNDAY	
27	28	29	30	1 JULY	2	3	
4 Independence Day	5	6	7	8	9	10	JULY
11	12	13	14	(15)	16	17	
18	19	20	21	22	23	24	
25	26	27	28	29	30	31	
1 AUGUST	2	3	4	5	6	7	
8	9	10	11	12	13	14	AUGUST
15	16	17	18	(19)	20	21	
22	23	24	25	26	27	28	
29	30	31	1 SEPTEMBER	2	3	4	
5 Labor Day	6	7	8	9	10	11	SEPTEMBER
12	13	14	15	(16)	17	18	
19	20	21	22	23	24	25	
26 Rosh Hashanah	27	28	29	30	1 OCTOBER	2	
3	4	5 Yom Kippur	6	7	8	9	
10 Columbus Day	11	12	13	14	15	16	OCTOBER
17	18	19	20	(21)	22	23	
24	25	26	27	28	29	30	
31 🎃	1 NOVEMBER	2	3	4	5	6 Daylight Saving Time Ends	
7	8 Election Day	9	10	11 Veterans' Day	12	13	NOVEMBER
14	15	16	17	(18)	19	20	
21	22	23	24 Thanksgiving Day	25	26	27	
28	29	30	1 DECEMBER	2	3	4	
5	6	7	8	9	10	11	
12	13	14	15	(16)	17	18	DECEMBER
19 Chanukah	20	21	22	23	24	25 Christmas	
26	27	28	29	30	31	1 JANUARY New Year's Day	

JANUARY ALMANAC

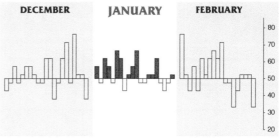

Market Probability Chart above is a graphic representation of the S&P 500 Recent Market Probability Calendar on page 126.

◆ January Barometer predicts year's course with .732 batting average (page 18) ◆ 10 of last 18 midterm election years followed January's direction ◆ Every down January on the S&P since 1950, *without exception*, preceded a new or extended bear market, a flat market, or a 10% correction (page 22) ◆ S&P gains January's first five days preceded full-year gains 82.6% of the time, 8 of last 18 midterm election years followed first five days' direction (page 16) ◆ November, December and January constitute the year's best three-month span, a 4.3% S&P gain (pages 52 & 149) ◆ January NASDAQ powerful 2.8% since 1971 (pages 60 & 150) ◆ "January Effect" now starts in mid-December and favors small-cap stocks (pages 112 & 114) ◆ 2009 has the dubious honor of the worst S&P 500 January on record ◆ Dow gained more than 1000 points in 2018 & 2019

January Vital Statistics

	DJIA		S&P 500		NASDAQ		Russell 1K		Russell 2K	
Rank	5		5		1		4		4	
Up	45		43		34		26		24	
Down	27		29		17		17		19	
Average % Change	0.9%		1.1%		2.8%		1.1%		1.6%	
Midterm-Election Year	−0.5%		−0.7%		0.01%		−0.6%		−0.6%	
Best & Worst January										
	% Change		% Change		% Change		% Change		% Change	
Best	1976	14.4	1987	13.2	1975	16.6	1987	12.7	1985	13.1
Worst	2009	−8.8	2009	−8.6	2008	−9.9	2009	−8.3	2009	−11.2
Best & Worst January Weeks										
Best	01/09/1976	6.1	01/02/2009	6.8	01/12/2001	9.1	01/02/2009	6.8	01/09/1987	7.0
Worst	01/08/2016	−6.2	01/08/2016	−6.0	01/28/2000	−8.2	01/08/2016	−6.0	01/08/2016	−7.9
Best & Worst January Days										
Best	01/17/1991	4.6	01/03/2001	5.0	01/03/2001	14.2	01/03/2001	5.3	01/21/2009	5.3
Worst	01/08/1988	−6.9	01/08/1988	−6.8	01/02/2001	−7.2	01/08/1988	−6.1	01/20/2009	−7.0
First Trading Day of Expiration Week: 1980–2021										
Record (#Up − #Down)	27–15		24–18		22–20		22–20		22–20	
Current streak	U2		U2		U2		U2		U2	
Avg % Change	0.09		0.07		0.09		0.05		0.04	
Options Expiration Day: 1980–2021										
Record (#Up − #Down)	24–18		24–18		25–17		24–18		25–17	
Current streak	D1		D1		U7		D1		U1	
Avg % Change	0.02		0.05		0.02		0.04		0.09	
Options Expiration Week: 1980–2021										
Record (#Up − #Down)	24–18		20–22		25–17		20–22		24–18	
Current streak	U4		U4		U4		U4		U4	
Avg % Change	0.01		0.12		0.47		0.12		0.36	
Week After Options Expiration: 1980–2021										
Record (#Up − #Down)	23–19		25–17		24–18		25–17		28–14	
Current streak	D2		D3		D2		D3		D2	
Avg % Change	0.002		0.16		0.12		0.14		0.08	
First Trading Day Performance										
% of Time Up	59.7		50.0		56.9		46.5		46.5	
Avg % Change	0.24		0.15		0.20		0.14		0.03	
Last Trading Day Performance										
% of Time Up	54.2		59.7		62.7		55.8		69.8	
Avg % Change	0.14		0.2		0.23		0.23		0.18	

Dow & S&P 1950-June 11, 2021, NASDAQ 1971-June 11, 2021, Russell 1K & 2K 1979-June 11, 2021.

20th Amendment made "lame ducks" disappear.
Now, "As January goes, so goes the year."

MONDAY
D 42.9
S 47.6
N 61.9
27

Major bottoms are usually made when analysts cut their earnings estimates
and companies report earnings which are below expectations.
— Edward Babbitt, Jr. (Avatar Associates)

TUESDAY
D 71.4
S 76.2
N 66.7
28

All a parent can give a child is roots and wings.
— Chinese proverb

WEDNESDAY
D 47.6
S 52.4
N 47.6
29

News on stocks is not important. How the stock reacts to it is important.
— Michael L. Burke (*Investors Intelligence*)

THURSDAY
D 47.6
S 52.4
N 47.6
30

My best shorts come from research reports where there are recommendations to buy stocks on weakness;
also, where a brokerage firm changes its recommendation from a buy to a hold.
— Marc Howard (Hedge fund manager, *New York Magazine* 1976, b. 1941)

Last Trading Day of the Year, NASDAQ Down 15 of Last 21
NASDAQ Was Up 29 Years in a Row 1971–1999

FRIDAY
D 42.9
S 38.1
N 28.6
31

You are your own Promised Land, your own new frontier.
— Julia Margaret Cameron (19th century English photographer)

New Year's Day

SATURDAY
1

January Almanac Investor Sector Seasonalities: See Pages 94, 96 and 98

SUNDAY
2

JANUARY'S FIRST FIVE DAYS: AN EARLY WARNING SYSTEM

The last 46 up First Five Days were followed by full-year gains 38 times for an 82.6% accuracy ratio and a 13.7% average gain in all 46 years. The eight exceptions include flat years 1994, 2011, 2015, four related to war, and 2018. Vietnam military spending delayed the start of the 1966 bear market. Ceasefire imminence early in 1973 raised stocks temporarily. Saddam Hussein turned 1990 into a bear. The war on terrorism, instability in the Mideast and corporate malfeasance shaped 2002 into one of the worst years on record. In 2018 a partially inverted yield curve and trade tensions triggered a fourth quarter sell-off. The 25 down First Five Days were followed by 14 up years and 11 down (44.0% accurate) and an average gain of 1.0%.

In midterm election years this indicator has a poor record. In the last 18 midterm election years, 8 full years followed the direction of the First Five Days.

THE FIRST-FIVE-DAYS-IN-JANUARY INDICATOR

	Chronological Data					Ranked by Performance		
	Previous Year's Close	January 5th Day	5-Day Change	Year Change	Rank		5-Day Change	Year Change
1950	16.76	17.09	2.0%	21.8%	1	1987	6.2%	2.0%
1951	20.41	20.88	2.3	16.5	2	1976	4.9	19.1
1952	23.77	23.91	0.6	11.8	3	1999	3.7	19.5
1953	26.57	26.33	−0.9	−6.6	4	2003	3.4	26.4
1954	24.81	24.93	0.5	45.0	5	2006	3.4	13.6
1955	35.98	35.33	−1.8	26.4	6	1983	3.3	17.3
1956	45.48	44.51	−2.1	2.6	7	1967	3.1	20.1
1957	46.67	46.25	−0.9	−14.3	8	1979	2.8	12.3
1958	39.99	40.99	2.5	38.1	9	2018	2.8	−6.2
1959	55.21	55.40	0.3	8.5	10	2019	2.7	28.9
1960	59.89	59.50	−0.7	−3.0	11	2010	2.7	12.8
1961	58.11	58.81	1.2	23.1	12	1963	2.6	18.9
1962	71.55	69.12	−3.4	−11.8	13	1958	2.5	38.1
1963	63.10	64.74	2.6	18.9	14	1984	2.4	1.4
1964	75.02	76.00	1.3	13.0	15	1951	2.3	16.5
1965	84.75	85.37	0.7	9.1	16	2013	2.2	29.6
1966	92.43	93.14	0.8	−13.1	17	1975	2.2	31.5
1967	80.33	82.81	3.1	20.1	18	1950	2.0	21.8
1968	96.47	96.62	0.2	7.7	19	2012	1.8	13.4
1969	103.86	100.80	−2.9	−11.4	20	2021	1.8	??
1970	92.06	92.68	0.7	0.1	21	2004	1.8	9.0
1971	92.15	92.19	0.04	10.8	22	1973	1.5	−17.4
1972	102.09	103.47	1.4	15.6	23	1972	1.4	15.6
1973	118.05	119.85	1.5	−17.4	24	1964	1.3	13.0
1974	97.55	96.12	−1.5	−29.7	25	2017	1.3	19.4
1975	68.56	70.04	2.2	31.5	26	1961	1.2	23.1
1976	90.19	94.58	4.9	19.1	27	1989	1.2	27.3
1977	107.46	105.01	−2.3	−11.5	28	2011	1.1	−0.003
1978	95.10	90.64	−4.7	1.1	29	2002	1.1	−23.4
1979	96.11	98.80	2.8	12.3	30	1997	1.0	31.0
1980	107.94	108.95	0.9	25.8	31	1980	0.9	25.8
1981	135.76	133.06	−2.0	−9.7	32	1966	0.8	−13.1
1982	122.55	119.55	−2.4	14.8	33	1994	0.7	−1.5
1983	140.64	145.23	3.3	17.3	34	1965	0.7	9.1
1984	164.93	168.90	2.4	1.4	35	2009	0.7	23.5
1985	167.24	163.99	−1.9	26.3	36	2020	0.7	16.3
1986	211.28	207.97	−1.6	14.6	37	1970	0.7	0.1
1987	242.17	257.28	6.2	2.0	38	1952	0.6	11.8
1988	247.08	243.40	−1.5	12.4	39	1954	0.5	45.0
1989	277.72	280.98	1.2	27.3	40	1996	0.4	20.3
1990	353.40	353.79	0.1	−6.6	41	1959	0.3	8.5
1991	330.22	314.90	−4.6	26.3	42	1995	0.3	34.1
1992	417.09	418.10	0.2	4.5	43	1992	0.2	4.5
1993	435.71	429.05	−1.5	7.1	44	1968	0.2	7.7
1994	466.45	469.90	0.7	−1.5	45	2015	0.2	−0.7
1995	459.27	460.83	0.3	34.1	46	1990	0.1	−6.6
1996	615.93	618.46	0.4	20.3	47	1971	0.04	10.8
1997	740.74	748.41	1.0	31.0	48	2007	−0.4	3.5
1998	970.43	956.04	−1.5	26.7	49	2014	−0.6	11.4
1999	1229.23	1275.09	3.7	19.5	50	1960	−0.7	−3.0
2000	1469.25	1441.46	−1.9	−10.1	51	1957	−0.9	−14.3
2001	1320.28	1295.86	−1.8	−13.0	52	1953	−0.9	−6.6
2002	1148.08	1160.71	1.1	−23.4	53	1974	−1.5	−29.7
2003	879.82	909.93	3.4	26.4	54	1998	−1.5	26.7
2004	1111.92	1131.91	1.8	9.0	55	1988	−1.5	12.4
2005	1211.92	1186.19	−2.1	3.0	56	1993	−1.5	7.1
2006	1248.29	1290.15	3.4	13.6	57	1986	−1.6	14.6
2007	1418.30	1412.11	−0.4	3.5	58	2001	−1.8	−13.0
2008	1468.36	1390.19	−5.3	−38.5	59	1955	−1.8	26.4
2009	903.25	909.73	0.7	23.5	60	2000	−1.9	−10.1
2010	1115.10	1144.98	2.7	12.8	61	1985	−1.9	26.3
2011	1257.64	1271.50	1.1	−0.003	62	1981	−2.0	−9.7
2012	1257.60	1280.70	1.8	13.4	63	1956	−2.1	2.6
2013	1426.19	1457.15	2.2	29.6	64	2005	−2.1	3.0
2014	1848.36	1837.49	−0.6	11.4	65	1977	−2.3	−11.5
2015	2058.90	2062.14	0.2	−0.7	66	1982	−2.4	14.8
2016	2043.94	1922.03	−6.0	9.5	67	1969	−2.9	−11.4
2017	2238.83	2268.90	1.3	19.4	68	1962	−3.4	−11.8
2018	2673.61	2747.71	2.8	−6.2	69	1991	−4.6	26.3
2019	2506.85	2574.41	2.7	28.9	70	1978	−4.7	1.1
2020	3230.78	3253.05	0.7	16.3	71	2008	−5.3	−38.5
2021	3756.07	3824.68	1.8	??	72	2016	−6.0	9.5

Based on S&P 500

First Trading Day of the Year, NASDAQ Up 17 of Last 24

MONDAY

D 66.7
S 57.1
N 71.4

3

*A bank is a place where they lend you an umbrella in fair weather
and ask for it back again when it begins to rain.*
— Robert Frost (American poet, 1874–1963)

Second Trading Day of the Year, Dow Up 19 of Last 28
Santa Claus Rally Ends (Page 118)

TUESDAY

D 57.1
S 47.6
N 42.9

4

*The number one thing that has made us successful, by far, is obsessive, compulsive focus on the customer,
as opposed to obsession over the competitor.*
— Jeff Bezos (Founder & CEO Amazon, technology entrepreneur, investor & philanthropist, b. 1964)

WEDNESDAY

D 52.4
S 61.9
N 57.1

5

*I write an email about every week to ten days…and within about 24 hours everyone will have read it.
The amazing thing is how I can change the direction of the entire company within 24 hours.
Ten years ago I couldn't do that.*
— Michael Marks (CEO Flextronics, *Forbes*, 7/7/03)

THURSDAY

D 52.4
S 57.1
N 52.4

6

Complexity is the enemy of execution.
— Tony Robbins (American author, coach, speaker, and philanthropist, b. 1960)

January's First Five Days Act as an "Early Warning" (Page 16)

FRIDAY

D 38.1
S 47.6
N 66.7

7

*The investor who concentrated on the 50 stocks in the S&P 500 that are followed by the fewest
Wall Street analysts wound up with a rousing 24.6% gain in [2006 versus] 13.6% [for] the S&P 500.*
— Rich Bernstein (Chief Investment Strategist, Merrill Lynch, *Barron's* 1/8/07)

SATURDAY

8

SUNDAY

9

THE INCREDIBLE JANUARY BAROMETER (DEVISED 1972): ONLY 11 SIGNIFICANT ERRORS IN 71 YEARS

Devised by Yale Hirsch in 1972, our January Barometer states that as the S&P 500 goes in January, so goes the year. The indicator has registered **11 major errors since 1950, for an 84.5% accuracy ratio**. Vietnam affected 1966 and 1968; 1982 saw the start of a major bull market in August; two January rate cuts and 9/11 affected 2001; the anticipation of military action in Iraq held down the market in January 2003; 2009 was the beginning of a new bull market; the Fed saved 2010 with QE2; QE3 likely staved off declines in 2014; global growth fears sparked selling in January 2016; a partially inverted yield curve and trade tensions fueled Q4 selling in 2018; and COVID-19 pandemic and recovery disrupted 2020. (*Almanac Investor* newsletter subscribers receive full analysis of each reading as well as its potential implications for the full year.)

Including the eight flat-year errors (less than +/- 5%) yields a 73.2% accuracy ratio. A full comparison of all monthly barometers for the Dow, S&P and NASDAQ can be seen at *www.stocktradersalmanac.com* in the January 9, 2020, Alert. Bear markets began or continued when Januarys suffered a loss (*see page 22*). Full years followed January's direction in 10 of the last 18 midterm election years. *See page 20 for more.*

AS JANUARY GOES, SO GOES THE YEAR

Market Performance in January

Year	Previous Year's Close	January Close	January Change	Year Change	
1950	16.76	17.05	1.7%	21.8%	
1951	20.41	21.66	6.1	16.5	
1952	23.77	24.14	1.6	11.8	
1953	26.57	26.38	-0.7	-6.6	
1954	24.81	26.08	5.1	45.0	
1955	35.98	36.63	1.8	26.4	
1956	45.48	43.82	-3.6	2.6	flat
1957	46.67	44.72	-4.2	-14.3	
1958	39.99	41.70	4.3	38.1	
1959	55.21	55.42	0.4	8.5	
1960	59.89	55.61	-7.1	-3.0	flat
1961	58.11	61.78	6.3	23.1	
1962	71.55	68.84	-3.8	-11.8	
1963	63.10	66.20	4.9	18.9	
1964	75.02	77.04	2.7	13.0	
1965	84.75	87.56	3.3	9.1	
1966	92.43	92.88	0.5	-13.1	X
1967	80.33	86.61	7.8	20.1	
1968	96.47	92.24	-4.4	7.7	X
1969	103.86	103.01	-0.8	-11.4	
1970	92.06	85.02	-7.6	0.1	flat
1971	92.15	95.88	4.0	10.8	
1972	102.09	103.94	1.8	15.6	
1973	118.05	116.03	-1.7	-17.4	
1974	97.55	96.57	-1.0	-29.7	
1975	68.56	76.98	12.3	31.5	
1976	90.19	100.86	11.8	19.1	
1977	107.46	102.03	-5.1	-11.5	
1978	95.10	89.25	-6.2	1.1	flat
1979	96.11	99.93	4.0	12.3	
1980	107.94	114.16	5.8	25.8	
1981	135.76	129.55	-4.6	-9.7	
1982	122.55	120.40	-1.8	14.8	X
1983	140.64	145.30	3.3	17.3	
1984	164.93	163.41	-0.9	1.4	flat
1985	167.24	179.63	7.4	26.3	
1986	211.28	211.78	0.2	14.6	
1987	242.17	274.08	13.2	2.0	flat
1988	247.08	257.07	4.0	12.4	
1989	277.72	297.47	7.1	27.3	
1990	353.40	329.08	-6.9	-6.6	
1991	330.22	343.93	4.2	26.3	
1992	417.09	408.79	-2.0	4.5	flat
1993	435.71	438.78	0.7	7.1	
1994	466.45	481.61	3.3	-1.5	flat
1995	459.27	470.42	2.4	34.1	
1996	615.93	636.02	3.3	20.3	
1997	740.74	786.16	6.1	31.0	
1998	970.43	980.28	1.0	26.7	
1999	1229.23	1279.64	4.1	19.5	
2000	1469.25	1394.46	-5.1	-10.1	
2001	1320.28	1366.01	3.5	-13.0	X
2002	1148.08	1130.20	-1.6	-23.4	
2003	879.82	855.70	-2.7	26.4	X
2004	1111.92	1131.13	1.7	9.0	
2005	1211.92	1181.27	-2.5	3.0	flat
2006	1248.29	1280.08	2.5	13.6	
2007	1418.30	1438.24	1.4	3.5	flat
2008	1468.36	1378.55	-6.1	-38.5	
2009	903.25	825.88	-8.6	23.5	X
2010	1115.10	1073.87	-3.7	12.8	X
2011	1257.64	1286.12	2.3	-0.003	flat
2012	1257.60	1312.41	4.4	13.4	
2013	1426.19	1498.11	5.0	29.6	
2014	1848.36	1782.59	-3.6	11.4	X
2015	2058.90	1994.99	-3.1	-0.7	flat
2016	2043.94	1940.24	-5.1	9.5	X
2017	2238.83	2278.87	1.8	19.4	
2018	2673.61	2823.81	5.6	-6.2	X
2019	2506.85	2704.10	7.9	28.9	
2020	3230.78	3225.52	-0.2	16.3	X
2021	3756.07	3714.24	-1.1	??	

January Performance by Rank

Rank	Year	January Change	Year Change	
1	1987	13.2%	2.0%	flat
2	1975	12.3	31.5	
3	1976	11.8	19.1	
4	2019	7.9	28.9	
5	1967	7.8	20.1	
6	1985	7.4	26.3	
7	1989	7.1	27.3	
8	1961	6.3	23.1	
9	1997	6.1	31.0	
10	1951	6.1	16.5	
11	1980	5.8	25.8	
12	2018	5.6	-6.2	X
13	1954	5.1	45.0	
14	2013	5.0	29.6	
15	1963	4.9	18.9	
16	2012	4.4	13.4	
17	1958	4.3	38.1	
18	1991	4.2	26.3	
19	1999	4.1	19.5	
20	1971	4.0	10.8	
21	1988	4.0	12.4	
22	1979	4.0	12.3	
23	2001	3.5	-13.0	X
24	1965	3.3	9.1	
25	1983	3.3	17.3	
26	1996	3.3	20.3	
27	1994	3.3	-1.5	flat
28	1964	2.7	13.0	
29	2006	2.5	13.6	
30	1995	2.4	34.1	
31	2011	2.3	-0.003	flat
32	1972	1.8	15.6	
33	1955	1.8	26.4	
34	2017	1.8	19.4	
35	1950	1.7	21.8	
36	2004	1.7	9.0	
37	1952	1.6	11.8	
38	2007	1.4	3.5	flat
39	1998	1.0	26.7	
40	1993	0.7	7.1	
41	1966	0.5	-13.1	X
42	1959	0.4	8.5	
43	1986	0.2	14.6	
44	2020	-0.2	16.3	X
45	1953	-0.7	-6.6	
46	1969	-0.8	-11.4	
47	1984	-0.9	1.4	flat
48	1974	-1.0	-29.7	
49	2021	-1.1	??	
50	2002	-1.6	-23.4	
51	1973	-1.7	-17.4	
52	1982	-1.8	14.8	X
53	1992	-2.0	4.5	flat
54	2005	-2.5	3.0	flat
55	2003	-2.7	26.4	X
56	2015	-3.1	-0.7	flat
57	2014	-3.6	11.4	X
58	1956	-3.6	2.6	flat
59	2010	-3.7	12.8	X
60	1962	-3.8	-11.8	
61	1957	-4.2	-14.3	
62	1968	-4.4	7.7	X
63	1981	-4.6	-9.7	
64	1977	-5.1	-11.5	
65	2000	-5.1	-10.1	
66	2016	-5.1	9.5	X
67	2008	-6.1	-38.5	
68	1978	-6.2	1.1	flat
69	1990	-6.9	-6.6	
70	1960	-7.1	-3.0	flat
71	1970	-7.6	0.1	flat
72	2009	-8.6	23.5	X

X = major error Based on S&P 500

MONDAY
D 57.1
S 66.7
N 66.7
10

The first rule is not to lose. The second rule is not to forget the first rule.
— Warren Buffett (CEO Berkshire Hathaway, investor and philanthropist, b. 1930)

TUESDAY
D 52.4
S 61.9
N 66.7
11

In investing, the return you want should depend on whether you want to eat well or sleep well.
— J. Kenfield Morley (Sales Manager Bell & Howell Co., "Some Things I Believe," *The Rotarian* February 1937)

January Ends "Best Three-Month Span" (Pages 52, 60, 149 and 150)

WEDNESDAY
D 52.4
S 42.9
N 47.6
12

Trading is not a science. It's an art. But it helps to know a lot of science.
— Senior Member of Central Bank of Spain (to Daniel Lacalle *The Energy World is Flat: Opportunities from the End of Peak Oil*)

THURSDAY
D 52.4
S 52.4
N 47.6
13

The way a young man spends his evenings is a part of that thin area between success and failure.
— Robert R. Young (U.S. financier and railroad tycoon, 1897–1958)

FRIDAY
D 57.1
S 57.1
N 42.9
14

The fear of capitalism has compelled socialism to widen freedom, and the fear of socialism has compelled capitalism to increase equality.
— Will and Ariel Durant (*The Lessons of History*, 1885–1981, 1898–1981)

SATURDAY
15

SUNDAY
16

JANUARY BAROMETER IN GRAPHIC FORM

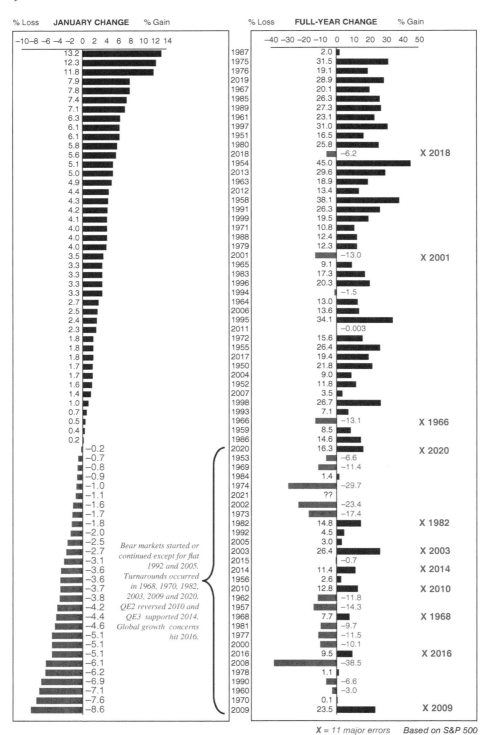

% Loss	JANUARY CHANGE	% Gain		% Loss	FULL-YEAR CHANGE	% Gain

January Change scale: −10 −8 −6 −4 −2 0 2 4 6 8 10 12 14
Full-Year Change scale: −40 −30 −20 −10 0 10 20 30 40 50

Year	January	Full-Year	Major error
1987	13.2	2.0	
1975	12.3	31.5	
1976	11.8	19.1	
2019	7.9	28.9	
1967	7.8	20.1	
1985	7.4	26.3	
1989	7.1	27.3	
1961	6.3	23.1	
1997	6.1	31.0	
1951	6.1	16.5	
1980	5.8	25.8	
2018	5.6	−6.2	X 2018
1954	5.1	45.0	
2013	5.0	29.6	
1963	4.9	18.9	
2012	4.4	13.4	
1958	4.3	38.1	
1991	4.2	26.3	
1999	4.1	19.5	
1971	4.0	10.8	
1988	4.0	12.4	
1979	4.0	12.3	
2001	3.5	−13.0	X 2001
1965	3.3	9.1	
1983	3.3	17.3	
1996	3.3	20.3	
1994	3.3	−1.5	
1964	2.7	13.0	
2006	2.5	13.6	
1995	2.4	34.1	
2011	2.3	−0.003	
1972	1.8	15.6	
1955	1.8	26.4	
2017	1.8	19.4	
1950	1.7	21.8	
2004	1.7	9.0	
1952	1.6	11.8	
2007	1.4	3.5	
1998	1.0	26.7	
1993	0.7	7.1	
1966	0.5	−13.1	X 1966
1959	0.4	8.5	
1986	0.2	14.6	
2020	−0.2	16.3	X 2020
1953	−0.7	−6.6	
1969	−0.8	−11.4	
1984	−0.9	1.4	
1974	−1.0	−29.7	
2021	−1.1	??	
2002	−1.6	−23.4	
1973	−1.7	−17.4	
1982	−1.8	14.8	X 1982
1992	−2.0	4.5	
2005	−2.5	3.0	
2003	−2.7	26.4	X 2003
2015	−3.1	−0.7	
2014	−3.6	11.4	X 2014
1956	−3.6	2.6	
2010	−3.7	12.8	X 2010
1962	−3.8	−11.8	
1957	−4.2	−14.3	
1968	−4.4	7.7	X 1968
1981	−4.6	−9.7	
1977	−5.1	−11.5	
2000	−5.1	−10.1	
2016	−5.1	9.5	X 2016
2008	−6.1	−38.5	
1978	−6.2	1.1	
1990	−6.9	−6.6	
1960	−7.1	−3.0	
1970	−7.6	0.1	
2009	−8.6	23.5	X 2009

Bear markets started or continued except for flat 1992 and 2005. Turnarounds occurred in 1968, 1970, 1982, 2003, 2009 and 2020. QE2 reversed 2010 and QE3 supported 2014. Global growth concerns hit 2016.

X = 11 major errors   *Based on S&P 500*

Martin Luther King Jr. Day *(Market Closed)*

I have a dream that my four little children will one day live in a nation where they will not be judged by the color of their skin but by the content of their character.
— Martin Luther King Jr. (Civil rights leader, 1964 Nobel Peace Prize–winner, 1929–1968)

First Trading Day of January Expiration Week, Dow Up 19 of Last 29, But Down 5 of Last 8

TUESDAY
D 52.4
S 66.7
N 71.4
18

Nothing will improve a person's hearing more than sincere praise.
— Harvey Mackay (*Pushing the Envelope*, 1999)

WEDNESDAY
D 42.9
S 47.6
N 52.4
19

An economist is someone who sees something happen, and then wonders if it would work in theory.
— Ronald Reagan (40th U.S. President, 1911–2004)

January Expiration Week, Dow Down 11 of Last 23, But Up 9 of Last 11

THURSDAY
D 42.9
S 47.6
N 42.9
20

Three passions, simple but overwhelmingly strong, have governed my life: the longing for love, the search for knowledge, and unbearable pity for the suffering of mankind.
— Bertrand Russell (British mathematician and philosopher, 1872–1970)

January Expiration Day Improving Since 2011, Dow Up 10 of Last 11

FRIDAY
D 33.3
S 52.4
N 42.9
21

When a falling stock becomes a screaming buy because it cannot conceivably drop further, try to buy it 30 percent lower.
— Al Rizzo (Investment Advisor, *Dynamic Growth Letter*, 1986)

SATURDAY
22

SUNDAY
23

DOWN JANUARYS: A REMARKABLE RECORD

In the first third of the 20th century, there was no correlation between January markets and the year as a whole. Then, in 1972, Yale Hirsch discovered that the 1933 "Lame Duck" Amendment to the Constitution changed the political calendar, and the January Barometer was born—its record has been quite accurate (page 18).

Down Januarys are harbingers of trouble ahead in the economic, political, or military arena. Eisenhower's heart attack in 1955 cast doubt on whether he could run in 1956—a flat year. Two other election years with down Januarys were also flat (1984 & 1992). Thirteen bear markets began, and ten continued into second years with poor Januarys. 1968 started down, as we were mired in Vietnam, but Johnson's "bombing halt" changed the climate. Imminent military action in Iraq held January 2003 down before the market triple-bottomed in March. After Baghdad fell, pre-election and recovery forces fueled 2003 into a banner year. 2005 was flat, registering the narrowest Dow trading range on record. 2008 was the worst January on record and preceded the worst bear market since the Great Depression. A negative reading in 2015 and 2016 preceded an official Dow bear market declaration in February 2016. In 2020 the shortest bear market in history began after the close on February 19. As of June 16, 2021, only NASDAQ has endured a 10% correction.

Unfortunately, bull and bear markets do not start conveniently at the beginnings and ends of months or years. Though some years ended higher, **every down January since 1950 was followed by a new or continuing bear market, a 10% correction, or a flat year**. **Down Januarys were followed by substantial declines averaging** *minus* **13.0%**, providing excellent buying opportunities later in most years.

FROM DOWN JANUARY S&P CLOSES TO LOW NEXT 11 MONTHS

Year	January Close	% Change	11-Month Low	Date of Low	Jan Close to Low %	% Feb to Dec	Year % Change	
1953	26.38	−0.7%	22.71	14-Sep	−13.9%	−6.0%	−6.6%	bear
1956	43.82	−3.6	43.42	14-Feb	−0.9	6.5	2.6	FLAT/bear
1957	44.72	−4.2	38.98	22-Oct	−12.8	−10.6	−14.3	Cont. bear
1960	55.61	−7.1	52.30	25-Oct	−6.0	4.5	−3.0	bear
1962	68.84	−3.8	52.32	26-Jun	−24.0	−8.3	−11.8	bear
1968	92.24	−4.4	87.72	5-Mar	−4.9	12.6	7.7	−10%/bear
1969	103.01	−0.8	89.20	17-Dec	−13.4	−10.6	−11.4	Cont. bear
1970	85.02	−7.6	69.20	26-May	−18.6	8.4	0.1	Cont. bear
1973	116.03	−1.7	92.16	5-Dec	−20.6	−15.9	−17.4	bear
1974	96.57	−1.0	62.28	3-Oct	−35.5	−29.0	−29.7	Cont. bear
1977	102.03	−5.1	90.71	2-Nov	−11.1	−6.8	−11.5	bear
1978	89.25	−6.2	86.90	6-Mar	−2.6	7.7	1.1	Cont. bear/bear
1981	129.55	−4.6	112.77	25-Sep	−13.0	−5.4	−9.7	bear
1982	120.40	−1.8	102.42	12-Aug	−14.9	16.8	14.8	Cont. bear
1984	163.42	−0.9	147.82	24-Jul	−9.5	2.3	1.4	Cont. bear/FLAT
1990	329.07	−6.9	295.46	11-Oct	−10.2	0.4	−6.6	bear
1992	408.79	−2.0	394.50	8-Apr	−3.5	6.6	4.5	FLAT
2000	1394.46	−5.1	1264.74	20-Dec	−9.3	−5.3	−10.1	bear
2002	1130.20	−1.6	776.76	9-Oct	−31.3	−22.2	−23.4	bear
2003	855.70	−2.7	800.73	11-Mar	−6.4	29.9	26.4	Cont. bear
2005	1181.27	−2.5	1137.50	20-Apr	−3.7	5.7	3.0	FLAT
2008	1378.55	−6.1	752.44	20-Nov	−45.4	−34.5	−38.5	bear
2009	825.88	−8.6	676.53	9-Mar	−18.1	35.0	23.5	Cont. bear
2010	1073.87	−3.7	1022.58	2-Jul	−4.8	17.1	12.8	−10%/no bear
2014	1782.59	−3.6	1741.89	3-Feb	−2.3	15.5	11.4	−10% intraday
2015	1994.99	−3.1	1867.61	25-Aug	−6.4	2.5	−0.7	bear
2016	1940.24	−5.1	1829.08	11-Feb	−5.7	15.4	9.5	Cont. bear
2020	3225.52	− 0.2	2237.40	23-Mar	− 30.6	16.4	16.3	bear
2021*	3714.24	− 1.1	3768.47	4-Mar	1.5	??	??	??
				Totals	−378.0%	48.7%	−59.7%	
				Average	−13.0%	1.7%	−2.1%	

*As of 6/11/2021. Not included in averages.

MONDAY

D 42.9
S 52.4
N 61.9

24

In this game, the market has to keep pitching, but you don't have to swing.
You can stand there with the bat on your shoulder for six months until you get a fat pitch.
— Warren Buffett (CEO Berkshire Hathaway, investor and philanthropist, b. 1930)

TUESDAY

D 61.9
S 61.9
N 52.4

25

The death of contrarians has been greatly exaggerated. The reason is that the crowd is the market
for most of any cycle. You cannot be contrarian all the time, otherwise you end up simply fighting
the tape the whole way up (or down), therefore being wildly wrong.
— Barry L. Ritholtz (Founder/CIO Ritholtz Wealth Management, *Bailout Nation*,
The Big Picture blog, Bloomberg View 12/20/2013, b. 1961)

FOMC Meeting (2 Days)

WEDNESDAY

D 61.9
S 47.6
N 66.7

26

If you have an important point to make, don't try to be subtle or clever. Use a pile driver.
Hit the point once. Then come back and hit it again. Then hit it a third time—a tremendous whack.
— Winston Churchill (British statesman, 1874–1965)

THURSDAY

D 52.4
S 42.9
N 57.1

27

Governments last as long as the under-taxed can defend themselves against the over-taxed.
— Bernard Berenson (American art critic, 1865–1959)

FRIDAY

D 42.9
S 47.6
N 42.9

28

"Be yourself!" is about the worst advice you can give to some people.
— Thomas Lansing Masson (American anthropologist, editor and author, 1866–1934)

SATURDAY

29

February Almanac Investor Sector Seasonalities:
See Pages 94, 96 and 98

SUNDAY

30

FEBRUARY ALMANAC

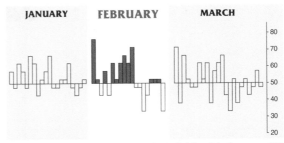

FEBRUARY						
S	M	T	W	T	F	S
				1	2	3	4	5
6	7	8	9	10	11	12
13	14	15	16	17	18	19
20	21	22	23	24	25	26
27	28					

MARCH						
S	M	T	W	T	F	S
		1	2	3	4	5
6	7	8	9	10	11	12
13	14	15	16	17	18	19
20	21	22	23	24	25	26
27	28	29	30	31		

Market Probability Chart above is a graphic representation of the S&P 500 Recent Market Probability Calendar on page 126.

◆ February is the weak link in "Best Six Months" (pages 52, 54 & 149) ◆ RECENT RECORD: S&P up 9, down 6, average change + 0.1% last 15 years ◆ #4 NASDAQ month in midterm election years average gain 0.7% up 6 down 6 (page 166), #6 Dow, up 12 down 6 and #6 S&P, up 10, down 8 (pages 156 & 162) ◆ Day before Presidents' Day weekend S&P down 17 of 30, 11 straight 1992–2002, day after up 8 of last 12 (see page 100 & 135) ◆ Many technicians modify market predictions based on January's market

February Vital Statistics

	DJIA		S&P 500		NASDAQ		Russell 1K		Russell 2K	
Rank	8		11		9		11		6	
Up	43		40		28		26		25	
Down	29		32		23		17		18	
Average % Change	0.2%		0.001%		0.6%		0.3%		1.1%	
Midterm-Election Year	0.7%		0.5%		0.7%		0.8%		1.4%	
Best & Worst February										
	% Change		% Change		% Change		% Change		% Change	
Best	1986	8.8	1986	7.1	2000	19.2	1986	7.2	2000	16.4
Worst	2009	−11.7	2009	−11.0	2001	−22.4	2009	−10.7	2009	−12.3
Best & Worst February Weeks										
Best	02/01/2008	4.4	02/06/2009	5.2	02/04/2000	9.2	02/06/2009	5.3	02/01/1991	6.6
Worst	02/28/2020	−12.4	02/28/2020	−11.5	02/28/2020	−10.5	02/28/2020	−11.6	02/28/2020	−12.0
Best & Worst February Days										
Best	02/24/2009	3.3	02/24/2009	4.0	02/11/1999	4.2	02/24/2009	4.1	02/24/2009	4.5
Worst	02/10/2009	−4.6	02/10/2009	−4.9	02/16/2001	−5.0	02/10/2009	−4.8	02/10/2009	−4.7
First Trading Day of Expiration Week: 1980–2021										
Record (#Up – #Down)	25–17		29–13		25–17		29–13		25–17	
Current Streak	U1		D2		D1		D2		D2	
Avg % Change	0.30		0.27		0.12		0.25		0.15	
Options Expiration Day: 1980–2021										
Record (#Up – #Down)	22–20		18–24		18–24		19–23		21–21	
Current Streak	I1		D2		U1		D2		U1	
Avg % Change	−0.02		−0.11		−0.24		−0.10		0.01	
Options Expiration Week: 1980–2021										
Record (#Up – #Down)	26–16		23–19		23–19		23–19		27–15	
Current Streak	U1		D2		D2		D2		D2	
Avg % Change	0.53		0.32		0.25		0.33		0.45	
Week After Options Expiration: 1980–2021										
Record (#Up – #Down)	20–22		20–22		24–18		20–22		22–20	
Current Streak	D2		D2		D2		D2		D2	
Avg % Change	−0.52		−0.45		−0.45		−0.43		−0.36	
First Trading Day Performance										
% of Time Up	63.9		62.5		70.6		67.4		67.4	
Avg % Change	0.15		0.18		0.37		0.23		0.38	
Last Trading Day Performance										
% of Time Up	45.8		51.4		49.0		48.8		51.2	
Avg % Change	−0.07		−0.06		−0.09		−0.13		−0.04	

Dow & S&P 1950-June 11, 2021, NASDAQ 1971-June 11, 2021, Russell 1K & 2K 1979-June 11, 2021.

Either go short, or stay away the day before Presidents' Day.

JANUARY 2022/FEBRUARY 2022

MONDAY
D 47.6
S 52.4
N 52.4
31

Little minds are tamed and subdued by misfortune; but great minds rise above them.
— Washington Irving (American essayist, historian, novelist, author of *The Legend of Sleepy Hollow*, U.S. ambassador to Spain 1842–46, 1783–1859)

First Day Trading in February, Dow Up 15 of Last 18

TUESDAY
D 81.0
S 76.2
N 76.2
1

The usual bull market successfully weathers a number of tests until it is considered invulnerable, whereupon it is ripe for a bust.
— George Soros (Financier, philanthropist, political activist, author and philosopher, b. 1930)

WEDNESDAY
D 42.9
S 52.4
N 52.4
2

There's no trick to being a humorist when you have the whole government working for you.
— Will Rogers (American humorist and showman, 1879–1935)

THURSDAY
D 52.4
S 42.9
N 38.1
3

If you bet on a horse, that's gambling. If you bet you can make three spades, that's entertainment. If you bet cotton will go up three points, that's business. See the difference?
— Blackie Sherrod (Sportswriter, 1919–2016)

FRIDAY
D 57.1
S 57.1
N 61.9
4

You can't grow long-term if you can't eat short-term. Anybody can manage short. Anybody can manage long. Balancing those two things is what management is.
— Jack Welch (CEO of General Electric, *Business Week*, June 8, 1998, 1935–2020)

SATURDAY
5

SUNDAY
6

MARKET CHARTS OF MIDTERM ELECTION YEARS

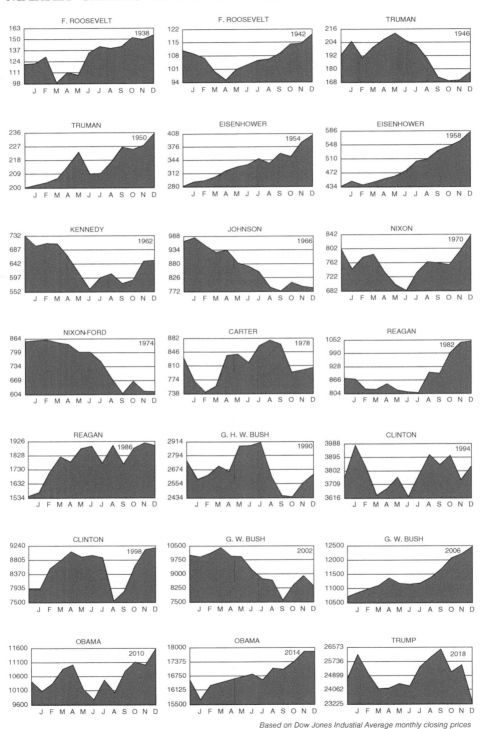

Based on Dow Jones Industial Average monthly closing prices

MONDAY
D 42.9
S 42.9
N 47.6
7

Don't be overly concerned about your heirs. Usually, unearned funds do them more harm than good.
— Gerald M. Loeb (E.F. Hutton, *The Battle for Investment Survival*, predicted 1929 Crash, 1900–1974)

TUESDAY
D 47.6
S 61.9
N 61.9
8

Letting your emotions override your plan or system is the biggest cause of failure.
— J. Welles Wilder Jr. (Creator of several technical indicators including Relative
Strength Index (RSI) 1935–2021)

**Week Before February Expiration Week, NASDAQ Down 11 of Last 21,
But Up 9 of Last 12**

WEDNESDAY
D 52.4
S 52.4
N 52.4
9

We are handicapped by policies based on old myths rather than current realities.
— James William Fulbright (U.S. Senator Arkansas 1944–1974, 1905–1995)

THURSDAY
D 52.4
S 61.9
N 66.7
10

*Welch's genius was the capacity to energize and inspire hundreds of thousands of people
across a range of businesses and countries.*
— Warren G. Bennis (USC Business professor, *Business Week*, September 10, 2001,
referring to retiring CEO Jack Welch of General Electric)

FRIDAY
D 57.1
S 66.7
N 66.7
11

*Bill [Gates] isn't afraid of taking long-term chances. He also understands that you have
to try everything because the real secret to innovation is failing fast.*
— Gary Starkweather (Inventor of laser printer in 1969 at Xerox, *Fortune*, July 8, 2002)

SATURDAY
12

SUNDAY
13

MIDTERM ELECTION YEARS: WHERE BOTTOM PICKER'S FIND PARADISE

American presidents have danced the Quadrennial Quadrille over the past two centuries. After the midterm congressional election and the invariable seat loss by his party, the president during the next two years jiggles fiscal policies to get federal spending, disposable income and social security benefits up and interest rates and inflation down. By Election Day, he will have danced his way into the wallets and hearts of the electorate and, hopefully, will have choreographed four more years in the White House for his party.

After the Inaugural Ball is over, however, we pay the piper. Practically all bear markets began and ended in the two years after presidential elections. Bottoms often occurred in an air of crisis: the Cuban Missile Crisis in 1962, tight money in 1966, Cambodia in 1970, Watergate and Nixon's resignation in 1974, and threat of international monetary collapse in 1982. But remember, the word for "crisis" in Chinese is composed of two characters: the first, the symbol for danger; the second, opportunity. In the last 15 quadrennial cycles since 1961, 9 of the 18 bear markets bottomed in the midterm year. *See pages 133–134 for further detail.*

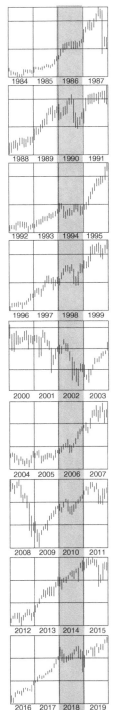

THE RECORD SINCE 1914

1914	Wilson (D)	Bottom in July. War closed markets.
1918	Wilson (D)	**Bottom 12 days prior to start of year.**
1922	Harding (R)	**Bottom 4½ months prior to start of year.**
1926	Coolidge (R)	Only drop (7 wks, −17%) ends Mar. 30.
1930	Hoover (R)	**'29 Crash continues through 1930. No bottom.**
1934	Roosevelt (D)	1st Roosevelt bear, Feb to July 26 bottom (−23%).
1938	Roosevelt (D)	Big 1937 break ends in March, DJI off 49%.
1942	Roosevelt (D)	World War II bottom in April.
1946	Truman (D)	Market tops in May, bottoms in October.
1950	Truman (D)	June 1949 bottom, June 1950 Korean War outbreak causes 14% drop.
1954	Eisenhower (R)	**September 1953 bottom, then straight up.**
1958	Eisenhower (R)	**October 1957 bottom, then straight up.**
1962	Kennedy (D)	Bottoms in June and October.
1966	Johnson (D)	Bottom in October.
1970	Nixon (R)	Bottom in May.
1974	Nixon, Ford (R)	December Dow bottom, S&P bottom in October.
1978	Carter (D)	March bottom, despite October massacre later.
1982	Reagan (R)	Bottom in August.
1986	Reagan (R)	**No bottom in 1985 or 1986.**
1990	Bush (R)	Bottom October 11 (Kuwaiti Invasion).
1994	Clinton (D)	Bottom April 4 after 10% drop.
1998	Clinton (D)	October 8 bottom (Asian currency crisis, hedge fund debacle).
2002	Bush, GW (R)	October 9 bottom (Corp malfeasance, terrorism, Iraq).
2006	Bush, GW (R)	**No Bottom in 2006** (Iraq success, credit bubble).
2010	Obama (D)	**No Bear**, July low, −13.6% from April high.
2014	Obama (D)	**No Bear, No Bottom** (Fed QE).
2018	Trump (R)	**No Bear, December bottom** (Fed, rates)

Bold = *No bottom in midterm election year*

Graph shows Midterm years screened.
Based on Dow Jones Industrial Average monthly ranges.

28

Valentine's Day ♥
First Trading Day of February Expiration Week Dow Down 9 of Last 17

MONDAY
14
D 52.4
S 61.9
N 81.0

*To find one man in a thousand who is your true friend from unselfish motives is to
find one of the great wonders of the world.*
— Leopold Mozart (Quoted by Maynard Solomon, *Mozart*)

TUESDAY
15
D 66.7
S 71.4
N 71.4

When I have to depend upon hope in a trade, I get out of it.
— Jesse Livermore (Early 20th century stock trader and speculator,
How to Trade in Stocks, 1877–1940)

WEDNESDAY
16
D 57.1
S 47.6
N 47.6

*To succeed in the markets, it is essential to make your own decisions.
Numerous traders cited listening to others as their worst blunder.*
— Jack D. Schwager (Investment manager, author, *Stock Market Wizards:
Interviews with America's Top Stock Traders*, b. 1948)

THURSDAY
17
D 42.9
S 47.6
N 47.6

*I hate to be wrong. That has aborted many a tempting error, but not all of them.
But I hate much more to stay wrong.*
— Paul A. Samuelson (American economist, 12/23/03 University of Kansas interview, 1915–2009)

February Expiration Day, NASDAQ Up 7 of Last 12
Day Before Presidents' Day Weekend, S&P Up 10 of Last 11

FRIDAY
18
D 33.3
S 33.3
N 33.3

The best minds are not in government. If any were, business would hire them away.
— Ronald Reagan (40th U.S. President, 1911–2004)

SATURDAY
19

SUNDAY
20

PROSPERITY MORE THAN PEACE DETERMINES THE OUTCOME OF MIDTERM CONGRESSIONAL RACES

Though the stock market in presidential election years very often is able to predict if the party in power will retain or lose the White House, the outcome of congressional races in midterm years is another matter entirely. Typically, the president's party will lose a number of House seats in these elections (1934, 1998 and 2002 were exceptions). It is considered a victory for the president when his party loses a small number of seats, and a repudiation of sorts when a large percentage of seats is lost.

The table below would seem to indicate that there is no relationship between the stock market's behavior in the ten months prior to the midterm election and the magnitude of seats lost in the House. Roaring bull markets preceded the elections of 1954 and 1958, yet Republicans lost few seats during one, and a huge number in the other.

If the market does not offer a clue to the outcome of House races, does anything besides the popularity and performance of the administration? Yes! In the two years prior to the elections in the first eleven midterm years listed, no war or major recession began. As a result, the percentage of House seats lost was minimal. A further observation is that the market gained ground in the last seven weeks of the year, except 2002.

Our five major wars began under four Democrats and one Republican in the shaded area. The percentage of seats lost was greater during these midterm elections. But the eight worst repudiations of the president are at the bottom of the list. These were preceded by: a Fed interest rate tightening cycle in 2018, the sick economy in 1930, the botched health proposals in 1994, the severe recession in 1937, the post-war contraction in 1946, the recession in 1957, financial crisis and the second worst bear market in history from 2007 to 2009, Watergate in 1974, and rumors of corruption (Teapot Dome) in 1922. **Obviously, prosperity is of greater importance to the electorate than peace!**

LAST 26 MIDTERM ELECTIONS RANKED BY % LOSS OF SEATS BY PRESIDENT'S PARTY

	% Seats Gained or Lost	Year	President	Dow Jones Industrials Jan 1 to Elec Day	Dow Jones Industrials Elec Day to Dec 31	Year's CPI % Change
1	3.6 %	2002	R: G.W. Bush	−14.5 %	−2.7 %	1.6 %
2	2.9	1934	D: Roosevelt	−3.8	8.3	1.5
3	2.4	1998	D: Clinton	10.1	5.5	1.6
4	−1.5	1962	D: Kennedy	−16.5	6.8	1.3
5	−2.7	1986	R: Reagan	22.5	0.1	1.1
6	−4.0	1926	R: Coolidge	−3.9	4.4	−1.1
7	−4.6	1990	R: G.H.W. Bush	−9.1	5.3	6.1
8	−5.1	1978	D: Carter	−3.7	0.6	9.0
9	−6.3	1970	R: Nixon	−5.3	10.7	5.6
10	−6.5	2014	D: Obama	7.3	3.5	0.8
11	−8.1	1954	R: Eisenhower	26.0	14.2	−0.7
12	−9.0	1918	D: Wilson (WW1)	15.2	−4.1	20.4
13	−11.0	1950	D: Truman (Korea)	11.2	−5.8	5.9
14	−12.9	2006	R: G.W. Bush (Iraq)	13.4	2.5	2.6
15	−13.5	1982	R: Reagan	14.9	4.1	3.8
16	−15.9	1966	D: Johnson (Vietnam)	−17.2	−2.1	3.5
17	−16.9	1942	D: Roosevelt (WW2)	3.4	4.1	9.0
18	−17.4	2018	R: Trump	3.0	−8.3	1.9
19	−18.4	1930	R: Hoover	−25.4	−11.2	−6.4
20	−20.9	1994	D: Clinton	1.5	0.7	2.7
21	−21.3	1938	D: Roosevelt	28.2	−0.1	−2.8
22	−22.6	1946	D: Truman	−9.6	1.6	18.1
23	−23.9	1958	R: Eisenhower	25.1	7.1	1.8
24	−24.6	2010	D: Obama	7.3	3.5	1.5
25	−25.0	1974	R: Ford	−22.8	−6.2	12.3
26	−25.0	1922	R: Harding	21.4	0.3	−2.3

Presidents' Day *(Market Closed)*

Towering genius disdains a beaten path. It scorns to tread in the footsteps of any predecessor,
however illustrious. It thirsts for distinction.
— Abraham Lincoln (16th U.S. President, 1809–1865)

Day After Presidents' Day, NASDAQ Down 16 of Last 27, But Up 7 of Last 9

D 47.6
S 42.9
N 47.6

I don't believe in intuition. When you get sudden flashes of perception,
it is just the brain working faster than usual.
— Katherine Anne Porter (American author, 1890–1980)

Week After February Expiration Week, Dow Down 13 of Last 23,
But Up 7 of Last 10, 2020 Down 12.4% 5th Worst Week Since 1950

D 47.6
S 52.4
N 57.1

The price of a stock varies inversely with the thickness of its research file.
— Martin Sosnoff (Atalanta Sosnoff Capital, Silent Investor, Silent Loser)

D 52.4
S 52.4
N 66.7

Oil has fostered massive corruption in almost every country that has been "blessed" with it, and the
expectation that oil wealth will transform economies has lead to disastrous policy choices.
— Ted Tyson (Chief Investment Officer, Mastholm Asset Management)

End of February Miserable in Recent Years, (Page 24 and 135)

D 47.6
S 52.4
N 57.1

You have powers you never dreamed of. You can do things you never thought you could do.
There are no limitations in what you can do except the limitations in your own mind.
— Darwin P. Kingsley (President New York Life, 1857–1932)

March Almanac Investor Sector Seasonalities: See Pages 94, 96 and 98

MARCH ALMANAC

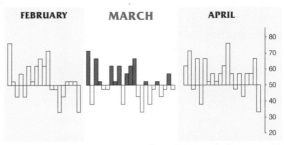

MARCH						
S	M	T	W	T	F	S
			1	2	3	4	5
6	7	8	9	10	11	12
13	14	15	16	17	18	19
20	21	22	23	24	25	26
27	28	29	30	31		

APRIL						
S	M	T	W	T	F	S
					1	2
3	4	5	6	7	8	9
10	11	12	13	14	15	16
17	18	19	20	21	22	23
24	25	26	27	28	29	30

Market Probability Chart above is a graphic representation of the S&P 500 Recent Market Probability Calendar on page 126.

◆ Mid-month strength and late-month weakness are most evident above ◆ RECENT RECORD: S&P 12 up, 9 down, average gain 0.7%, sixth best ◆ Rather turbulent in recent years, with wild fluctuations and large gains and losses ◆ March 2020 Dow declined 13.7%, worst March loss since 1938 ◆ March has been taking some mean end-of-quarter hits (page 136), down 1469 Dow points March 9–22, 2001 ◆ Last three or four days Dow a net loser 20 out of last 32 years ◆ NASDAQ hard hit in 2001, down 14.5% after 22.4% drop in February ◆ Third best NASDAQ month during midterm election years average gain 1.3%, up 7, down 5 ◆ Third Dow month to gain more than 1000 points in 2016

March Vital Statistics

	DJIA	S&P 500	NASDAQ	Russell 1K	Russell 2K
Rank	6	6	7	7	8
Up	46	46	32	28	30
Down	26	26	19	15	13
Average % Change	0.9%	1.0%	0.6%	0.8%	0.8%
Midterm-Election Year	1.0%	1.1%	1.3%	1.6%	2.7%
Best & Worst March					
	% Change	% Change	% Change	% Change	% Change
Best	2000 7.8	2000 9.7	2009 10.9	2000 8.9	1979 9.7
Worst	2020 –13.7	2020 –12.5	1980 –17.1	2020 –13.4	2020 –21.9
Best & Worst March Weeks					
Best	03/27/2020 12.8	03/13/2009 10.7	03/13/2009 10.6	03/13/2009 10.7	03/13/2009 12.0
Worst	03/20/2020 –17.3	03/20/2020 –15.0	03/20/2020 –12.6	03/20/2020 –15.3	03/13/2020 –16.5
Best & Worst March Days					
Best	03/24/2020 11.4	03/24/2020 9.4	03/13/2020 9.4	03/24/2020 9.5	03/24/2020 9.4
Worst	03/16/2020 –12.9	03/16/2020 –12.0	03/16/2020 –12.3	03/16/2020 –12.2	03/16/2020 –14.3
First Trading Day of Expiration Week: 1980–2021					
Record (#Up – #Down)	27–15	27–15	22–20	25–17	23–19
Current Streak	U1	U1	U1	U1	U1
Avg % Change	–0.12	–0.17	–0.44	–0.22	–0.56
Options Expiration Day: 1980–2021					
Record (#Up – #Down)	22–20	24–18	22–20	23–19	21–20
Current Streak	D2	D2	U1	U1	U1
Avg % Change	–0.03	–0.06	–0.08	–0.06	–0.06
Options Expiration Week: 1980–2021					
Record (#Up – #Down)	28–13	27–15	25–17	26–16	23–19
Current Streak	D2	D2	D2	D2	D2
Avg % Change	0.41	0.36	–0.16	0.30	–0.15
Week After Options Expiration: 1980–2021					
Record (#Up – #Down)	18–24	14–28	19–23	14–28	18–24
Current Streak	U2	U2	D1	U2	D1
Avg % Change	–0.09	–0.06	–0.01	–0.07	–0.12
First Trading Day Performance					
% of Time Up	68.1	65.3	64.7	62.8	67.4
Avg % Change	0.26	0.27	0.41	0.32	0.40
Last Trading Day Performance					
% of Time Up	41.7	41.7	64.7	48.8	81.4
Avg % Change	–0.10	–0.02	0.21	0.09	0.40

Dow & S&P 1950–June 11, 2021, NASDAQ 1971–June 11, 2021, Russell 1K & 2K 1979–June 11, 2021.

March has Ides and St. Patrick's Day;
Begins bullishly, then fades away.

MONDAY
D 33.3
S 33.3
N 28.6
28

My dad always said that you don't live in the world you were born into, and that's not going to change. The rate of change is only going to accelerate.
— Mark Cuban (American billionaire entrepreneur, b. 1958)

First Trading Day in March, S&P Up 16 of Last 22

TUESDAY
D 61.9
S 71.4
N 66.7
1

Stock prices tend to discount what has been unanimously reported by the mass media.
— Louis Ehrenkrantz (Wall Street broker, money manager, executive 1934–1999)

Ash Wednesday

WEDNESDAY
D 38.1
S 38.1
N 38.1
2

No other country can substitute for the U.S. The U.S. is still No. 1 in military, No. 1 in economy, No. 1 in promoting human rights and No. 1 in idealism. Only the U.S. can lead the world. No other country can.
— Senior Korean official (to Thomas L. Friedman *NY Times* Foreign Affairs columnist, 2/25/2009)

THURSDAY
D 61.9
S 66.7
N 61.9
3

Whoso neglects learning in his youth, loses the past and is dead for the future.
— Euripides (Greek tragedian, *Medea*, 485–406 BC)

March Historically Strong Early in the Month (Pages 32 and 136)

FRIDAY
D 47.6
S 52.4
N 42.9
4

Exercising the right of occasional suppression and slight modification, it is truly absurd to see how plastic a limited number of observations become, in the hands of men with preconceived ideas.
— Sir Francis Galton, FRS (English Victorian polymath: pioneer of statistical correlation and regression, *Meteorographica* 1863, 1822–1911)

SATURDAY
5

SUNDAY
6

WHY A 50% GAIN IN THE DOW IS POSSIBLE FROM ITS 2022 LOW TO ITS 2023 HIGH

Normally, major corrections occur sometime in the first or second years following presidential elections. In the last 14 midterm election years, bear markets began or were in progress nine times—we experienced bull years in 1986, 2006, 2010 and 2014, while 1994 was flat. A correction in 2018 ended on Christmas Eve day.

The puniest midterm advance, 14.5% from the 1946 low, was during the industrial contraction after World War II. The next five smallest advances were: 2014 (tepid global growth) 19.1%, 1978 (OPEC–Iran) 21.0%, 1930 (economic collapse) 23.4%, 1966 (Vietnam) 26.7%, and 2018 (Fed interest rate tightening) 31.4%.

Since 1914 the Dow has gained 46.8% on average from its midterm election year low to its subsequent high in the following pre-election year. A swing of such magnitude is equivalent to a move from 20000 to 30000 or from 30000 to 45000.

POST-ELECTION HIGH TO MIDTERM LOW: –20.1%

Conversely, since 1913 the Dow has dropped –20.1% on average from its post-election-year high to its subsequent low in the following midterm year. At press-time the Dow's 2021 post-election year high is 34777.76. A 20.1% decline would put the Dow back at 27787 at the 2022 midterm bottom. Spiking inflation could trigger the Fed to raise rates more quickly than expected which makes a decline to this level possible. Whatever the level, the rally off the 2022 midterm low could be another great buying opportunity.

Pretty impressive seasonality! There is no reason to think the quadrennial Presidential Election/Stock Market Cycle will not continue. Page 132 shows how effectively most presidents "managed" to have much stronger economies in the third and fourth years of their terms than in their first two.

% CHANGE IN DOW JONES INDUSTRIALS BETWEEN THE MIDTERM YEAR LOW AND THE HIGH IN THE FOLLOWING YEAR

	Midterm Year Low			Pre-Election Year High			
	Date of Low		Dow	Date of High		Dow	% Gain
1	Jul 30	1914*	52.32	Dec 27	1915	99.21	89.6%
2	Jan 15	1918**	73.38	Nov 3	1919	119.62	63.0
3	Jan 10	1922**	78.59	Mar 20	1923	105.38	34.1
4	Mar 30	1926*	135.20	Dec 31	1927	202.40	49.7
5	Dec 16	1930*	157.51	Feb 24	1931	194.36	23.4
6	Jul 26	1934*	85.51	Nov 19	1935	148.44	73.6
7	Mar 31	1938*	98.95	Sep 12	1939	155.92	57.6
8	Apr 28	1942*	92.92	Jul 14	1943	145.82	56.9
9	Oct 9	1946	163.12	Jul 24	1947	186.85	14.5
10	Jan 13	1950**	196.81	Sep 13	1951	276.37	40.4
11	Jan 11	1954**	279.87	Dec 30	1955	488.40	74.5
12	Feb 25	1958**	436.89	Dec 31	1959	679.36	55.5
13	Jun 26	1962**	535.74	Dec 18	1963	767.21	43.2
14	Oct 7	1966*	744.32	Sep 25	1967	943.08	26.7
15	May 26	1970*	631.16	Apr 28	1971	950.82	50.6
16	Dec 6	1974*	577.60	Jul 16	1975	881.81	52.7
17	Feb 28	1978*	742.12	Oct 5	1979	897.61	21.0
18	Aug 12	1982*	776.92	Nov 29	1983	1287.20	65.7
19	Jan 22	1986	1502.29	Aug 25	1987	2722.42	81.2
20	Oct 11	1990*	2365.10	Dec 31	1991	3168.84	34.0
21	Apr 4	1994	3593.35	Dec 13	1995	5216.47	45.2
22	Aug 31	1998*	7539.07	Dec 31	1999	11497.12	52.5
23	Oct 9	2002*	7286.27	Dec 31	2003	10453.92	43.5
24	Jan 20	2006	10667.39	Oct 9	2007	14164.53	32.8
25	Jul 2	2010**	9686.48	Apr 29	2011	12810.54	32.3
26	Feb 3	2014	15372.80	May 19	2015	18312.39	19.1
27	Dec 24	2018	21792.20	Dec 27	2019	28645.26	31.4

*Bear Market ended   **Bear previous year   **Average   46.8%**

Cumulative Growth Chart (1/1/2008 – 7/31/2020)

296.98%

207.88%

51.58%

■ Probabilities I Share   ■ S&P 500   ■ Morningstar Diversified Alternatives Index

Past Performance is no indication of future returns. Since inception, January 1, 2008 to present. The Morningstar Diversified Alternatives Index is comprised of seven alternative asset classes that broadly represent the alternative landscape, hedge funds, long/short equity, merger arbitrage, managed futures, breakeven Inflation, global Infrastructure, and listed private equity. The hypothetical scenario does not take into account federal, state or municipal takes. If taxes were taken into account, the hypothetical values shown would have been lower.

Using historical trends and patterns to obtain dynamic exposure to the US stock market.

Statistical Analysis vs S&P 500

	Probabilities I Share	MDAI	S&P 500
Cumulative Performance	207.88%	51.58%	296.98%
Annualized Alpha	2.27%	-1.05%	0.00%
Beta	0.65	0.35	1.00
Sharpe Ratio	0.54	0.40	0.69
Standard Deviation	17.27%	6.82%	15.67%
Maximum Drawdown	-27.33%	-15.25%	-48.45%
Correlation	0.59	0.80	1.00
Up Capture of S&P 500	77.33%	33.78%	100%
Down Capture of S&P 500	75.53%	37.12%	100%

Standardized Returns As of 6/30/2021 (Greater than one year, annualized)

Updated Quarterly	YTD	1 Year	3 Years	5 Years	10 Years	Since Inception
Probabilities Fund I Share (Inception 01/01/2008)	1.26%	18.40%	4.38%	4.45%	6.33%	8.65%
Probabilities Fund A at NAV (Inception 01/16/2014)	1.19%	18.16%	4.16%	4.19%	N/A	3.09%
Probabilities Fund A at Maximum Load	-4.66%	11.38%	2.14%	2.97%	N/A	2.27%
Probabilities Fund C (Inception 01/16/2014)	0.87%	17.36%	3.39%	3.42%	N/A	2.32%
S&P 500 Total Return	15.25%	40.79%	18.67%	17.65%	14.84%	10.56%

Disclosures

	Jan	Feb	Mar	Apr	May	Jun	Jul	Aug	Sep	Oct	Nov	Dec	YTD	MDAI*	S&P 500	ITD
2021	-3.69%	1.68%	3.67%	5.58%	-4.45%	-1.14%	0.62%						1.89%	7.70%	17.99%	207.88%
2020	0.74%	-7.04%	-21.83%	11.60%	-1.51%	-2.56%	4.63%	-0.10%	0.91%	-7.98%	13.98%	5.70%	-8.33%	-2.58%	18.40%	202.18%
2019	2.92%	5.68%	2.09%	5.56%	-3.97%	4.81%	3.76%	-2.03%	1.44%	2.76%	6.49%	1.49%	35.10%	7.42%	31.49%	229.62%
2018	4.40%	-6.50%	-4.13%	1.18%	-1.94%	0.69%	0.39%	0.29%	-0.49%	-1.65%	5.47%	-12.73%	-15.21%	-3.49%	-4.38%	143.98%
2017	1.05%	4.26%	-0.27%	2.27%	0.18%	0.98%	0.79%	-0.61%	0.26%	1.84%	2.67%	1.65%	16.03%	2.70%	21.83%	187.76%
2016	-6.02%	-1.36%	9.89%	0.19%	-0.48%	0.78%	0.10%	-1.64%	-0.39%	-2.85%	3.74%	1.95%	3.16%	2.31%	11.96%	148.01%
2015	-7.56%	7.58%	-1.95%	-1.14%	0.29%	-0.95%	1.35%	-3.61%	0.39%	3.83%	1.04%	-3.93%	-5.35%	-3.66%	1.38%	140.42%
2014	-4.46%	2.98%	1.35%	0.19%	0.10%	-0.47%	0.00%	1.62%	-0.66%	2.27%	1.85%	0.61%	5.30%	3.04%	13.69%	154.02%
2013	5.91%	0.53%	6.57%	-0.24%	0.62%	0.28%	0.71%	-2.23%	-0.35%	0.71%	2.53%	2.61%	18.73%	8.64%	32.39%	141.29%
2012	6.19%	5.83%	2.04%	2.38%	-2.80%	0.18%	4.19%	1.77%	-0.26%	0.70%	5.13%	0.07%	28.07%	6.82%	16.00%	103.17%
2011	4.16%	7.75%	2.12%	6.09%	0.81%	-3.26%	-0.49%	-8.86%	-6.67%	5.79%	4.38%	2.54%	13.65%	-3.67%	2.11%	58.64%
2010	-6.75%	10.41%	4.41%	2.16%	-3.56%	0.62%	-2.97%	1.22%	1.70%	0.62%	3.09%	5.45%	16.43%	11.83%	15.06%	39.48%
2009	-0.94%	-15.90%	1.44%	10.98%	15.15%	0.75%	3.01%	-1.84%	-1.82%	-7.96%	8.31%	5.76%	13.88%	21.73%	26.46%	19.89%
2008	1.68%	-15.28%	-8.28%	5.59%	6.07%	-0.61%	-0.07%	-2.56%	-2.33%	10.19%	11.65%	2.30%	5.27%	-12.21%	-37.00%	5.28%

Morningstar Diversified Alternatives Index.

Important Disclosures

Investors should carefully consider the investment objectives, risks, charges and expenses of the Probabilities Fund. This and other importantinformation about the Fund is contained in the Prospectus, which can be obtained by contacting your financial advisor, or by calling 1.888.868.9501. The Prospectus should be read carefully before investing. Probabilities Fund is distributed by Northern Lights Distributors, LLC member FINRA/SIPC. Probabilities Fund Management, LLC and Northern Lights Distributors are not affiliated.

Performance shown before the inception date of the mutual fund, December 12, 2013, is for the Fund's predecessor limited partnership. The prior performance is net of management fee and other expenses, including the effect of the performance fee. The Fund's investment goals, policies, guidelines and restrictions are similar to the predecessor limited partnership. From its inception date, the predecessor limited partnership was not subject to certain investment restrictions,diversification requirements and other restrictions of the Investment Company Act of 1940 which if they had been applicable, it might have adversely affected its performance. In addition, the predecessor limited partnership was not subject to sales loads that would have adversely affected performance. Performance of the predecessor fund is not an indicator of future results.

Mutual Funds involve risk including the possible loss of principal.

The Fund's advisor has contractually agreed to reduce the fees and/or absorb expenses of the Fund, at least until January 31, 2022, to ensure that the net annual fund operating expenses will not exceed 2.14% for Class A, 2.89% for Class C and 1.89% for Class I, subject to possible recoupment from the Fund in future years.

ETFs are subject to investment advisory and other expenses, which will be indirectly paid by the Fund. As a result, your cost of investing in the Fund will behigher than the cost of investing directly in the ETFs and may be higher than other mutual funds that invest directly in stocks and bonds. Each ETF is subject to specific risks, depending on its investments. Leveraged ETFs employ leverage, which magnifies the changes in the value of the Leveraged ETFs, which could result in significant losses to the Fund. The Fund invests in Leveraged ETFs in an effort to deliver daily performance at twice the rate of the underlying index and if held over long periods of time, particularly in volatile markets, the ETFs may not achieve their objective and may, in fact, perform contrary to expectations. Inverse ETFs are designed to rise in price when stock prices are falling.

Inverse ETFs tend to limit the Fund's participation in overall market-wide gains. Accordingly, their performance over longer terms can perform very differently than underlying assets and benchmarks, and volatile markets can amplify this effect.

The advisor's judgment about the attractiveness, value and potential appreciation of particular security or derivative in which the Fund invests or sells short may prove to be incorrect and may not produce the desired results. Equity prices can fall rapidly in response to developments affecting a specific company or industry, or to changing economic, political or market conditions. A higher portfolio turnover may result in higher transactional and brokerage costs. The indices shown are for informational purposes only and are not reflective of any investment. As it is not possible to invest in the indices, the data shown does not reflect or compare features of an actual investment, such as its objectives, costs and expenses, liquidity, safety, guarantees or insurance, fluctuation of principal or return, or tax features. Past performance does not guaranteed future results. The S&P 500 Index is an unmanaged composite of 500 large capitalization companies. This index is widely used by professional investors as a performance benchmark for large-cap stocks.

Alpha (Jensen's alpha) is a risk-adjusted performance measure that represents the average return on an investment, above or below that predicted by the capital asset pricing model (CAPM), given the investment's beta and the average market return. This metric is also commonly referred to as simply alpha. Beta is a measure of a fund's volatility relative to market movements. Sharpe Ratio is a measure of risk adjusted performance calculated by subtracting the risk-free rate from the rate of return of the portfolio and dividing the result by the standard deviation of the portfolio returns. The 3 month T-Bill rate was used in the calculation.

Standard Deviation is a statistical measurement of volatility risk based on historical returns. Maximum Drawdown represents the largest peak-to-trough decline during a specific period of time. Correlation is a statistical measure of how two investments move inrelation to each other.

Up and Down Capture ratios reflect how a particular investment performed when a specific index has either risen or fallen. Long positions entail buying asecurity such as a stock, commodity or currency, with the expectation that the asset will rise in value. Short positions entail a sale that is completed by thedelivery of a security borrowed by the seller. Short sellers assume they will be able to buy the stock at a lower amount that the price at which they sold short.

MONDAY

D 47.6
S 47.6
N 33.3

7

In the end, we will remember not the words of our enemies, but the silence of our friends.
— Martin Luther King Jr. (Civil rights leader, 1964 Nobel Peace Prize, 1929–1968)

TUESDAY

D 47.6
S 47.6
N 47.6

8

What counts more than luck, is determination and perseverance. If the talent is there,
it will come through. Don't be too impatient.
— Fred Astaire (The report from his first screen test stated, "Can't act. Can't sing. Balding. Can dance a little.")

Dow Down 1469 Points March 9–22 in 2001

WEDNESDAY

D 61.9
S 61.9
N 52.4

9

I will never knowingly buy any company that has a real time quote of their stock price in the building lobby.
— Robert Mahan (A trader commenting on Enron)

THURSDAY

D 47.6
S 52.4
N 47.6

10

Washington is run by people who think there is a 1% difference between 2% growth and 3% growth.
— George Will (American political commentator & journalist, b. 1941)

FRIDAY

D 57.1
S 61.9
N 61.9

11

He who knows nothing is confident of everything.
— Anonymous

SATURDAY

12

Daylight Saving Time Begins

SUNDAY

13

THE DECEMBER LOW INDICATOR: A USEFUL PROGNOSTICATING TOOL

When the Dow closes below its December closing low in the first quarter, it is frequently an excellent warning sign. Jeffrey Saut, Market Strategist and Board Member at Capital Wealth Planning, brought this to our attention years ago. The December Low Indicator was originated by Lucien Hooper, a *Forbes* columnist and Wall Street analyst back in the 1970s. Hooper dismissed the importance of January and January's first week as reliable indicators. He noted that the trend could be random or even manipulated during a holiday-shortened week. Instead, said Hooper, "Pay much more attention to the December low. If that low is violated during the first quarter of the New Year, watch out!"

Twenty-one of the 36 occurrences were followed by gains for the rest of the year—and 19 full-year gains—after the low for the year was reached. For perspective we've included the January Barometer readings for the selected years. Hooper's "Watch Out" warning was absolutely correct, though. All but two of the instances since 1952 experienced further declines, as the Dow fell an additional 11% on average when December's low was breached in Q1.

Only three significant drops occurred (not shown) when December's low was not breached in Q1 (1974, 1981 and 1987). Both indicators were wrong eight times and nine years ended flat. If the December low is not crossed, turn to our January Barometer for guidance (page 18).

YEARS DOW FELL BELOW DECEMBER LOW IN FIRST QUARTER

Year	Previous Dec Low	Date Crossed	Crossing Price	Subseq. Low	% Change Cross-Low	Rest of Year % Change	Full Year % Change	Jan Bar
1952	262.29	2/19/52	261.37	256.35	−1.9%	11.7%	8.4%	1.6%[2]
1953	281.63	2/11/53	281.57	255.49	−9.3	−0.2	−3.8	−0.7[3]
1956	480.72	1/9/56	479.74	462.35	−3.6	4.1	2.3	−3.6[1, 2, 3]
1957	480.61	1/18/57	477.46	419.79	−12.1	−8.7	−12.8	−4.2
1960	661.29	1/12/60	660.43	566.05	−14.3	−6.7	−9.3	−7.1
1962	720.10	1/5/62	714.84	535.76	−25.1	−8.8	−10.8	−3.8
1966	939.53	3/1/66	938.19	744.32	−20.7	−16.3	−18.9	0.5[1]
1968	879.16	1/22/68	871.71	825.13	−5.3	8.3	4.3	−4.4[1, 2, 3]
1969	943.75	1/6/69	936.66	769.93	−17.8	−14.6	−15.2	−0.8
1970	769.93	1/26/70	768.88	631.16	−17.9	9.1	4.8	−7.6[2, 3]
1973	1000.00	1/29/73	996.46	788.31	−20.9	−14.6	−16.6	−1.7
1977	946.64	2/7/77	946.31	800.85	−15.4	−12.2	−17.3	−5.1
1978	806.22	1/5/78	804.92	742.12	−7.8	0.01	−3.1	−6.2[3]
1980	819.62	3/10/80	818.94	759.13	−7.3	17.7	14.9	5.8[2]
1982	868.25	1/5/82	865.30	776.92	−10.2	20.9	19.6	−1.8[1, 2]
1984	1236.79	1/25/84	1231.89	1086.57	−11.8	−1.6	−3.7	−0.9[3]
1990	2687.93	1/15/90	2669.37	2365.10	−11.4	−1.3	−4.3	−6.9[3]
1991	2565.59	1/7/91	2522.77	2470.30	−2.1	25.6	20.3	4.2[2]
1993	3255.18	1/8/93	3251.67	3241.95	−0.3	15.5	13.7	0.7[2]
1994	3697.08	3/30/94	3626.75	3593.35	−0.9	5.7	2.1	3.3[2, 3]
1996	5059.32	1/10/96	5032.94	5032.94	NC	28.1	26.0	3.3[2]
1998	7660.13	1/9/98	7580.42	7539.07	−0.5	21.1	16.1	1.0[2]
2000	10998.39	1/4/00	10997.93	9796.03	−10.9	−1.9	−6.2	−5.1
2001	10318.93	3/12/01	10208.25	8235.81	−19.3	−1.8	−7.1	3.5[1]
2002	9763.96	1/16/02	9712.27	7286.27	−25.0	−14.1	−16.8	−1.6
2003	8303.78	1/24/03	8131.01	7524.06	−7.5	28.6	25.3	−2.7[1, 2]
2005	10440.58	1/21/05	10392.99	10012.36	−3.7	3.1	−0.6	−2.5[3]
2006	10717.50	1/20/06	10667.39	10667.39	NC	16.8	16.3	2.5
2007	12194.13	3/2/07	12114.10	12050.41	−0.5	9.5	6.4	1.4[2]
2008	13167.20	1/2/08	13043.96	7552.29	−42.1	−32.7	−33.8	−6.1
2009	8149.09	1/20/09	7949.09	6547.05	−17.6	31.2	18.8	−8.6[1, 2]
2010	10285.97	1/22/10	10172.98	9686.48	−4.8	13.8	11.0	−3.7[1, 2]
2014	15739.43	1/31/14	15698.85	15372.80	−2.1	13.5	7.5	−3.6[1, 2]
2016	17128.55	1/6/16	16906.51	15660.18	−7.4	16.9	13.4	−5.1[1, 2]
2018	24140.91	2/8/18	23860.46	21792.20	−8.7	−2.2	−5.6	5.6[1]
2020	27502.81	2/25/20	27081.36	18591.93	−31.3	13.0	7.2	−0.2[1, 2]
			Average Drop		**−11.0%**			

[1]January Barometer wrong. [2]December Low Indicator wrong. [3]Year Flat.

Monday Before March Triple Witching, Dow Up 24 of Last 34
2020 Down 12.9% 2nd Worst Dow Day Since 1901

MONDAY
D 61.9
S 38.1
N 42.9
14

Learn from the mistakes of others; you can't live long enough to make them all yourself.
— Eleanor Roosevelt (First Lady, 1884–1962)

TUESDAY
D 71.4
S 57.1
N 42.9
15

Moses Shapiro (of General Instrument) told me, "Son, this is Talmudic wisdom. Always ask the question 'If not?' Few people have good strategies for when their assumptions are wrong." That's the best business advice I ever got.
— John Malone (CEO of cable giant TCI, Fortune, 2/16/98)

FOMC Meeting (2 Days)

WEDNESDAY
D 57.1
S 61.9
N 66.7
16

If more of us valued food and cheer and song above hoarded gold, it would be a merrier world.
— J. R. R. Tolkien (English writer, poet, philologist, and academic, The Hobbit, 1892–1973)

St. Patrick's Day ♣

THURSDAY
D 61.9
S 66.7
N 71.4
17

You don't learn to hold your own in the world by standing on guard, but by attacking and getting well hammered yourself.
— George Bernard Shaw (Irish dramatist, 1856–1950)

March Triple Witching Day Mixed Last 30 Years, But NASDAQ Up 6 of Last 7

FRIDAY
D 57.1
S 42.9
N 66.7
18

With globalization, the big [countries] don't eat the small, the fast eat the slow.
— Thomas L. Friedman (NY Times Foreign Affairs columnist, referring to the Arab nations)

SATURDAY
19

SUNDAY
20

HOW TO TRADE BEST MONTHS SWITCHING STRATEGIES

Our Best Months Switching Strategies found on pages 54, 56, 62 and 64 are simple and reliable, with a proven 71-year track record. Thus far we have failed to find a similar trading strategy that even comes close over the past six decades. And to top it off, the strategy has only been improving since we first discovered it in 1986.

Exogenous factors and cultural shifts must be considered. "Backward" tests that go back to 1925 or even 1896 and conclude that the pattern does not work are best ignored. They do not take into account these factors. Farming made August the best month from 1900 to 1951. Since 1987 it is the worst month of the year for the Dow and S&P. Panic caused by the financial crisis in 2007–08 caused every asset class aside from U.S. Treasuries to decline substantially. But the bulk of the major decline in equities in the worst months of 2008 was sidestepped using these strategies.

Our Best Months Switching Strategy will not make you an instant millionaire as other strategies claim they can do. What it will do is steadily build wealth over time with probably less risk than a buy-and-hold approach.

A sampling of tradable funds for the best and worst months appears in the table below. These are just a starting point and only skim the surface of possible trading vehicles currently available to take advantage of these strategies. Your specific situation and risk tolerance will dictate a suitable choice. If you are trading in a tax-advantaged account such as a company-sponsored 401(k) or individual retirement account (IRA), your investment options may be limited to what has been selected by your employer or IRA administrator. But if you are a self-directed trader with a brokerage account, then you likely have unlimited choices (perhaps too many).

TRADABLE BEST AND WORST MONTHS SWITCHING STRATEGY FUNDS

Best Months		Worst Months	
Exchange Traded Funds (ETF)		**Exchange Traded Funds (ETF)**	
Symbol	Name	Symbol	Name
DIA	SPDR Dow Jones Industrial Average	SHY	iShares 1–3 Year Treasury Bond
SPY	SPDR S&P 500	IEI	iShares 3–7 Year Treasury Bond
QQQ	Invesco QQQ	IEF	iShares 7–10 Year Treasury Bond
IWM	iShares Russell 2000	TLT	iShares 20+ Year Treasury Bond
Mutual Funds		**Mutual Funds**	
Symbol	Name	Symbol	Name
VWNDX	Vanguard Windsor Fund	VFSTX	Vanguard Short-Term Investment-Grade Bond Fund
FMAGX	Fidelity Magellan Fund	FBNDX	Fidelity Investment Grade Bond Fund
AMCPX	American Funds AMCAP Fund	ABNDX	American Funds Bond Fund of America
FCGAX	Franklin Growth Fund	FKUSX	Franklin U.S. Government Securities Fund
SECEX	Guggenheim Large Cap Core Fund	SIUSX	Guggenheim Investment Grade Bond Fund

Generally speaking, during the best months you want to be invested in equities that offer similar exposure to the companies that constitute the Dow, S&P 500, and NASDAQ indices. These would typically be large-cap growth and value stocks as well as technology concerns. Reviewing the holdings of a particular ETF or mutual fund and comparing them to the index members is an excellent way to correlate.

During the Worst Months switch into Treasury bonds, money market funds or a bear/short fund. **Grizzly Short** (GRZZX) and **AdvisorShares Ranger Equity Bear** (HDGE) are two possible choices. Money market funds will be the safest, but are likely to offer the smallest return, while bear/short funds offer potentially greater returns, but more risk. If the market moves sideways or higher during the Worst Months, a bear/short fund is likely to lose money. Treasuries can offer a combination of fair returns with limited risk.

Additional Worst Month possibilities include precious metals and the companies that mine them. **SPDR Gold Shares** (GLD), **VanEck Vectors Gold Miners** (GDX) and **Aberdeen Standard Gold** (SGOL) are a few well-recognized names available from the ETF universe.

BECOME AN ALMANAC INVESTOR

Almanac Investor subscribers receive specific buy and sell trade ideas based upon the Best Months Switching Strategies online and via email. Sector Index Seasonalities, found on page 92, are also put into action throughout the year with corresponding ETF trades. Buy limits, stop losses, and auto-sell price points for the majority of seasonal trades are delivered directly to your inbox. Visit *www.stocktradersalmanac.com* or see the insert for details and a special offer for new subscribers.

Dow Lost 4012 Points (17.3%) on the Week Ending 3/20/2020
Worst Dow Weekly Point Loss and 2nd Worst Percent Loss Overall

MONDAY
D 38.1
S 33.3
N 42.9
21

Based on my own personal experience—both as an investor in recent years and an expert witness in years past—
rarely do more than three or four variables really count. Everything else is noise.
— Martin J. Whitman (Founder Third Avenue Funds, b. 1924)

TUESDAY
D 47.6
S 52.4
N 61.9
22

People won't have time for you if you're always angry or complaining.
— Professsor Stephen Hawking (English theoretical physicist, cosmologist, and author, 1942–2018)

Week After Triple Witching, Dow Down 22 of Last 34, 2000 Up 4.9%,
2007 Up 3.1%, 2009 Up 6.8%, 2011 Up 3.1%,
2020 Up 12.8% Best Week Since 1931

WEDNESDAY
D 42.9
S 38.1
N 47.6
23

People somehow think you must buy at the bottom and sell at the top. That's nonsense.
The idea is to buy when the probability is greatest that the market is going to advance.
— Martin Zweig (Fund manager, Winning on Wall Street, 1943–2013)

THURSDAY
D 33.3
S 47.6
N 52.4
24

Small volume is usually accompanied by a fall in price; large volume by a rise in price.
— Charles C. Ying ("Stock Market Prices and Volumes of Sales," Econometrica, July 1966)

March Historically Weak Later in the Month (Pages 32 and 136)

FRIDAY
D 57.1
S 52.4
N 61.9
25

If I had eight hours to chop down a tree, I'd spend six sharpening my axe.
— Abraham Lincoln (16th U.S. President, 1809–1865)

SATURDAY
26

April Almanac Investor Sector Seasonalities: See Pages 94, 96 and 98

SUNDAY
27

APRIL ALMANAC

APRIL						
S	M	T	W	T	F	S
					1	2
3	4	5	6	7	8	9
10	11	12	13	14	15	16
17	18	19	20	21	22	23
24	25	26	27	28	29	30

MAY						
S	M	T	W	T	F	S
1	2	3	4	5	6	7
8	9	10	11	12	13	14
15	16	17	18	19	20	21
22	23	24	25	26	27	28
29	30	31				

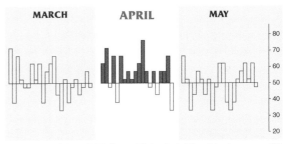

Market Probability Chart above is a graphic representation of the S&P 500 Recent Market Probability Calendar on page 126.

◆ April is still the best Dow month (average 2.0%) since 1950 (page 52) ◆ April 1999 first month ever to gain 1000 Dow points, 856 in 2001, knocked off its high horse in 2002 down 458, 2003 up 488 ◆ Up 16 straight, average gain 2.5% ◆ April 2020 Dow +11.1%, best April since 1938 ◆ Exhibits strength after tax deadline recent years ◆ Stocks anticipate great first quarter earnings by rising sharply before earnings are reported, rather than after ◆ Rarely a dangerous month, recent exceptions are 2002, 2004 and 2005 ◆ "Best Six Months" of the year end with April (page 54) ◆ Midterm election year Aprils since 1950 (Dow 0.7%, S&P 0.2%, NASDAQ –0.1%) ◆ End of April NASDAQ strength fading (pages 127 & 128)

April Vital Statistics

	DJIA		S&P 500		NASDAQ		Russell 1K		Russell 2K	
Rank	1		1		3		2		3	
Up	50		52		34		31		28	
Down	22		20		17		12		15	
Average % Change	2.0%		1.7%		1.8%		1.9%		1.8%	
Midterm Election Year	0.7%		0.2%		–0.1%		–0.1%		0.7%	
Best & Worst April										
	% Change		% Change		% Change		% Change		% Change	
Best	2020	11.1	2020	12.7	2020	15.4	2020	13.1	2009	15.3
Worst	1970	–6.3	1970	–9.0	2000	–15.6	2002	–5.8	2000	–6.1
Best & Worst April Weeks										
Best	4/9/2020	12.7	4/9/2020	12.1	4/12/2001	14.0	4/9/2020	12.6	4/9/2020	18.5
Worst	4/14/2000	–7.3	4/14/2000	–10.5	4/14/2000	–25.3	4/14/2000	–11.2	4/14/2000	–16.4
Best & Worst April Days										
Best	4/6/2020	7.7	4/6/2020	7.0	4/5/2001	8.9	4/6/2020	7.1	4/6/2020	8.2
Worst	4/14/2000	–5.7	4/14/2000	–5.8	4/14/2000	–9.7	4/14/2000	–6.0	4/14/2000	–7.3
First Trading Day of Expiration Week: 1980–2021										
Record (#Up – #Down)	24–18		22–20		22–20		22–20		18–24	
Current Streak	D3		D3		D1		U1		D3	
Avg % Change	0.16		0.10		0.12		0.09		–0.07	
Options Expiration Day: 1980–2021										
Record (#Up – #Down)	27–15		27–15		24–18		27–15		26–16	
Current Streak	U3		U3		U3		U3		U2	
Avg % Change	0.22		0.20		–0.03		0.19		0.26	
Options Expiration Week: 1980–2021										
Record (#Up – #Down)	34–8		30–12		29–13		28–14		30–12	
Current Streak	U6		U2		U6		U2		U1	
Avg % Change	1.06		0.90		1.03		0.89		0.74	
Week After Options Expiration: 1980–2021										
Record (#Up – #Down)	26–16		27–15		28–14		27–15		29–13	
Current Streak	D4		D2		D2		D2		U3	
Avg % Change	0.36		0.41		0.68		0.42		0.83	
First Trading Day Performance										
% of Time Up	58.3		61.1		47.1		58.1		48.8	
Avg % Change	0.10		0.08		–0.16		0.05		–0.23	
Last Trading Day Performance										
% of Time Up	48.6		52.8		58.8		51.2		58.1	
Avg % Change	0.04		0.03		0.06		–0.02		–0.12	

Dow & S&P 1950-June 11, 2021, NASDAQ 1971-June 11, 2021, Russell 1K & 2K 1979-June 11, 2021.

April "Best Month" for Dow since 1950;
Day-before-Good Friday gains are nifty.

Start Looking for Dow and S&P MACD SELL Signal on April 1 (Pages 54 & 56)
Almanac Investor Subscribers Emailed When It Triggers (See Insert)

MONDAY
D 42.9
S 42.9
N 33.3
28

The advice of the elders to young men is very apt to be as unreal as a list of the best books.
— Oliver Wendell Holmes Jr. (U.S. Supreme Court Justice 1902–1932, in *The Mind and Faith of Justice Holmes*, edited by Max Lerner, 1841–1935)

TUESDAY
D 42.9
S 47.6
N 42.9
29

I was absolutely unemotional about numbers. Losses did not have an effect on me because I viewed them as purely probability driven, which meant sometimes you came up with a loss. Bad days, bad weeks, bad months never impacted the way I approached markets the next day.
— James Leitner (Trader, hedge fund manager, Falcon Management Corp, b. 1953)

WEDNESDAY
D 66.7
S 57.1
N 66.7
30

Choose a job you love, and you will never have to work a day in your life.
— Confucius (Chinese philosopher, 551–478 B.C.)

Last Day of March, Dow Down 20 of Last 32, Russell 2000 Up 24 of Last 32

THURSDAY
D 42.9
S 47.6
N 57.1
31

Spend at least as much time researching a stock as you would choosing a refrigerator.
— Peter Lynch (Fidelity Investments, *One Up On Wall Street*, b. 1944)

First Trading Day in April, Dow and S&P Up 19 of Last 27

FRIDAY
D 61.9
S 61.9
N 57.1
1

The knowledge of past times… is both an ornament and nutriment to the human mind.
— Leonardo da Vinci (Italian Renaissance polymath, 1452–1519)

SATURDAY
2

SUNDAY
3

DOW JONES INDUSTRIALS ONE-YEAR SEASONAL PATTERN CHARTS SINCE 1901

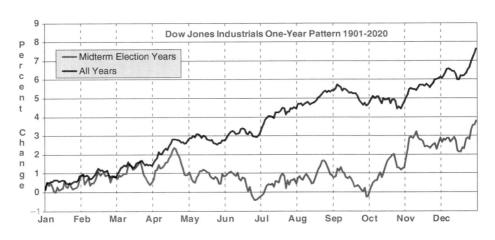

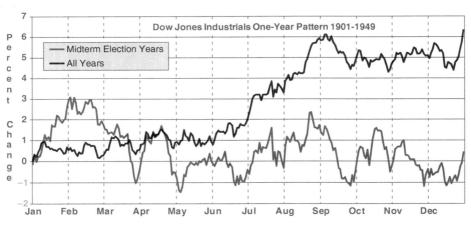

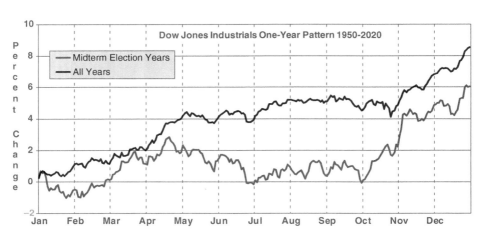

MONDAY

D 66.7
S 71.4
N 66.7

4

Everyone times the market. Some people buy when they have money, and sell when they need money, while others use methods that are more sophisticated.
— Marian McClellan (Co-creator of the McClellan Oscillator and Summation Index, 1934–2003)

April is the Best Month for the Dow, Average 2.0% Gain Since 1950

TUESDAY

D 47.6
S 47.6
N 57.1

5

A good general [or trader] plans in two ways: for an absolute victory and for absolute defeat. The one enables him to squeeze the last ounce of success out of a triumph; the other keeps a failure from turning into a catastrophe.
— Frederick Schiller Faust (AKA Max Brand, American author, *Way of the Lawless*, 1892–1944)

WEDNESDAY

D 66.7
S 66.7
N 61.9

6

History shows that once the United States fully recognizes an economic problem and thereby places all its efforts on solving it, the problem is about to be solved by natural forces.
— James L. Fraser (Investment counselor, writer, editor, publisher, CFA, *Contrary Investor,* 1930–2013)

April is now the Best Month for S&P, 3rd Best for NASDAQ (Since 1971)

THURSDAY

D 38.1
S 38.1
N 28.6

7

If you torture the data long enough, it will confess to anything.
— Ronald Coase (British economist, 1991 Nobel Prize in Economics, 1910–2013)

FRIDAY

D 61.9
S 66.7
N 66.7

8

Technology has no respect for tradition.
— Peter C. Lee (Merchants' Exchange CEO, quoted in *Stocks, Futures & Options Magazine*, May 2003)

SATURDAY

9

SUNDAY

10

S&P 500 ONE-YEAR SEASONAL PATTERN CHARTS SINCE 1930

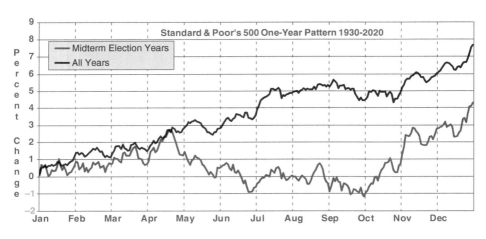

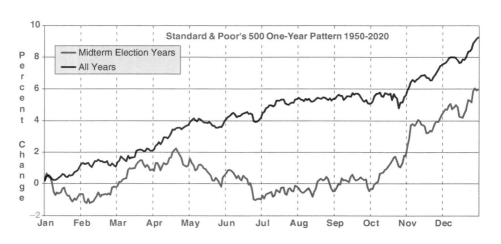

Monday Before April Expiration, Dow Up 20 of Last 33, Down 10 of Last 17

MONDAY

D 57.1
S 52.4
N 47.6

11

There's nothing wrong with cash. It gives you time to think.
— Robert Prechter, Jr. (American financial author & stock market analyst, *The Elliott Wave Theorist,* b. 1949)

TUESDAY

D 52.4
S 57.1
N 66.7

12

If the winds of fortune are temporarily blowing against you, remember that you can harness them and make them carry you toward your definite purpose, through the use of your imagination.
— Napoleon Hill (Author, *Think and Grow Rich*, 1883–1970)

WEDNESDAY

D 47.6
S 52.4
N 42.9

13

Industrial capitalism has generated the greatest productive power in human history.
To date, no other socioeconomic system has been able to generate comparable productive power.
— Peter L. Berger (*The Capitalist Revolution*)

April Expiration Day Dow Up 17 of Last 25, But Down 5 of Last 8
NASDAQ Up 20 of Last 21 Days Before Good Friday

THURSDAY

D 66.7
S 57.1
N 42.9

14

New issues: The closest thing to a "Sure Thing" Wall Street has to offer.
— Norm Fosback (*Stock Market Logic, Fosback's Fund Forecaster, New Issues Newsletter*)

Good Friday *(Market Closed)*

FRIDAY

15

To affect the quality of the day, that is the highest of the arts.
— Henry David Thoreau (American writer, naturalist and philosopher, 1817–1862)

Passover

SATURDAY

16

Easter

SUNDAY

17

NASDAQ, RUSSELL 1000 & 2000 ONE-YEAR SEASONAL PATTERN CHARTS SINCE 1971

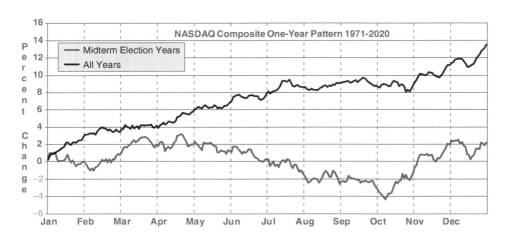

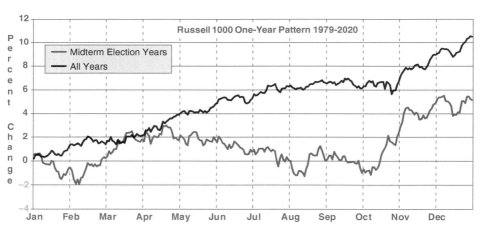

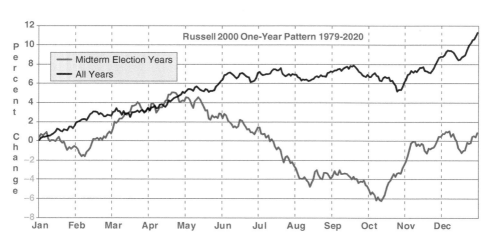

Income Tax Deadline

Day After Easter, Second Worst Post-Holiday (Page 100)

MONDAY
D 61.9
S 61.9
N 52.4
18

Fight until death over taxes? Oh, no. Women, country, God, things like that. Taxes? No.
— Daniel Patrick Moynihan (U.S. Senator New York 1977–2001, "Meet The Press" 5/23/1993, 1927–2003)

April Exhibits Strength After Tax Deadline Recent Years (Pages 40 and 136)

TUESDAY
D 66.7
S 76.2
N 76.2
19

In business, the competition will bite you if you keep running; if you stand still, they will swallow you.
— William Knudsen (Former President of GM)

April 1999 First Month Ever to Gain 1000 Dow Points

WEDNESDAY
D 52.4
S 57.1
N 42.9
20

The only way to even begin to manage this new world is by focusing on…nation building—helping others restructure their economies and put in place decent non-corrupt government.
— Thomas L. Friedman (*NY Times* Foreign Affairs columnist)

THURSDAY
D 57.1
S 47.6
N 47.6
21

The very purpose of existence is to reconcile the glowing opinion we hold of ourselves with the appalling things that other people think about us.
— Quentin Crisp (Author, performer, 1908–1999)

FRIDAY
D 61.9
S 57.1
N 42.9
22

You know you're right when the other side starts to shout.
— I. A. O'Shaughnessy (American oilman, 1885–1973)

SATURDAY
23

May Almanac Investor Sector Seasonalities: See Pages 94, 96 and 98

SUNDAY
24

MAY ALMANAC

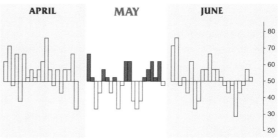

	MAY							JUNE				
S	M	T	W	T	F	S	S	M	T	W	T	F	S

Market Probability Chart above is a graphic representation of the S&P 500 Recent Market Probability Calendar on page 126.

◆ "May/June disaster area" between 1965 and 1984 with S&P down 15 out of 20 Mays ◆ Between 1985 and 1997 May was the best month with 13 straight gains, gaining 3.3% per year on average, up 15, down 9 since ◆ Worst six months of the year begin with May (page 54) ◆ A $10,000 investment compounded to a gain of $1,230,865 for November–April in 71 years compared to a $2693 gain for May–October ◆ Dow Memorial Day week record: up 12 years in a row (1984–1995), down 15 of the last 26 years ◆ Since 1950 midterm election year Mays rank, #10 Dow, #11 S&P and #8 NASDAQ

May Vital Statistics

	DJIA		S&P 500		NASDAQ		Russell 1K		Russell 2K	
Rank	9		8		5		5		5	
Up	39		43		31		30		28	
Down	33		29		20		13		15	
Average % Change	−0.01%		0.2%		1.0%		0.9%		1.3%	
Midterm Election Year	−0.6%		−0.7%		−0.7%		0.1%		−1.1%	
Best & Worst May										
	% Change		% Change		% Change		% Change		% Change	
Best	1990	8.3	1990	9.2	1997	11.1	1990	8.9	1997	11.0
Worst	2010	−7.9	1962	−8.6	2000	−11.9	2010	−8.1	2019	−7.9
Best & Worst May Weeks										
Best	05/29/1970	5.8	05/02/1997	6.2	05/17/2002	8.8	05/02/1997	6.4	05/22/2020	7.8
Worst	05/25/1962	−6.0	05/25/1962	−6.8	05/07/2010	−8.0	05/07/2010	−6.6	05/07/2010	−8.9
Best & Worst May Days										
Best	05/27/1970	5.1	05/27/1970	5.0	05/30/2000	7.9	05/10/2010	4.4	05/18/2020	6.1
Worst	05/28/1962	−5.7	05/28/1962	−6.7	05/23/2000	−5.9	05/20/2010	−3.9	05/20/2010	−5.1
First Trading Day of Expiration Week: 1980–2021										
Record (#Up – #Down)	25–17		27–15		23–19		25–1		21–21	
Current Streak	D3		D1		D1		D1		U1	
Avg % Change	0.11		0.11		0.09		0.08		−0.06	
Options Expiration Day: 1980–2021										
Record (#Up – #Down)	22–20		23–19		20–22		23–19		22–20	
Current Streak	U2		D1		D1		D1		U2	
Avg % Change	−0.06		−0.07		−0.09		−0.06		0.05	
Options Expiration Week: 1980–2021										
Record (#Up – #Down)	19–23		19–23		21–21		18–24		21–21	
Current Streak	D6		D5		U1		D5		D3	
Avg % Change	−0.06		−0.07		0.10		−0.07		−0.29	
Week After Options Expiration: 1980–2021										
Record (#Up – #Down)	24–18		27–15		29–13		27–15		31–11	
Current Streak	U2		U2		U2		U2		U2	
Avg % Change	0.13		0.26		0.37		0.29		0.57	
First Trading Day Performance										
% of Time Up	55.6		58.3		60.8		58.1		60.5	
Avg % Change	0.16		0.19		0.25		0.18		0.16	
Last Trading Day Performance										
% of Time Up	56.9		59.7		64.7		53.5		58.1	
Avg % Change	0.13		0.22		0.17		0.15		0.21	

Dow & S&P 1950–June 11, 2021, NASDAQ 1971–June 11, 2021, Russell 1K & 2K 1979–June 11, 2021.

*Trading in May used to be a disaster
Now it's prime time for portfolio masters*

MONDAY

D 47.6
S 42.9
N 47.6

25

Three billion new people will be active on the Internet within ten years,
as wireless broadband becomes ubiquitous.
— John Mauldin (Mauldin Economics, Millennium Wave Advisors, 2/2/07)

TUESDAY

D 61.9
S 57.1
N 47.6

26

Any fool can buy. It is the wise man who knows how to sell.
— Albert W. Thomas (Trader, investor, *Over My Shoulder*, mutualfundmagic.com,
If It Doesn't Go Up, Don't Buy It!, b. 1927)

WEDNESDAY

D 66.7
S 57.1
N 47.6

27

Become more humble as the market goes your way.
— Bernard Baruch (Financier, speculator, statesman, presidential adviser, 1870–1965)

THURSDAY

D 61.9
S 66.7
N 76.2

28

The game is lost only when we stop trying.
— Mario Cuomo (Former NY Governor, *C-Span*)

End of "Best Six Months" of the Year (Pages 54, 56, 64 and 149)

FRIDAY

D 28.6
S 33.3
N 38.1

29

Over the last 25 years, computer processing capacity has risen more than a millionfold,
while communication capacity has risen over a thousandfold.
— Richard Worzel (Futurist, *Facing the Future*, b. 1950)

SATURDAY

30

SUNDAY

1

SUMMER MARKET VOLUME DOLDRUMS DRIVE WORST SIX MONTHS

In recent years, Memorial Day weekend has become the unofficial start of summer. Not long afterward trading activity typically begins to slowly decline (barring any external event triggers) toward a later summer low. We refer to this summertime slowdown in trading as the doldrums due to the anemic volume and uninspired trading on Wall Street. The individual trader, if he is looking to sell a stock, is generally met with disinterest from The Street. It becomes difficult to sell a stock at a good price. That is also why many summer rallies tend to be short lived and are quickly followed by a pullback or correction.

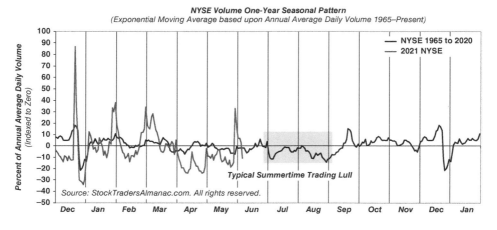

NYSE Volume One-Year Seasonal Pattern
(Exponential Moving Average based upon Annual Average Daily Volume 1965–Present)

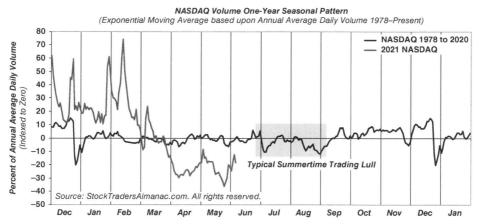

NASDAQ Volume One-Year Seasonal Pattern
(Exponential Moving Average based upon Annual Average Daily Volume 1978–Present)

Above are plotted the one-year seasonal volume patterns since 1965 for the NYSE and since 1978 for NASDAQ against the annual average daily volume moving average for 2021 as of the close on June 4, 2021. The typical summer lull is highlighted in the shaded box. A prolonged surge in volume during the typically quiet summer months, especially when accompanied by gains, can be an encouraging sign that the bull market will continue. However, should traders lose their conviction and participate in the annual summer exodus from The Street, a market pullback or correction could quickly unfold.

First Trading Day in May, S&P Up 17 of Last 24

MONDAY
2

D 57.1
S 66.7
N 71.4

A man should always hold something in reserve, a surprise to spring when things get tight.
— Christy Mathewson (MLB Hall of Fame Pitcher, one of the first 5 members, 3rd most wins, 1880–1925)

TUESDAY
3

D 61.9
S 52.4
N 57.1

The mind is like the stomach. It is not how much you put into it that counts,
but how much it digests — if you try to feed it with a shovel you get bad results.
— Albert Jay Nock (Libertarian writer and social theorist, 1873–1945)

FOMC Meeting (2 Days)

WEDNESDAY
4

D 38.1
S 33.3
N 38.1

The facts are unimportant! It's what they are perceived to be that determines the course of events.
— R. Earl Hadady (*Bullish Consensus, Contrary Opinion*)

THURSDAY
5

D 38.1
S 42.9
N 52.4

Almost any insider purchase is worth investigating for a possible lead to a superior speculation.
But very few insider sales justify concern.
— William Chidester (*Scientific Investing*)

Friday Before Mother's Day, Dow Up 19 of Last 27

FRIDAY
6

D 61.9
S 57.1
N 52.4

The worst bankrupt in the world is the person who has lost his enthusiasm.
— H.W. Arnold

SATURDAY
7

Mother's Day

SUNDAY
8

TOP-PERFORMING MONTHS:
STANDARD & POOR'S 500 AND DOW JONES INDUSTRIALS

Monthly performance of the S&P and the Dow is ranked over the past 71 1/2 years. NASDAQ monthly performance is shown on page 58.

April, November and December still hold the top three positions in both the Dow and the S&P. Disastrous Januarys in 2008, 2009 and 2016 knocked January into fifth. This, in part, led to our discovery in 1986 of the market's most consistent seasonal pattern. You can divide the year into two sections and have practically all the gains in one six-month section and very little in the other. September is the worst month on both lists. (See "Best Six Months" on page 54.)

MONTHLY % CHANGES (JANUARY 1950–MAY 2021)

	Standard & Poor's 500					Dow Jones Industrials			
Month	Total % Change	Avg. % Change	# Up	# Down	Month	Total % Change	Avg. % Change	# Up	# Down
Jan	76.8%	1.1%	43	29	Jan	68.2%	0.9%	45	27
Feb	0.1	0.002	40	32	Feb	11.4	0.2	43	29
Mar	74.2	1.0	46	26	Mar	66.2	0.9	46	26
Apr	121.8	1.7	52	20	Apr	145.5	2.0	50	22
May	16.3	0.2	43	29	May	−0.6	−0.01	39	33
Jun	7.6	0.1	39	32	Jun	−11.2	−0.2	34	37
Jul	80.4	1.1	41	30	Jul	89.3	1.3	46	25
Aug	2.2	0.03	39	32	Aug	−3.8	−0.1	40	31
Sep*	−34.2	−0.5	32	38	Sep	−47.0	−0.7	29	42
Oct	54.9	0.8	42	29	Oct	37.5	0.5	42	29
Nov	121.2	1.7	49	22	Nov	125.5	1.8	49	22
Dec	106.9	1.5	53	18	Dec	109.2	1.5	50	21
% Rank					**% Rank**				
Apr	121.8%	1.7%	52	20	Apr	145.5%	2.0%	50	22
Nov	121.2	1.7	49	22	Nov	125.5	1.8	49	22
Dec	106.9	1.5	53	18	Dec	109.2	1.5	50	21
Jul	80.4	1.1	41	30	Jul	89.3	1.3	46	25
Jan	76.8	1.1	43	29	Jan	68.2	0.9	45	27
Mar	74.2	1.0	46	26	Mar	66.2	0.9	46	26
Oct	54.9	0.8	42	29	Oct	37.5	0.5	42	29
May	16.3	0.2	43	29	Feb	11.4	0.2	43	29
Jun	7.6	0.1	39	32	May	−0.6	−0.01	39	33
Aug	2.2	0.03	39	32	Aug	−3.8	−0.1	40	31
Feb	0.1	0.002	40	32	Jun	−11.2	−0.2	34	37
Sep*	−34.2	−0.5	32	38	Sep	−47.0	−0.7	29	42
Totals	**628.2%**	**8.7%**			**Totals**	**590.2%**	**8.1%**		
Average		**0.73%**			**Average**		**0.67%**		

*No change 1979

Anticipators, shifts in cultural behavior and faster information flow have altered seasonality in recent years. Here is how the months ranked over the past 15 years (186 months) using total percentage gains on the S&P 500: April 49.9, July 31.1, November 22.5, March 18.9, December 11.4, October 5.9, September 3.3, August 2.1, February 1.0, January –0.5, May –0.7 and June –5.5.

January has declined in 11 of the last 22 years. Sizable turnarounds in "bear killing" October were a common occurrence from 1999 to 2007. Recent big Dow losses in the 21-year period were: September 2001 (9/11 attack), off 11.1%; September 2002 (Iraq war drums), off 12.4%; June 2008, off 10.2%; October 2008, off 14.1%; and February 2009, off 11.7% (financial crisis) and March 2020, off 13.7% (Covid-19 pandemic shutdown).

Monday After Mother's Day, Dow Up 17 of Last 27, But Down 7 of Last 10

MONDAY

9

D 71.4
S 52.4
N 71.4

No man's life, liberty, or property is safe while Congress is in session.
— Mark Twain (American novelist and satirist, pen name of Samuel Longhorne Clemens, 1835–1910)

TUESDAY

10

D 38.1
S 42.9
N 47.6

Unless you've interpreted changes before they've occurred, you'll be decimated trying to follow them.
— Robert J. Nurock (Stock market analyst, Wall Street Week panelist, 1938–2017)

WEDNESDAY

11

D 61.9
S 52.4
N 42.9

A successful man is one who can lay a firm foundation with the bricks that others throw at him.
— Sidney Greenberg (Rabbi, author, 1918–2003)

THURSDAY

12

D 33.3
S 33.3
N 42.9

Never lend money to someone who must borrow money to pay interest [on other money owed].
— (A Swiss Banker's First Rule quoted by Lester Thurow)

FRIDAY

13

D 57.1
S 47.6
N 52.4

Regardless of current economic conditions, it's always best to remember that the stock market is a barometer and not a thermometer.
— Yale Hirsch (Creator of *Stock Trader's Almanac*, b. 1923)

SATURDAY

14

SUNDAY

15

"BEST SIX MONTHS": STILL AN EYE-POPPING STRATEGY

Our Best Six Months Switching Strategy consistently delivers. Investing in the Dow Jones Industrial Average between November 1 and April 30 each year and then switching into fixed income for the other six months has produced reliable returns with reduced risk since 1950.

The chart on page 149 shows November, December, January, March and April to be top months since 1950. Add February, and an excellent strategy is born! These six consecutive months gained 27726.69 Dow points in 71 years, while the remaining May-through-October months gained 6588.43 points. The S&P gained 3194.78 points in the same best six months versus 968.32 points in the worst six.

Percentage changes are shown along with a compounding $10,000 investment. The November–April $1,230,865 gain overshadows May–October's $2,693 gain. (S&P results were $1,011,918 to $12,623.) Just four November–April losses were double-digit: April 1970 (Cambodian invasion), 1973 (OPEC oil embargo), 2008 (financial crisis) and March 2020 (Covid-19 economic shutdown). Similarly, Iraq muted the Best Six and inflated the Worst Six in 2003. When we discovered this strategy in 1986, November–April outperformed May–October by $88,163 to minus $1,522. Results improved substantially these past 34 years, $1,142,702 to $1,171. A simple timing indicator nearly triples results (page 56).

	SIX-MONTH SWITCHING STRATEGY			
	DJIA % Change May 1–Oct 31	Investing $10,000	DJIA % Change Nov 1–Apr 30	Investing $10,000
1950	5.0%	$10,500	15.2%	$11,520
1951	1.2	10,626	−1.8	11,313
1952	4.5	11,104	2.1	11,551
1953	0.4	11,148	15.8	13,376
1954	10.3	12,296	20.9	16,172
1955	6.9	13,144	13.5	18,355
1956	−7.0	12,224	3.0	18,906
1957	−10.8	10,904	3.4	19,549
1958	19.2	12,998	14.8	22,442
1959	3.7	13,479	−6.9	20,894
1960	−3.5	13,007	16.9	24,425
1961	3.7	13,488	−5.5	23,082
1962	−11.4	11,950	21.7	28,091
1963	5.2	12,571	7.4	30,170
1964	7.7	13,539	5.6	31,860
1965	4.2	14,108	−2.8	30,968
1966	−13.6	12,189	11.1	34,405
1967	−1.9	11,957	3.7	35,678
1968	4.4	12,483	−0.2	35,607
1969	−9.9	11,247	−14.0	30,622
1970	2.7	11,551	24.6	38,155
1971	−10.9	10,292	13.7	43,382
1972	0.1	10,302	−3.6	41,820
1973	3.8	10,693	−12.5	36,593
1974	−20.5	8,501	23.4	45,156
1975	1.8	8,654	19.2	53,826
1976	−3.2	8,377	−3.9	51,727
1977	−11.7	7,397	2.3	52,917
1978	−5.4	6,998	7.9	57,097
1979	−4.6	6,676	0.2	57,211
1980	13.1	7,551	7.9	61,731
1981	−14.6	6,449	−0.5	61,422
1982	16.9	7,539	23.6	75,918
1983	−0.1	7,531	−4.4	72,578
1984	3.1	7,764	4.2	75,626
1985	9.2	8,478	29.8	98,163
1986	5.3	8,927	21.8	119,563
1987	−12.8	7,784	1.9	121,835
1988	5.7	8,228	12.6	137,186
1989	9.4	9,001	0.4	137,735
1990	−8.1	8,272	18.2	162,803
1991	6.3	8,793	9.4	178,106
1992	−4.0	8,441	6.2	189,149
1993	7.4	9,066	0.03	189,206
1994	6.2	9,628	10.6	209,262
1995	10.0	10,591	17.1	245,046
1996	8.3	11,470	16.2	284,743
1997	6.2	12,181	21.8	346,817
1998	−5.2	11,548	25.6	435,602
1999	−0.5	11,490	0.04	435,776
2000	2.2	11,743	−2.2	426,189
2001	−15.5	9,923	9.6	467,103
2002	−15.6	8,375	1.0	471,774
2003	15.6	9,682	4.3	492,060
2004	−1.9	9,498	1.6	499,933
2005	2.4	9,726	8.9	544,427
2006	6.3	10,339	8.1	588,526
2007	6.6	11,021	−8.0	541,444
2008	−27.3	8,012	−12.4	474,305
2009	18.9	9,526	13.3	537,388
2010	1.0	9,621	15.2	619,071
2011	−6.7	8,976	10.5	684,073
2012	−0.9	8,895	13.3	775,055
2013	4.8	9,322	6.7	826,984
2014	4.9	9,779	2.6	848,486
2015	−1.0	9,681	0.6	853,577
2016	2.1	$9,884	15.4	$985,223
2017	11.6	$11,031	3.4	$1,018,721
2018	3.9	$11,461	5.9	$1,078,826
2019	1.7	$11,656	−10.0	$970,943
2020	8.9	$12,693	27.8	$1,240,865
Average/Gain	**0.8%**	**$2,693**	**7.5%**	**$1,230,865**
# Up/Down	**44/27**		**56/15**	

Monday Before May Expiration, Dow Up 24 of Last 34, But Down 7 of Last 11

MONDAY

D 61.9
S 61.9
N 57.1

16

A senior European diplomat said he was convinced that the choice of starting a war this spring was made for political as well as military reasons. [The President] clearly does not want to have a war raging on the eve of his presumed reelection campaign.
— Reported by Steven R. Weisman (*NY Times* 3/14/03)

TUESDAY

D 57.1
S 61.9
N 66.7

17

We spend $500 million a year just in training our people. We've developed some technology that lets us do simulations. Think of Flight Simulation. What we've found is that the retention rate from simulation is about 75%, opposed to 25% from classroom work.
— Joe Forehand (CEO, Accenture, *Forbes*, 7/7/03)

WEDNESDAY

D 38.1
S 38.1
N 42.9

18

The reason the market did so well in the last several years is because the Federal Reserve drove interest rates down to extraordinary low levels—like 1%.
— George Roche (Chairman, T. Rowe Price, *Barron's* 12/18/06)

THURSDAY

D 38.1
S 33.3
N 33.3

19

Show me a good phone receptionist and I'll show you a good company.
— Harvey Mackay (*Pushing the Envelope*, 1999)

May Expiration Day, Dow Up 14 of Last 21

FRIDAY

D 28.6
S 38.1
N 42.9

20

It is the growth of total government spending as a percentage of gross national product—not the way it is financed—that crowds out the private sector.
— Paul Craig Roberts (*Business Week*, 1984)

SATURDAY

21

SUNDAY

22

MACD-TIMING TRIPLES "BEST SIX MONTHS" RESULTS

Using the simple MACD (moving average convergence divergence) indicator developed by our late friend Gerald Appel to better time entries and exits into and out of the Best Six Months (page 54) period nearly triples the results. Several years ago, Sy Harding (RIP) enhanced our Best Six Months Switching Strategy with MACD triggers, dubbing it the "best mechanical system ever." In 2006, we improved it even more, achieving similar results with just four trades every four years (page 60).

Our *Almanac Investor eNewsletter* (see ad insert) implements this system with quite a degree of success. Starting on the first trading day of October, we look to catch the market's first hint of an up-trend after the summer doldrums, and beginning on the first trading day of April, we prepare to exit these seasonal positions as soon as the market falters.

In up-trending markets, MACD signals get you in earlier and keep you in longer. But if the market is trending down, entries are delayed until the market turns up, and exit points can come a month earlier.

The results are astounding, applying the simple MACD signals. Instead of $10,000 gaining $1,230,865 over the 71 recent years when invested only during the Best Six Months (page 54), the gain nearly tripled to $3,081,967. The $2,693 gain during the Worst Six Months became a loss of $4,872.

Impressive results for being invested during only 6.3 months of the year on average! For the rest of the year consider money markets, bonds, puts, bear funds, covered calls, or credit call spreads.

Updated signals are emailed to our *Almanac Investor eNewsletter* subscribers as soon as they are triggered. Visit *www .stocktradersalmanac.com,* or see the ad insert for details and a special offer for new subscribers.

BEST SIX-MONTH SWITCHING STRATEGY+TIMING

	DJIA		DJIA	
	% Change	Investing	% Change	Investing
	May 1–Oct 31*	$10,000	Nov 1–Apr 30*	$10,000
1950	7.3%	$10,730	13.3%	$11,330
1951	0.1	10,741	1.9	11,545
1952	1.4	10,891	2.1	11,787
1953	0.2	10,913	17.1	13,803
1954	13.5	12,386	16.3	16,053
1955	7.7	13,340	13.1	18,156
1956	−6.8	12,433	2.8	18,664
1957	−12.3	10,904	4.9	19,579
1958	17.3	12,790	16.7	22,849
1959	1.6	12,995	−3.1	22,141
1960	−4.9	12,358	16.9	25,883
1961	2.9	12,716	−1.5	25,495
1962	−15.3	10,770	22.4	31,206
1963	4.3	11,233	9.6	34,202
1964	6.7	11,986	6.2	36,323
1965	2.6	12,298	−2.5	35,415
1966	−16.4	10,281	14.3	40,479
1967	−2.1	10,065	5.5	42,705
1968	3.4	10,407	0.2	42,790
1969	−11.9	9,169	−6.7	39,923
1970	−1.4	9,041	20.8	48,227
1971	−11.0	8,046	15.4	55,654
1972	−0.6	7,998	−1.4	54,875
1973	−11.0	7,118	0.1	54,930
1974	−22.4	5,524	28.2	70,420
1975	0.1	5,530	18.5	83,448
1976	−3.4	5,342	−3.0	80,945
1977	−11.4	4,733	0.5	81,350
1978	−4.5	4,520	9.3	88,916
1979	−5.3	4,280	7.0	95,140
1980	9.3	4,678	4.7	99,612
1981	−14.6	3,995	0.4	100,010
1982	15.5	4,614	23.5	123,512
1983	2.5	4,729	−7.3	114,496
1984	3.3	4,885	3.9	118,961
1985	7.0	5,227	38.1	164,285
1986	−2.8	5,081	28.2	210,613
1987	−14.9	4,324	3.0	216,931
1988	6.1	4,588	11.8	242,529
1989	9.8	5,038	3.3	250,532
1990	−6.7	4,700	15.8	290,116
1991	4.8	4,926	11.3	322,899
1992	−6.2	4,621	6.6	344,210
1993	5.5	4,875	5.6	363,486
1994	3.7	5,055	13.1	411,103
1995	7.2	5,419	16.7	479,757
1996	9.2	5,918	21.9	584,824
1997	3.6	6,131	18.5	693,016
1998	−12.4	5,371	39.9	969,529
1999	−6.4	5,027	5.1	1,018,975
2000	−6.0	4,725	5.4	1,074,000
2001	−17.3	3,908	15.8	1,243,692
2002	−25.2	2,923	6.0	1,318,314
2003	16.4	3,402	7.8	1,421,142
2004	−0.9	3,371	1.8	1,446,723
2005	−0.5	3,354	7.7	1,558,121
2006	4.7	3,512	14.4	1,782,490
2007	5.6	3,709	−12.7	1,556,114
2008	−24.7	2,793	−14.0	1,338,258
2009	23.8	3,458	10.8	1,482,790
2010	4.6	3,617	7.3	1,591,034
2011	−9.4	3,277	18.7	1,888,557
2012	0.3	3,287	10.0	2,077,413
2013	4.1	3,422	7.1	2,224,909
2014	2.3	3,501	7.4	2,389,552
2015	−6.0	3,291	4.9	2,506,640
2016	3.5	3,406	13.1	2,835,010
2017	15.7	3,941	0.4	2,846,350
2018	5.0	4,138	5.2	2,994,360
2019	1.5	4,200	−13.3	2,596,110
2020	22.1	5,128	19.1	3,091,967
Average	**−0.4%**		**8.9%**	
# Up	**40**		**61**	
# Down	**31**		**10**	
70-Year Gain (Loss)		**($4,872)**		**$3,081,967**

MACD generated entry and exit points (earlier or later) can lengthen or shorten six-month periods.

MONDAY

D 47.6
S 52.4
N 52.4

23

The higher a people's intelligence and moral strength, the lower will be the prevailing rate of interest.
— Eugen von Bohm-Bawerk (Austrian economist, *Capital and Interest*, 1851–1914)

TUESDAY

D 47.6
S 57.1
N 52.4

24

The key to long-term profits on Wall Street is not making big killings, it's not getting killed.
— Daniel Turov (*Turov on Timing*)

Start Looking for NASDAQ MACD Sell Signal on June 1 (Page 62)
Almanac Investor Subscribers Emailed When It Triggers (See Insert)

WEDNESDAY

D 57.1
S 61.9
N 61.9

25

Let me tell you the secret that has led me to my goal. My strength lies solely in my tenacity.
— Louis Pasteur (French chemist, founder of microbiology, 1822–1895)

THURSDAY

D 47.6
S 52.4
N 57.1

26

All the features and achievements of modern civilization are, directly or indirectly,
the products of the capitalist process.
— Joseph A. Schumpeter (Austrian-American economist, *Theory of Economic Development*, 1883–1950)

Friday Before Memorial Day Tends to Be Lackluster with Light Trading,
Dow Down 12 of Last 22, Average –0.2%

FRIDAY

D 61.9
S 61.9
N 71.4

27

The market can stay irrational longer than you can stay solvent.
— John Maynard Keynes (British economist, 1883–1946)

SATURDAY

28

June Almanac Investor Sector Seasonalities: See Pages 94, 96 and 98

SUNDAY

29

JUNE ALMANAC

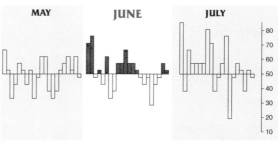

JUNE						
S	M	T	W	T	F	S
				1	2	3	4
5	6	7	8	9	10	11
12	13	14	15	16	17	18
19	20	21	22	23	24	25
26	27	28	29	30		

JULY						
S	M	T	W	T	F	S
					1	2
3	4	5	6	7	8	9
10	11	12	13	14	15	16
17	18	19	20	21	22	23
24	25	26	27	28	29	30
31						

Market Probability Chart above is a graphic representation of the S&P 500 Recent Market Probability Calendar on page 126.

◆ The "summer rally" in most years is the weakest rally of all four seasons (page 76) ◆ Week after June Triple-Witching Day Dow down 27 of last 31 (page 108) ◆ RECENT RECORD: S&P up 12, down 9, average loss 0.5%, ranks tenth ◆ Stronger for NASDAQ, average gain 0.7% last 21 years ◆ Watch out for end-of-quarter "portfolio pumping" on last day of June, Dow down 17 of last 30, NASDAQ up 9 of last 10 ◆ Midterm election year Junes: #12 S&P, #12 Dow, #11 NASDAQ ◆ June ends NASDAQ's Best Eight Months

June Vital Statistics

	DJIA		S&P 500		NASDAQ		Russell 1K		Russell 2K	
Rank	11		9		6		9		7	
Up	34		39		28		26		27	
Down	37		32		22		16		15	
Average % Change	−0.2%		0.1%		0.8%		0.3%		0.8%	
Midterm Election Year	−1.7%		−1.8%		−1.4%		−1.2%		−1.4%	
Best & Worst June										
	% Change		% Change		% Change		% Change		% Change	
Best	2019	7.2	1955	8.2	2000	16.6	2019	6.9	2000	8.6
Worst	2008	−10.2	2008	−8.6	2002	−9.4	2008	−8.5	2010	−7.9
Best & Worst June Weeks										
Best	6/5/2020	6.8	6/2/2000	7.2	6/2/2000	19.0	6/2/2000	8.0	6/2/2000	12.2
Worst	6/30/1950	−6.8	6/30/1950	−7.6	6/15/2001	−8.4	6/12/2020	−4.2	6/12/2020	−4.9
Best & Worst June Days										
Best	6/28/1962	3.8	6/28/1962	3.4	6/2/2000	6.4	6/10/2010	3.0	6/2/2000	4.2
Worst	6/11/2020	−6.9	6/11/2020	−5.9	6/11/2020	−5.3	6/11/2020	−5.9	6/11/2020	−7.6
First Trading Day of Expiration Week: 1980–2021										
Record (#Up – #Down)	22–19		24–17		19–22		22–19		17–23	
Current Streak	U3		U3		U3		U3		U3	
Avg % Change	−0.02		−0.08		−0.20		−0.09		−0.24	
Options Expiration Day: 1980–2021										
Record (#Up – #Down)	23–18		24–17		21–20		24–17		21–20	
Current Streak	D3		D3		U1		D3		D6	
Avg % Change	−0.08		0.003		−0.04		−0.02		−0.03	
Options Expiration Week: 1980–2021										
Record (#Up – #Down)	24–17		23–18		19–22		21–20		20–21	
Current Streak	U2		U4		U3		U4		U3	
Avg % Change	0.01		0.003		−0.11		−0.05		−0.15	
Week After Options Expiration: 1980–2021										
Record (#Up – #Down)	12–29		18–23		22–19		18–23		21–20	
Current Streak	D3		D3		D3		D3		D1	
Avg % Change	−0.56		−0.27		0.06		−0.24		−0.13	
First Trading Day Performance										
% of Time Up	58.3		54.2		58.8		60.5		67.4	
Avg % Change	0.16		0.13		0.12		0.10		0.23	
Last Trading Day Performance										
% of Time Up	56.3		53.5		70.0		57.1		66.7	
Avg % Change	0.08		0.13		0.36		0.10		0.45	

Dow & S&P 1950-June 11, 2021, NASDAQ 1971-June 11, 2021, Russell 1K & 2K 1979-June 11, 2021.

Last Day of June not hot for the Dow;
Down 17 of 30, WOW!

Memorial Day *(Market Closed)*

I have but one lamp by which my feet (or "investments") are guided, and that is the lamp of experience.
I know of no way of judging the future but by the past.
— Patrick Henry (U.S. Founding Father, twice Governor of VA, 1736–1799, March 23, 1775 speech)

Day After Memorial Day, Dow Up 23 of Last 36, But Down 5 of Last 7

D 33.3
S 47.6
N 47.6

Whatever method you use to pick stocks…, your ultimate success or failure will depend on your ability
to ignore the worries of the world long enough to allow your investments to succeed.
It isn't the head but the stomach that determines the fate of the stockpicker.
— Peter Lynch (Fidelity Investments, *Beating the Street*, 1994)

First Trading Day in June, Dow Up 26 of Last 33, Down 4 of 5 2008–2012

D 76.2
S 71.4
N 61.9

Live beyond your means; then you're forced to work hard, you have to succeed.
— Edward G. Robinson (American actor)

Memorial Day Week Dow Down 15 of Last 26, Up 12 Straight 1984–1995

D 61.9
S 76.2
N 71.4

When a country lives on borrowed time, borrowed money and borrowed energy, it is just begging the
markets to discipline it in their own way at their own time. Usually the markets do it in an orderly way—
except when they don't.
— Thomas L. Friedman (*NY Times* Foreign Affairs columnist, 2/24/05)

D 47.6
S 47.6
N 57.1

The heights by great men reached and kept, were not attained by sudden flight, but they, while their
companions slept, were toiling upward in the night.
— Henry Wadsworth Longfellow (American poet, 1807–1882)

TOP-PERFORMING NASDAQ MONTHS

NASDAQ stocks continue to run away during three consecutive months, November, December and January, with an average gain of 6.4% despite the slaughter of November 2000, −22.9%, December 2000, −4.9%, December 2002, −9.7%, November 2007, −6.9%, January 2008, −9.9%, November 2008, −10.8%, January 2009, −6.4%, January 2010, −5.4%, January 2016, −7.9%, and December 2018, −9.5%. Solid gains in November and December 2004 offset January 2005's 5.2% Iraq turmoil–fueled drop.

You can see the months graphically on page 148. January by itself is impressive, up 2.8% on average. April, May and June also shine, creating our NASDAQ Best Eight Months strategy. What appears as a Death Valley abyss occurs during NASDAQ's leanest months: July, August and September. NASDAQ's Best Eight Months seasonal strategy using MACD timing is displayed on page 62.

MONTHLY % CHANGES (JANUARY 1971–MAY 2021)

	NASDAQ Composite*					Dow Jones Industrials			
Month	Total % Change	Avg. % Change	# Up	# Down	Month	Total % Change	Avg. % Change	# Up	# Down
Jan	140.4%	2.8	34	17	Jan	60.5%	1.2	31	19
Feb	30.4	0.6	28	23	Feb	13.8	0.3	30	20
Mar	32.7	0.6	32	19	Mar	38.4	0.8	32	18
Apr	89.7	1.8	34	17	Apr	111.8	2.2	34	16
May	48.6	1.0	31	20	May	10.9	0.2	28	22
Jun	44.5	0.9	28	22	Jun	4.3	0.1	25	24
Jul	30.6	0.6	28	22	Jul	43.4	0.9	29	20
Aug	19.4	0.4	28	22	Aug	−14.1	−0.3	27	22
Sep	−28.8	−0.6	27	23	Sep	−40.8	−0.8	19	30
Oct	30.2	0.6	27	23	Oct	30.7	0.6	30	19
Nov	93.3	1.9	35	15	Nov	69.7	1.4	34	15
Dec	84.9	1.7	30	20	Dec	69.6	1.4	34	15
% Rank					**% Rank**				
Jan	140.4%	2.8	34	17	Apr	111.8%	2.2	34	16
Apr	93.3	1.9	35	15	Nov	69.7	1.4	34	15
Nov	89.7	1.8	34	17	Dec	69.6	1.4	34	15
Dec	84.9	1.7	30	20	Jan	60.5	1.2	31	19
May	48.6	1.0	31	20	Jul	43.4	0.9	29	20
Jun	44.5	0.9	28	22	Mar	38.4	0.8	32	18
Oct	32.7	0.6	32	19	Oct	30.7	0.6	30	19
Mar	30.6	0.6	28	22	Feb	13.8	0.3	30	20
Feb	30.4	0.6	28	23	May	10.9	0.2	28	22
Jul	30.2	0.6	27	23	Jun	4.3	0.1	25	24
Aug	19.4	0.4	28	22	Aug	−14.1	−0.3	27	22
Sep	−28.8	−0.6	27	23	Sep	−40.8	−0.8	19	30
Totals	**615.9%**	**12.3%**			**Totals**	**398.2%**	**8.0%**		
Average		**1.03%**			**Average**		**0.67%**		

Based on NASDAQ composite, prior to Feb. 5, 1971 based on National Quotation Bureau indices.

For comparison, Dow figures are shown. During this period, NASDAQ averaged a 1.03% gain per month, 53.7% more than the Dow's 0.67% per month. Between January 1971 and January 1982, NASDAQ's composite index doubled in 12 years, while the Dow stayed flat. But while NASDAQ plummeted 77.9% from its 2000 highs to the 2002 bottom, the Dow only lost 37.8%. The Great Recession and bear market of 2007–2009 spread its carnage equally across the Dow and NASDAQ. Recent market moves are increasingly more correlated, but NASDAQ still has an advantage.

MONDAY

D 57.1
S 52.4
N 52.4

6

Life is what happens, while you're busy making other plans.
— John Lennon (Beatle, 1940–1980)

June Ends NASDAQ's "Best Eight Months" (Pages 60, 62 and 150)

TUESDAY

D 66.7
S 42.9
N 42.9

7

What investors really get paid for is holding dogs. Small stocks tend to have higher average returns than big stocks, and value stocks tend to have higher average returns than growth stocks.
— Kenneth R. French (Economist, Dartmouth, NBER, b. 1954)

WEDNESDAY

D 66.7
S 61.9
N 47.6

8

There are many people who think they want to be matadors [or money managers or traders] only to find themselves in the ring with two thousand pounds of bull bearing down on them, and then discover that what they really wanted was to wear tight pants and hear the crowd roar.
— Terry Pearce (Founder and President of Leadership Communication, b. 1941)

2008 Second Worst June Ever, Dow –10.2%, S&P –8.6%, Only 1930 Was Worse, NASDAQ June 2008 –9.1%, June 2002 –9.4%

THURSDAY

D 38.1
S 33.3
N 38.1

9

Stocks are super-attractive when the Fed is loosening and interest rates are falling. In sum: Don't fight the Fed!
— Martin Zweig (Fund manager, *Winning on Wall Street*, 1943–2013)

FRIDAY

D 38.1
S 38.1
N 38.1

10

Your chances for success in any undertaking can be measured by your belief in yourself.
— Robert Collier (Direct marketing copywriter & author, 1885–1950)

SATURDAY

11

SUNDAY

12

GET MORE OUT OF NASDAQ'S "BEST EIGHT MONTHS" WITH MACD TIMING

NASDAQ's amazing eight-month run from November through June is hard to miss on pages 58 and 148. A $10,000 investment in these eight months since 1971 gained $1,191,446 versus $863 during the void that is the four-month period July–October (as of June 11, 2021).

Using the same MACD timing indicators on the NASDAQ as is done for the Dow (page 56) has enabled us to capture much of October's improved performance, pumping up NASDAQ's results considerably. Over the 50 years since NASDAQ began, the gain on the same $10,000 more than doubles to $2,878,871 and the gain during the four-month void becomes a loss of $5,563. Only four sizable losses occurred during the favorable period, and the bulk of NASDAQ's bear markets were avoided, including the worst of the 2000–2002 bear.

Updated signals are emailed to our monthly newsletter subscribers as soon as they are triggered. Visit *www.stocktradersalmanac.com*, or see the ad insert for details and a special offer for new subscribers.

BEST EIGHT MONTHS STRATEGY + TIMING

MACD Signal Date	Worst 4 Months July 1–Oct 31* NASDAQ	% Change	Investing $10,000	MACD Signal Date	Best 8 Months Nov 1–June 30* NASDAQ	% Change	Investing $10,000
22-Jul-71	109.54	–3.6	$9,640	4-Nov-71	105.56	24.1	$12,410
7-Jun-72	131.00	–1.8	9,466	23-Oct-72	128.66	–22.7	9,593
25-Jun-73	99.43	–7.2	8,784	7-Dec-73	92.32	–20.2	7,655
3-Jul-74	73.66	–23.2	6,746	7-Oct-74	56.57	47.8	11,314
11-Jun-75	83.60	–9.2	6,125	7-Oct-75	75.88	20.8	13,667
22-Jul-76	91.66	–2.4	5,978	19-Oct-76	89.45	13.2	15,471
27-Jul-77	101.25	–4.0	5,739	4-Nov-77	97.21	26.6	19,586
7-Jun-78	123.10	–6.5	5,366	6-Nov-78	115.08	19.1	23,327
3-Jul-79	137.03	–1.1	5,307	30-Oct-79	135.48	15.5	26,943
20-Jun-80	156.51	26.2	6,697	9-Oct-80	197.53	11.2	29,961
4-Jun-81	219.68	–17.6	5,518	1-Oct-81	181.09	–4.0	28,763
7-Jun-82	173.84	12.5	6,208	7-Oct-82	195.59	57.4	45,273
1-Jun-83	307.95	–10.7	5,544	3-Nov-83	274.86	–14.2	38,844
1-Jun-84	235.90	5.0	5,821	15-Oct-84	247.67	17.3	45,564
3-Jun-85	290.59	–3.0	5,646	1-Oct-85	281.77	39.4	63,516
10-Jun-86	392.83	–10.3	5,064	1-Oct-86	352.34	20.5	76,537
30-Jun-87	424.67	–22.7	3,914	2-Nov-87	328.33	20.1	91,921
8-Jul-88	394.33	–6.6	3,656	29-Nov-88	368.15	22.4	112,511
13-Jun-89	450.73	0.7	3,682	9-Nov-89	454.07	1.9	114,649
11-Jun-90	462.79	–23.0	2,835	2-Oct-90	356.39	39.3	159,706
11-Jun-91	496.62	6.4	3,016	1-Oct-91	528.51	7.4	171,524
11-Jun-92	567.68	1.5	3,061	14-Oct-92	576.22	20.5	206,686
7-Jun-93	694.61	9.9	3,364	1-Oct-93	763.23	–4.4	197,592
17-Jun-94	729.35	5.0	3,532	11-Oct-94	765.57	13.5	224,267
1-Jun-95	868.82	17.2	4,140	13-Oct-95	1018.38	21.6	272,709
3-Jun-96	1238.73	1.0	4,181	7-Oct-96	1250.87	10.3	300,798
4-Jun-97	1379.67	24.4	5,201	3-Oct-97	1715.87	1.8	306,212
1-Jun-98	1746.82	–7.8	4,795	15-Oct-98	1611.01	49.7	458,399
1-Jun-99	2412.03	18.5	5,682	6-Oct-99	2857.21	35.7	622,047
29-Jun-00	3877.23	–18.2	4,648	18-Oct-00	3171.56	–32.2	421,748
1-Jun-01	2149.44	–31.1	3,202	1-Oct-01	1480.46	5.5	444,944
3-Jun-02	1562.56	–24.0	2,434	2-Oct-02	1187.30	38.5	616,247
20-Jun-03	1644.72	15.1	2,802	6-Oct-03	1893.46	4.3	642,746
21-Jun-04	1974.38	–1.6	2,757	1-Oct-04	1942.20	6.1	681,954
8-Jun-05	2060.18	1.5	2,798	19-Oct-05	2091.76	6.1	723,553
1-Jun-06	2219.86	3.9	2,907	5-Oct-06	2306.34	9.5	792,291
7-Jun-07	2541.38	7.9	3,137	1-Oct-07	2740.99	–9.1	724,796
2-Jun-08	2491.53	–31.3	2,155	17-Oct-08	1711.29	6.1	769,000
15-Jun-09	1816.38	17.8	2,539	9-Oct-09	2139.28	1.6	781,313
7-Jun-10	2173.90	18.6	3,011	4-Nov-10	2577.34	7.4	839,130
1-Jun-11	2769.19	–10.5	2,695	7-Oct-11	2479.35	10.8	929,756
1-Jun-12	2747.48	9.6	2,954	6-Nov-12	3011.93	16.2	1,080,376
4-Jun-13	3445.26	10.1	3,252	15-Oct-13	3794.01	15.4	1,227,442
26-Jun-14	4379.05	0.9	3,281	21-Oct-14	4419.48	14.5	1,405,421
4-Jun-15	5059.12	–5.5	3,101	5-Oct-15	4781.26	1.4	1,425,097
13-Jun-16	4848.44	9.5	3,396	24-Oct-16	5309.83	18.8	1,693,015
9-Jun-17	6207.92	11.3	3,780	28-Nov-17	6912.36	11.6	1,859,187
21-Jun-18	7712.95	–5.3	3,580	31-Oct-18	7305.90	7.9	2,006,063
19-Jul-19	8146.49	–1.1	3,541	11-Oct-19	8057.04	17.8	2,441,987
11-Jun-20	9492.73	25.3	4,437	5-Nov-20	11890.93	18.3	2,888,871
11-Jun-21**	14069.42						
	50-Year Loss		**($5,563)**		**50-Year Gain**		**$2,878,871**

** As of 6/11/2021 – NASDAQ Seasonal Sell NOT triggered yet
* MACD-generated entry and exit points (earlier or later) can lengthen or shorten eight-month periods.

Monday of Triple Witching Week, Dow Down 14 of Last 25 **MONDAY**

D 57.1
S 57.1
N 52.4

13

There is no one who can replace America. Without American leadership, there is no leadership.
That puts a tremendous burden on the American people to do something positive.
You can't be tempted by the usual nationalism.
— Lee Hong-koo (South Korean prime minister 1994–1995 and ambassador to U.S. 1998–2000,
NY Times 2/25/2009)

TUESDAY

D 57.1
S 57.1
N 57.1

14

If a battered stock refuses to sink any lower no matter how many negative articles appear in the papers,
that stock is worth a close look.
— James L. Fraser (Investment counselor, writer, editor, publisher, CFA, *Contrary Investor*, 1930–2013)

FOMC Meeting (2 Days) **WEDNESDAY**

D 57.1
S 66.7
N 66.7

15

Another factor contributing to productivity is technology, particularly the rapid introduction
of new microcomputers based on single-chip circuits.... The results over the next decade
will be a second industrial revolution.
— Yale Hirsch (Creator of *Stock Trader's Almanac, Smart Money Newsletter* 9/22/1976, b. 1923)

Triple Witching Week Often Up in Bull Markets and Down in Bears (Page 108) **THURSDAY**

D 61.9
S 57.1
N 57.1

16

English stocks...are springing up like mushrooms this year...forced up to a quite unreasonable level and
then, for most part, collapse. In this way, I have made over 400 pounds...[Speculating] makes small
demands on one's time, and it's worth while running some risk in order to relieve the enemy of his money.
— Karl Marx (German social philosopher and revolutionary, in an 1864 letter to his uncle, 1818–1883)

June Triple Witching Day, Dow Up 10 of Last 19, But Down 6 of Last 7 **FRIDAY**

D 52.4
S 57.1
N 66.7

17

Bill Gates' One-Minus Staffing: *For every project, figure out the bare minimum of people needed to staff*
it. Cut to the absolute muscle and bones, then take out one more. When you understaff, people jump on the
loose ball. You find out who the real performers are. Not so when you're overstaffed. People sit around
waiting for somebody else to do it.
— Quoted by Rich Karlgaard (Publisher, *Forbes* Dec. 25, 2000)

SATURDAY

18

Father's Day **SUNDAY**

19

TRIPLE RETURNS, FEWER TRADES: BEST 6 + 4-YEAR CYCLE

We first introduced this strategy to *Almanac Investor* newsletter subscribers in October 2006. Recurring seasonal stock market patterns and the four-year Presidential Election/ Stock Market Cycle (page 132) have been integral to our research since the first Almanac more than 50 years ago. Yale Hirsch discovered the Best Six Months in 1986 (page 54), and it has been a cornerstone of our seasonal investment analysis and strategies ever since.

Most of the market's gains have occurred during the Best Six Months, and the market generally hits a low point every four years in the first (post-election) year or second (midterm) year and exhibits the greatest gains in the third (pre-election) year. This strategy combines the best of these two market phenomena, the Best Six Months and the 4-Year Cycle, timing entries and exits with MACD (pages 56 and 62).

We've gone back to 1949 to include the full four-year cycle that began with post-election year 1949. Only four trades every four years are needed to nearly triple the results of the Best Six Months. Buy and sell during the post-election and midterm years and then hold from the midterm MACD seasonal buy signal sometime after October 1 until the post-election MACD seasonal sell signal sometime after April 1, approximately 2.5 years: solid returns, less effort, lower transaction fees and fewer taxable events.

BEST SIX MONTHS+TIMING+4-YEAR CYCLE STRATEGY			
	DJIA		DJIA
	% Change	Investing	% Change	Investing
	May 1–Oct 31*	$10,000	Nov 1–Apr 30*	$10,000
1949	3.0%	$10,300	17.5%	$11,750
1950	7.3	11,052	19.7	14,065
1951		11,052		14,065
1952		11,052		14,065
1953	0.2	11,074	17.1	16,470
1954	13.5	12,569	35.7	22,350
1955		12,569		22,350
1956		12,569		22,350
1957	−12.3	11,023	4.9	23,445
1958	17.3	12,930	27.8	29,963
1959		12,930		29,963
1960		12,930		29,963
1961	2.9	13,305	−1.5	29,514
1962	−15.3	11,269	58.5	46,780
1963		11,269		46,780
1964		11,269		46,780
1965	2.6	11,562	−2.5	45,611
1966	−16.4	9,666	22.2	55,737
1967		9,666		55,737
1968		9,666		55,737
1969	−11.9	8,516	−6.7	52,003
1970	−1.4	8,397	21.5	63,184
1971		8,397		63,184
1972		8,397		63,184
1973	−11.0	7,473	0.1	63,247
1974	−22.4	5,799	42.5	90,127
1975		5,799		90,127
1976		5,799		90,127
1977	−11.4	5,138	0.5	90,578
1978	−4.5	4,907	26.8	114,853
1979		4,907		114,853
1980		4,907		114,853
1981	−14.6	4,191	0.4	115,312
1982	15.5	4,841	25.9	145,178
1983		4,841		145,178
1984		4,841		145,178
1985	7.0	5,180	38.1	200,491
1986	−2.8	5,035	33.2	267,054
1987		5,035		267,054
1988		5,035		267,054
1989	9.8	5,528	3.3	275,867
1990	−6.7	5,158	35.1	372,696
1991		5,158		372,696
1992		5,158		372,696
1993	5.5	5,442	5.6	393,455
1994	3.7	5,643	88.2	740,482
1995		5,643		740,482
1996		5,643		740,482
1997	3.6	5,846	18.5	877,471
1998	−12.4	5,121	36.3	1,195,993
1999		5,121		1,195,993
2000		5,121		1,195,993
2001	−17.3	4,235	15.8	1,384,960
2002	−25.2	3,168	34.2	1,858,616
2003		3,168		1,858,616
2004		3,168		1,858,616
2005	−0.5	3,152	7.7	2,001,729
2006	4.7	3,300	−31.7	1,367,181
2007		3,300		1,367,181
2008		3,300		1,367,181
2009	23.8	4,085	10.8	1,514,738
2010	4.6	4,273	27.4	1,929,777
2011		4,273		1,929,777
2012		4,273		1,929,777
2013	4.1	4,448	7.1	2,066,791
2014	2.3	4,550	24.0	2,562,820
2015		4,550		2,562,820
2016		4,550		2,562,820
2017	15.7	$5,265	0.4	$2,573,072
2018**	5.0	$5,528	34.6	$3,463,354
Average	−0.5%		9.7%	
# Up	20		32	
# Down	16		4	
72-Year Gain (Loss)		($4,472)		$3,453,354

* MACD and 2.5-year hold lengthen and shorten six-month periods.
** As of April 22, 2021 Seasonal Sell signal.

FOUR TRADES EVERY FOUR YEARS		
	Worst	Best
	Six Months	Six Months
Year	May–Oct	Nov–April
Post-election	Sell	Buy
Midterm	Sell	Buy
Pre-election	Hold	Hold
Election	Hold	Hold

MONDAY

D 47.6
S 52.4
N 52.4

20

Two signposts on the road to wisdom: 1. Nothing is the end of the world and, 2.
Nobody gives a hoot what you think.
— Phil Pearlman (Chief Behavioral Officer at Osprey Funds, b. 1967)

TUESDAY

D 38.1
S 47.6
N 61.9

21

First-rate people hire first-rate people; second-rate people hire third-rate people.
— Leo Rosten (American author, 1908–1997)

Week After June Triple Witching, Dow Down 27 of Last 31
Average Loss Since 1990, 1.1%

WEDNESDAY

D 38.1
S 42.9
N 42.9

22

Every man with a new idea is a crank until the idea succeeds.
— Mark Twain (American novelist and satirist, pen name of Samuel Longhorne Clemens, 1835–1910)

THURSDAY

D 42.9
S 47.6
N 38.1

23

Follow the course opposite to custom and you will almost always do well.
— Jean-Jacques Rousseau (Swiss philosopher, 1712–1778)

FRIDAY

D 28.6
S 28.6
N 23.8

24

If banking institutions are protected by the taxpayer and they are given free reign to speculate,
I may not live long enough to see the crisis, but my soul is going to come back and haunt you.
— Paul A. Volcker (Fed Chairman 1979–1987, Chair Economic Recovery Advisory Board, 2/2/2010, b. 1927)

SATURDAY

25

July Almanac Investor Sector Seasonalities: See Pages 94, 96 and 98

SUNDAY

26

JULY ALMANAC

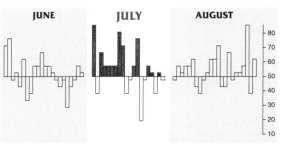

JULY							AUGUST						
S	M	T	W	T	F	S	S	M	T	W	T	F	S
					1	2		1	2	3	4	5	6
3	4	5	6	7	8	9	7	8	9	10	11	12	13
10	11	12	13	14	15	16	14	15	16	17	18	19	20
17	18	19	20	21	22	23	21	22	23	24	25	26	27
24	25	26	27	28	29	30	28	29	30	31			
31													

Market Probability Chart above is a graphic representation of the S&P 500 Recent Market Probability Calendar on page 126.

◆ July is the best month of the third quarter (page 68) ◆ Start of 2nd half brings an inflow of retirement funds ◆ First trading day Dow up 26 of last 32 ◆ Graph above shows strength in the first half of July ◆ Huge gain in July usually provides better buying opportunity over next 4 months ◆ Start of NASDAQ's worst four months of the year (page 60) ◆ Midterm election Julys are ranked #3 Dow (up 11, down 7), #5 S&P (up 10, down 8), and #12 NASDAQ (up 4, down 8)

July Vital Statistics

	DJIA	S&P 500	NASDAQ	Russell 1K	Russell 2K
Rank	4	4	8	6	10
Up	46	41	28	22	22
Down	25	30	22	20	20
Average % Change	1.3%	1.1%	0.6%	0.9%	−0.2%
Midterm Election Year	1.3%	0.9%	−1.9%	−0.7%	−3.8%

		Best & Worst July								
		% Change		% Change		% Change		% Change		% Change
Best	1989	9.0	1989	8.8	1997	10.5	1989	8.2	1980	11.0
Worst	1969	−6.6	2002	−7.9	2002	−9.2	2002	−7.5	2002	−15.2

		Best & Worst July Weeks								
Best	7/17/2009	7.3	7/17/2009	7.0	7/17/2009	7.4	7/17/2009	7.0	7/17/2009	8.0
Worst	7/19/2002	−7.7	7/19/2002	−8.0	7/28/2000	−10.5	7/19/2002	−7.4	7/2/2010	−7.2

		Best & Worst July Days								
Best	7/24/2002	6.4	7/24/2002	5.7	7/29/2002	5.8	7/24/2002	5.6	7/29/2002	4.9
Worst	7/19/2002	−4.6	7/19/2002	−3.8	7/28/2000	−4.7	7/19/2002	−3.6	7/23/2002	−4.1

First Trading Day of Expiration Week: 1980–2021					
Record (#Up − #Down)	26–15	25–16	27–14	25–16	22–19
Current Streak	U3	D1	D1	D1	D3
Avg % Change	0.12	0.03	0.01	0.008	−0.07

Options Expiration Day: 1980–2021					
Record (#Up − #Down)	17–22	20–21	17–24	20–21	16–25
Current Streak	D4	U1	U1	U1	U1
Avg % Change	−0.23	−0.26	−0.38	−0.27	−0.42

Options Expiration Week: 1980–2021					
Record (#Up − #Down)	26–15	24–17	21–20	24–17	23–18
Current Streak	U1	U1	D3	U1	U1
Avg % Change	0.49	0.19	0.09	−0.27	0.03

Week After Options Expiration: 1980–2021					
Record (#Up − #Down)	22–19	20–21	18–23	21–20	15–26
Current Streak	D1	D1	D1	D1	D1
Avg % Change	−0.08	−0.11	−0.38	−0.12	−0.36

First Trading Day Performance					
% of Time Up	66.2	73.2	64.0	76.2	66.7
Avg % Change	0.26	0.27	0.17	0.33	0.11

Last Trading Day Performance					
% of Time Up	50.7	60.6	50.0	57.1	61.9
Avg % Change	0.02	0.06	−0.02	−0.02	−0.04

Dow & S&P 1950-June 11, 2021, NASDAQ 1971-June 11, 2021, Russell 1K & 2K 1979-June 11, 2021.

When Dow and S&P in July are inferior,
NASDAQ days tend to be even drearier.

Studying Market History Can Produce Gains

LIKE THESE

▶ iShares PHLX Semiconductor (SOXX) **up 19.2%** in 2 months
▶ iShares DJ Transports (IYT) **up 25.5%** in 5 months
▶ Global X Copper Miners (COPX) **up 30.1%** in 6 months
▶ iShares Russell 2000 (IWM) **up 28.9%** in 6 months

AND THESE

▶ Avid Tech Inc (AVID) **up 177.5%** in 8 months
▶ Customers Bancp (CUBI) **up 116.7%** in 8 months
▶ Kansas City Southern (KSU) **up 51.8%** in 8 months
▶ Abbott Labs (ABT) **up 42.8%** in 1.25 years

Jeffrey A. Hirsch
Editor Stock Trader's Almanac,
Chief Market Strategist
Probabilities Fund Management, LLC

What do all these big winners have in common? All were undervalued and off Wall Street's radar screen when we selected them. All were chosen by my team of highly-trained veteran market analysts with decades of experience trading and investing in the market with real money. All passed through our multi-disciplined approach that combines our renowned *Stock Trader's Almanac* behavioral finance analysis of the 4-Year Election Cycle, market and sector seasonality in conjunction with our proprietary fundamental stock screening criteria with the entries and exits pinpointed using old-school technical analysis. We refer to our blend of historical rules-based strategy with technical and fundamental tactical signals as DYNAMIC Investing.

My name is Jeffrey A. Hirsch, I am the editor-in chief of the *Stock Trader's Almanac* and I want to introduce you to my **eNewsletter ALMANAC INVESTOR**. ALMANAC INVESTOR is a unique service that brings you top stocks and top sectors at the right time every week. Subscribe to my highly acclaimed weekly digital subscription service, *Almanac Investor* eNewsletter, which culminates over 50 years of independent market research and publishing every Thursday you will receive a detailed report updating our market outlook and portfolio positions plus timely Alerts as warranted on our seasonal signals and indicators, bringing you actionable trades and investment ideas with clear and specific buy and sell points.

600.4% Gain Since 2001 Vs. 253.9% for S&P 500

Almanac Investor eNewsletter, is the culmination of all we've done with the *Almanac* and newsletters over the years. Our *Almanac Investor* Stock Portfolio currently has a Total Return of 600.4% since inception in 2001 versus a 253.9% return for the S&P 500 over the same timeframe. This includes all of our sold positions.

▶ Excludes dividends, fees and any foreign currency gains or losses
▶ No margin or leverage used
▶ Long and Short stock trades across Small, Mid and Large-Cap companies
▶ Rarely fully invested, some cash balance maintained

Get The *2023 Stock Trader's Almanac* FREE

Save up to 57% Off the Regular Pricing and get a **FREE** *Stock Trader's Almanac (Retail value $50).* Your subscription includes, weekly Email Alerts, interim buy and sell signal alerts, full access to the website and a **FREE** annual copy of the *Stock Trader's Almanac*. **Subscribe today at www.StockTradersAlmanac.com click "Subscribe Now". TWO WAYS TO SAVE:**

▶ **1-Year @ $150** – 48% Off vs. Monthly – Use promo code **1YRSTA22**
▶ **2-Years @ $250 – BEST DEAL**, 57% Off – Use promo code **2YRSTA22**

Go to **www.STOCKTRADERSALMANAC.com**
and click "**Subscribe Now**" or CALL 914-750-5860

Those who study market history are bound to profit from it!

Now you can find out which seasonal trends are on schedule and which are not, and how to take advantage of them. You will be kept abreast of upcoming market-moving events and what our indicators are saying about the next major market move. Every week you will receive timely dispatches about bullish and bearish seasonal patterns.

Our digital subscription service, *Almanac Investor*, provides all this plus unusual investing opportunities – exciting small-, mid- and large-cap stocks; seasoned, under-valued equities; timely sector ETF trades and more. Our **Data-Rich and Data-Driven Market Cycle Analysis** is the only investment tool of its kind that helps traders and investors forecast market trends with accuracy and confidence.

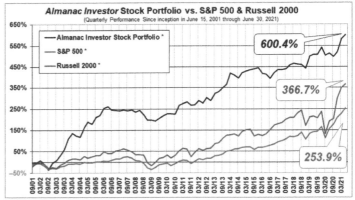

Almanac Investor Stock Portfolio vs. S&P 500 & Russell 2000
(Quarterly Performance Since inception in June 15, 2001 through June 30, 2021)
- Almanac Investor Stock Portfolio *
- S&P 500 *
- Russell 2000 *
600.4% / 366.7% / 253.9%

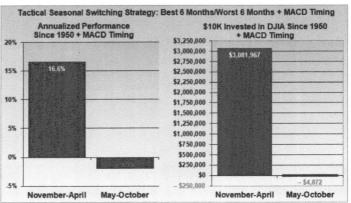

Tactical Seasonal Switching Strategy: Best 6 Months/Worst 6 Months + MACD Timing
Annualized Performance Since 1950 + MACD Timing — 16.6% (November-April)
$10K Invested in DJIA Since 1950 + MACD Timing — $3,081,967 (November-April), –$4,872 (May-October)

YOU RECEIVE WEEKLY EMAIL ALERTS CONTAINING:	
	▸ Opportune ETF and Stock Trading Ideas with Specific Buy and Sell Price Limits
	▸ Timely Data-Rich and Data-Driven Market Analysis
	▸ Access to Webinars, Videos, Tools and Resources
	▸ Market-Tested and Time-Proven Short- and Long-term Trading Strategies
	▸ Best Six-Months Switching Strategy MACD Timing Signals.

MONDAY
D 38.1
S 42.9
N 52.4
27

The market is a voting machine, whereon countless individuals register choices which are the product partly of reason and partly of emotion.
— Graham & Dodd

TUESDAY
D 52.4
S 47.6
N 66.7
28

The CROWD is always wrong at market turning points but often times right once a trend sets in. The reason many market fighters go broke is they believe the CROWD is always wrong. There is nothing further from the truth. Unless volatility is extremely low or very high one should think twice before betting against the CROWD.
— Shawn Andrew (Trader, Ricercar Fund /SA, 12/21/01)

WEDNESDAY
D 52.4
S 57.1
N 61.9
29

If you are ready to give up everything else to study the whole history of the market as carefully as a medical student studies anatomy and you have the cool nerves of a great gambler, the sixth sense of a clairvoyant, and the courage of a lion, you have a ghost of a chance.
— Bernard Baruch (Financier, speculator, statesman, presidential adviser, 1870–1965)

Last Day of Q2 Bearish for Dow, Down 17 of Last 30, But Up 8 of Last 10, Bullish for NASDAQ, Up 21 of 29

THURSDAY
D 52.4
S 52.4
N 61.9
30

Develop interest in life as you see it; in people, things, literature, music—the world is so rich, simply throbbing with rich treasures, beautiful souls and interesting people. Forget yourself.
— Henry Miller (American writer, *Tropic of Cancer, Tropic of Capricorn*, 1891–1980)

First Trading Day in July, S&P Up 28 of Last 32, Average Gain 0.5%

FRIDAY
D 76.2
S 85.7
N 76.2
1

There is nothing as invigorating as the ego boost that comes from having others sign on when your company is just a dream. What they are saying when they agree to service customers, suppliers, employers or distributors is that they believe in you.
— Joshua Hyatt (*Inc. Magazine, Mapping the Entrepreneurial Mind*, August 1991)

SATURDAY
2

SUNDAY
3

FIRST MONTH OF QUARTERS IS THE MOST BULLISH

We have observed over the years that the investment calendar reflects the annual, semiannual and quarterly operations of institutions during January, April and July. The opening month of the first three quarters produces the greatest gains in the Dow Jones Industrials, the S&P 500 and NASDAQ.

The fourth quarter had behaved quite differently, since it is affected by year-end portfolio adjustments and presidential and congressional elections in even-numbered years. Since 1991, major turnarounds have helped October join the ranks of bullish first months of quarters. October transformed into a bear-killing-turnaround month, posting Dow gains in 16 of the last 23 years; 2008 was a significant exception. (See pages 156–171.)

After experiencing the most powerful bull market of all time during the 1990s, followed by two ferocious bear markets early in the millennium, we divided the monthly average percentage changes into two groups: before 1991 and after. Comparing the month-by-month quarterly behavior of the three major U.S. averages in the table, you'll see that first months of the first three quarters perform best overall. Nasty sell-offs in April 2000, 2002, 2004 and 2005, and July 2000–2002 and 2004 hit the NASDAQ hardest. The bear market of October 2007–March 2009, which cut the markets more than in half, took a toll on every first month except April. October 2008 was the worst month in a decade. January was also a difficult month in eight of the last fourteen years, pulling its performance lower. (See pages 156–171.)

Between 1950 and 1990, the S&P 500 gained 1.3% (Dow, 1.4%) on average in first months of the first three quarters. Second months barely eked out any gain, while third months, thanks to March, moved up 0.23% (Dow, 0.07%) on average. NASDAQ's first month of the first three quarters averages 1.67% from 1971 to 1990, with July being a negative drag.

DOW JONES INDUSTRIALS, S&P 500 AND NASDAQ
AVERAGE MONTHLY % CHANGES BY QUARTER

	DJIA 1950–1990			S&P 500 1950–1990			NASDAQ 1971–1990		
	1st Mo	2nd Mo	3rd Mo	1st Mo	2nd Mo	3rd Mo	1st Mo	2nd Mo	3rd Mo
1Q	1.5%	−0.01%	1.0%	1.5%	−0.1%	1.1%	3.8%	1.2%	0.9%
2Q	1.6	−0.4	0.1	1.3	−0.1	0.3	1.7	0.8	1.1
3Q	1.1	0.3	−0.9	1.1	0.3	−0.7	−0.5	0.1	−1.6
Tot	4.2%	−0.1%	0.2%	3.9%	0.1%	0.7%	5.0%	2.1%	0.4%
Avg	1.40%	−0.04%	0.07%	1.30%	0.03%	0.23%	1.67%	0.70%	0.13%
4Q	−0.1%	1.4%	1.7%	0.4%	1.7%	1.6%	−1.4%	1.6%	1.4%
	DJIA 1991-May 2021			S&P 500 1991-May 2021			NASDAQ 1991-May 2021		
1Q	0.3%	0.4%	0.8%	0.5%	0.1%	0.9%	2.1%	0.2%	0.5%
2Q	2.5	0.5	−0.5	2.2	0.7	−0.1	1.8	1.0	0.8
3Q	1.5	−0.5	−0.4	1.2	−0.3	−0.2	1.4	0.6	0.1
Tot	4.3%	0.4%	−0.1%	3.9%	0.5%	0.6%	5.3%	1.8%	1.4%
Avg	1.43%	0.13%	−0.03%	1.30%	0.17%	0.20%	1.77%	0.59%	0.47%
4Q	1.4%	2.2%	1.4%	1.3%	1.8%	1.4%	1.9%	2.1%	1.9%
	DJIA 1950-May 2021			S&P 500 1950-May 2021			NASDAQ 1971-May 2021		
1Q	0.9%	0.2%	0.9%	1.1%	0.002%	1.0%	2.8%	0.6%	0.6%
2Q	2.0	−0.01	−0.2	1.7	0.2	0.1	1.8	1.0	0.9
3Q	1.3	−0.1	−0.7	1.1	0.03	−0.5	0.6	0.4	−0.6
Tot	4.2%	0.1%	0.0%	3.9%	0.2%	0.6%	5.2%	2.0%	0.9%
Avg	1.40%	0.03%	0.00%	1.30%	0.08%	0.20%	1.74%	0.66%	0.30%
4Q	0.5%	1.8%	1.5%	0.8%	1.7%	1.5%	0.6%	1.9%	1.7%

Independence Day  *(Market Closed)*

Amongst democratic nations, each generation is a new people.
— Alexis de Tocqueville (Author, *Democracy in America*, 1840, 1805–1859)

Market Subject to Elevated Volatility After July 4th

TUESDAY
5

D 33.3
S 38.1
N 38.1

We all want progress, but if you're on the wrong road, progress means doing an about-turn and walking back to the right road; in that case, the man who turns back soonest is the most progressive.
— C. S. Lewis (Irish novelist, poet, academic, 1898–1963)

July Begins NASDAQ's "Worst Four Months" (Pages 60, 62 and 150)

WEDNESDAY
6

D 57.1
S 66.7
N 61.9

A good manager is a man who isn't worried about his own career but rather the careers of those who work for him… Don't worry about yourself! Take care of those who work for you and you'll float to greatness on their achievements.
— H.S.M. Burns (Scottish CEO Shell Oil 1947–1960, 1900–1971)

THURSDAY
7

D 57.1
S 57.1
N 61.9

Charts not only tell what was, they tell what is; and a trend from was to is (projected linearly into the will be) contains better percentages than clumsy guessing.
— Robert A. Levy (Chairman, Cato Institute, founder, CDA Investment Technologies, *The Relative Strength Concept of Common Stock Forecasting*, 1968, b. 1941)

July is the Best Performing Dow and S&P Month of the Third Quarter (Page 68)

FRIDAY
8

D 61.9
S 57.1
N 57.1

The game [or market] can be reduced to a social science; that it is simply a matter of figuring out the odds, and exploiting the laws of probability; that baseball players [or investors] follow strikingly predictable patterns.
— Michael Lewis (American author & journalist, what Oakland A's GM Billy Beane claims to believe, *Moneyball: The Art of Winning an Unfair Game*, b. 1960)

SATURDAY
9

SUNDAY
10

2020 DAILY DOW POINT CHANGES (DOW JONES INDUSTRIAL AVERAGE)

Week #		Monday**	Tuesday	Wednsday	Thursday	Friday** 2019 Close	Weekly Dow Close 28538.44	Net Point Change
1			Holiday		330.36	−233.92	28634.88	96.44
2	J	68.50	−119.70	161.41	211.81	−133.13	28823.77	188.89
3	A	83.28	32.62	90.55	267.42	50.46	29348.10	524.33
4	N	Holiday	−152.06	−9.77	−26.18	−170.36	28989.73	−358.37
5		−453.93	187.05	11.60	124.99	−603.41	28256.03	−733.70
6		143.78	407.82	483.22	88.92	−277.26	29102.51	846.48
7	F	174.31	−0.48	275.08	−128.11	−25.23	29398.08	295.57
8	E B	Holiday	−165.89	115.84	−128.05	−227.57	28992.41	−405.67
9		−1031.61	−879.44	−123.77	−1190.95	−357.28	25409.36	−3583.05
10	M	1293.96	−785.91	1173.45	−969.58	−256.50	25864.78	455.42
11	A	−2013.76	1167.14	−1464.94	−2352.60	1985.00	23185.62	−2679.16
12	R	−2997.10	1048.86	−1338.46	188.27	−913.21	19173.98	−4011.64
13		−582.05	2112.98	495.64	1351.62	−915.39	21636.78	2462.80
14		690.70	−410.32	−973.65	469.93	−360.91	21052.53	−584.25
15	A	1627.46	−26.13	779.71	285.80	Holiday	23719.37	2666.84
16	P	−328.60	558.99	−445.41	33.33	704.81	24242.49	523.12
17	R	−592.05	−631.56	456.94	39.44	260.01	23775.27	−467.22
18		358.51	−32.23	532.31	−288.14	−622.03	23723.69	−51.58
19	M	26.07	133.33	−218.45	211.25	455.43	24331.32	607.63
20	A	−109.33	−457.21	−516.81	377.37	60.08	23685.42	−645.90
21	Y	911.95	−390.51	369.04	−101.78	−8.96	24465.16	779.74
22		Holiday	529.95	553.16	−147.63	−17.53	25383.11	917.95
23		91.91	267.63	527.24	11.93	829.16	27110.98	1727.87
24	J U	461.46	−300.14	−282.31	−1861.82	477.37	25605.54	−1505.44
25	N	157.62	526.82	−170.37	−39.51	−208.64	25871.46	265.92
26		153.50	131.14	−710.16	299.66	−730.05	25015.55	−855.91
27		580.25	217.08	−77.91	92.39	Holiday	25827.36	811.81
28	J	459.67	−396.85	177.10	−361.19	369.21	26075.30	247.94
29	U	10.50	556.79	227.51	−135.39	−62.76	26671.95	596.65
30	L	8.92	159.53	165.44	−353.51	−182.44	26469.89	−202.06
31		114.88	−205.49	160.29	−225.92	114.67	26428.32	−41.57
32		236.08	164.07	373.05	185.46	46.50	27433.48	1005.16
33	A	357.96	−104.53	289.93	−80.12	34.30	27931.02	497.54
34	U	−86.11	−66.84	−85.19	46.85	190.60	27930.33	−0.69
35	G	378.13	−60.02	83.48	160.35	161.60	28653.87	723.54
36		−223.82	215.61	454.84	−807.77	−159.42	28133.31	−520.56
37	S	Holiday	−632.42	439.58	−405.89	131.06	27665.64	−467.67
38	E	327.69	2.27	36.78	−130.40	−244.56	27657.42	−8.22
39	P	−509.72	140.48	−525.05	52.31	358.52	27173.96	−483.46
40		410.10	−131.40	329.04	35.20	−134.09	27682.81	508.85
41	O	465.83	−375.88	530.70	122.05	161.39	28586.90	904.09
42	C	250.62	−157.71	−165.81	−19.80	112.11	28606.31	19.41
43	T	−410.89	113.37	−97.97	152.84	−28.09	28335.57	−270.74
44		−650.19	−222.19	−943.24	139.16	−157.51	26501.60	−1833.97
45		423.45	554.98	367.63	542.52	−66.78	28323.40	1821.80
46	N	834.57	262.95	−23.29	−317.46	399.64	29479.81	1156.41
47	O V	470.63	−167.09	−344.93	44.81	−219.75	29263.48	−216.33
48		327.79	454.97	−173.77	Holiday	37.90*	29910.37	646.89
49		−271.73	185.28	59.87	85.73	248.74	30218.26	307.89
50	D	−148.47	104.09	−105.07	−69.55	47.11	30046.37	−171.89
51	E	−184.82	337.76	−44.77	148.83	−124.32	30179.05	132.68
52	C	37.40	−200.94	114.32	70.04*	Holiday	30199.87	20.82
53		204.10	−68.30	73.89	196.92		30606.48	406.61
TOTALS		1126.98	3852.74	1067.54	−4418.94	439.72		2068.04

Outline Bold Color: Down Friday, Down Monday
*Shortened trading day: Nov 27, Dec 24
** Monday denotes first trading day of week, Friday denotes last trading day of week

Monday Before July Expiration, Dow Up 14 of Last 18

MONDAY

D 57.1
S 57.1
N 66.7

11

Only buy stocks when the market declines 10% from that date a year ago,
which happens once or twice a decade.
— Eugene D. Brody (Oppenheimer Capital)

TUESDAY

D 52.4
S 57.1
N 61.9

12

There has never been a commercial technology like this (Internet) in the history of the world,
whereby the minute you adopt it, it forces you to think and act globally.
— Robert D. Hormats (Under Secretary of State Economic, Energy and the Environment 2009–2013,
Goldman Sachs 1982–2009, b.1943)

WEDNESDAY

D 81.0
S 81.0
N 66.7

13

Some traders are born with an innate discipline. Most have to learn it the hard way.
— J. Welles Wilder Jr. (Creator of several technical indicators including Relative Strength Index (RSI) 1935–2021)

THURSDAY

D 76.2
S 71.4
N 76.2

14

A realist believes that what is done or left undone in the short run determines the long run.
— Sydney J. Harris (American journalist and author, 1917–1986)

July Expiration Day, Dow Down 14 of Last 21, –4.6% 2002, –2.5% 2010

FRIDAY

D 52.4
S 38.1
N 52.4

15

The only function of economic forecasting is to make astrology look respectable.
— John Kenneth Galbraith (Canadian/American economist and diplomat, 1908–2006)

SATURDAY

16

SUNDAY

17

DON'T SELL STOCKS ON MONDAY OR FRIDAY

Since 1989, Monday*, Tuesday and Wednesday have been the most consistently bullish days of the week for the Dow, and Thursday and Friday* the least bullish, as traders have become reluctant to stay long going into the weekend. Since 1989 Mondays and Tuesdays gained 20471.73 Dow points, while Thursdays and Fridays have gained 4950.52 points. Also broken out are the last twenty and a half years to illustrate Monday's and Friday's poor performance in bear market years 2001–2002 and 2008–2009. See pages 70, 78 and 143–146 for more.

ANNUAL DOW POINT CHANGES FOR DAYS OF THE WEEK SINCE 1953

Year	Monday*	Tuesday	Wednesday	Thursday	Friday*	Year's DJIA Closing	Year's Point Change
1953	−36.16	−7.93	19.63	5.76	7.70	280.90	−11.00
1954	15.68	3.27	24.31	33.96	46.27	404.39	123.49
1955	−48.36	26.38	46.03	−0.66	60.62	488.40	84.01
1956	−27.15	−9.36	−15.41	8.43	64.56	499.47	11.07
1957	−109.50	−7.71	64.12	3.32	−14.01	435.69	−63.78
1958	17.50	23.59	29.10	22.67	55.10	583.65	147.96
1959	−44.48	29.04	4.11	13.60	93.44	679.36	95.71
1960	−111.04	−3.75	−5.62	6.74	50.20	615.89	−63.47
1961	−23.65	10.18	87.51	−5.96	47.17	731.14	115.25
1962	−101.60	26.19	9.97	−7.70	−5.90	652.10	−79.04
1963	−8.88	47.12	16.23	22.39	33.99	762.95	110.85
1964	−0.29	−17.94	39.84	5.52	84.05	874.13	111.18
1965	−73.23	39.65	57.03	3.20	68.48	969.26	95.13
1966	−153.24	−27.73	56.13	−46.19	−12.54	785.69	−183.57
1967	−68.65	31.50	25.42	92.25	38.90	905.11	119.42
1968†	6.41	34.94	25.16	−72.06	44.19	943.75	38.64
1969	−164.17	−36.70	18.33	23.79	15.36	800.36	−143.39
1970	−100.05	−46.09	116.07	−3.48	72.11	838.92	38.56
1971	−2.99	9.56	13.66	8.04	23.01	890.20	51.28
1972	−87.40	−1.23	65.24	8.46	144.75	1020.02	129.82
1973	−174.11	10.52	−5.94	36.67	−36.30	850.86	−169.16
1974	−149.37	47.51	−20.31	−13.70	−98.75	616.24	−234.62
1975	39.46	−109.62	56.93	124.00	125.40	852.41	236.17
1976	70.72	71.76	50.88	−33.70	−7.42	1004.65	152.24
1977	−65.15	−44.89	−79.61	−5.62	21.79	831.17	−173.48
1978	−31.29	−70.84	71.33	−64.67	69.31	805.01	−26.16
1979	−32.52	9.52	−18.84	75.18	0.39	838.74	33.73
1980	−86.51	135.13	137.67	−122.00	60.96	963.99	125.25
1981	−45.68	−49.51	−13.95	−14.67	34.82	875.00	−88.99
1982	5.71	86.20	28.37	−1.47	52.73	1046.54	171.54
1983	30.51	−30.92	149.68	61.16	1.67	1258.64	212.10
1984	−73.80	78.02	−139.24	92.79	−4.84	1211.57	−47.07
1985	80.36	52.70	51.26	46.32	104.46	1546.67	335.10
1986	−39.94	97.63	178.65	29.31	83.63	1895.95	349.28
1987	−559.15	235.83	392.03	139.73	−165.56	1938.83	42.88
1988	268.12	166.44	−60.48	−230.84	86.50	2168.57	229.74
1989	−53.31	143.33	233.25	90.25	171.11	2753.20	584.63
Subtotal	*−1937.20*	*941.79*	*1708.54*	*330.82*	*1417.35*		*2461.30*
1990	219.90	−25.22	47.96	−352.55	−9.63	2633.66	−119.54
1991	191.13	47.97	174.53	254.79	−133.25	3168.83	535.17
1992	237.80	−49.67	3.12	108.74	−167.71	3301.11	132.28
1993	322.82	−37.03	243.87	4.97	−81.65	3754.09	452.98
1994	206.41	−95.33	29.98	−168.87	108.16	3834.44	80.35
1995	262.97	210.06	357.02	140.07	312.56	5117.12	1282.68
1996	626.41	155.55	−34.24	268.52	314.91	6448.27	1331.15
1997	1136.04	1989.17	−590.17	−949.80	−125.26	7908.25	1459.98
1998	649.10	679.95	591.63	−1579.43	931.93	9181.43	1273.18
1999	980.49	−1587.23	826.68	735.94	1359.81	11497.12	2315.69
2000	2265.45	306.47	−1978.34	238.21	−1542.06	10786.85	−710.27
Subtotal	*7098.52*	*1594.69*	*−327.96*	*−1299.41*	*967.81*		*8033.65*
2001	−389.33	336.86	−396.53	976.41	−1292.76	10021.50	−765.35
2002	−1404.94	−823.76	1443.69	−428.12	−466.74	8341.63	−1679.87
2003	978.87	482.11	−425.46	566.22	510.55	10453.92	2112.29
2004	201.12	523.28	358.76	−409.72	−344.35	10783.01	329.00
2005	316.23	−305.62	27.67	−128.75	24.96	10717.50	−65.51
2006	95.74	573.98	1283.87	193.34	−401.28	12463.15	1745.65
2007	278.23	−157.93	1316.74	−766.63	131.26	13264.82	801.67
2008	−1387.20	1704.51	−3073.72	−940.88	−791.14	8776.39	−4488.43
2009	−45.22	161.76	617.56	932.68	−15.12	10428.05	1651.66
2010	1236.88	−421.80	1019.66	−76.73	−608.55	11577.51	1149.46
2011	−571.02	1423.66	−776.05	246.27	317.19	12217.56	640.05
2012	254.59	−49.28	−456.37	847.34	299.30	13104.14	886.58
2013	−79.63	1091.75	170.93	653.64	1635.83	16576.66	3472.52
2014	−171.63	817.56	265.07	−337.48	672.89	17823.07	1246.41
2015	308.28	−879.14	926.70	982.16	−1736.04	17425.03	−398.04
2016	602.00	594.09	636.92	678.40	−173.84	19762.60	2337.57
2017	1341.29	1184.32	882.40	445.43	1103.18	24719.22	4956.62
2018	−1694.23	252.29	754.24	−47.39	−656.67	23327.46	−1391.76
2019	−1723.31	1364.93	656.12	1156.52	3756.72	28538.44	5210.98
2020	1126.98	3852.74	1067.54	−4418.94	439.72	30606.48	2068.04
2021‡	1966.68	−1188.17	618.16	1304.52	1448.72		
Subtotal	*1240.38*	*10538.14*	*6917.90*	*1428.29*	*3853.83*		*19819.63*
Totals	6401.70	13074.62	8298.48	459.70	6238.99		30314.58

* Monday denotes first trading day of week, Friday denotes last trading day of week
† Most Wednesdays closed last 7 months of 1968   ‡ Partial year through June 4, 2021

72

MONDAY

D 47.6
S 47.6
N 52.4

18

Education is our passport to the future, for tomorrow belongs only to the people who prepare for it today.
— Malcom X (Minister, human rights activist and civil rights leader, 1925–1965)

Week After July Expiration Prone to Wild Swings, Dow Up 13 of Last 23
1998 –4.3%, 2002 +3.1%, 2006 +3.2%, 2007 –4.2%, 2009 +4.0%, 2010 +3.2

TUESDAY

D 57.1
S 57.1
N 61.9

19

If you could kick the person in the pants responsible for most of your trouble, you wouldn't sit for a month.
— Theodore Roosevelt (26th U.S. President, 1858–1919)

WEDNESDAY

D 76.2
S 76.2
N 76.2

20

Nobody can be a great economist who is only an economist—and I am even tempted to add that the economist who is only an economist is likely to become a nuisance if not a positive danger.
— Friedrich Hayek (Austrian-British economist & philosopher, 1899–1992)

Beware the "Summer Rally" Hype
Historically the Weakest Rally of All Seasons (Page 76)

THURSDAY

D 14.3
S 19.0
N 9.5

21

I have learned as a composer chiefly through my mistakes and pursuits of false assumptions, not by my exposure to founts of wisdom and knowledge.
— Igor Stravinsky (Russian composer)

FRIDAY

D 33.3
S 47.6
N 42.9

22

Under capitalism man exploits man: under socialism the reverse is true.
— Polish proverb

SATURDAY

23

August Almanac Investor Sector Seasonalities: See Pages 94, 96 and 98

SUNDAY

24

AUGUST ALMANAC

AUGUST							SEPTEMBER						
S	M	T	W	T	F	S	S	M	T	W	T	F	S
	1	2	3	4	5	6				1	2	3	
7	8	9	10	11	12	13	4	5	6	7	8	9	10
14	15	16	17	18	19	20	11	12	13	14	15	16	17
21	22	23	24	25	26	27	18	19	20	21	22	23	24
28	29	30	31				25	26	27	28	29	30	

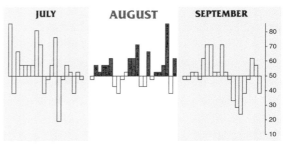

Market Probability Chart above is a graphic representation of the S&P 500 Recent Market Probability Calendar on page 126.

◆ Harvesting made August the best stock market month 1901–1951 ◆ Now that about 2% farm, August is the worst Dow and S&P and second worst NASDAQ (2000 up 11.7%, 2001 down 10.9%, 2021 up 9.6%) month since 1987 ◆ The second-shortest bear in history (45 days) caused by turmoil in Russia, currency crisis and hedge fund debacle ended here in 1998, 1344.22-point drop in the Dow, sixth worst point loss, off 15.1% ◆ Saddam Hussein triggered a 10.0% slide in 1990 ◆ Best Dow gains: 1982 (11.5%) and 1984 (9.8%) as bear markets ended ◆ Next to last day S&P up only eight times last 25 years ◆ Midterm election year Augusts' rankings #8 S&P, #8 Dow, and #10 NASDAQ

August Vital Statistics

	DJIA		S&P 500		NASDAQ		Russell 1K		Russell 2K	
Rank	10		10		11		10		9	
Up	40		39		28		26		24	
Down	31		32		22		16		18	
Average % Change	−0.1%		0.03%		0.4%		0.4%		0.3%	
Midterm Election Year	−0.5%		−0.2%		−1.2%		0.2%		−1.3%	
Best & Worst August										
	% Change		% Change		% Change		% Change		% Change	
Best	1982	11.5	1982	11.6	2000	11.7	1982	11.3	1984	11.5
Worst	1998	−15.1	1998	−14.6	1998	−19.9	1998	−15.1	1998	−19.5
Best & Worst August Weeks										
Best	08/20/1982	10.3	08/20/1982	8.8	08/03/1984	7.4	08/20/1982	8.5	08/03/1984	7.0
Worst	08/23/1974	−6.1	08/05/2011	−7.2	08/28/1998	−8.8	08/05/2011	−7.7	08/05/2011	−10.3
Best & Worst August Days										
Best	08/17/1982	4.9	08/17/1982	4.8	08/09/2011	5.3	08/09/2011	5.0	08/09/2011	6.9
Worst	08/31/1998	−6.4	08/31/1998	−6.8	08/31/1998	−8.6	08/08/2011	−6.9	08/08/2011	−8.9
First Trading Day of Expiration Week: 1980–2021										
Record (#Up - #Down)	25–16		29–12		30–11		29–12		26–15	
Current streak	D3		U1		U1		U1		U1	
Avg % Change	0.21		0.25		0.32		0.23		0.27	
Options Expiration Day: 1980–2021										
Record (#Up - #Down)	21–20		22–19		23–18		23–18		23–18	
Current streak	U3		U3		U3		U3		D1	
Avg % Change	−0.08		−0.03		−0.09		−0.03		0.10	
Options Expiration Week: 1980–2021										
Record (#Up - #Down)	19–22		23–18		22–19		23–18		24–17	
Current streak	D2		U1		U1		U1		D2	
Avg % Change	0.01		0.18		0.35		0.20		0.33	
Week After Options Expiration: 1980–2021										
Record (#Up - #Down)	25–16		27–14		26–15		27–14		27–14	
Current streak	U1		U1		U1		U1		U1	
Avg % Change	0.32		0.37		0.57		0.37		0.16	
First Trading Day Performance										
% of Time Up	46.5		49.3		54.0		45.2		47.6	
Avg % Change	0.02		0.04		−0.02		0.09		−0.001	
Last Trading Day Performance										
% of Time Up	59.2		63.4		66.0		59.5		66.7	
Avg % Change	0.11		0.11		0.06		−0.03		0.04	

Dow & S&P 1950-June 11, 2021, NASDAQ 1971-June 11, 2021, Russell 1K & 2K 1979-June 11, 2021.

August's a good month to go on vacation;
Trading stocks will likely lead to frustration.

MONDAY

D 61.9
S 57.1
N 57.1

25

The reading of all good books is indeed like a conversation with the noblest men of past centuries, in which they reveal to us the best of their thoughts.
— René Descartes (French philosopher, mathematician & scientist, 1596–1650)

TUESDAY

D 52.4
S 52.4
N 57.1

26

There is no tool to change human nature…people are prone to recurring bouts of optimism and pessimism that manifest themselves from time to time in the buildup or cessation of speculative excesses.
— Alan Greenspan (Fed Chairman 1987–2006, July 18, 2001 monetary policy report to the Congress)

FOMC Meeting (2 Days)

WEDNESDAY

D 47.6
S 38.1
N 38.1

27

When Paris sneezes, Europe catches cold.
— Prince Klemens Metternich (Austrian statesman, 1773–1859)

THURSDAY

D 33.3
S 52.4
N 61.9

28

In nature there are no rewards or punishments; there are consequences.
— Horace Annesley Vachell (English writer, *The Face of Clay*, 1861–1955)

Last Trading Day in July, NASDAQ and S&P Down 11 of Last 16, Dow Down 12 of Last 16

FRIDAY

D 42.9
S 47.6
N 42.9

29

The only things that evolve by themselves in an organization are disorder, friction and malperformance.
— Peter Drucker (Austrian-born pioneer management theorist, 1909–2005)

SATURDAY

30

SUNDAY

31

A RALLY FOR ALL SEASONS

Most years, especially when the market sells off during the first half, prospects for the perennial summer rally become the buzz on the Street. Parameters for this "rally" were defined by the late Ralph Rotnem as the lowest close in the Dow Jones Industrials in May or June to the highest close in July, August, or September. Such a big deal is made of the "summer rally" that one might get the impression the market puts on its best performance in the summertime. Nothing could be further from the truth! Not only does the market "rally" in every season of the year, but it does so with more gusto in the winter, spring and fall than in the summer.

Winters in 58 years averaged a 13.1% gain as measured from the low in November or December to the first quarter closing high. Spring rose 11.9%, followed by fall with 11.0%. Last and least was the average 9.4% "summer rally." Even 2020's impressive 25.2% "summer rally" was outmatched by spring. Nevertheless, no matter how thick the gloom or grim the outlook, don't despair! There's always a rally for all seasons, statistically.

SEASONAL GAINS IN DOW JONES INDUSTRIALS

	WINTER RALLY Nov/Dec Low to Q1 High	SPRING RALLY Feb/Mar Low to Q2 High	SUMMER RALLY May/Jun Low to Q3 High	FALL RALLY Aug/Sep Low to Q4 High
1964	15.3%	6.2%	9.4%	8.3%
1965	5.7	6.6	11.6	10.3
1966	5.9	4.8	3.5	7.0
1967	11.6	8.7	11.2	4.4
1968	7.0	11.5	5.2	13.3
1969	0.9	7.7	1.9	6.7
1970	5.4	6.2	22.5	19.0
1971	21.6	9.4	5.5	7.4
1972	19.1	7.7	5.2	11.4
1973	8.6	4.8	9.7	15.9
1974	13.1	8.2	1.4	11.0
1975	36.2	24.2	8.2	8.7
1976	23.3	6.4	5.9	4.6
1977	8.2	3.1	2.8	2.1
1978	2.1	16.8	11.8	5.2
1979	11.0	8.9	8.9	6.1
1980	13.5	16.8	21.0	8.5
1981	11.8	9.9	0.4	8.3
1982	4.6	9.3	18.5	37.8
1983	15.7	17.8	6.3	10.7
1984	5.9	4.6	14.1	9.7
1985	11.7	7.1	9.5	19.7
1986	31.1	18.8	9.2	11.4
1987	30.6	13.6	22.9	5.9
1988	18.1	13.5	11.2	9.8
1989	15.1	12.9	16.1	5.7
1990	8.8	14.5	12.4	8.6
1991	21.8	11.2	6.6	9.3
1992	14.9	6.4	3.7	3.3
1993	8.9	7.7	6.3	7.3
1994	9.7	5.2	9.1	5.0
1995	13.6	19.3	11.3	13.9
1996	19.2	7.5	8.7	17.3
1997	17.7	18.4	18.4	7.3
1998	20.3	13.6	8.2	24.3
1999	15.1	21.6	8.2	12.6
2000	10.8	15.2	9.8	3.5
2001	6.4	20.8	1.7	23.1
2002	14.8	7.9	2.8	17.6
2003	6.5	23.9	14.3	15.7
2004	11.6	5.2	4.4	10.6
2005	9.0	2.1	5.6	5.3
2006	8.8	8.3	9.5	13.0
2007	6.7	13.5	6.6	10.3
2008	2.5	11.2	3.8	4.5
2009	19.6	34.4	19.7	15.5
2010	11.6	13.1	11.1	16.0
2011	12.6	10.3	7.0	14.7
2012	18.0	4.5	12.4	5.7
2013	16.2	11.8	6.9	12.2
2014	6.0	10.2	5.5	10.3
2015	7.1	5.5	3.0	14.4
2016	3.4	15.6	8.7	10.8
2017	18.0	8.3	8.8	14.6
2018	14.4	7.6	11.8	6.6
2019	19.7	6.8	10.3	12.4
2020	8.1	48.3	25.2	14.8
2021	23.2	15.1*		
Totals	**758.1%**	**690.5%**	**535.7%**	**629.4%**
Average	**13.1%**	**11.9%**	**9.4%**	**11.0%**

*As of 6/11/2021

First Trading Day in August, Dow Down 16 of Last 24

MONDAY

D 38.1
S 47.6
N 52.4

1

Most people can bear adversity. But if you wish to know what a man really is, give him power.
— Robert G. Ingersoll (American lawyer, politician and orator, "The Great Agnostic," 1833–1899)

TUESDAY

D 52.4
S 57.1
N 42.9

2

For a country, everything will be lost when the jobs of an economist and a banker become highly respected professions.
— Montesquieu (French philosopher and historian, 1689–1755)

First Nine Trading Days of August Are Historically Weak (Pages 74 and 126)

WEDNESDAY

D 57.1
S 52.4
N 52.4

3

When someone told me "We're going with you guys because no one ever got fired for buying Cisco (products)." That's what they used to say in IBM's golden age.
— Mark Dickey (Former Cisco sales exec, then at SmartPipes, *Fortune* 5/15/00).

THURSDAY

D 52.4
S 57.1
N 52.4

4

Methodology is the last refuge of a sterile mind.
— Marianne L. Simmel (Psychologist)

FRIDAY

D 57.1
S 57.1
N 42.9

5

The worst mistake investors make is taking their profits too soon, and their losses too long.
— Michael Price (Mutual Shares Fund)

SATURDAY

6

SUNDAY

7

TAKE ADVANTAGE OF DOWN FRIDAY/ DOWN MONDAY WARNING

Fridays and Mondays are the most important days of the week. Friday is the day for squaring positions—trimming longs or covering shorts before taking off for the weekend. Traders want to limit their exposure (particularly to stocks that are not acting well) since there could be unfavorable developments before trading resumes two or more days later.

Monday is important because the market then has the chance to reflect any weekend news, plus what traders think after digesting the previous week's action and the many Monday morning research and strategy comments.

For over 30 years, a down Friday followed by down Monday has frequently corresponded to important market inflection points that exhibit a clearly negative bias, often coinciding with market tops and, on a few climactic occasions, such as in October 2002, March 2009 and March 2020, near-major market bottoms.

One simple way to get a quick reading on which way the market may be heading is to keep track of the performance of the Dow Jones Industrial Average on Fridays and the following Mondays. Since 1995, there have been 261 occurrences of Down Friday/ Down Monday (DF/DM), with 77 falling in the bear market years of 2001, 2002, 2008, 2011, 2015 and 2020, producing an average decline of 13.3%.

To illustrate how Down Friday/ Down Monday can telegraph market inflection points we created the chart below of the Dow Jones Industrials from November 2019 to June 11, 2021, with arrows pointing to occurrences of DF/ DM. Use DF/DM as a warning to examine market conditions carefully.

DOWN FRIDAY/DOWN MONDAY

Year	Total Number Down Friday/ Down Monday	Subsequent Average % Dow Loss*	Average Number of Days it took
1995	8	−1.2%	18
1996	9	−3.0%	28
1997	6	−5.1%	45
1998	9	−6.4%	47
1999	9	−6.4%	39
2000	11	−6.6%	32
2001	13	−13.5%	53
2002	18	−11.9%	54
2003	9	−3.0%	17
2004	9	−3.7%	51
2005	10	−3.0%	37
2006	11	−2.0%	14
2007	8	−6.0%	33
2008	15	−17.0%	53
2009	10	−8.7%	15
2010	7	−3.1%	10
2011	11	−9.0%	53
2012	11	−4.0%	38
2013	7	−2.4%	15
2014	7	−2.5%	8
2015	12	−9.2%	44
2016	10	−2.7%	25
2017	11	−1.2%	18
2018	14	−5.8%	45
2019	7	−4.3%	32
2020	8	−19.0%	27
2021**	1	−3.2%	4
Average	**10**	**−6.1%**	**32**

* Over next 3 months, ** Ending June 11, 2021

DOW JONES INDUSTRIALS (November 2019 - June 11, 2021)

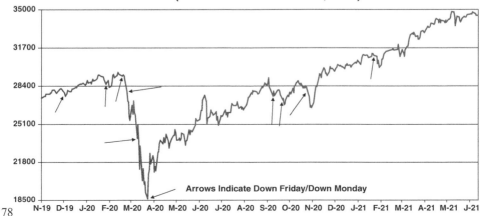

Arrows Indicate Down Friday/Down Monday

N-19 D-19 J-20 F-20 M-20 A-20 M-20 J-20 J-20 A-20 S-20 O-20 N-20 D-20 J-21 F-21 M-21 A-21 M-21 J-21

MONDAY
D 57.1
S 61.9
N 42.9
8

The trend is your friend...until it ends.
— Anonymous

TUESDAY
D 42.9
S 42.9
N 47.6
9

The public may boo me, but when I go home and think of my money, I clap.
— Horace (Roman poet-critic, *Epistles*, c. 20 BC)

August Worst Dow and S&P Month 1988–2020
Harvesting Made August Best Dow Month 1901–1951

WEDNESDAY
D 33.3
S 38.1
N 38.1
10

I am young, powerful and successful, and I produce at least $10,000 a month.
— (Mantra of Suze Orman, *The 9 Steps to Financial Freedom*, as a young Merrill Lynch broker)

THURSDAY
D 47.6
S 47.6
N 57.1
11

Trending markets require different strategies than none trending markets.
— Larry Williams (Trader, author, politician, b. 1942)

FRIDAY
D 61.9
S 52.4
N 57.1
12

It wasn't raining when Noah built the ark.
— Warren Buffett (CEO Berkshire Hathaway, investor & philanthropist, b. 1930)

SATURDAY
13

SUNDAY
14

MARTY ZWEIG'S INVESTING RULES

Longtime *Almanac* proponent and good friend Danny Riley put out one of his morning missives in early April 2021 that caught our eye. Danny – or DBOY as his trading jacket used to say – is a 39-year veteran of the CME trading floor. He ran one of the largest S&P desks on the floor of the CME Group since 1985 where he executed customer flow for clients that included Martin "Pit Bull" Schwartz, Paul Tudor Jones, George Soros, Bank of America, UBS, Société Générale and many others.

Before he left the floor in December of 2014 he founded a company called *MrTopStep. com* to help educate both professional and retail traders about many of the rules and methods he learned while on the floor. MrTopStep launched in January 2009. The name is derived from the Chicago Board of Trade pits. The most senior member in the "pit" was given the distinction of being able to stand at the "top step."

In his "Opening Print" morning note Danny was opining on the fickle nature of market timers and newsletter writers (present company not included) and the fact that at the time the stock market was being propped up by the super accommodative Fed and the trillions in fiscal stimulus from U.S. Government pouring into the economy and market.

He was reminded of a couple of famous rules from legendary trader and investor Marty Zweig (1942–2013): "Don't Fight The Tape" and Don't Fight The Fed." Many people these days think "Don't Fight the Fed" comes from the massive quantitative easing programs the Fed implemented after the 2007 global credit crisis. Danny recalls he first heard it from the "Pit Bull" back in the late 1980s.

Marty Zweig was a brilliant and generous individual who left us too soon. Over the years he contributed to the *Almanac*. He was a believer in market seasonality and cycles. But he was most famous for his evidence-based methodology that combined fundamental analysis, technical analysis and market timing.

We all struggle to contain our emotions when trading and following our own rules. Sometimes we add to losers and hold too long. Other times we get out of winning positions too soon. So for the benefit of all *Almanac* readers we present to you Marty Zweig's famous trading rules that Danny shared that morning. Marty Zweig's rules should be heeded by all.

Marty Zweig's Investing Rules

1. The trend is your friend: Don't fight the tape.
2. Let profits run, take losses quickly.
3. If you buy for a reason and that reason is discounted or is no longer valid, sell!
4. If the values don't make sense, then don't participate (2 + 2 = 4).
5. The cheap get cheaper, the dear get dearer.
6. Don't fight the Fed.
7. Every indicator eventually bites the dust.
8. Adapt to change.
9. Don't let your opinion of what should happen bias your trading strategy.
10. Don't blame your mistakes on the market.
11. Don't play all the time.
12. The market is not efficient but it is still tough to beat.
13. You'll never know all the answers.
14. If you can't sleep at night, reduce your positions or get out.
15. Don't put too much faith in the "experts."
16. Don't focus too much on short-term information flows.
17. Beware "new era" thinking (i.e. "it's different this time because…")

Mid-August Stronger Than Beginning and End
Monday Before August Expiration, Dow Up 16 of Last 26, Avg. 0.2%

MONDAY
D 52.4
S 61.9
N 61.9
15

It's no coincidence that three of the top five stock option traders in a recent trading contest were all former Marines.
— Robert Prechter, Jr. (American financial author & stock market analyst, *The Elliott Wave Theorist*, b. 1949)

TUESDAY
D 52.4
S 61.9
N 66.7
16

Don't delay! A good plan, violently executed now, is better than a perfect plan next week. War is a very simple thing, [like stock trading] and the determining characteristics are self-confidence, speed, and audacity.
— General George S. Patton, Jr. (U.S. Army field commander WWII, 1885–1945)

WEDNESDAY
D 71.4
S 71.4
N 66.7
17

If a man can see both sides of a problem, you know that none of his money is tied up in it.
— Verda Ross

THURSDAY
D 47.6
S 42.9
N 42.9
18

I sold enough papers last year of high school to pay cash for a BMW.
— Michael Dell (Founder Dell Computer, *Forbes*)

August Expiration Day Less Bullish Lately, Dow Down 7 of Last 11
Down 531 Points (3.1%) in 2015

FRIDAY
D 33.3
S 42.9
N 33.3
19

Have not great merchants, great manufacturers, great inventors done more for the world than preachers and philanthropists. Can there be any doubt that cheapening the cost of necessities and conveniences of life is the most powerful agent of civilization and progress?
— Charles Elliott Perkins (Railroad magnate, 1888, 1840–1907)

SATURDAY
20

SUNDAY
21

FOURTH QUARTER MARKET MAGIC

Examining market performance on a quarterly basis reveals several intriguing and helpful patterns. Fourth quarter market gains have been magical, providing the greatest and most consistent gains over the years. First quarter performance runs a respectable second. This should not be surprising as cash inflows, trading volume and buying bias are generally elevated during these two quarters.

Positive market psychology hits a fever pitch as the holiday season approaches and does not begin to wane until spring. Professionals drive the market higher as they make portfolio adjustments to maximize yearend numbers. Bonuses are paid and invested around the turn of the year.

The market's sweet spot of the Four-Year Cycle begins in the fourth quarter of the midterm year. The best two-quarter span runs from the fourth quarter of the midterm year through the first quarter of the pre-election year, averaging 13.7% for the Dow, 14.4% for the S&P 500 and an amazing 19.9% for NASDAQ. Pre-election Q2 is smoking too, the third best quarter of the cycle, creating a three-quarter sweet spot from midterm Q4 to pre-election Q2.

Quarterly strength fades in the latter half of the pre-election year, but stays impressively positive through the election year. Losses dominate the first quarter of post-election years and the second and third quarters of midterm years.

QUARTERLY % CHANGES

	Q1	Q2	Q3	Q4	Year	Q2–Q3	Q4–Q1
Dow Jones Industrials (1949–March 2021)							
Average	2.0%	1.8%	0.7%	3.9%	8.6%	2.5%	6.2%
Post Election	0.3%	1.7%	0.5%	4.2%	6.7%	2.3%	5.5%
Midterm	1.2%	−1.4%	0.1%	6.1%	6.0%	−1.2%	13.7%
Pre-Election	7.3%	4.8%	1.0%	2.7%	16.2%	5.8%	2.3%
Election	−0.5%	1.9%	1.1%	2.8%	5.4%	3.2%	3.3%
S&P 500 (1949–March 2021)							
Average	2.1%	1.9%	0.9%	4.1%	9.3%	2.9%	6.4%
Post Election	0.1%	2.2%	0.9%	3.6%	7.0%	3.2%	4.7%
Midterm	0.9%	−2.1%	0.5%	6.6%	6.0%	−1.5%	14.4%
Pre-Election	7.4%	4.9%	0.6%	3.5%	16.8%	5.5%	3.7%
Election	0.2%	2.8%	1.5%	2.5%	7.3%	4.4%	2.9%
NASDAQ Composite (1971–March 2021)							
Average	4.1%	3.7%	0.6%	4.4%	13.5%	4.6%	8.7%
Post Election	−0.9%	6.3%	2.5%	5.0%	12.6%	8.8%	6.9%
Midterm	2.0%	−1.9%	−3.5%	6.4%	2.2%	−5.0%	19.9%
Pre-Election	13.2%	7.2%	0.9%	5.9%	29.3%	8.1%	8.3%
Election	2.0%	3.0%	2.5%	0.6%	8.9%	6.0%	0.3%

Time and Money are two sides of a single coin. No person gives you his money until he has first given you his time.
WIN THE TIME OF THE PEOPLE, THEIR MONEY WILL FOLLOW.
— Roy H. Williams (*The Wizard of Ads*)

TUESDAY
D 52.4
S 47.6
N 47.6
23

If you destroy a free market you create a black market. If you have ten thousand regulations you destroy all respect for the law.
— Winston Churchill (British statesman, 1874–1965)

Week After August Expiration Mixed, Dow Up 8, Down 8 Last 16

WEDNESDAY
D 57.1
S 52.4
N 52.4
24

We are nowhere near a capitulation point because it's at that point where it's despair, not hope, that reigns supreme, and there was scant evidence of any despair at any of the meetings I gave.
— David Rosenberg (Economist, Merrill Lynch, *Barron's* 4/21/2008)

THURSDAY
D 47.6
S 52.4
N 52.4
25

One thing John Chambers (Cisco CEO) does well is stretch people's responsibilities and change the boxes they are in. It makes our jobs new all the time.
— Mike Volpi (Senior VP of business development and alliances at Cisco, *Fortune*)

FRIDAY
D 47.6
S 57.1
N 57.1
26

The world hates change, but it is the only thing that has brought progress.
— Charles Kettering (Inventor of electric ignition, founded Delco in 1909, 1876–1958)

SATURDAY
27

September Almanac Investor Sector Seasonalities:
See Pages 94, 96 and 98

SUNDAY
28

SEPTEMBER ALMANAC

SEPTEMBER						
S	M	T	W	T	F	S
				1	2	3
4	5	6	7	8	9	10
11	12	13	14	15	16	17
18	19	20	21	22	23	24
25	26	27	28	29	30	

OCTOBER						
S	M	T	W	T	F	S
						1
2	3	4	5	6	7	8
9	10	11	12	13	14	15
16	17	18	19	20	21	22
23	24	25	26	27	28	29
30	31					

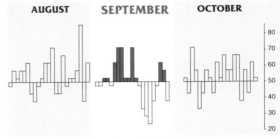

Market Probability Chart above is a graphic representation of the S&P 500 Recent Market Probability Calendar on page 126.

◆ Start of business year, end of vacations, and back to school made September a leading barometer month in first 60 years of 20th century; now portfolio managers back after Labor Day tend to clean house ◆ Biggest % loser on the S&P, Dow and NASDAQ since 1950 (pages 52 & 60) ◆ Streak of four great Dow Septembers averaging 4.2% gains ended in 1999 with six losers in a row averaging –5.9% (see page 156), up three straight 2005–2007, down 6% in 2008 and 2011 ◆ Day after Labor Day Dow up 16 of last 27 ◆ S&P opened strong 15 of last 26 years but tends to close weak due to end-of-quarter mutual fund portfolio restructuring, last trading day: S&P down 17 of past 28 ◆ September Triple-Witching Week can be dangerous, week after is pitiful (see page 108)

September Vital Statistics

	DJIA		S&P 500		NASDAQ		Russell 1K		Russell 2K	
Rank	12		12		12		12		12	
Up	29		32		27		21		23	
Down	42		38		23		21		19	
Average % Change	–0.7%		–0.5%		–0.6%		–0.6%		–0.4%	
Midterm Election Year	–0.8%		–0.4%		–0.8%		–1.0%		–0.8%	
Best & Worst September										
	% Change		% Change		% Change		% Change		% Change	
Best	2010	7.7	2010	8.8	1998	13.0	2010	9.0	2010	12.3
Worst	2002	–12.4	1974	–11.9	2001	–17.0	2002	–10.9	2001	–13.6
Best & Worst September Weeks										
Best	09/28/2001	7.4	09/28/2001	7.8	09/16/2011	6.3	09/28/2001	7.6	09/28/2001	6.9
Worst	09/21/2001	–14.3	09/21/2001	–11.6	09/21/2001	–16.1	09/21/2001	–11.7	09/21/2001	–14.0
Best & Worst September Days										
Best	09/08/1998	5.0	09/30/2008	5.4	09/08/1998	6.0	09/30/2008	5.3	09/18/2008	7.0
Worst	09/17/2001	–7.1	09/29/2008	–8.8	09/29/2008	–9.1	09/29/2008	–8.7	09/29/2008	–6.7
First Trading Day of Expiration Week: 1980–2021										
Record (#Up - #Down)	26–15		22–19		16–25		22–19		18–23	
Current streak	U1		U1		U1		U1		U2	
Avg % Change	–0.01		–0.04		–0.23		–0.06		–0.11	
Options Expiration Day: 1980–2021										
Record (#Up - #Down)	20–21		20–21		24–17		21–20		24–17	
Current streak	D2		D3		D3		D3		D3	
Avg % Change	–0.07		0.04		0.04		0.02		0.09	
Options Expiration Week: 1980–2021										
Record (#Up - #Down)	22–19		24–17		23–18		24–17		22–19	
Current streak	D2		D2		D3		D2		U1	
Avg % Change	–0.10		0.07		0.09		0.07		0.20	
Week After Options Expiration: 1980–2021										
Record (#Up - #Down)	14–27		12–29		18–23		12–28		14–27	
Current streak	D3		D3		U1		D3		D3	
Avg % Change	–0.70		–0.73		–0.80		–0.74		–1.34	
First Trading Day Performance										
% of Time Up	59.2		59.2		56.0		52.4		50.0	
Avg % Change	–0.01		–0.02		–0.04		–0.07		–0.01	
Last Trading Day Performance										
% of Time Up	42.3		43.7		52.0		52.4		64.3	
Avg % Change	–0.08		–0.02		0.05		0.08		0.26	

Dow & S&P 1950-June 11, 2021, NASDAQ 1971-June 11, 2021, Russell 1K & 2K 1979-June 11, 2021

September is when leaves and stocks tend to fall;
On Wall Street it's the worst month of all.

August's Third-to-Last Trading Day, S&P Up 18 Years In A Row 2003–2020

MONDAY
D 81.0
S 85.7
N 81.0
29

It isn't as important to buy as cheap as possible as it is to buy at the right time.
— Jesse Livermore (Early 20th century stock trader and speculator, *How to Trade in Stocks*, 1877–1940)

August's Next-to-Last Trading Day, S&P Down 17 of Last 25 Years

TUESDAY
D 38.1
S 38.1
N 61.9
30

I measure what's going on, and I adapt to it. I try to get my ego out of the way.
The market is smarter than I am so I bend.
— Martin Zweig (Fund manager, *Winning on Wall Street*, 1943–2013)

Last Trading Day in August, S&P Up 13 of Last 21 Years

WEDNESDAY
D 57.1
S 61.9
N 57.1
31

Liberties voluntarily forfeited are not easily retrieved. All the more so for those that are removed surreptitiously.
— Ted Koppel (Newsman, managing editor Discovery Channel, *NY Times* 11/6/06, b. 1940)

First Trading Day in September, S&P Up 14 of Last 26,
But Down 9 of Last 13

THURSDAY
D 47.6
S 47.6
N 57.1
1

One determined person can make a significant difference;
a small group of determined people can change the course of history.
— Sonia Johnson (Author, lecturer)

FRIDAY
D 76.2
S 47.6
N 47.6
2

You know a country is falling apart when even the government will not accept its own currency.
— Jim Rogers (Financier, *Adventure Capitalist*, b. 1942)

SATURDAY
3

SUNDAY
4

MARKET GAINS MORE ON SUPER-8 DAYS EACH MONTH THAN ON ALL 13 REMAINING DAYS COMBINED

For many years, the last day plus the first four days were the best days of the month. The market currently exhibits greater bullish bias from the last three trading days of the previous month through the first two days of the current month, and now shows significant bullishness during the middle three trading days, 9 to 11, due to 401(k) cash inflows (see pages 147 & 148). This pattern was not as pronounced during the boom years of the 1990s, with market strength all month long. Since the 2009 market bottom, the "Super Eight" advantage has been sporadic. In 2015, the "Super Eight" had a clear advantage. The "Super Eight" were destroyed in 2020 through the end of June. When compared to the last twenty-two and half year record (at the bottom of the page), the "Super Eight" edge has dulled recently.

SUPER-8 DAYS* DOW % CHANGES VS. REST OF MONTH

	Super 8 Days	Rest of Month	Super 8 Days	Rest of Month	Super 8 Days	Rest of Month
	2013		**2014**		**2015**	
Jan	2.28%	3.47%	0.92%	−4.26%	−3.64%	−0.07%
Feb	−0.27	−0.41	−1.99	3.66	2.65	2.00
Mar	2.93	1.82	0.77	−0.21	1.91	−4.78
Apr	0.11	1.65	2.44	−1.82	1.20	0.83
May	1.93	2.81	−0.56	2.50	1.31	−1.28
Jun	−0.27	−3.96	−0.09	1.24	−1.32	0.49
Jul	1.11	4.23	1.79	−1.10	−0.11	−1.31
Aug	−1.35	−3.75	−1.81	2.61	0.37	−8.02
Sep	2.55	0.83	0.32	−1.26	2.27	−2.04
Oct	−0.64	2.60	−3.28	3.82	1.03	6.57
Nov	1.79	1.41	2.42	2.28	0.68	0.68
Dec	−0.72	3.30	−1.66	3.14	−0.74	−0.86
Totals	**9.45%**	**14.00%**	**−0.73%**	**10.60%**	**5.61%**	**−7.79%**
Average	**0.79%**	**1.17%**	**−0.06%**	**0.88%**	**0.47%**	**−0.65%**
	2016		**2017**		**2018**	
Jan	−2.95%	−4.93%	−0.44%	1.24%	2.83%	4.54%
Feb	1.69	0.30	0.62	2.90	−1.68	−3.17
Mar	4.02	2.21	1.16	−1.66	−4.26	−0.09
Apr	2.14	0.43	−0.39	1.83	0.89	−1.34
May	−1.33	0.57	−0.03	0.45	−0.79	3.59
Jun	−1.33	−2.68	1.18	−0.09	−0.67	−1.17
Jul	4.97	2.66	0.89	0.98	0.33	4.72
Aug	−0.11	−0.30	2.12	−1.65	−1.39	3.53
Sep	0.84	−1.72	0.53	1.65	0.05	1.59
Oct	−0.65	0.49	1.97	2.96	−0.30	−6.62
Nov	−0.71	5.93	−0.15	0.93	1.97	−1.68
Dec	0.38	3.73	3.61	1.27	−2.63	−5.08
Totals	**6.96%**	**6.69%**	**11.07%**	**10.81%**	**−5.65%**	**−1.18%**
Average	**0.58%**	**0.56%**	**0.92%**	**0.90%**	**−0.47%**	**−0.10%**
	2019		**2020**		**2021**	
Jan	0.04%	7.10%	1.40%	−1.01%	−0.46%	2.22%
Feb	4.70	1.54	−0.78	−4.78	−0.54	2.49
Mar	0.11	−1.77	−18.59	2.59	1.57	3.25
Apr	2.90	0.21	−4.42	11.77	2.92	−0.18
May	−1.71	−2.56	−1.92	5.59	2.64	−1.64
Jun	0.35	4.32	−1.56	4.78		
Jul	1.81	0.60	2.81	−0.33		
Aug	−3.87	−1.41	1.23	6.03		
Sep	1.98	2.62	4.04	−7.99		
Oct	−1.32	1.85	0.68	0.55		
Nov	2.50	1.05	1.94	7.30		
Dec	−0.85	2.85	0.13	1.06		
Totals	**6.64%**	**16.40%**	**−15.04%**	**25.56%**	**6.13%**	**6.14%**
Average	**0.55%**	**1.37%**	**−1.25%**	**2.13%**	**1.23%**	**1.23%**

	Super Eight Days		Rest of Month (13 days)	
269	Net % Changes	120.85%	Net % Changes	41.91%
Month	Average Period	0.47%	Average Period	0.16%
Totals	Average Day	0.06%	Average Day	0.01%

86

* Super 8 Days = Last 3 + First 2 + Middle 3

Labor Day *(Market Closed)* MONDAY

5

If you don't keep [your employees] happy, they're not going to keep the [customers] happy.
— David Longest (Red Lobster VP, *NY Times* 4/23/89)

Day After Labor Day, Dow Up 16 of Last 27, But Down 8 of Last 11 TUESDAY

D 61.9
S 52.4
N 47.6

6

The inherent vice of capitalism is the unequal sharing of blessings; the inherent virtue of socialism is the equal sharing of miseries.
— Winston Churchill (British statesman, 1874–1965)

WEDNESDAY

D 42.9
S 52.4
N 52.4

7

Liberals have practiced tax and tax, spend and spend, elect and elect but conservatives have perfected borrow and borrow, spend and spend, elect and elect.
— George Will (*Newsweek*, 1989)

THURSDAY

D 52.4
S 47.6
N 52.4

8

Pullbacks near the 30-week moving average are often good times to take action.
— Michael L. Burke (*Investors Intelligence*)

2001 4-Day Closing, Longest Since 9-Day Banking Moratorium in March 1933 FRIDAY

D 57.1
S 61.9
N 57.1

9

Corporate guidance has become something of an art. The CFO has refined and perfected his art, gracefully leading on the bulls with the calculating grace and cunning of a great matador.
— Joe Kalinowski (I/B/E/S)

SATURDAY

10

 SUNDAY

11

"In Memory"

A CORRECTION FOR ALL SEASONS

While there's a rally for every season (page 76), almost always there's a decline or correction, too. Fortunately, corrections tend to be smaller than rallies, and that's what gives the stock market its long-term upward bias. In each season the average bounce outdoes the average setback. On average, the net gain between the rally and the correction is smallest in summer and fall.

The summer setback tends to be slightly outdone by the average correction in the fall. Tax selling and portfolio cleaning are the usual explanations—individuals sell to register a tax loss, and institutions like to get rid of their losers before preparing year-end statements. The October jinx also plays a major part. Since 1964, there have been 19 fall declines of over 10%, and in 11 of them (1966, 1974, 1978, 1979, 1987, 1990, 1997, 2000, 2002, 2008 and 2018) much damage was done in October, where so many bear markets end. Recent October lows were also seen in 1998, 1999, 2004, 2005 and 2011. Most often, it has paid to buy after fourth quarter or late third quarter "waterfall declines" for a rally that may continue into January or even beyond. Anticipation of war in Iraq put the market down in 2003 Q1. Quick success rallied stocks through Q3. Covid-19 economic shutdown in late Q1/early Q2 of 2020 caused the worst winter and spring slumps since 1932. Easy monetary policy and strong corporate earnings spared Q1 2011 and 2012 from a seasonal slump. Tax cut expectations lifted the market in Q4 2017.

SEASONAL CORRECTIONS IN DOW JONES INDUSTRIALS

	WINTER SLUMP Nov/Dec High to Q1 Low	SPRING SLUMP Feb/Mar High to Q2 Low	SUMMER SLUMP May/Jun High to Q3 Low	FALL SLUMP Aug/Sep High to Q4 Low
1964	−0.1%	−2.4%	−1.0%	−2.1%
1965	−2.5	−7.3	−8.3	−0.9
1966	−6.0	−13.2	−17.7	−12.7
1967	−4.2	−3.9	−5.5	−9.9
1968	−8.8	−0.3	−5.5	+0.4
1969	−8.7	−8.7	−17.2	−8.1
1970	−13.8	−20.2	−8.8	−2.5
1971	−1.4	−4.8	−10.7	−13.4
1972	−0.5	−2.6	−6.3	−5.3
1973	−11.0	−12.8	−10.9	−17.3
1974	−15.3	−10.8	−29.8	−27.6
1975	−6.3	−5.5	−9.9	−6.7
1976	−0.2	−5.1	−4.7	−8.9
1977	−8.5	−7.2	−11.5	−10.2
1978	−12.3	−4.0	−7.0	−13.5
1979	−2.5	−5.8	−3.7	−10.9
1980	−10.0	−16.0	−1.7	−6.8
1981	−6.9	−5.1	−18.6	−12.9
1982	−10.9	−7.5	−10.6	−3.3
1983	−4.1	−2.8	−6.8	−3.6
1984	−11.9	−10.5	−8.4	−6.2
1985	−4.8	−4.4	−2.8	−2.3
1986	−3.3	−4.7	−7.3	−7.6
1987	−1.4	−6.6	−1.7	−36.1
1988	−6.7	−7.0	−7.6	−4.5
1989	−1.7	−2.4	−3.1	−6.6
1990	−7.9	−4.0	−17.3	−18.4
1991	−6.3	−3.6	−4.5	−6.3
1992	+0.1	−3.3	−5.4	−7.6
1993	−2.7	−3.1	−3.0	−2.0
1994	−4.4	−9.6	−4.4	−7.1
1995	−0.8	−0.1	−0.2	−2.0
1996	−3.5	−4.6	−7.5	+0.2
1997	−1.8	−9.8	−2.2	−13.3
1998	−7.0	−3.1	−18.2	−13.1
1999	−2.7	−1.7	−8.0	−11.5
2000	−14.8	−7.4	−4.1	−11.8
2001	−14.5	−13.6	−27.4	−16.2
2002	−5.1	−14.2	−26.7	−19.5
2003	−15.8	−5.3	−3.1	−2.1
2004	−3.9	−7.7	−6.3	−5.7
2005	−4.5	−8.5	−3.3	−4.5
2006	−2.4	−5.4	−7.8	−0.4
2007	−3.7	−3.2	−6.1	−8.4
2008	−14.5	−11.0	−20.6	−35.9
2009	−32.0	−6.3	−7.4	−3.5
2010	−6.1	−10.4	−13.1	−1.0
2011	+0.2	−4.0	−16.3	−12.2
2012	+0.5	−8.7	−5.3	−7.8
2013	−0.2	−0.3	−4.1	−5.7
2014	−7.3	−2.6	−3.4	−6.7
2015	−4.9	−3.8	−14.4	−7.6
2016	−12.6	−3.3	−0.9	−4.0
2017	−1.2	−3.4	−1.0	+0.6
2018	−5.3	−9.7	−4.5	−18.5
2019	−13.4	−4.9	−4.8	−4.2
2020	−35.1	−29.1	−6.8	−8.9
2021*	−2.0	−0.1*		
Totals	**−399.4%**	**−387.4%**	**−485.2%**	**−504.5%**
Average	**−6.9%**	**−6.7%**	**−8.5%**	**−6.9%**

As of 6/11/2021

Monday Before September Triple Witching, NASDAQ Down 13 of Last 22

MONDAY

D 76.2
S 71.4
N 61.9

12

*Never doubt that a small group of thoughtful, committed citizens can change the world:
indeed it's the only thing that ever has.*
— Margaret Mead (American anthropologist)

TUESDAY

D 61.9
S 71.4
N 66.7

13

People do not change when you tell them they should; they change when they tell themselves they must.
— Michael Mandelbaum (Johns Hopkins foreign policy specialist, *NY Times*, 6/24/2009, b. 1946)

*Expiration Week 2001, Dow Lost 1370 Points (14.3%)
9th Worst Weekly Point Loss Ever, 6th Worst Week Overall*

WEDNESDAY

D 52.4
S 52.4
N 66.7

14

*So at last I was going to America! Really, really going, at last! The boundaries burst. The arch of heaven soared! A
million suns shone out for every star. The winds rushed in from outer space, roaring in my ears, "America! America!"*
— Mary Antin (1881–1949, Immigrant writer, *The Promised Land*, 1912)

THURSDAY

D 57.1
S 52.4
N 38.1

15

The time to buy is when blood is running in the streets.
— Baron Nathan Rothschild (London Financier, 1777–1836)

September Triple Witching, Dow Up 11 of Last 17, Down 6 of Last 9

FRIDAY

D 81.0
S 71.4
N 76.2

16

I went to a restaurant that serves "breakfast at any time." So I ordered French toast during the Renaissance.
— Steven Wright (Comedian, b. 1955)

SATURDAY

17

SUNDAY

18

FIRST-TRADING-DAY-OF-THE-MONTH PHENOMENON

While the Dow Jones Industrial Average has gained 26,857.18 points between September 2, 1997 (7622.42) and June 11, 2021 (34,479.60), it is incredible that 7,756.95 points were gained on the first trading days of these 285 months. The remaining 5699 trading days combined gained 19,100.23 points during the period. This averages out to gains of 27.22 points on first days, in contrast to just 3.35 points on all others.

Note September 1997 through October 2000 racked up a total gain of 2632.39 Dow points on the first trading days of these 38 months (winners except for seven occasions). But between November 2000 and September 2002, when the 2000–2002 bear markets did the bulk of their damage, frightened investors switched from pouring money into the market on that day to pulling it out, 14 months out of 23, netting a 404.80 Dow point loss. The 2007–2009 bear market lopped off 964.14 Dow points on first days in 17 months November 2007–March 2009. First days had their worst year in 2014, declining eight times for a total loss of 820.86 Dow points.

First days of August have performed worst, declining 15 times in the last 23 years. July's first trading day is third best by points but best based upon frequency of gains with only five declines in the last 27 years. In rising market trends, first days tend to perform much better, as institutions are likely anticipating strong performance at each month's outset. S&P 500 and NASDAQ first days differ slightly from Dow's. October's first trading day is worst for S&P 500. April is worst for NASDAQ while October also has a loss.

DOW POINTS GAINED FIRST DAY OF MONTH
SEPTEMBER 1997–JUNE 11, 2021

	Jan	Feb	Mar	Apr	May	Jun	Jul	Aug	Sep	Oct	Nov	Dec	Totals
1997									257.36	70.24	232.31	189.98	749.89
1998	56.79	201.28	4.73	68.51	83.70	22.42	96.65	−96.55	288.36	−210.09	114.05	16.99	646.84
1999	2.84	−13.13	18.20	46.35	225.65	36.52	95.62	−9.19	108.60	−63.95	−81.35	120.58	486.74
2000	−139.61	100.52	9.62	300.01	77.87	129.87	112.78	84.97	23.68	49.21	−71.67	−40.95	636.30
2001	−140.70	96.27	−45.14	−100.85	163.37	78.47	91.32	−12.80	47.74	−10.73	188.76	−87.60	268.11
2002	51.90	−12.74	262.73	−41.24	113.41	−215.46	−133.47	−229.97	−355.45	346.86	120.61	−33.52	−126.34
2003	265.89	56.01	−53.22	77.73	−25.84	47.55	55.51	−79.83	107.45	194.14	57.34	116.59	819.32
2004	−44.07	11.11	94.22	15.63	88.43	14.20	−101.32	39.45	−5.46	112.38	26.92	162.20	413.69
2005	−53.58	62.00	63.77	−99.46	59.19	82.39	28.47	−17.76	−21.97	−33.22	−33.30	106.70	143.23
2006	129.91	89.09	60.12	35.62	−23.85	91.97	77.80	−59.95	83.00	−8.72	−49.71	−27.80	397.48
2007	11.37	51.99	−34.29	27.95	73.23	40.47	126.81	150.38	91.12	191.92	−362.14	−57.15	311.66
2008	−220.86	92.83	−7.49	391.47	189.87	−134.50	32.25	−51.70	−26.63	−19.59	−5.18	−679.95	−439.48
2009	258.30	−64.03	−299.64	152.68	44.29	221.11	57.06	114.95	−185.68	−203.00	76.71	126.74	299.49
2010	155.91	118.20	78.53	70.44	143.22	−112.61	−41.49	208.44	254.75	41.63	6.13	249.76	1172.91
2011	93.24	148.23	−168.32	56.99	−3.18	−279.65	168.43	−10.75	−119.96	−258.08	−297.05	−25.65	−695.75
2012	179.82	83.55	28.23	52.45	65.69	−274.88	−8.70	−37.62	−54.90	77.98	136.16	−59.98	187.80
2013	308.41	149.21	35.17	−5.69	−138.85	138.46	65.36	128.48	23.65	62.03	69.80	−77.64	758.39
2014	−135.31	−326.05	−153.68	74.95	−21.97	26.46	129.47	−69.93	−30.89	−238.19	−24.28	−51.44	−820.86
2015	9.92	196.09	155.93	−77.94	185.54	29.69	138.40	−91.66	−469.68	−11.99	165.22	168.43	395.95
2016	−276.09	−17.12	348.58	107.66	117.52	2.47	19.38	−27.73	18.42	−54.30	−105.32	68.35	201.82
2017	119.16	26.85	303.31	−13.01	−27.05	135.53	129.64	72.80	39.46	152.51	57.77	−40.76	956.21
2018	104.79	37.32	−420.22	−458.92	−64.10	219.37	35.77	−81.37	−12.34	192.90	264.98	287.97	106.15
2019	18.78	64.22	110.32	329.74	−162.77	4.74	117.47	−280.85	−285.26	−343.79	301.13	−268.37	−394.64
2020	330.36	143.78	1293.96	−973.65	−622.03	91.91	−77.91	236.08	215.61	35.20	423.45	185.28	1282.04
2021	−382.59	229.29	603.14	171.66	238.38	45.86							905.74
Totals	704.58	1524.77	2288.56	209.08	777.72	442.36	1215.30	−122.11	−9.02	71.35	1211.34	348.76	8662.69

SUMMARY FIRST DAYS VS. OTHER DAYS OF MONTH

	# of Days	Total Points Gained	Average Daily Point Gain
First days	285	7756.95	27.22
Other days	5699	19100.23	3.35

MONDAY

D 47.6
S 52.4
N 47.6

19

Knowledge born from actual experience is the answer to why one profits; lack of it is the reason one loses.
— Gerald M. Loeb (E.F. Hutton, *The Battle for Investment Survival*, predicted 1929 Crash, 1900–1974)

TUESDAY

D 52.4
S 47.6
N 52.4

20

I look at the future from the standpoint of probabilities. It's like a branching stream of probabilities, and there are actions that we can take that affect those probabilities or that accelerate one thing or slow down another thing.
— Elon Musk (South African engineer & industrialist, CEO Tesla, Founder SpaceX, b. 1971)

FOMC Meeting (2 Days)

WEDNESDAY

D 52.4
S 33.3
N 38.1

21

I have a simple philosophy. Fill what's empty. Empty what's full. And scratch where it itches.
— Alice Roosevelt Longworth (American writer, socialite, daughter of Teddy, 1884–1980)

THURSDAY

D 38.1
S 28.6
N 28.6

22

If a political party does not have its foundation in the determination to advance a cause that is right and that is moral, then it is not a political party; it is merely a conspiracy to seize power.
— Dwight D. Eisenhower (34th U.S. President, 1890–1969)

Week After September Triple Witching Dow Down 24 of Last 31, Average Loss Since 1990, 1.0%

FRIDAY

D 28.6
S 23.8
N 33.3

23

All you need is to look over the earnings forecasts publicly made a year ago to see how much care you need to give those being made now for next year.
— Gerald M. Loeb (E.F. Hutton, *The Battle for Investment Survival*, predicted 1929 Crash, 1900–1974)

SATURDAY

24

October Almanac Investor Sector Seasonalities: See Pages 94, 96 and 98

SUNDAY

25

OCTOBER ALMANAC

OCTOBER								NOVEMBER						
S	M	T	W	T	F	S		S	M	T	W	T	F	S
						1						1	2	3	4	5
2	3	4	5	6	7	8		6	7	8	9	10	11	12
9	10	11	12	13	14	15		13	14	15	16	17	18	19
16	17	18	19	20	21	22		20	21	22	23	24	25	26
23	24	25	26	27	28	29		27	28	29	30			
30	31													

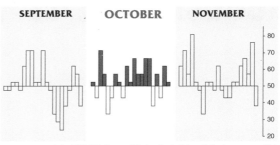

Market Probability Chart above is a graphic representation of the S&P 500 Recent Market Probability Calendar on page 126.

◆ Known as the jinx month because of crashes in 1929 and 1987, the 554-point drop on October 27, 1997, back-to-back massacres in 1978 and 1979, Friday the 13th in 1989 and the meltdown in 2008 ◆ Yet October is a "bear killer" and turned the tide in 12 post–WWII bear markets: 1946, 1957, 1960, 1962, 1966, 1974, 1987, 1990, 1998, 2001, 2002 and 2011 ◆ First October Dow top in 2007, 20-year 1987 Crash anniversary –2.6% ◆ Worst six months of the year ends with October (page 52) ◆ No longer worst month (pages 52 & 60) ◆ Best Dow, S&P and NASDAQ month from 1993 to 2007 ◆ Midterm election year Octobers since 1950, #1 Dow (2.6%), #1 S&P (2.7%) and #2 NASDAQ (3.1%) ◆ October is a great time to buy ◆ Big October gains five years 1999–2003 after atrocious Septembers ◆ Can get into Best Six Months earlier using MACD (page 56) ◆ October 2011, second month to gain 1000 Dow points and again in 2015

October Vital Statistics

	DJIA	S&P 500	NASDAQ	Russell 1K	Russell 2K
Rank	7	7	10	8	11
Up	42	42	27	26	24
Down	29	29	23	16	18
Average % Change	0.5%	0.8%	0.6%	0.8%	–0.4%
Midterm Election Year	2.6%	2.7%	3.1%	3.5%	2.4%
Best & Worst October					
	% Change	% Change	% Change	% Change	% Change
Best	1982 10.7	1974 16.3	1974 17.2	1982 11.3	2011 15.0
Worst	1987 –23.2	1987 –21.8	1987 –27.2	1987 –21.9	1987 –30.8
Best & Worst October Weeks					
Best	10/11/1974 12.6	10/11/1974 14.1	10/31/2008 10.9	10/31/2008 10.8	10/31/2008 14.1
Worst	10/10/2008 –18.2	10/10/2008 –18.2	10/23/1987 –19.2	10/10/2008 –18.2	10/23/1987 –20.4
Best & Worst October Days					
Best	10/13/2008 11.1	10/13/2008 11.6	10/13/2008 11.8	10/13/2008 11.7	10/13/2008 9.3
Worst	10/19/1987 –22.6	10/19/1987 –20.5	10/19/1987 –11.4	10/19/1987 –19.0	10/19/1987 –12.5
First Trading Day of Expiration Week: 1980–2021					
Record (#Up - #Down)	31–10	29–12	27–14	30–11	29–12
Current streak	U1	U1	U1	U1	U1
Avg % Change	0.66	0.63	0.53	0.61	0.37
Options Expiration Day: 1980–2021					
Record (#Up - #Down)	20–21	21–20	22–19	20–21	16–25
Current streak	U1	U1	D3	D3	D3
Avg % Change	–0.12	–0.19	–0.12	–0.18	–0.20
Options Expiration Week: 1980–2021					
Record (#Up - #Down)	29–12	30–11	24–17	29–12	24–17
Current streak	U1	U6	U2	U2	D1
Avg % Change	0.59	0.63	0.66	0.62	0.40
Week After Options Expiration: 1980–2021					
Record (#Up - #Down)	20–21	18–23	21–20	18–23	19–22
Current streak	D1	D1	D1	D1	U2
Avg % Change	–0.34	–0.36	–0.34	–0.39	–0.60
First Trading Day Performance					
% of Time Up	49.3	50.7	48.0	54.8	47.6
Avg % Change	0.05	0.04	–0.13	0.19	–0.25
Last Trading Day Performance					
% of Time Up	52.1	53.5	62.0	61.9	69.0
Avg % Change	0.06	0.13	0.44	0.29	0.51

Dow & S&P 1950-June 11, 2021, NASDAQ 1971-June 11, 2021, Russell 1K & 2K 1979-June 11, 2021.

October has killed many a bear;
Buy techs and small caps and soon wear a grin ear to ear.

Rosh Hashanah

🐻 MONDAY

D 38.1
S 38.1
N 47.6

26

Pretend that every single person you meet has a sign around his or her neck that says, "Make me feel important." Not only will you succeed in sales, you will succeed in life.
— Mary Kay Ash (Founder, Mary Kay Cosmetics)

TUESDAY

D 52.4
S 47.6
N 52.4

27

In the realm of ideas, everything depends on enthusiasm; in the real world, all rests on perseverance.
— Johann Wolfgang von Goethe (German poet and polymath, 1749–1832)

🐂 WEDNESDAY

D 61.9
S 61.9
N 47.6

28

As for it being different this time, it is different every time. The question is in what way, and to what extent.
— Tom McClellan (*The McClellan Market Report*)

End of September Prone to Weakness
From End-of-Q3 Institutional Portfolio Restructuring

THURSDAY

D 57.1
S 57.1
N 42.9

29

The difference between genius and stupidity is that genius has its limits.
— Anonymous

Last Day of Q3, S&P Down 15 of Last 24, But Up 5 of Last 6,
Massive 5.4% Rally in 2008

🐻 FRIDAY

D 42.9
S 38.1
N 47.6

30

Early in March (1960), Dr. Arthur F. Burns called on me…Burns' conclusion was that unless some decisive action was taken, and taken soon, we were heading for another economic dip which would hit its low point in October, just before the elections.
— Richard M. Nixon (37th U.S. President, *Six Crises*, 1913–1994)

SATURDAY

1

SUNDAY

2

SECTOR SEASONALITY: SELECTED PERCENTAGE PLAYS

Sector seasonality was featured in the first *Almanac* in 1968. A Merrill Lynch study showed that buying seven sectors around September or October and selling in the first few months of 1954–1964 tripled the gains of holding them for 10 years. Over the years we have honed this strategy significantly and now devote a significant portion of our time and resources to investing and trading during positive and negative seasonal periods for the different sector indexes below with highly correlated Exchange Traded Funds (ETFs).

Updated seasonalities appear in the table below. We specify whether the seasonality starts or finishes in the beginning third (B), middle third (M), or last third (E) of the month. These selected percentage plays are geared to take advantage of the bulk of seasonal sector strength or weakness.

By design, entry points are in advance of the major seasonal moves, providing traders ample opportunity to accumulate positions at favorable prices. Conversely, exit points have been selected to capture the majority of the move.

From the major seasonalities in the table below, we created the Sector Index Seasonality Strategy Calendar on pages 96 and 98. Note the concentration of bullish sector seasonalities during the Best Six Months, November to April, and bearish sector seasonalities during the Worst Six Months, May to October.

Almanac Investor eNewsletter subscribers receive specific entry and exit points for highly correlated ETFs and detailed analysis in ETF Trade Alerts. Visit *www.stocktradersalmanac.com*, or see the ad insert for additional details and a special offer for new subscribers.

SECTOR INDEX SEASONALITY TABLE

Ticker	Sector Index	Type	Seasonality Start		Finish		Average % Return[†] 15-Year	10-Year	5-Year
XCI	Computer Tech	Short	January	B	March	B	−2.8	0.9	0.4
XNG	Natural Gas	Long	February	E	June	B	13.8	11.5	19.3
MSH	High-Tech	Long	March	M	July	B	10.9	11.3	20.1
UTY	Utilities	Long	March	M	October	B	8.3	8.2	11.6
XCI	Computer Tech	Long	April	M	July	M	8.1	9.8	12.5
BKX	Banking	Short	May	B	July	B	−7.9	−2.9	−3.8
XAU	Gold & Silver	Short	May	M	June	E	−5.9	−3.7	−0.01
S5MATR	Materials	Short	May	M	October	M	−2.5	−1.0	4.4
XNG	Natural Gas	Short	June	M	July	E	−5.7	−4.4	−5.1
XAU	Gold & Silver	Long	July	E	December	E	1.9	−3.4	0.4
S5INDU	Industrials	Short	July	M	October	B	−2.7	−3.2	0.9
DJT	Transports	Short	July	M	October	M	−2.6	−2.1	1.8
BTK	Biotech	Long	August	B	March	B	13.5	16.3	10.4
MSH	High-Tech	Long	August	M	January	M	11.2	13.3	17.6
SOX	Semiconductor	Short	August	M	October	E	−3.8	−0.6	0.7
XOI	Oil	Short	September	B	November	E	−3.5	−2.7	−1.7
BKX	Banking	Long	October	B	May	B	12.8	18.0	19.3
XBD	Broker/Dealer	Long	October	B	April	M	15.0	21.4	21.2
XCI	Computer Tech	Long	October	B	January	B	8.2	8.0	8.2
S5COND	Consumer Discretionary	Long	October	B	June	B	14.1	16.4	12.8
S5CONS	Consumer Staples	Long	October	B	June	B	7.9	9.4	5.9
S5HLTH	Healthcare	Long	October	B	May	B	9.9	11.8	7.7
S5INDU	Industrials	Long	October	E	May	M	11.0	10.9	11.0
S5MATR	Materials	Long	October	B	May	B	14.3	13.6	10.7
DRG	Pharmaceutical	Long	October	M	January	B	6.0	6.3	4.8
RMZ	Real Estate	Long	October	E	May	B	9.0	8.0	3.9
SOX	Semiconductor	Long	October	E	December	B	8.9	9.7	12.0
XTC	Telecom	Long	October	M	December	E	2.7	1.7	0.3
DJT	Transports	Long	October	B	May	B	14.4	14.0	9.4
XOI	Oil	Long	December	M	July	B	5.8	5.0	−0.4

[†] *Average % Return based on full seasonality completion through June 4, 2021*

First Trading Day in October, Dow Down 9 of Last 16, Off 2.4% in 2011　　　MONDAY

D 52.4
S 52.4
N 47.6

3

I'm a trader that uses whatever he can find to get a leg up in a short legged game. Sure, I use technical analysis, but much of it is mumbo jumbo, redundant, lacks a logical premise or does not hold up in testing. Fundamentals and technicals are both important and merge.
— Larry Williams (Trader, author, politician, b. 1942)

Start Looking for MACD BUY Signals on October 1 (Pages 54, 56, 62 and 64)　　　TUESDAY
Almanac Investor Subscribers Emailed When It Triggers (See Insert)

D 42.9
S 42.9
N 47.6

4

There are very few instances in history when any government has ever paid off debt.
— Walter Wriston (Retired CEO of Citicorp and Citibank)

Yom Kippur　　　🐷 WEDNESDAY

D 71.4
S 71.4
N 76.2

5

Try to surround yourself with people who can give you a little happiness, because you can only pass through this life once, Jack. You don't come back for an encore.
— Elvis Presley (Musician, 1935–1977)

October Ends Dow and S&P "Worst Six Months" (Pages 52, 54, 56, 64 and 149)　　　THURSDAY
And NASDAQ "Worst Four Months" (Pages 60, 62 and 150)

D 57.1
S 57.1
N 52.4

6

It isn't the incompetent who destroy an organization. It is those who have achieved something and want to rest upon their achievements who are forever clogging things up.
— Charles E. Sorenson (Danish-American engineer, officer, director of Ford Motor Co. 1907–1950, helped develop 1st auto assembly line, 1881–1968)

Dow Lost 1874 Points (18.2%) on the Week Ending 10/10/2008　　　🐻 FRIDAY
Worst Dow Week in the History of Wall Street

D 33.3
S 33.3
N 42.9

7

I am not a member of any organized party—I am a Democrat.
— Will Rogers (American humorist and showman, 1879–1935)

SATURDAY

8

SUNDAY

9

SECTOR INDEX SEASONALITY STRATEGY CALENDAR*

Index		Jan	Feb	Mar	Apr	May	Jun	Jul	Aug	Sep	Oct	Nov	Dec
BKX	L / S												
BTK	L / S												
S5COND & S5CONS	L / S												
S5INDU	L / S												
DJT	L / S												
DRG	L / S												
S5HLTH	L / S												
MSH	L / S												
RMZ	L / S												

* Graphic representation of the Sector Index Seasonality Percentage Plays on page 92.
L = Long Trade, S = Short Trade, ⟶ = Start of Trade

(continued on page 98)

96

Columbus Day *(Bond Market Closed)*

MONDAY
10

D 47.6
S 42.9
N 52.4

Throughout the centuries there were men who took first steps down new roads armed with nothing but their own vision.
— Ayn Rand (Russian-born American novelist and philosopher, *The Fountainhead*, 1957, 1905–1982)

TUESDAY
11

D 57.1
S 57.1
N 57.1

Executives owe it to the organization and to their fellow workers not to tolerate nonperforming individuals in important jobs.
— Peter Drucker (Austria-born pioneer management theorist, 1909–2005)

WEDNESDAY
12

D 52.4
S 52.4
N 57.1

Why is it right-wing [conservatives] always stand shoulder to shoulder in solidarity,
while liberals always fall out among themselves?
— Yevgeny Yevtushenko (Russian poet, *Babi Yar*, quoted in London *Observer* December 15, 1991, b. 1933)

October 2011, Second Dow Month to Gain 1000 Points

THURSDAY
13

D 38.1
S 42.9
N 52.4

No horse gets anywhere until he is harnessed. No steam or gas ever drives anything until it is confined. No Niagara is
ever turned into light and power until it is tunneled. No life ever grows great until it is focused, dedicated, disciplined.
— Harry Emerson Fosdick (Protestant minister, author, 1878–1969)

FRIDAY
14

D 61.9
S 61.9
N 66.7

The thing you do obsessively between age 13 and 18 that's the thing you have the most chance of being world class at.
— William H. Gates (Microsoft founder, "Charlie Rose" interview 2/22/2016, b. 1955)

SATURDAY
15

SUNDAY
16

SECTOR INDEX SEASONALITY STRATEGY CALENDAR*

* Graphic representation of the Sector Index Seasonality Percentage Plays on page 92.
L = Long Trade, S = Short Trade, ⟶ = Start of Trade

Monday Before October Expiration, Dow Up 30 of 39

MONDAY
D 52.4
S 52.4
N 47.6
17

There is always plenty of capital for those who can create practical plans for using it.
— Napoleon Hill (Author, *Think and Grow Rich*, 1883–1970)

TUESDAY
D 57.1
S 66.7
N 57.1
18

Companies that announce mass layoffs or a series of firings underperform the stock market over a three-year period.
— Bain & Company (*Smart Money Magazine*, August 2001)

Crash of October 19, 1987, Dow down 22.6% in One Day

WEDNESDAY
D 47.6
S 57.1
N 52.4
19

Taxes are what we pay for civilized society.
— Oliver Wendell Holmes Jr. (U.S. Supreme Court Justice 1902–1932, "The Great Dissenter," inscribed above IRS HQ entrance, 1841–1935)

THURSDAY
D 52.4
S 57.1
N 57.1
20

To know values is to know the meaning of the market.
— Charles Dow (Co-founder Dow Jones & Co, 1851–1902)

October Expiration Day, Dow Down 6 Straight 2005–2010, But Up 6 of Last 8

FRIDAY
D 61.9
S 66.7
N 61.9
21

The dissenter (or "contrary investor") is every human at those moments of his life when he resigns momentarily from the herd and thinks for himself.
— Archibald MacLeish (American poet, writer and political activist, 1892–1982)

SATURDAY
22

SUNDAY
23

MARKET BEHAVIOR THREE DAYS BEFORE AND THREE DAYS AFTER HOLIDAYS

The *Stock Trader's Almanac* has tracked holiday seasonality annually since the first edition in 1968. Stocks used to rise on the day before holidays and sell off the day after, but nowadays, each holiday moves to its own rhythm. Eight holidays are separated into six groups. Average percentage changes for the Dow, S&P 500, NASDAQ, and Russell 2000 are shown.

The Dow and S&P consist of blue chips and the largest cap stocks, whereas NASDAQ and the Russell 2000 would be more representative of smaller-cap stocks. This is evident on the last day of the year, with NASDAQ and the Russell 2000 having a field day, while their larger brethren in the Dow and S&P are showing losses on average.

Thanks to the Santa Claus Rally, the three days before and after New Year's Day and Christmas are best. NASDAQ and the Russell 2000 average gains of 1.1% to 1.5% over the six-day spans. However, trading around the first day of the year has been mixed recently. Traders have been selling more the first trading day of the year, pushing gains and losses into the New Year.

Bullishness before Labor Day and after Memorial Day is affected by strength the first day of September and June. The second worst day after a holiday is the day after Easter. Surprisingly, the following day is the best second day after a holiday, eclipsing the second day after New Year's Day.

Presidents' Day is the least bullish of all the holidays, bearish the day before and three days after. NASDAQ has dropped 20 of the last 32 days before Presidents' Day (Dow, 17 of 32; S&P, 18 of 32; Russell 2000, 15 of 32).

	−3	−2	−1	Mixed	+1	+2	+3
HOLIDAYS: 3 DAYS BEFORE, 3 DAYS AFTER (Average % change 1980–May 2021)							
S&P 500	0.04	0.17	−0.09	New Year's	0.19	0.21	0.10
DJIA	0.02	0.12	−0.14	Day	0.28	0.19	0.22
NASDAQ	0.08	0.20	0.14	1/1/22	0.21	0.46	0.21
Russell 2K	0.01	0.35	0.35		0.01	0.20	0.21
S&P 500	0.35	0.04	−0.08	Negative Before & After	−0.14	−0.03	−0.14
DJIA	0.34	0.01	−0.02	Presidents'	−0.10	−0.05	−0.14
NASDAQ	0.55	0.30	−0.22	Day	−0.40	−0.02	−0.13
Russell 2K	0.41	0.19	0.01	2/21/22	−0.30	−0.13	−0.11
S&P 500	0.10	0.02	0.42	Positive Before &	−0.19	0.40	0.07
DJIA	0.09	−0.01	0.32	Negative After	−0.14	0.36	0.06
NASDAQ	0.27	0.25	0.51	Good Friday	−0.26	0.47	0.18
Russell 2K	0.19	0.13	0.60	4/15/22	−0.37	0.34	0.02
S&P 500	0.10	0.01	0.01	Positive After	0.25	0.15	0.21
DJIA	0.07	−0.02	−0.04	Memorial	0.30	0.16	0.11
NASDAQ	0.17	0.17	0.06	Day	0.21	0.01	0.40
Russell 2K	0.07	0.25	0.13	5/30/22	0.30	0.13	0.30
S&P 500	0.21	0.15	0.09	Negative After	−0.08	0.02	0.09
DJIA	0.15	0.12	0.09	Independence	−0.03	0.02	0.07
NASDAQ	0.34	0.18	0.07	Day	−0.06	−0.11	0.26
Russell 2K	0.33	0.02	0.04	7/4/22	−0.19	−0.09	0.07
S&P 500	0.26	−0.24	0.11	Positive Before	0.00	0.13	−0.08
DJIA	0.23	−0.27	0.11	& Mixed After	0.02	0.17	−0.14
NASDAQ	0.45	−0.07	0.11	Labor Day	−0.10	0.02	0.04
Russell 2K	0.53	0.02	0.11	9/5/22	−0.01	0.16	0.02
S&P 500	0.13	0.03	0.24	Positive Before	0.16	−0.39	0.32
DJIA	0.14	0.03	0.22	& After	0.12	−0.34	0.31
NASDAQ	0.06	−0.15	0.41	Thanksgiving	0.41	−0.38	0.15
Russell 2K	0.22	−0.01	0.39	11/24/22	0.27	−0.53	0.27
S&P 500	0.14	0.14	0.13	Christmas	0.28	0.02	0.22
DJIA	0.19	0.19	0.16	12/25/22	0.31	0.03	0.18
NASDAQ	−0.06	0.30	0.31		0.28	0.04	0.26
Russell 2K	0.21	0.29	0.28		0.29	−0.01	0.42

MONDAY
D 52.4
S 66.7
N 57.1
24

Some men see things as they are and say "why?" I dream things that never were and say "why not?"
— George Bernard Shaw (Irish dramatist, 1856–1950)

Late October is Time to Buy Depressed Stocks
Especially Techs and Small Caps

TUESDAY
D 42.9
S 38.1
N 47.6
25

Securities pricing is, in every sense a psychological phenomenon that arises from the interaction of human beings with fear. Why not greed and fear as the equation is usually stated? Because greed is simply fear of not having enough.
— John Bollinger (Bollinger Capital Management, *Capital Growth Letter, Bollinger on Bollinger Bands*)

WEDNESDAY
D 66.7
S 57.1
N 52.4
26

The men who can manage men manage the men who manage only things, and the men who can manage money manage all.
— Will and Ariel Durant (*The Story of Civilization*, 1885–1981, 1898–1981)

THURSDAY
D 47.6
S 42.9
N 52.4
27

People who can take a risk, who believe in themselves enough to walk away [from a company] are generally people who bring about change.
— Cynthia Danaher (Exiting GM of Hewlett-Packard's Medical Products Group, *Newsweek*)

88th Anniversary of 1929 Crash, Dow Down 23.0% in Two Days,
October 28 and 29

FRIDAY
D 61.9
S 61.9
N 57.1
28

In Wall Street, the man who does not change his mind will soon have no change to mind.
— William D. Gann (Trader, technical analyst, author, publisher, 1878–1955)

SATURDAY
29

November Almanac Investor Sector Seasonalities:
See Pages 94, 96 and 98

SUNDAY
30

NOVEMBER ALMANAC

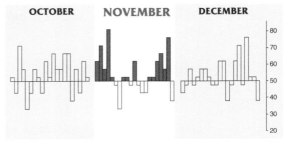

NOVEMBER						
S	M	T	W	T	F	S
		1	2	3	4	5
6	7	8	9	10	11	12
13	14	15	16	17	18	19
20	21	22	23	24	25	26
27	28	29	30			

DECEMBER						
S	M	T	W	T	F	S
				1	2	3
4	5	6	7	8	9	10
11	12	13	14	15	16	17
18	19	20	21	22	23	24
25	26	27	28	29	30	31

Market Probability Chart above is a graphic representation of the S&P 500 Recent Market Probability Calendar on page 126.

◆ #2 S&P and Dow month since 1950, #2 on NASDAQ since 1971 (pages 52 & 60) ◆ Start of the "Best Six Months" of the year (page 54), NASDAQ's Best Eight Months and Best Three Months (pages 149 & 150) ◆ Simple timing indicator almost triples "Best Six Months" strategy (page 56), doubles NASDAQ's Best Eight (page 62) ◆ Day before and after Thanksgiving Day combined, only 18 losses in 69 years (page 106) ◆ Week before Thanksgiving Dow up 19 of last 28 ◆ Midterm election year Novembers rank #2 Dow and #2 S&P, NASDAQ #1

November Vital Statistics

	DJIA		S&P 500		NASDAQ		Russell 1K		Russell 2K	
Rank	2		2		2		1		1	
Up	49		49		35		32		29	
Down	22		22		15		10		13	
Average % Change	1.8%		1.7%		1.9%		2.0%		2.5%	
Midterm Election Year	2.5%		2.6%		3.5%		2.6%		3.3%	
Best & Worst November										
	% Change		% Change		% Change		% Change		% Change	
Best	2020	11.8	2020	10.8	2001	14.2	2020	11.6	2020	18.3
Worst	1973	−14.0	1973	−11.4	2000	−22.9	2000	−9.3	2008	−12.0
Best & Worst November Weeks										
Best	11/28/2008	9.7	11/28/2008	12.0	11/28/2008	10.9	11/28/2008	12.5	11/28/2008	16.4
Worst	11/21/2008	−5.3	11/21/2008	−8.4	11/10/2000	−12.2	11/21/2008	−8.8	11/21/2008	−11.0
Best & Worst November Days										
Best	11/13/2008	6.7	11/13/2008	6.9	11/13/2008	6.5	11/13/2008	7.0	11/13/2008	8.5
Worst	11/20/2008	−5.6	11/20/2008	−6.7	11/19/2008	−6.5	11/20/2008	−6.9	11/19/2008	−7.9
First Trading Day of Expiration Week: 1980–2021										
Record (#Up – #Down)	23–18		19–22		16–25		21–20		18–23	
Current streak	U2		U1		U1		U1		U10	
Avg % Change	−0.02		−0.06		−0.17		−0.06		−0.05	
Options Expiration Day: 1980–2021										
Record (#Up – #Down)	26–15		24–17		21–20		24–17		24–16	
Current streak	D1		D1		D1		D1		U11	
Avg % Change	0.22		0.15		0.04		0.15		0.16	
Options Expiration Week: 1980–2021										
Record (#Up – #Down)	26–15		24–17		23–18		23–18		21–20	
Current streak	D1		D1		U2		D1		U1	
Avg % Change	0.27		0.08		0.07		0.08		−0.09	
Week After Options Expiration: 1980–2021										
Record (#Up – #Down)	24–17		26–15		27–14		26–15		25–16	
Current streak	U1		U1		U1		U1		U1	
Avg % Change	0.58		0.59		0.72		0.61		0.83	
First Trading Day Performance										
% of Time Up	64.8		64.8		66.0		73.8		61.9	
Avg % Change	0.31		0.32		0.33		0.42		0.30	
Last Trading Day Performance										
% of Time Up	54.9		52.1		62.0		45.2		64.3	
Avg % Change	0.11		0.13		−0.07		0.02		0.08	

Dow & S&P 1950–June 11, 2021, NASDAQ 1971–June 11, 2021, Russell 1K & 2K 1979–June 11, 2021.

Astute investors always smile and remember,
When stocks seasonally start soaring, and salute November.

Halloween

MONDAY
D 47.6
S 52.4
N 52.4
31

Between two evils, I always pick the one I never tried before.
— Mae West (American actress and playwright, 1893–1980)

First Trading Day in November, Dow Up 9 of Last 12

TUESDAY
D 61.9
S 61.9
N 61.9
1

When teachers held high expectations of their students that alone was enough to cause an increase of 25 points in the students' IQ scores.
— Warren Bennis (Author, *The Unconscious Conspiracy: Why Leaders Can't Lead*, 1976)

FOMC Meeting (2 Days)

WEDNESDAY
D 61.9
S 71.4
N 61.9
2

Intense concentration hour after hour can bring out resources in people they didn't know they had.
— Edwin Land (Polaroid inventor and founder, 1909–1991)

THURSDAY
D 61.9
S 57.1
N 61.9
3

Those companies that the market expects will have the best futures, as measured by the price/earnings ratios they are accorded, have consistently done worst subsequently.
— David Dreman (Dreman Value Management, author, *Forbes* columnist, b. 1936)

FRIDAY
D 76.2
S 81.0
N 66.7
4

If you can't deal with emotion, get out of trading.
— J. Welles Wilder Jr. (Creator of several technical indicators including Relative Strength Index (RSI) 1935–2021)

SATURDAY
5

Daylight Saving Time Ends

SUNDAY
6

MIDTERM ELECTION TIME UNUSUALLY BULLISH

Presidential election years tend to produce high drama and frenetic campaigns. Midterm years with only local or state candidates running are less stressful. Could this be the reason for the bullishness that seems to occur in the five days before and three days after midterm congressional elections? We don't think so.

So many bear markets seem to occur in midterm years, very often bottoming in October. Also, major military involvements began or were in their early stages in midterm years, such as World War II, Korea, Vietnam, Kuwait and Iraq. Solidly bullish midterm years as 1954, 1958, 1986, 2006, 2010 and 2014 were exceptions.

With so many negative occurrences in midterm years, perhaps the opportunity for investors to make a change for the better by casting their votes translates into an inner bullish feeling before and after midterm elections.

An impressive 2.8% has been the average gain during the eight trading days surrounding midterm election days since 1934. This is equivalent to roughly 966 Dow points per day at present levels. There was only one losing period: in 1994 when the Republicans took control of both the House and the Senate for the first time in 40 years.

Four other midterm switches occurred in 1946, when control of Congress passed to the Republicans for just two years; in 1954, when Democrats took back control; in 2006 when Democrats regained control; in 2010, when Republicans reclaimed the House; and in 2018 when Democrats recaptured the majority.

There were twelve occasions when the percentage of House seats lost by the president's party was in double digits. The average market gain during the eight-day trading period was 2.3%. In contrast, the average gain in the ten occasions when there were no losses, or losses were in single digits, gains averaged 3.4%.

BULLS WIN BATTLE BETWEEN ELEPHANTS AND DONKEYS

Midterm Year	Dow Jones Industrials 5 Trading Days Before E. Day	Dow Jones Industrials 3 Trading Days After E. Day	% Change	President's Party % Seats Lost	President in Power
1934	93.36	99.02	6.1%	2.9%	Dem
1938	152.21	158.41	4.1	−21.3	Dem
1942	113.11	116.12	2.7	−16.9	Dem
1946	164.20	170.79	4.0	−22.6	Dem*
1950	225.69	229.29	1.6	−11.0	Dem
1954	356.32	366.00	2.7	−8.1	Rep*
1958	536.88	554.26	3.2	−23.9	Rep
1962	588.98	616.13	4.6	−1.5	Dem
1966	809.63	819.09	1.2	−15.9	Dem
1970	754.45	771.97	2.3	−6.3	Rep
1974	659.34	667.16	1.2	−25.0	Rep
1978	792.45	807.09	1.8	−5.1	Dem
1982	1006.07	1051.78	4.5	−13.5	Rep
1986	1845.47	1886.53	2.2	−2.7	Rep
1990	2448.02	2488.61	1.7	−4.6	Rep
1994	3863.37	3801.47	−1.6	−20.9	Dem*
1998	8366.04	8975.46	7.3	2.4	Dem
2002	8368.94	8537.13	2.0	3.6	Rep
2006	12080.73	12108.43	0.2	−12.9	Rep*
2010	11169.46	11444.08	2.5	−24.6	Dem*
2014	17005.75	17573.93	3.3	−6.5	Dem*
2018	24874.64	25989.30	4.5	−17.4	Rep*
		Total	62.1%		
		Average	2.8%	−11.4	

* Control switches to other party

104

November Begins Dow and S&P "Best Six Months" (Pages 52, 54, 56, 64 and 149) And NASDAQ "Best Eight Months" (Pages 60, 62 and 150)

MONDAY

7

D 61.9
S 52.4
N 61.9

The single best predictor of overall excellence is a company's ability to attract, motivate, and retain talented people.
— Bruce Pfau (Vice chair human resources KPMG, *Fortune* 1998)

Election Day

TUESDAY

8

D 57.1
S 47.6
N 47.6

The only title in our democracy superior to that of president is the title of citizen.
— Louis D. Brandeis (U.S. Supreme Court Justice 1916–1939, 1856–1941)

WEDNESDAY

9

D 47.6
S 33.3
N 33.3

The stock market is a device for transferring money from the impatient to the patient.
— Warren Buffett (CEO Berkshire Hathaway, investor & philanthropist, b. 1930)

THURSDAY

10

D 38.1
S 52.4
N 61.9

In the business world, everyone is paid in two coins: cash and experience. Take the experience first; the cash will come later.
— Harold S. Geneen (British-American businessman, CEO ITT Corp, 1910–1977)

Veterans' Day *(Bond Market Closed)*

FRIDAY

11

D 61.9
S 52.4
N 61.9

A day will come when all nations on our continent will form a European brotherhood…A day will come when we shall see…the United States of Europe…reaching out for each other across the seas.
— Victor Hugo (French novelist, playwright, *Hunchback of Notre Dame* and *Les Misérables*, 1802–1885)

SATURDAY

12

SUNDAY

13

TRADING THE THANKSGIVING MARKET

For 35 years, the "holiday spirit" gave the Wednesday before Thanksgiving and the Friday after a great track record, except for two occasions. Publishing it in the 1987 *Almanac* was the kiss of death. Since 1988, Wednesday–Friday gained 18 of 33 times, with a total Dow point gain of 395.18 versus Monday's total Dow point loss of 1086.29, down 16 of 23 since 1998. The best strategy appears to be coming into the week long and exiting into strength before Friday.

DOW JONES INDUSTRIALS BEFORE AND AFTER THANKSGIVING

	Tuesday Before	Wednesday Before		Friday After	Total Gain Dow Points	Dow Close	Next Monday
1952	−0.18	1.54		1.22	2.76	283.66	0.04
1953	1.71	0.65		2.45	3.10	280.23	1.14
1954	3.27	1.89		3.16	5.05	387.79	0.72
1955	4.61	0.71		0.26	0.97	482.88	−1.92
1956	−4.49	−2.16		4.65	2.49	472.56	−2.27
1957	−9.04	10.69		3.84	14.53	449.87	−2.96
1958	−4.37	8.63		8.31	16.94	557.46	2.61
1959	2.94	1.41		1.42	2.83	652.52	6.66
1960	−3.44	1.37		4.00	5.37	606.47	−1.04
1961	−0.77	1.10		2.18	3.28	732.60	−0.61
1962	6.73	4.31		7.62	11.93	644.87	−2.81
1963	32.03	−2.52		9.52	7.00	750.52	1.39
1964	−1.68	−5.21	T	−0.28	−5.49	882.12	−6.69
1965	2.56	N/C		−0.78	−0.78	948.16	−1.23
1966	−3.18	1.84	H	6.52	8.36	803.34	−2.18
1967	13.17	3.07		3.58	6.65	877.60	4.51
1968	8.14	−3.17	A	8.76	5.59	985.08	−1.74
1969	−5.61	3.23		1.78	5.01	812.30	−7.26
1970	5.21	1.98	N	6.64	8.62	781.35	12.74
1971	−5.18	0.66		17.96	18.62	816.59	13.14
1972	8.21	7.29	K	4.67	11.96	1025.21	−7.45
1973	−17.76	10.08		−0.98	9.10	854.00	−29.05
1974	5.32	2.03	S	−0.63	1.40	618.66	−15.64
1975	9.76	3.15		2.12	5.27	860.67	−4.33
1976	−6.57	1.66	G	5.66	7.32	956.62	−6.57
1977	6.41	0.78		1.12	1.90	844.42	−4.85
1978	−1.56	2.95	I	3.12	6.07	810.12	3.72
1979	−6.05	−1.80		4.35	2.55	811.77	16.98
1980	3.93	7.00	G	3.66	10.66	993.34	−23.89
1981	18.45	7.90		7.80	15.70	885.94	3.04
1982	−9.01	9.01	I	7.36	16.37	1007.36	−4.51
1983	7.01	−0.20		1.83	1.63	1277.44	−7.62
1984	9.83	6.40	V	18.78	25.18	1220.30	−7.95
1985	0.12	18.92		−3.56	15.36	1472.13	−14.22
1986	6.05	4.64	I	−2.53	2.11	1914.23	−1.55
1987	40.45	−16.58		−36.47	−53.05	1910.48	−76.93
1988	11.73	14.58	N	−17.60	−3.02	2074.68	6.76
1989	7.25	17.49		18.77	36.26	2675.55	19.42
1990	−35.15	9.16	G	−12.13	−2.97	2527.23	5.94
1991	14.08	−16.10		−5.36	−21.46	2894.68	40.70
1992	25.66	17.56		15.94	33.50	3282.20	22.96
1993	3.92	13.41		−3.63	9.78	3683.95	−6.15
1994	−91.52	−3.36		33.64	30.28	3708.27	31.29
1995	40.46	18.06		7.23*	25.29	5048.84	22.04
1996	−19.38	−29.07		22.36*	−6.71	6521.70	N/C
1997	41.03	−14.17	D	28.35*	14.18	7823.13	189.98
1998	−73.12	13.13		18.80*	31.93	9333.08	−216.53
1999	−93.89	12.54	A	−19.26*	−6.72	10988.91	−40.99
2000	31.85	−95.18		70.91*	−24.27	10470.23	75.84
2001	−75.08	−66.70	Y	125.03*	58.33	9959.71	23.04
2002	−172.98	255.26		−35.59*	219.67	8896.09	−33.52
2003	16.15	15.63		2.89*	18.52	9782.46	116.59
2004	3.18	27.71		1.92*	29.63	10522.23	−46.33
2005	51.15	44.66		15.53*	60.19	10931.62	−40.90
2006	5.05	5.36		−46.78*	−41.42	12280.17	−158.46
2007	51.70	−211.10		181.84*	−29.26	12980.88	−237.44
2008	36.08	247.14		102.43*	349.57	8829.04	−679.95
2009	−17.24	30.69		−154.48*	−123.79	10309.92	34.92
2010	−142.21	150.91		−95.28*	55.63	11092.00	−39.51
2011	−53.59	−236.17		−25.77*	−261.94	11231.78	291.23
2012	−7.45	48.38		172.79*	221.17	13009.68	−42.31
2013	0.26	24.53		−10.92*	13.61	16086.41	−77.64
2014	−2.96	−2.69		15.99*	13.30	17828.24	−51.44
2015	19.51	1.20		−14.90*	−13.70	17798.49	−78.57
2016	67.18	59.31		68.96*	128.27	19152.14	−54.24
2017	160.50	−64.65		31.81*	−32.84	23557.99	22.79
2018	−551.80	−0.95		−178.74*	−179.69	24285.95	354.29
2019	55.21	42.32		−112.59*	−70.27	28051.41	−268.37
2020	454.97	−173.77		37.90*	−135.87	29910.37	−271.73

Shortened trading day

106

Monday Before November Expiration, Dow Up 12 of Last 17,
2008 –2.6%, 2018 –2.3%

MONDAY

D 47.6
S 47.6
N 42.9

14

Those who are of the opinion that money will do everything may very well be suspected to do everything for money.
— Sir George Savile (British statesman and author, 1633–1695)

TUESDAY

D 71.4
S 61.9
N 52.4

15

An inventor fails 999 times, and if he succeeds once, he's in. He treats his failures simply as practice shots.
— Charles Kettering (Inventor of electric ignition, founded Delco in 1909, 1876–1958)

Week Before Thanksgiving, Dow Up 19 of Last 28, Down Last 4
2003 –1.4%, 2004 –0.8%, 2008 –5.3%, 2011 –2.9%, 2012 –1.8%, 2018 –2.2%

WEDNESDAY

D 52.4
S 47.6
N 52.4

16

The big guys are the status quo, not the innovators.
— Kenneth L. Fisher (*Forbes* columnist)

THURSDAY

D 38.1
S 42.9
N 42.9

17

Men, it has been well said, think in herds; it will be seen that they go mad in herds, while they only recover their senses slowly, and one by one.
— Charles Mackay (Scottish poet, journalist, author, anthologist, novelist, and songwriter, *Extraordinary Popular Delusions and the Madness of Crowds*, 1814–1889)

November Expiration Day, Dow Up 14 of Last 19
Dow Surged in 2008, Up 494 Points (6.5%)

FRIDAY

D 42.9
S 42.9
N 47.6

18

There have been three great inventions since the beginning of time: Fire, the wheel, and central banking.
— Will Rogers (American humorist and showman, 1879–1935)

SATURDAY

19

SUNDAY

20

AURA OF THE TRIPLE WITCH—4TH QUARTER MOST BULLISH: DOWN WEEKS TRIGGER MORE WEAKNESS WEEK AFTER

Standard options expire the third Friday of every month, but in March, June, September, and December, a powerful coven gathers. Since the S&P index futures began trading on April 21, 1982, stock options, index options, and index futures all expire at the same time four times each year—known as Triple Witching. Traders have long sought to understand and master the magic of this quarterly phenomenon.

The market for single-stock and ETF futures and weekly options continues to grow. However, their impact on the market has thus far been subdued. As their availability continues to expand, trading volumes and market influence could broaden. Until such time, we do not believe the term "quadruple witching" is applicable just yet.

We have analyzed what the market does prior to, during, and following Triple-Witching expirations in search of consistent trading patterns. Here are some of our findings of how the Dow Jones Industrials perform around Triple-Witching Week (TWW).

- TWWs have become more bullish since 1990, except in the second quarter.
- Following weeks have become more bearish. Since Q1 2000, only 32 of 84 were up, and 16 occurred in December, 9 in March, 5 in September, 2 in June.
- TWWs have tended to be down in flat periods and dramatically so during bear markets.
- DOWN WEEKS TEND TO FOLLOW DOWN TWWs is a most interesting pattern. Since 1991, of 41 down TWWs, 28 following weeks were also down. This is surprising, inasmuch as the previous decade had an exactly opposite pattern: There were 13 down TWWs then, but 12 up weeks followed them.
- TWWs in the second and third quarter (Worst Six Months May through October) are much weaker, and the weeks following, horrendous. But in the first and fourth quarter (Best Six Months period November through April), only the week after Q1 expiration is negative.

Throughout the *Almanac* you will also see notations on the performance of Mondays and Fridays of TWW, as we place considerable significance on the beginnings and ends of weeks (pages 72, 78 and 143–146).

TRIPLE-WITCHING WEEK AND WEEK AFTER DOW POINT CHANGES

	Expiration Week Q1	Week After	Expiration Week Q2	Week After	Expiration Week Q3	Week After	Expiration Week Q4	Week After
1991	−6.93	−89.36	−34.98	−58.81	33.54	−13.19	20.12	167.04
1992	40.48	−44.95	−69.01	−2.94	21.35	−76.73	9.19	12.97
1993	43.76	−31.60	−10.24	−3.88	−8.38	−70.14	10.90	6.15
1994	32.95	−120.92	3.33	−139.84	58.54	−101.60	116.08	26.24
1995	38.04	65.02	86.80	75.05	96.85	−33.42	19.87	−78.76
1996	114.52	51.67	55.78	−50.60	49.94	−15.54	179.53	76.51
1997	−130.67	−64.20	14.47	−108.79	174.30	4.91	−82.01	−76.98
1998	303.91	−110.35	−122.07	231.67	100.16	133.11	81.87	314.36
1999	27.20	−81.31	365.05	−303.00	−224.80	−524.30	32.73	148.33
2000	666.41	517.49	−164.76	−44.55	−293.65	−79.63	−277.95	200.60
2001	−821.21	−318.63	−353.36	−19.05	−1369.70	611.75	224.19	101.65
2002	34.74	−179.56	−220.42	−10.53	−326.67	−284.57	77.61	−207.54
2003	662.26	−376.20	83.63	−211.70	173.27	−331.74	236.06	46.45
2004	−53.48	26.37	6.31	−44.57	−28.61	−237.22	106.70	177.20
2005	−144.69	−186.80	110.44	−325.23	−36.62	−222.35	97.01	7.68
2006	203.31	0.32	122.63	−25.46	168.66	−52.67	138.03	−102.30
2007	−165.91	370.60	215.09	−279.22	377.67	75.44	110.80	−84.78
2008	410.23	−144.92	−464.66	−496.18	−33.55	−245.31	−50.57	−63.56
2009	54.40	497.80	−259.53	−101.34	214.79	−155.01	−142.61	191.21
2010	117.29	108.38	239.57	−306.83	145.08	252.41	81.59	81.58
2011	−185.88	362.07	52.45	−69.78	516.96	−737.61	−317.87	427.61
2012	310.60	−151.89	212.97	−126.39	−13.90	−142.34	55.83	−252.73
2013	117.04	−2.08	−270.78	110.20	75.03	−192.85	465.78	257.27
2014	237.10	20.29	171.34	−95.24	292.23	−166.59	523.97	248.91
2015	378.34	−414.99	117.11	−69.27	−48.51	−69.91	−136.66	423.62
2016	388.99	−86.57	−190.18	−274.41	38.35	137.65	86.56	90.40
2017	11.64	−317.90	112.31	10.48	470.55	81.25	322.58	102.32
2018	−389.23	−1413.31	−226.05	−509.59	588.83	−285.19	−1655.14	617.03
2019	398.63	−346.55	629.52	−119.17	−284.45	−114.82	319.71	190.17
2020	−4011.64	2462.80	265.92	−855.91	−8.22	−483.46	132.68	20.82
2021	−150.67	444.91						
Up	21	12	18	4	18	7	23	23
Down	10	19	12	26	12	23	7	7

OCTOBER 2022/NOVEMBER 2022

Trading Thanksgiving Market: Long into Weakness Prior,
Exit into Strength After (Page 106)

MONDAY

D 47.6
S 52.4
N 47.6

21

In this age of instant information, investors can experience both fear and greed at the exact same moment.
— Sam Stovall (Chief Investment Strategist CFRA Research, October 2003)

TUESDAY

D 52.4
S 52.4
N 61.9

22

Leadership is the ability to hide your panic from others
— Lau Tzu (Chinese philosopher, Shaolin monk, founder of Taoism, 6th century BCE)

WEDNESDAY

D 66.7
S 61.9
N 66.7

23

He who knows how will always work for he who knows why.
— David Lee Roth (Lead singer of Van Halen, b. 1954)

Thanksgiving *(Market Closed)*

THURSDAY

24

Remember to look up at the stars and not down at your feet.
— Professsor Stephen Hawking (English theoretical physicist, cosmologist, and author, 1942–2018)

(Shortened Trading Day)

FRIDAY

D 76.2
S 66.7
N 66.7

25

He who hesitates is poor.
— Mel Brooks (Writer, director, comedian, b. 1926)

SATURDAY

26

December Almanac Investor Sector Seasonalities: See Pages 94, 96 and 98

SUNDAY

27

DECEMBER ALMANAC

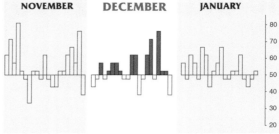

DECEMBER							JANUARY						
S	M	T	W	T	F	S	S	M	T	W	T	F	S
				1	2	3						1	2
4	5	6	7	8	9	10	3	4	5	6	7	8	9
11	12	13	14	15	16	17	10	11	12	13	14	15	16
18	19	20	21	22	23	24	17	18	19	20	21	22	23
25	26	27	28	29	30	31	24	25	26	27	28		
							31						

Market Probability Chart above is a graphic representation of the S&P 500 Recent Market Probability Calendar on page 126.

◆ #3 S&P (+1.5%) and Dow (+1.8%) month since 1950 (page 52), #2 NASDAQ 1.9% since 1971 (page 60) ◆ 2018 worst December since 1931, down over 8% Dow and S&P, –9.5% on NASDAQ (pages 156, 162 and 166) ◆ "Free lunch" served on Wall Street before Christmas (page 116) ◆ Small caps start to outperform larger caps near middle of month (pages 112 and 114) ◆ "Santa Claus Rally" visible in graph above and on page 118 ◆ In 1998 was part of best fourth quarter since 1928 (page 178) ◆ Fourth-quarter expiration week most bullish triple-witching week, Dow up 23 of last 30 (page 108) ◆ Midterm election years Decembers rankings: #5 Dow, #3 S&P and #7 NASDAQ

December Vital Statistics

	DJIA		S&P 500		NASDAQ		Russell 1K		Russell 2K	
Rank	3		3		4		3		2	
Up	50		53		30		32		32	
Down	21		18		20		10		10	
Average % Change	1.5%		1.5%		1.7%		1.4%		2.3%	
Midterm Election Year	0.9%		1.2%		–0.3%		0.1%		0.3%	
Best & Worst December										
	% Change		% Change		% Change		% Change		% Change	
Best	1991	9.5	1991	11.2	1999	22.0	1991	11.2	1999	11.2
Worst	2018	–8.7	2018	–9.2	2002	–9.7	2018	–9.3	2018	–12.0
Best & Worst December Weeks										
Best	12/2/2011	7.0	12/2/2011	7.4	12/8/2000	10.3	12/2/2011	7.4	12/2/2011	10.3
Worst	12/4/1987	–7.5	12/6/1974	–7.1	12/15/2000	–9.1	12/21/2018	–7.1	12/21/2018	–8.4
Best & Worst December Days										
Best	12/26/2018	5.0	12/16/2008	5.1	12/5/2000	10.5	12/16/2008	5.2	12/16/2008	6.7
Worst	12/1/2008	–7.7	12/1/2008	–8.9	12/1/2008	–9.0	12/1/2008	–9.1	12/1/2008	–11.9
First Trading Day of Expiration Week: 1980–2021										
Record (#Up – #Down)	24–17		24–17		19–22		24–17		18–23	
Current Streak	D1		D1		U2		D1		U2	
Avg % Change	0.11		0.08		–0.07		0.05		–0.21	
Options Expiration Day: 1980–2021										
Record (#Up – #Down)	25–16		28–13		27–14		28–13		25–16	
Current Streak	D1		D1		D1		D1		D1	
Avg % Change	0.19		0.26		0.23		0.25		0.33	
Options Expiration Week: 1980–2021										
Record (#Up – #Down)	31–10		29–12		24–17		28–13		22–19	
Current Streak	U2		U2		U2		U2		U2	
Avg % Change	0.56		0.60		0.20		0.56		0.49	
Week After Options Expiration: 1980–2021										
Record (#Up – #Down)	30–10		26–15		28–13		26–15		29–12	
Current Streak	U8		D1		U8		D1		U1	
Avg % Change	0.81		0.57		0.77		0.60		0.93	
First Trading Day Performance										
% of Time Up	47.9		49.3		58.0		50.0		50.0	
Avg % Change	–0.03		–0.02		0.12		–0.02		–0.13	
Last Trading Day Performance										
% of Time Up	53.5		60.6		70.0		52.4		64.3	
Avg % Change	0.07		0.10		28.0		–0.05		0.35	

Dow & S&P 1950-June 11, 2021, NASDAQ 1971-June 11, 2021, Russell 1K & 2K 1979-June 11, 2021.

*If Santa Claus should fail to call,
Bears may come to Broad and Wall.*

MONDAY

D 61.9
S 57.1
N 57.1

28

The stock market is that creation of man which humbles him the most.
— Anonymous

TUESDAY

D 66.7
S 76.2
N 66.7

29

We may face more inflation pressure than currently shows up in formal data.
— William Poole (Economist, president Federal Reserve Bank St. Louis 1998–2008, June 2006 speech, b. 1937)

Last Trading Day of November, S&P Down 15 of Last 23

WEDNESDAY

D 52.4
S 38.1
N 42.9

30

Behold, my son, with what little wisdom the world is ruled.
— Count Axel Gustafsson Oxenstierna (1648 letter to his son at conclusion of Thirty Years War, 1583–1654)

First Trading Day in December, NASDAQ Up 22 of 34,
But Down 6 of Last 9

THURSDAY

D 42.9
S 42.9
N 52.4

1

Vietnam, the original domino in the Cold War, now faces the prospect of becoming, in the words of political scientist Sunai Phasuk of Chulalongkorn University in Bangkok, one of the new "dominos of democracy."
— Seth Mydans (*NY Times*, Jan. 6, 2001)

FRIDAY

D 38.1
S 47.6
N 47.6

2

Success is going from failure to failure without loss of enthusiasm.
— Winston Churchill (British statesman, 1874–1965)

SATURDAY

3

SUNDAY

4

MOST OF THE SO-CALLED JANUARY EFFECT TAKES PLACE IN THE LAST HALF OF DECEMBER

Over the years we have reported annually on the fascinating January Effect, showing that small-cap stocks handily outperformed large-cap stocks during January 40 out of 43 years between 1953 and 1995. Readers saw that "Cats and Dogs" on average quadrupled the returns of blue chips in this period. Then the January Effect disappeared over the next four years.

Looking at the graph on page 114, comparing the Russell 1000 index of large-capitalization stocks to the Russell 2000 smaller-capitalization stocks, shows small-cap stocks beginning to outperform the blue chips in mid-December. Narrowing the comparison down to half-month segments was an inspiration and proved to be quite revealing, as you can see in the table below.

34-YEAR AVERAGE RATES OF RETURN (DEC 1987 – FEB 2021)

| From 12/15 | Russell 1000 | | Russell 2000 | |
	Change	Annualized	Change	Annualized
12/15–12/31	1.6%	43.9%	2.9%	92.5%
12/15–01/15	2.1	26.9	3.6	49.9
12/15–01/31	2.2	19.4	3.6	33.3
12/15–02/15	3.5	22.9	5.5	37.9
12/15–02/28	2.5	13.3	4.9	27.3
From 12/31				
12/31–01/15	0.5	11.0	0.7	15.8
12/31–01/31	0.6	7.4	0.7	8.7
12/31–02/15	1.9	16.0	2.6	22.4
12/31–02/28	1.0	6.5	2.0	13.3

42-YEAR AVERAGE RATES OF RETURN (DEC 1979 – FEB 2021)

| From 12/15 | Russell 1000 | | Russell 2000 | |
	Change	Annualized	Change	Annualized
12/15–12/31	1.5%	40.6%	2.7%	84.1%
12/15–01/15	2.3	29.8	4.0	56.7
12/15–01/31	2.5	22.2	4.1	38.6
12/15–02/15	3.6	23.6	5.9	41.1
12/15–02/28	2.9	15.2	5.4	29.7
From 12/31				
12/31–01/15	0.8	18.2	1.3	31.2
12/31–01/31	1.0	12.7	1.4	18.2
12/31–02/15	2.1	17.8	3.2	28.2
12/31–02/28	1.4	9.2	2.7	18.3

* Mid-month dates are the 11th trading day of the month, month end dates are monthly closes.

Small-cap strength in the last half of December became even more magnified after the 1987 market crash. Note the dramatic shift in gains in the last half of December during the 34-year period starting in 1987, versus the 42 years from 1979 to 2021. With all the beaten-down small stocks being dumped for tax-loss purposes, it generally pays to get a head start on the January Effect in mid-December. You don't have to wait until December either; the small-cap sector often begins to turn around near the beginning of November.

MONDAY

D 66.7
S 57.1
N 66.7

5

Man's mind, once stretched by a new idea, never regains its original dimensions.
— Oliver Wendell Holmes (American author, poet and physician, 1809–1894)

Small Cap Strength Starts in Mid-December (Pages 112 and 114)

TUESDAY

D 47.6
S 47.6
N 61.9

6

An entrepreneur tends to lie some of the time. An entrepreneur in trouble tends to lie most of the time.
— Anonymous

WEDNESDAY

D 57.1
S 52.4
N 47.6

7

…the most successful positions I've taken have been those about which I've been most nervous (and ignored that emotion anyway). Courage is not about being fearless; courage is about acting appropriately even when you are fearful.
— Daniel Turov (*Turov on Timing*)

THURSDAY

D 57.1
S 57.1
N 61.9

8

People become attached to their burdens sometimes more than the burdens are attached to them.
— George Bernard Shaw (Irish dramatist, 1856–1950)

FRIDAY

D 52.4
S 57.1
N 66.7

9

Every age has a blind eye and sees nothing wrong in practices and institutions, which its successors view with just horror.
— Sir Richard Livingstone (*On Education*, 1880–1960)

SATURDAY

10

SUNDAY

11

JANUARY EFFECT NOW STARTS IN MID-DECEMBER

Small-cap stocks tend to outperform big caps in January. Known as the "January Effect," the tendency is clearly revealed by the graph below. Daily data for the Russell 2000 index of smaller companies are divided by the Russell 1000 index of largest companies since July 1, 1979, and then compressed into a single year to show an idealized yearly pattern. When the graph is descending, big blue chips are outperforming smaller companies; when the graph is rising, smaller companies are moving up faster than their larger brethren.

In a typical year, the smaller fry stay on the sidelines while the big boys are on the field. Then, around early November, small stocks begin to wake up, and in mid-December they take off. Anticipated year-end dividends, payouts and bonuses could be a factor. Other major moves are quite evident just before Labor Day—possibly because individual investors are back from vacation. Small caps hold the lead through the beginning of June, though the bulk of the move is complete by early March.

RUSSELL 2000/RUSSELL 1000 ONE-YEAR SEASONAL PATTERN

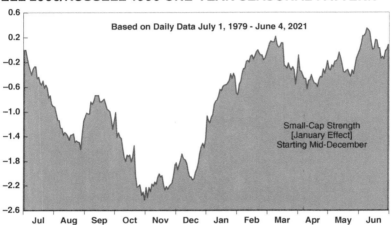

The bottom graph shows the actual ratio of the Russell 2000 divided by the Russell 1000 from 1979. Smaller companies had the upper hand for five years into 1983, as the last major bear trend wound to a close and the nascent bull market logged its first year. After falling behind for about eight years, they came back after the Persian Gulf War bottom in 1990, moving up until 1994, when big caps ruled the latter stages of the millennial bull. For six years, the picture was bleak for small fry, as the blue chips and tech stocks moved to stratospheric PE ratios. Small caps spiked in late 1999 and early 2000 and reached a peak in early 2006, as the four-year-old bull entered its final year. Note how the small-cap advantage has waned during major bull moves and intensified during weak market times.

RUSSELL 2000/RUSSELL 1000 (1979 – MAY 2021)

Monday Before December Triple Witching S&P Up 13 of Last 21, 2018 Down 2.1%

MONDAY

D 57.1
S 52.4
N 47.6

12

Make money and the whole nation will conspire to call you a gentleman.
— George Bernard Shaw (Irish dramatist, 1856–1950)

TUESDAY

D 61.9
S 47.6
N 42.9

13

Self-discipline is a form of freedom. Freedom from laziness and lethargy, freedom from expectations and demands of others, freedom from weakness and fear—and doubt.
— Harvey A. Dorfman (Sports psychologist, *The Mental ABC's of Pitching*, b. 1935)

FOMC Meeting (2 Days)

WEDNESDAY

D 52.4
S 47.6
N 52.4

14

Edison has done more toward abolishing poverty than all the reformers and statesmen.
— Henry Ford (Founder Ford Motors, father of moving assembly line, 1863–1947)

December Triple Witching Week, S&P Up 28 of Last 37, 2018 Down 7.1%

THURSDAY

D 61.9
S 61.9
N 61.9

15

Drawing on my fine command of language, I said nothing.
— Robert Benchley (American writer, actor and humorist, 1889–1945)

December Triple Witching Day, S&P Up 26 of Last 39, 2018–2.1%

FRIDAY

D 52.4
S 61.9
N 57.1

16

Pretending to know everything closes the door to finding out what's really there.
— Neil deGrasse Tyson (American astrophysicist, cosmologist, Director Hayden Planetarium, *Cosmos: A Spacetime Odyssey*, b. 1958)

The Only FREE LUNCH on Wall Street is Served (Page 116)
Almanac Investors Emailed Alert Before the Open, Monday (See Insert)

SATURDAY

17

SUNDAY

18

WALL STREET'S ONLY "FREE LUNCH" SERVED BEFORE CHRISTMAS

Investors tend to get rid of their losers near year-end for tax purposes, often hammering these stocks down to bargain levels. Over the years, the *Almanac* has shown that NYSE stocks selling at their lows on December 15 will usually outperform the market by February 15 in the following year. Preferred stocks, closed-end funds, splits and new issues are eliminated.

BARGAIN STOCKS VS. THE MARKET*

Short Span* Late Dec–Jan/Feb	New Lows Late Dec	% Change Jan/Feb	% Change NYSE Composite	Bargain Stocks Advantage
1974–75	112	48.9%	22.1%	26.8%
1975–76	21	34.9	14.9	20.0
1976–77	2	1.3	−3.3	4.6
1977–78	15	2.8	−4.5	7.3
1978–79	43	11.8	3.9	7.9
1979–80	5	9.3	6.1	3.2
1980–81	14	7.1	−2.0	9.1
1981–82	21	−2.6	−7.4	4.8
1982–83	4	33.0	9.7	23.3
1983–84	13	−3.2	−3.8	0.6
1984–85	32	19.0	12.1	6.9
1985–86	4	−22.5	3.9	−26.4
1986–87	22	9.3	12.5	−3.2
1987–88	23	13.2	6.8	6.4
1988–89	14	30.0	6.4	23.6
1989–90	25	−3.1	−4.8	1.7
1990–91	18	18.8	12.6	6.2
1991–92	23	51.1	7.7	43.4
1992–93	9	8.7	0.6	8.1
1993–94	10	−1.4	2.0	−3.4
1994–95	25	14.6	5.7	8.9
1995–96	5	−11.3	4.5	−15.8
1996–97	16	13.9	11.2	2.7
1997–98	29	9.9	5.7	4.2
1998–99	40	−2.8	4.3	−7.1
1999–00	26	8.9	−5.4	14.3
2000–01	51	44.4	0.1	44.3
2001–02	12	31.4	−2.3	33.7
2002–03	33	28.7	3.9	24.8
2003–04	15	16.7	2.3	14.4
2004–05	36	6.8	−2.8	9.6
2005–06	71	12.0	2.6	9.4
2006–07	43	5.1	−0.5	5.6
2007–08	71	−3.2	−9.4	6.2
2008–09	88	11.4	−2.4	13.8
2009–10	25	1.8	−3.0	4.8
2010–11	20	8.3	3.4	4.9
2011–12	65	18.1	6.1	12.0
2012–13	17	20.9	3.4	17.5
2013–14	18	25.7	1.7	24.0
2014–15	17	0.2	−0.4	0.6
2015–16	38	−9.2	5.6	−14.8
2016–17	19	2.8	0.6	2.2
2017–18	18	3.3	1.2	2.1
2018–19	23	24.9	15.1	9.8
2019–20	13	−1.1%	−0.3%	−0.7%
2020–21	3	−4.9%	3.6%	−8.5%
47-Year Totals		**543.8%**	**150.0%**	**393.8%**
Average		**11.6%**	**3.2%**	**8.4%**

Dec 15–Feb 15 (1974–1999), Dec 1999–2021 based on actual newsletter portfolio

In response to changing market conditions, we tweaked the strategy the last 22 years, adding selections from NASDAQ and AMEX, and selling in mid-January some years. We email the list of stocks to our *Almanac Investor eNewsletter* subscribers. Visit *www.stocktradersalmanac.com*, or see the ad insert for additional details and a special offer for new subscribers.

We have come to the conclusion that the most prudent course of action is to compile our list from the stocks making new lows on Triple-Witching Friday before Christmas, capitalizing on the Santa Claus Rally (page 118). This also gives us the weekend to evaluate the issues in greater depth and weed out any glaringly problematic stocks. Subscribers will receive the list of stocks selected from the new lows made on December 17, 2021, and December 16, 2022, via email.

This "Free Lunch" strategy is an extremely short-term strategy reserved for the nimblest traders. It has performed better after market corrections and when there are more new lows to choose from. The object is to buy bargain stocks near their 52-week lows and sell after any quick, generous gains, as these issues can be real dogs.

Chanukah

Imagination is more important than knowledge.
— Albert Einstein (German/American physicist, 1921 Nobel Prize, 1879–1955)

Successful investing is anticipating the anticipations of others.
— John Maynard Keynes (British economist, 1883–1946)

*Week After December Triple Witching Dow Up 23 of Last 30,
Average Gain 0.8% Since 1991*

Don't confuse brains with a bull market.
— Humphrey B. Neill (Investor, analyst, author, *Neill Letters of Contrary Opinion*, 1895–1977)

A committee is a cul-de-sac down which ideas are lured and then quietly strangled.
— Sir Barnett Cocks (Member of Parliament, 1907–1989)

*Santa Claus Rally Begins December 23 (Page 118)
Last Trading Day Before Christmas, NASDAQ Up 10 of Last 14, 2018 –2.2%*

The test of success is not what you do when you are on top. Success is how high you bounce when you hit bottom.
— General George S. Patton, Jr. (U.S. Army field commander WWII, 1885–1945)

Christmas Day
January Almanac Investor Sector Seasonalities: See Pages 94, 96 and 98

IF SANTA CLAUS SHOULD FAIL TO CALL, BEARS MAY COME TO BROAD AND WALL

Santa Claus tends to come to Wall Street nearly every year, bringing a short, sweet, respectable rally within the last five days of the year and the first two in January. This has been good for an average 1.3% gain since 1969 (1.3% since 1950 as well). Santa's failure to show tends to precede bear markets, or times stocks could be purchased later in the year at much lower prices. We discovered this phenomenon in 1972.

DAILY % CHANGE IN S&P 500 AT YEAR-END

	Trading Days Before Year-End						First Days in January			Rally %
	6	5	4	3	2	1	1	2	3	Change
1969	−0.4	1.1	0.8	−0.7	0.4	0.5	1.0	0.5	−0.7	3.6
1970	0.1	0.6	0.5	1.1	0.2	−0.1	−1.1	0.7	0.6	1.9
1971	−0.4	0.2	1.0	0.3	−0.4	0.3	−0.4	0.4	1.0	1.3
1972	−0.3	−0.7	0.6	0.4	0.5	1.0	0.9	0.4	−0.1	3.1
1973	−1.1	−0.7	3.1	2.1	−0.2	0.01	0.1	2.2	−0.9	6.7
1974	−1.4	1.4	0.8	−0.4	0.03	2.1	2.4	0.7	0.5	7.2
1975	0.7	0.8	0.9	−0.1	−0.4	0.5	0.8	1.8	1.0	4.3
1976	0.1	1.2	0.7	−0.4	0.5	0.5	−0.4	−1.2	−0.9	0.8
1977	0.8	0.9	N/C	0.1	0.2	0.2	−1.3	−0.3	−0.8	−0.3
1978	0.03	1.7	1.3	−0.9	−0.4	−0.2	0.6	1.1	0.8	3.3
1979	−0.6	0.1	0.1	0.2	−0.1	0.1	−2.0	−0.5	1.2	−2.2
1980	−0.4	0.4	0.5	−1.1	0.2	0.3	0.4	1.2	0.1	2.0
1981	−0.5	0.2	−0.2	−0.5	0.5	0.2	0.2	−2.2	−0.7	−1.8
1982	0.6	1.8	−1.0	0.3	−0.7	0.2	−1.6	2.2	0.4	1.2
1983	−0.2	−0.03	0.9	0.3	−0.2	0.05	−0.5	1.7	1.2	2.1
1984	−0.5	0.8	−0.2	−0.4	0.3	0.6	−1.1	−0.5	−0.5	−0.6
1985	−1.1	−0.7	0.2	0.9	0.5	0.3	−0.8	0.6	−0.1	1.1
1986	−1.0	0.2	0.1	−0.9	−0.5	−0.5	1.8	2.3	0.2	2.4
1987	1.3	−0.5	−2.6	−0.4	1.3	−0.3	3.6	1.1	0.1	2.2
1988	−0.2	0.3	−0.4	0.1	0.8	−0.6	−0.9	1.5	0.2	0.9
1989	0.6	0.8	−0.2	0.6	0.5	0.8	1.8	−0.3	−0.9	4.1
1990	0.5	−0.6	0.3	−0.8	0.1	0.5	−1.1	−1.4	−0.3	−3.0
1991	2.5	0.6	1.4	0.4	2.1	0.5	0.04	0.5	−0.3	5.7
1992	−0.3	0.2	−0.1	−0.3	0.2	−0.7	−0.1	−0.2	0.04	−1.1
1993	0.01	0.7	0.1	−0.1	−0.4	−0.5	−0.2	0.3	0.1	−0.1
1994	0.01	0.2	0.4	−0.3	0.1	−0.4	−0.03	0.3	−0.1	0.2
1995	0.8	0.2	0.4	0.04	−0.1	0.3	0.8	0.1	−0.6	1.8
1996	−0.3	0.5	0.6	0.1	−0.4	−1.7	−0.5	1.5	−0.1	0.1
1997	−1.5	−0.7	0.4	1.8	1.8	−0.04	0.5	0.2	−1.1	4.0
1998	2.1	−0.2	−0.1	1.3	−0.8	−0.2	−0.1	1.4	2.2	1.3
1999	1.6	−0.1	0.04	0.4	0.1	0.3	−1.0	−3.8	0.2	−4.0
2000	0.8	2.4	0.7	1.0	0.4	−1.0	−2.8	5.0	−1.1	5.7
2001	0.4	−0.02	0.4	0.7	0.3	−1.1	0.6	0.9	0.6	1.8
2002	0.2	−0.5	−0.3	−1.6	0.5	0.05	3.3	−0.05	2.2	1.2
2003	0.3	−0.2	0.2	1.2	0.01	0.2	−0.3	1.2	0.1	2.4
2004	0.1	−0.4	0.7	−0.01	0.01	−0.1	−0.8	−1.2	−0.4	−1.8
2005	0.4	0.04	−1.0	0.1	−0.3	−0.5	1.6	0.4	0.002	0.4
2006	−0.4	−0.5	0.4	0.7	−0.1	−0.5	−0.1	0.1	−0.6	0.003
2007	1.7	0.8	0.1	−1.4	0.1	−0.7	−1.4	N/C	−2.5	−2.5
2008	−1.0	0.6	0.5	−0.4	2.4	1.4	3.2	−0.5	0.8	7.4
2009	0.2	0.5	0.1	−0.1	0.02	−1.0	1.6	0.3	0.05	1.4
2010	−0.2	0.1	0.1	0.1	−0.2	−0.02	1.1	−0.1	0.5	1.1
2011	0.8	0.9	0.01	−1.3	1.1	−0.4	1.6	0.02	0.3	1.9
2012	−0.9	−0.2	−0.5	−0.1	−1.1	1.7	2.5	−0.2	0.5	2.0
2013	0.5	0.3	0.5	−0.03	−0.02	0.4	−0.9	−0.03	−0.3	0.2
2014	0.2	−0.01	0.3	0.1	−0.5	−1.0	−0.03	−1.8	−0.9	−3.0
2015	1.2	−0.2	−0.2	1.1	−0.7	−0.9	−1.5	0.2	−1.3	−2.3
2016	−0.2	0.1	0.2	−0.8	−0.03	−0.5	0.9	0.6	−0.1	0.4
2017	0.2	−0.05	−0.1	0.1	0.2	−0.5	0.8	0.6	0.4	1.1
2018	−2.1	−2.7	5.0	0.9	−0.1	0.9	0.1	−2.5	3.4	1.3
2019	0.1	−0.02	0.5	0.003	−0.6	0.3	0.8	−0.7	0.4	0.3
2020	0.1	0.4	0.9	−0.2	0.1	0.6	−1.5	0.7	0.6	1.0
Avg	0.08	0.23	0.36	0.06	0.14	0.03	0.21	0.29	0.08	1.3

The couplet above was certainly on the mark in 1999, as the period suffered a horrendous 4.0% loss. On January 14, 2000, the Dow started its 33-month 37.8% slide to the October 2002 midterm election year bottom. NASDAQ cracked eight weeks later, falling 37.3% in 10 weeks, eventually dropping 77.9% by October 2002. Energy prices and Middle East terror woes may have grounded Santa in 2004. In 2007, the third worst reading since 1950 was recorded, as a full-blown financial crisis led to the second worst bear market in history. In 2016, the period was hit again as global growth concerns escalated and the market digested the first interest rate hike in nearly a decade.

DECEMBER 2022/JANUARY 2023

(Market Closed - Christmas Day Observed)

MONDAY
26

Anyone who has achieved excellence knows that it comes as a result of ceaseless concentration.
— Louise Brooks (Actress, 1906–1985)

TUESDAY
D 71.4
S 76.2
N 66.7
27

I never buy at the bottom and I always sell too soon.
— Baron Nathan Rothchild's success formula (London Financier, 1777–1836)

WEDNESDAY
D 47.6
S 52.4
N 47.6
28

On Wall Street, to know what everyone else knows is to know nothing.
— Newton Zinder (Investment advisor and analyst, E.F. Hutton, b. 1927)

THURSDAY
D 47.6
S 52.4
N 47.6
29

The average bottom-of-the-ladder person is potentially as creative as the top executive who sits in the big office. The problem is that the person on the bottom of the ladder doesn't trust his own brilliance and doesn't, therefore, believe in his own ideas.
— Robert Schuller (Minister)

Last Trading Day of the Year, NASDAQ Down 15 of last 21
NASDAQ Was Up 29 Years in a Row 1971–1999

FRIDAY
D 42.9
S 38.1
N 28.6
30

A fundamental analyst goes into each store and studies the products to decide whether to buy or not. A technical analyst sits on a bench watching people go into stores. Disregarding the intrinsic value, the technical analyst's decision is be based on the patterns or activity of people.
— Investopedia.com on Technical Analysis (Hat tip JC Parets of All Star Charts via Ari Wald of Oppenheimer)

SATURDAY
31

New Year's Day

SUNDAY
1

2023 STRATEGY CALENDAR

(Option expiration dates circled)

	MONDAY	TUESDAY	WEDNESDAY	THURSDAY	FRIDAY	SATURDAY	SUNDAY
JANUARY	26	27	28	29	30	31	1 JANUARY New Year's Day
	2	3	4	5	6	7	8
	9	10	11	12	13	14	15
	16 Martin Luther King Day	17	18	19	(20)	21	22
	23	24	25	26	27	28	29
FEBRUARY	30	31	1 FEBRUARY	2	3	4	5
	6	7	8	9	10	11	12
	13	14 ♥	15	16	(17)	18	19
	20 Presidents' Day	21	22 Ash Wednesday	23	24	25	26
MARCH	27	28	1 MARCH	2	3	4	5
	6	7	8	9	10	11	12 Daylight Saving Time Begins
	13	14	15	16	(17) ♣ St. Patrick's Day	18	19
	20	21	22	23	24	25	26
	27	28	29	30	31	1 APRIL	2
APRIL	3	4	5	6 Passover	7 Good Friday	8	9 Easter
	10	11	12	13	14	15	16
	17	18	19	20	(21)	22	23
	24	25	26	27	28	29	30
MAY	1 MAY	2	3	4	5	6	7
	8	9	10	11	12	13	14 Mother's Day
	15	16	17	18	(19)	20	21
	22	23	24	25	26	27	28
	29 Memorial Day	30	31	1 JUNE	2	3	4
JUNE	5	6	7	8	9	10	11
	12	13	14	15	(16)	17	18 Father's Day
	19	20	21	22	23	24	25
	26	27	28	29	30	1 JULY	2

Market closed on shaded weekdays; closes early when half-shaded.

2023 STRATEGY CALENDAR

(Option expiration dates circled)

MONDAY	TUESDAY	WEDNESDAY	THURSDAY	FRIDAY	SATURDAY	SUNDAY	
3	4 Independence Day	5	6	7	8	9	JULY
10	11	12	13	14	15	16	
17	18	19	20	(21)	22	23	
24	25	26	27	28	29	30	
31	1 AUGUST	2	3	4	5	6	
7	8	9	10	11	12	13	AUGUST
14	15	16	17	(18)	19	20	
21	22	23	24	25	26	27	
28	29	30	31	1 SEPTEMBER	2	3	
4 Labor Day	5	6	7	8	9	10	SEPTEMBER
11	12	13	14	(15)	16 Rosh Hashanah	17	
18	19	20	21	22	23	24	
25 Yom Kippur	26	27	28	29	30	1 OCTOBER	
2	3	4	5	6	7	8	OCTOBER
9 Columbus Day	10	11	12	13	14	15	
16	17	18	19	(20)	21	22	
23	24	25	26	27	28	29	
30	31 🎃	1 NOVEMBER	2	3	4	5 Daylight Saving Time Ends	
6	7 Election Day	8	9	10	11 Veterans' Day	12	NOVEMBER
13	14	15	16	(17)	18	19	
20	21	22	23 Thanksgiving Day	24	25	26	
27	28	29	30	1 DECEMBER	2	3	
4	5	6	7	8 Chanukah	9	10	DECEMBER
11	12	13	14	(15)	16	17	
18	19	20	21	22	23	24	
25 Christmas	26	27	28	29	30	31	

DIRECTORY OF TRADING PATTERNS AND DATABANK

CONTENTS

DOW JONES INDUSTRIALS MARKET PROBABILITY CALENDAR 2022

THE % CHANCE OF THE MARKET RISING ON ANY TRADING DAY OF THE YEAR*
(Based on the number of times the DJIA rose on a particular trading day during **January 1954–December 2020**)

Date	Jan	Feb	Mar	Apr	May	Jun	Jul	Aug	Sep	Oct	Nov	Dec
1	S	61.2	65.7	58.2	S	61.2	65.7	43.3	56.7	S	62.7	46.3
2	S	53.7	59.7	S	53.7	53.7	S	46.3	61.2	S	53.7	50.7
3	59.7	43.3	59.7	S	62.7	52.2	S	50.7	S	47.8	67.2	S
4	70.1	56.7	49.3	61.2	52.2	S	H	52.2	S	55.2	59.7	S
5	49.3	S	S	52.2	46.3	S	56.7	55.2	H	56.7	S	62.7
6	56.7	S	S	59.7	49.3	59.7	61.2	S	61.2	61.2	S	58.2
7	46.3	46.3	44.8	49.3	S	55.2	55.2	S	43.3	43.3	50.7	50.7
8	S	41.8	52.2	61.2	S	49.3	61.2	47.8	47.8	S	62.7	46.3
9	S	47.8	61.2	S	55.2	37.3	S	44.8	46.3	S	53.7	53.7
10	50.7	61.2	50.7	S	47.8	52.2	S	44.8	S	52.2	53.7	S
11	47.8	47.8	55.2	62.7	52.2	S	56.7	47.8	S	44.8	49.3	S
12	47.8	S	S	61.2	44.8	S	52.2	64.2	61.2	43.3	S	58.2
13	56.7	S	S	55.2	53.7	58.2	47.8	S	61.2	49.3	S	46.3
14	55.2	50.7	52.2	70.1	S	56.7	68.7	S	49.3	58.2	47.8	50.7
15	S	56.7	61.2	H	S	50.7	52.2	56.7	55.2	S	59.7	50.7
16	S	44.8	61.2	S	56.7	52.2	S	52.2	58.2	S	52.2	55.2
17	H	47.8	56.7	S	46.3	50.7	S	49.3	S	50.7	47.8	S
18	61.2	47.8	53.7	62.7	50.7	S	46.3	53.7	S	53.7	49.3	S
19	41.8	S	S	58.2	43.3	S	50.7	41.8	41.8	44.8	S	47.8
20	40.3	S	S	53.7	41.8	44.8	53.7	S	50.7	59.7	S	53.7
21	41.8	H	43.3	53.7	S	49.3	38.8	S	46.3	43.3	56.7	58.2
22	S	38.8	41.8	53.7	S	46.3	44.8	58.2	41.8	S	64.2	53.7
23	S	46.3	47.8	S	35.8	43.3	S	49.3	37.3	S	61.2	58.2
24	47.8	59.7	35.8	S	52.2	35.8	S	52.2	S	49.3	H	S
25	58.2	46.3	50.7	50.7	46.3	S	59.7	49.3	S	29.9	67.2	S
26	58.2	S	S	58.2	44.8	S	53.7	46.3	47.8	53.7	S	H
27	49.3	S	S	56.7	56.7	47.8	46.3	S	53.7	52.2	S	71.6
28	58.2	47.8	47.8	50.7	S	46.3	55.2	S	52.2	59.7	59.7	49.3
29	S		52.2	49.3	S	55.2	49.3	64.2	49.3	S	53.7	53.7
30	S		47.8	S	H	55.2	S	41.8	43.3	S	52.2	53.7
31	55.2		43.3		53.7		S	59.7		52.2		S

See new trends developing on pages 72, 86, 143–148

RECENT DOW JONES INDUSTRIALS MARKET PROBABILITY CALENDAR 2022

THE % CHANCE OF THE MARKET RISING ON ANY TRADING DAY OF THE YEAR*

(Based on the number of times the DJIA rose on a particular trading day during **January 2000–December 2020****)

Date	Jan	Feb	Mar	Apr	May	Jun	Jul	Aug	Sep	Oct	Nov	Dec
1	S	81.0	61.9	61.9	S	76.2	76.2	38.1	47.6	S	61.9	42.9
2	S	42.9	38.1	S	57.1	61.9	S	52.4	76.2	S	61.9	38.1
3	66.7	52.4	61.9	S	61.9	47.6	S	57.1	S	52.4	61.9	S
4	57.1	57.1	47.6	66.7	38.1	S	H	52.4	S	42.9	76.2	S
5	52.4	S	S	47.6	38.1	S	33.3	57.1	H	71.4	S	66.7
6	52.4	S	S	66.7	61.9	57.1	57.1	S	61.9	57.1	S	47.6
7	38.1	42.9	47.6	38.1	S	66.7	57.1	S	42.9	33.3	61.9	57.1
8	S	47.6	47.6	61.9	S	66.7	61.9	57.1	52.4	S	57.1	57.1
9	S	52.4	61.9	S	71.4	38.1	S	42.9	57.1	S	47.6	52.4
10	57.1	52.4	47.6	S	38.1	38.1	S	33.3	S	47.6	38.1	S
11	52.4	57.1	57.1	57.1	61.9	S	57.1	47.6	S	57.1	61.9	S
12	52.4	S	S	52.4	33.3	S	52.4	61.9	76.2	52.4	S	57.1
13	52.4	S	S	47.6	57.1	57.1	81.0	S	61.9	38.1	S	61.9
14	57.1	52.4	61.9	66.7	S	57.1	76.2	S	52.4	61.9	47.6	52.4
15	S	66.7	71.4	H	S	57.1	52.4	52.4	57.1	S	71.4	61.9
16	S	57.1	57.1	S	61.9	61.9	S	52.4	81.0	S	52.4	52.4
17	H	42.9	61.9	S	57.1	52.4	S	71.4	S	52.4	38.1	S
18	52.4	33.3	57.1	61.9	38.1	S	47.6	47.6	S	57.1	42.9	S
19	42.9	S	S	66.7	38.1	S	57.1	33.3	47.6	47.6	S	33.3
20	42.9	S	S	52.4	28.6	47.6	76.2	S	52.4	52.4	S	47.6
21	33.3	H	38.1	57.1	S	38.1	14.3	S	52.4	61.9	47.6	61.9
22	S	47.6	47.6	61.9	S	38.1	33.3	61.9	38.1	S	52.4	71.4
23	S	47.6	42.9	S	47.6	42.9	S	52.4	28.6	S	66.7	42.9
24	42.9	52.4	33.3	S	47.6	28.6	S	57.1	S	52.4	H	S
25	61.9	47.6	57.1	47.6	57.1	S	61.9	47.6	S	42.9	76.2	S
26	61.9	S	S	61.9	47.6	S	52.4	47.6	38.1	66.7	S	H
27	52.4	S	S	66.7	61.9	38.1	47.6	S	52.4	47.6	S	71.4
28	42.9	33.3	42.9	61.9	S	52.4	33.3	S	61.9	61.9	61.9	47.6
29	S		42.9	28.6	S	52.4	42.9	81.0	57.1	S	66.7	47.6
30	S		66.7	S	H	52.4	S	38.1	42.9	S	52.4	42.9
31	47.6		42.9		33.3		S	57.1		47.6		S

See new trends developing on pages 72, 86, 143–148   ** Based on most recent 21-year period

124

S&P 500 MARKET PROBABILITY CALENDAR 2022

THE % CHANCE OF THE MARKET RISING ON ANY TRADING DAY OF THE YEAR*

(Based on the number of times the S&P 500 rose on a particular trading day during January 1954–December 2020)

Date	Jan	Feb	Mar	Apr	May	Jun	Jul	Aug	Sep	Oct	Nov	Dec
1	S	61.2	62.7	62.7	S	58.2	73.1	46.3	58.2	S	62.7	46.3
2	S	58.2	56.7	S	56.7	62.7	S	46.3	53.7	S	58.2	50.7
3	50.7	49.3	62.7	S	65.7	53.7	S	50.7	S	49.3	67.2	S
4	67.2	52.2	47.8	62.7	53.7	S	H	53.7	S	62.7	58.2	S
5	53.7	S	S	53.7	43.3	S	55.2	56.7	H	58.2	S	59.7
6	52.2	S	S	56.7	47.8	56.7	56.7	S	59.7	61.2	S	56.7
7	46.3	49.3	46.3	50.7	S	47.8	58.2	S	44.8	44.8	47.8	46.3
8	S	46.3	55.2	64.2	S	47.8	61.2	47.8	47.8	S	59.7	50.7
9	S	44.8	61.2	S	52.2	40.3	S	50.7	53.7	S	56.7	55.2
10	53.7	62.7	50.7	S	49.3	53.7	S	44.8	S	49.3	56.7	S
11	53.7	55.2	62.7	62.7	53.7	S	56.7	47.8	S	43.3	47.8	S
12	52.2	S	S	53.7	43.3	S	53.7	62.7	61.2	47.8	S	49.3
13	58.2	S	S	52.2	50.7	61.2	53.7	S	65.7	49.3	S	47.8
14	61.2	49.3	43.3	61.2	S	56.7	73.1	S	50.7	53.7	49.3	43.3
15	S	56.7	59.7	H	S	56.7	52.2	62.7	53.7	S	52.2	50.7
16	S	40.3	62.7	S	56.7	50.7	S	56.7	56.7	S	50.7	58.2
17	H	50.7	55.2	S	50.7	55.2	S	55.2	S	50.7	50.7	S
18	59.7	41.8	50.7	61.2	52.2	S	44.8	52.2	S	58.2	52.2	S
19	50.7	S	S	61.2	38.8	S	47.8	44.8	47.8	44.8	S	44.8
20	49.3	S	S	53.7	49.3	44.8	53.7	S	53.7	64.2	S	46.3
21	49.3	H	43.3	53.7	S	50.7	38.8	S	46.3	43.3	56.7	55.2
22	S	41.8	46.3	47.8	S	50.7	46.3	61.2	46.3	S	61.2	50.7
23	S	41.8	41.8	S	44.8	46.3	S	46.3	34.3	S	61.2	58.2
24	59.7	56.7	49.3	S	53.7	34.3	S	50.7	S	47.8	H	S
25	55.2	49.3	43.3	47.8	50.7	S	56.7	49.3	S	32.8	67.2	S
26	52.2	S	S	58.2	47.8	S	53.7	47.8	46.3	58.2	S	H
27	43.3	S	S	50.7	56.7	41.8	46.3	S	50.7	55.2	S	73.1
28	61.2	53.7	49.3	49.3	S	49.3	61.2	S	58.2	59.7	59.7	53.7
29	S		53.7	55.2	S	59.7	59.7	64.2	49.3	S	59.7	59.7
30	S		41.8	S	H	53.7	S	46.3	44.8	S	49.3	61.2
31	61.2		41.8		56.7		S	64.2		53.7		S

*See new trends developing on pages 72, 86, 143–148

RECENT S&P 500 MARKET PROBABILITY CALENDAR 2022

THE % CHANCE OF THE MARKET RISING ON ANY TRADING DAY OF THE YEAR*

(Based on the number of times the S&P 500 rose on a particular trading day during January 2000–December 2020**)

Date	Jan	Feb	Mar	Apr	May	Jun	Jul	Aug	Sep	Oct	Nov	Dec
1	S	76.2	71.4	61.9	S	71.4	85.7	47.6	47.6	S	61.9	42.9
2	S	52.4	38.1	S	66.7	76.2	S	57.1	47.6	S	71.4	47.6
3	57.1	42.9	66.7	S	52.4	47.6	S	52.4	S	52.4	57.1	S
4	47.6	57.1	52.4	71.4	33.3	S	H	57.1	S	42.9	81.0	S
5	61.9	S	S	47.6	42.9	S	38.1	57.1	H	71.4	S	57.1
6	57.1	S	S	66.7	57.1	52.4	66.7	S	52.4	57.1	S	47.6
7	47.6	42.9	47.6	38.1	S	42.9	57.1	S	52.4	33.3	52.4	52.4
8	S	61.9	47.6	66.7	S	61.9	57.1	61.9	47.6	S	47.6	57.1
9	S	52.4	61.9	S	52.4	33.3	S	42.9	61.9	S	33.3	57.1
10	66.7	61.9	52.4	S	42.9	38.1	S	38.1	S	42.9	52.4	S
11	61.9	66.7	61.9	52.4	52.4	S	57.1	47.6	S	57.1	52.4	S
12	42.9	S	S	57.1	33.3	S	57.1	52.4	71.4	52.4	S	52.4
13	52.4	S	S	52.4	47.6	57.1	81.0	S	71.4	42.9	S	47.6
14	57.1	61.9	38.1	57.1	S	57.1	71.4	S	52.4	61.9	47.6	47.6
15	S	71.4	57.1	H	S	66.7	38.1	61.9	52.4	S	61.9	61.9
16	S	47.6	61.9	S	61.9	57.1	S	61.9	71.4	S	47.6	61.9
17	H	47.6	66.7	S	61.9	57.1	S	71.4	S	52.4	42.9	S
18	66.7	33.3	42.9	61.9	38.1	S	47.6	42.9	S	66.7	42.9	S
19	47.6	S	S	76.2	33.3	S	57.1	42.9	52.4	57.1	S	38.1
20	47.6	S	S	57.1	38.1	52.4	76.2	S	47.6	57.1	S	47.6
21	52.4	H	33.3	47.6	S	47.6	19.0	S	33.3	66.7	52.4	61.9
22	S	42.9	52.4	57.1	S	42.9	47.6	66.7	28.6	S	52.4	71.4
23	S	52.4	38.1	S	52.4	47.6	S	47.6	23.8	S	61.9	47.6
24	52.4	52.4	47.6	S	57.1	28.6	S	52.4	S	66.7	H	S
25	61.9	52.4	52.4	42.9	61.9	S	57.1	52.4	S	38.1	66.7	S
26	47.6	S	S	57.1	52.4	S	52.4	57.1	38.1	57.1	S	H
27	42.9	S	S	57.1	61.9	42.9	38.1	S	47.6	42.9	S	76.2
28	47.6	33.3	42.9	66.7	S	47.6	52.4	S	61.9	61.9	57.1	52.4
29	S		47.6	33.3	S	57.1	47.6	85.7	57.1	S	76.2	52.4
30	S		57.1	H	52.4	52.4	S	38.1	38.1	S	38.1	38.1
31	52.4		47.6		47.6		S	61.9		52.4		S

* See new trends developing on pages 72, 86, 143–148   ** Based on most recent 21-year period

NASDAQ COMPOSITE MARKET PROBABILITY CALENDAR 2022

THE % CHANCE OF THE MARKET RISING ON ANY TRADING DAY OF THE YEAR*

(Based on the number of times the NASDAQ rose on a particular trading day during January 1972–December 2020)

Date	Jan	Feb	Mar	Apr	May	Jun	Jul	Aug	Sep	Oct	Nov	Dec
1	S	69.4	63.3	44.9	S	59.2	63.3	53.1	55.1	S	67.3	57.1
2	S	65.3	53.1	S	63.3	73.5	S	42.9	59.2	S	55.1	57.1
3	57.1	55.1	67.3	S	67.3	57.1	S	53.1	S	46.9	67.3	S
4	63.3	63.3	49.0	65.3	57.1	S	H	61.2	S	57.1	57.1	S
5	59.2	S	S	61.2	53.1	S	46.9	55.1	H	61.2	S	65.3
6	63.3	S	S	55.1	57.1	59.2	49.0	S	57.1	59.2	S	61.2
7	57.1	53.1	46.9	42.9	S	51.0	53.1	S	55.1	55.1	53.1	46.9
8	S	53.1	55.1	65.3	S	51.0	61.2	42.9	53.1	S	55.1	55.1
9	S	53.1	59.2	S	65.3	42.9	S	51.0	51.0	S	53.1	49.0
10	61.2	67.3	51.0	S	55.1	51.0	S	46.9	S	59.2	63.3	S
11	57.1	61.2	69.4	61.2	42.9	S	67.3	57.1	S	53.1	55.1	S
12	57.1	S	S	61.2	51.0	S	61.2	59.2	55.1	51.0	S	42.9
13	61.2	S	S	51.0	57.1	59.2	69.4	S	63.3	67.3	S	42.9
14	61.2	67.3	49.0	57.1	S	63.3	77.6	S	59.2	63.3	49.0	42.9
15	S	63.3	51.0	H	S	57.1	63.3	57.1	38.8	S	46.9	51.0
16	S	51.0	65.3	S	57.1	51.0	S	53.1	55.1	S	49.0	57.1
17	H	55.1	59.2	S	59.2	55.1	S	59.2	S	51.0	51.0	S
18	71.4	38.8	67.3	51.0	49.0	S	51.0	51.0	S	53.1	53.1	S
19	59.2	S	S	63.3	40.8	S	55.1	34.7	51.0	44.9	S	49.0
20	44.9	S	S	55.1	49.0	51.0	61.2	S	63.3	65.3	S	51.0
21	49.0	H	40.8	55.1	S	63.3	34.7	S	49.0	49.0	53.1	59.2
22	S	49.0	46.9	51.0	S	49.0	51.0	71.4	49.0	S	67.3	63.3
23	S	53.1	55.1	S	49.0	49.0	S	51.0	42.9	S	61.2	69.4
24	57.1	63.3	53.1	S	55.1	36.7	S	51.0	S	49.0	H	S
25	46.9	57.1	49.0	51.0	57.1	S	57.1	53.1	S	36.7	61.2	S
26	65.3	S	S	46.9	59.2	S	51.0	57.1	51.0	44.9	S	H
27	59.2	S	S	63.3	57.1	46.9	44.9	S	49.0	55.1	S	71.4
28	55.1	46.9	44.9	65.3	S	59.2	57.1	S	49.0	59.2	69.4	49.0
29	S		51.0	61.2	S	67.3	51.0	65.3	44.9	S	65.3	61.2
30	S		57.1	S	H	69.4	S	61.2	51.0	S	61.2	69.4
31	63.3		63.3		63.3		S	67.3		61.2		S

* See new trends developing on pages 72, 86, 143–148
Based on NASDAQ composite, prior to Feb. 5, 1971 based on National Quotation Bureau indices

RECENT NASDAQ COMPOSITE MARKET PROBABILITY CALENDAR 2022

THE % CHANCE OF THE MARKET RISING ON ANY TRADING DAY OF THE YEAR*

(Based on the number of times the NASDAQ rose on a particular trading day during January 2000–December 2020**)

Date	Jan	Feb	Mar	Apr	May	Jun	Jul	Aug	Sep	Oct	Nov	Dec
1	S	76.2	66.7	57.1	S	61.9	76.2	52.4	57.1	S	61.9	52.4
2	S	52.4	38.1	S	71.4	71.4	S	42.9	47.6	S	61.9	47.6
3	71.4	38.1	61.9	S	57.1	57.1	S	52.4	S	47.6	61.9	S
4	42.9	61.9	42.9	66.7	38.1	S	H	52.4	S	47.6	66.7	S
5	57.1	S	S	57.1	52.4	S	38.1	42.9	H	76.2	S	66.7
6	52.4	S	S	61.9	52.4	52.4	61.9	S	47.6	52.4	S	61.9
7	66.7	47.6	33.3	28.6	S	42.9	61.9	S	52.4	42.9	61.9	47.6
8	S	61.9	47.6	66.7	S	47.6	57.1	42.9	52.4	S	47.6	61.9
9	S	52.4	52.4	S	71.4	38.1	S	47.6	57.1	S	33.3	66.7
10	66.7	66.7	47.6	S	47.6	38.1	S	38.1	S	52.4	61.9	S
11	66.7	66.7	61.9	47.6	42.9	S	66.7	57.1	S	57.1	61.9	S
12	47.6	S	S	66.7	42.9	S	61.9	57.1	61.9	57.1	S	47.6
13	47.6	S	S	42.9	52.4	52.4	66.7	S	66.7	52.4	S	42.9
14	42.9	81.0	42.9	42.9	S	57.1	76.2	S	66.7	66.7	42.9	52.4
15	S	71.4	42.9	H	S	66.7	52.4	61.9	38.1	S	52.4	61.9
16	S	47.6	66.7	S	57.1	57.1	S	66.7	76.2	S	52.4	57.1
17	H	47.6	71.4	S	66.7	66.7	S	66.7	S	47.6	42.9	S
18	71.4	33.3	66.7	52.4	42.9	S	52.4	42.9	S	57.1	47.6	S
19	52.4	S	S	76.2	33.3	S	61.9	33.3	47.6	52.4	S	33.3
20	42.9	S	S	42.9	42.9	52.4	76.2	S	52.4	57.1	S	42.9
21	42.9	H	42.9	47.6	S	61.9	9.5	S	38.1	61.9	47.6	61.9
22	S	47.6	61.9	42.9	S	42.9	42.9	81.0	28.6	S	61.9	61.9
23	S	57.1	47.6	S	52.4	38.1	S	47.6	33.3	S	66.7	61.9
24	61.9	66.7	52.4	S	52.4	23.8	S	52.4	S	57.1	H	S
25	52.4	57.1	61.9	47.6	61.9	S	57.1	52.4	S	47.6	66.7	S
26	66.7	S	S	47.6	57.1	S	57.1	57.1	47.6	52.4	S	H
27	57.1	S	S	47.6	71.4	52.4	38.1	S	52.4	52.4	S	66.7
28	42.9	28.6	33.3	76.2	S	66.7	61.9	S	47.6	57.1	57.1	47.6
29	S		42.9	38.1	S	61.9	42.9	81.0	42.9	S	66.7	47.6
30	S		66.7	S	H	61.9	S	61.9	47.6	S	42.9	28.6
31	52.4		57.1		47.6		S	57.1		52.4		S

*See new trends developing on pages 72, 86, 143–148   ** Based on most recent 21-year period*

RUSSELL 1000 INDEX MARKET PROBABILITY CALENDAR 2022

THE % CHANCE OF THE MARKET RISING ON ANY TRADING DAY OF THE YEAR*
(Based on the number of times the Russell 1000 rose on a particular trading day during January 1980–December 2020)

Date	Jan	Feb	Mar	Apr	May	Jun	Jul	Aug	Sep	Oct	Nov	Dec
1	S	65.9	61.0	58.5	S	61.0	78.0	43.9	53.7	S	73.2	51.2
2	S	61.0	46.3	S	58.5	61.0	S	41.5	51.2	S	58.5	51.2
3	46.3	58.5	61.0	S	61.0	51.2	S	51.2	S	56.1	61.0	S
4	56.1	53.7	43.9	63.4	51.2	S	H	51.2	S	53.7	63.4	S
5	58.5	S	S	51.2	39.0	S	41.5	53.7	H	58.5	S	61.0
6	53.7	S	S	58.5	48.8	56.1	48.8	S	53.7	56.1	S	43.9
7	53.7	53.7	41.5	43.9	S	39.0	56.1	S	41.5	39.0	48.8	48.8
8	S	51.2	53.7	70.7	S	48.8	58.5	56.1	46.3	S	56.1	48.8
9	S	46.3	58.5	S	56.1	39.0	S	43.9	58.5	S	46.3	53.7
10	65.9	73.2	43.9	S	56.1	46.3	S	43.9	S	53.7	56.1	S
11	56.1	65.9	61.0	56.1	53.7	S	53.7	43.9	S	41.5	56.1	S
12	53.7	S	S	51.2	48.8	S	61.0	58.5	65.9	46.3	S	46.3
13	56.1	S	S	51.2	53.7	56.1	68.3	S	68.3	58.5	S	43.9
14	65.9	51.2	41.5	56.1	S	58.5	82.9	S	56.1	63.4	53.7	39.0
15	S	65.9	56.1	H	S	58.5	48.8	63.4	53.7	S	53.7	58.5
16	S	43.9	61.0	S	58.5	56.1	S	63.4	53.7	S	48.8	61.0
17	H	43.9	53.7	S	56.1	61.0	S	63.4	S	56.1	56.1	S
18	68.3	39.0	51.2	63.4	48.8	S	53.7	61.0	S	56.1	48.8	S
19	43.9	S	S	61.0	43.9	S	51.2	46.3	48.8	46.3	S	48.8
20	41.5	S	S	51.2	48.8	41.5	63.4	S	46.3	68.3	S	43.9
21	51.2	H	39.0	51.2	S	48.8	34.1	S	39.0	48.8	53.7	65.9
22	S	46.3	46.3	53.7	S	51.2	41.5	68.3	43.9	S	58.5	61.0
23	S	46.3	41.5	S	43.9	46.3	S	48.8	36.6	S	63.4	58.5
24	51.2	58.5	43.9	S	61.0	31.7	S	53.7	S	46.3	H	S
25	53.7	56.1	51.2	46.3	61.0	S	70.7	46.3	S	34.1	68.3	S
26	61.0	S	S	56.1	56.1	S	51.2	56.1	39.0	53.7	S	H
27	51.2	S	S	58.5	56.1	41.5	41.5	S	48.8	51.2	S	70.7
28	58.5	48.8	41.5	58.5	S	48.8	61.0	S	63.4	63.4	70.7	56.1
29	S		48.8	53.7	S	61.0	56.1	63.4	53.7	S	65.9	61.0
30	S		48.8	S	H	56.1	S	48.8	53.7	S	46.3	51.2
31	58.5		48.8		51.2		S	58.5		63.4		S

* See new trends developing on pages 72, 86, 143–148

RUSSELL 2000 INDEX MARKET PROBABILITY CALENDAR 2022

THE % CHANCE OF THE MARKET RISING ON ANY TRADING DAY OF THE YEAR*

(Based on the number of times the Russell 2000 rose on a particular trading day during January 1980–December 2020)

Date	Jan	Feb	Mar	Apr	May	Jun	Jul	Aug	Sep	Oct	Nov	Dec
1	S	68.3	65.9	48.8	S	65.9	68.3	46.3	51.2	S	61.0	51.2
2	S	61.0	56.1	S	58.5	70.7	S	43.9	61.0	S	70.7	58.5
3	46.3	56.1	63.4	S	65.9	51.2	S	48.8	S	48.8	63.4	S
4	61.0	65.9	53.7	58.5	56.1	S	H	51.2	S	48.8	63.4	S
5	58.5	S	S	46.3	56.1	S	46.3	48.8	H	53.7	S	63.4
6	58.5	S	S	56.1	58.5	53.7	46.3	S	53.7	63.4	S	61.0
7	58.5	58.5	56.1	43.9	S	58.5	56.1	S	58.5	39.0	56.1	46.3
8	S	58.5	46.3	61.0	S	43.9	51.2	46.3	56.1	S	56.1	53.7
9	S	48.8	56.1	S	56.1	43.9	S	53.7	61.0	S	51.2	48.8
10	63.4	70.7	43.9	S	61.0	51.2	S	43.9	S	48.8	65.9	S
11	56.1	65.9	61.0	61.0	51.2	S	61.0	46.3	S	48.8	46.3	S
12	65.9	S	S	63.4	48.8	S	56.1	70.7	61.0	51.2	S	46.3
13	63.4	S	S	48.8	48.8	56.1	61.0	S	61.0	61.0	S	41.5
14	63.4	68.3	48.8	56.1	S	63.4	68.3	S	56.1	56.1	46.3	39.0
15	S	58.5	48.8	H	S	58.5	53.7	58.5	41.5	S	51.2	43.9
16	S	56.1	63.4	S	48.8	53.7	S	61.0	53.7	S	29.3	56.1
17	H	43.9	63.4	S	58.5	43.9	S	58.5	S	63.4	58.5	S
18	73.2	41.5	56.1	61.0	51.2	S	51.2	46.3	S	46.3	48.8	S
19	65.9	S	S	61.0	53.7	S	51.2	46.3	41.5	48.8	S	61.0
20	36.6	S	S	51.2	48.8	46.3	53.7	S	41.5	63.4	S	58.5
21	48.8	H	48.8	53.7	S	48.8	34.1	S	41.5	48.8	39.0	65.9
22	S	51.2	43.9	53.7	S	46.3	46.3	65.9	48.8	S	63.4	68.3
23	S	53.7	58.5	S	53.7	48.8	S	43.9	36.6	S	65.9	73.2
24	56.1	58.5	46.3	S	61.0	36.6	S	61.0	S	46.3	H	S
25	48.8	65.9	56.1	51.2	53.7	S	61.0	61.0	S	34.1	61.0	S
26	65.9	S	S	58.5	63.4	S	61.0	58.5	46.3	39.0	S	H
27	53.7	S	S	68.3	63.4	48.8	46.3	S	39.0	53.7	S	65.9
28	53.7	51.2	46.3	58.5	S	53.7	53.7	S	53.7	53.7	63.4	51.2
29	S		51.2	61.0	S	70.7	61.0	68.3	51.2	S	68.3	61.0
30	S		56.1	S	H	65.9	S	63.4	65.9	S	63.4	63.4
31	73.2		80.5		61.0		S	65.9		70.7		S

* See new trends developing on pages 72, 86, 143–148

DECENNIAL CYCLE: A MARKET PHENOMENON

By arranging each year's market gain or loss so that the first and succeeding years of each decade fall into the same column, certain interesting patterns emerge—strong fifth and eighth years; weak first, seventh, and zero years.

This fascinating phenomenon was first presented by Edgar Lawrence Smith in *Common Stocks and Business Cycles* (William-Frederick Press, 1959). Anthony Gaubis co-pioneered the decennial pattern with Smith.

When Smith first cut graphs of market prices into 10-year segments and placed them above one another, he observed that each decade tended to have three bull market cycles and that the longest and strongest bull markets seemed to favor the middle years of a decade.

Don't place too much emphasis on the decennial cycle nowadays, other than the extraordinary fifth and zero years, as the stock market is more influenced by the quadrennial presidential election cycle, shown on page 130. Also, the last half-century, which has been the most prosperous in U.S. history, has distributed the returns among most years of the decade. Interestingly, NASDAQ suffered its worst bear market ever in a zero year.

Second years have the fourth worst record of the decennial cycle. This year is also a midterm-election year which has the second weakest record in the four-year-presidential-election cycle. Waning economic stimulus and the elevated probability that the Fed will be less accommodative in 2022 combined with hotly contested mid-term elections could easily zap the post-Covid-19 bull market.

THE 10-YEAR STOCK MARKET CYCLE
Annual % Change in Dow Jones Industrial Average
Year of Decade

DECADES	1st	2nd	3rd	4th	5th	6th	7th	8th	9th	10th
1881–1890	3.0%	−2.9%	−8.5%	−18.8%	20.1%	12.4%	−8.4%	4.8%	5.5%	−14.1%
1891–1900	17.6	−6.6	−24.6	−0.6	2.3	−1.7	21.3	22.5	9.2	7.0
1901–1910	−8.7	−0.4	−23.6	41.7	38.2	−1.9	−37.7	46.6	15.0	−17.9
1911–1920	0.4	7.6	−10.3	−5.4	81.7	−4.2	−21.7	10.5	30.5	−32.9
1921–1930	12.7	21.7	−3.3	26.2	30.0	0.3	28.8	48.2	−17.2	−33.8
1931–1940	−52.7	−23.1	66.7	4.1	38.5	24.8	−32.8	28.1	−2.9	−12.7
1941–1950	−15.4	7.6	13.8	12.1	26.6	−8.1	2.2	−2.1	12.9	17.6
1951–1960	14.4	8.4	−3.8	44.0	20.8	2.3	−12.8	34.0	16.4	−9.3
1961–1970	18.7	−10.8	17.0	14.6	10.9	−18.9	15.2	4.3	−15.2	4.8
1971–1980	6.1	14.6	−16.6	−27.6	38.3	17.9	−17.3	−3.1	4.2	14.9
1981–1990	−9.2	19.6	20.3	−3.7	27.7	22.6	2.3	11.8	27.0	−4.3
1991–2000	20.3	4.2	13.7	2.1	33.5	26.0	22.6	16.1	25.2	−6.2
2001–2010	−7.1	−16.8	25.3	3.1	−0.6	16.3	6.4	−33.8	18.8	11.0
2011–2020	5.5	7.3	26.5	7.5	−2.2	13.4	25.1	−5.6	22.3	7.2
Total % Change	**5.6%**	**30.4%**	**92.6%**	**99.3%**	**365.8%**	**101.2%**	**−6.8%**	**182.3%**	**151.7%**	**−68.7%**
Avg % Change	**0.4%**	**2.2%**	**6.6%**	**7.1%**	**26.1%**	**7.2%**	**−0.5%**	**13.0%**	**10.8%**	**−4.9%**
Up Years	9	8	7	9	12	9	8	10	11	6
Down Years	5	6	7	5	2	5	6	4	3	8

Based on annual close; Cowles indices 1881–1885; 12 Mixed Stocks, 10 Rails, 2 Inds 1886–1889;
20 Mixed Stocks, 18 Rails, 2 Inds 1890–1896; Railroad average 1897 (First industrial average published May 26, 1896).

PRESIDENTIAL ELECTION/STOCK MARKET CYCLE: THE 188-YEAR SAGA CONTINUES

It is no mere coincidence that the last two years (pre-election year and election year) of the 47 administrations since 1833 produced a total net market gain of 772.0%, dwarfing the 326.6% gain of the first two years of these administrations.

Presidential elections every four years have a profound impact on the economy and the stock market. Wars, recessions, and bear markets tend to start or occur in the first half of the term; prosperous times and bull markets, in the latter half. After nine straight annual Dow gains during the millennial bull, the four-year election cycle reasserted its overarching domination of market behavior until 2008. Recovery from the worst recession since the Great Depression produced six straight annual gains, until 2015, when the Dow suffered its first pre-election year loss since 1939.

STOCK MARKET ACTION SINCE 1833
Annual % Change in Dow Jones Industrial Average[1]

4-Year Cycle Beginning	President Elected	Post-Election Year	Midterm Year	Pre-Election Year	Election Year
1833	Jackson (D)	−0.9	13.0	3.1	−11.7
1837	Van Buren (D)	−11.5	1.6	−12.3	5.5
1841*	W.H. Harrison (W)**	−13.3	−18.1	45.0	15.5
1845*	Polk (D)	8.1	−14.5	1.2	−3.6
1849*	Taylor (W)	N/C	18.7	−3.2	19.6
1853*	Pierce (D)	−12.7	−30.2	1.5	4.4
1857	Buchanan (D)	−31.0	14.3	−10.7	14.0
1861*	Lincoln (R)	−1.8	55.4	38.0	6.4
1865	Lincoln (R)**	−8.5	3.6	1.6	10.8
1869	Grant (R)	1.7	5.6	7.3	6.8
1873	Grant (R)	−12.7	2.8	−4.1	−17.9
1877	Hayes (R)	−9.4	6.1	43.0	18.7
1881	Garfield (R)**	3.0	−2.9	−8.5	−18.8
1885*	Cleveland (D)	20.1	12.4	−8.4	4.8
1889*	B. Harrison (R)	5.5	−14.1	17.6	−6.6
1893*	Cleveland (D)	−24.6	−0.6	2.3	−1.7
1897*	McKinley (R)	21.3	22.5	9.2	7.0
1901	McKinley (R)**	−8.7	−0.4	−23.6	41.7
1905	T. Roosevelt (R)	38.2	−1.9	−37.7	46.6
1909	Taft (R)	15.0	−17.9	0.4	7.6
1913*	Wilson (D)	−10.3	−5.4	81.7	−4.2
1917	Wilson (D)	−21.7	10.5	30.5	−32.9
1921*	Harding (R)**	12.7	21.7	−3.3	26.2
1925	Coolidge (R)	30.0	0.3	28.8	48.2
1929	Hoover (R)	−17.2	−33.8	−52.7	−23.1
1933*	F. Roosevelt (D)	66.7	4.1	38.5	24.8
1937	F. Roosevelt (D)	−32.8	28.1	−2.9	−12.7
1941	F. Roosevelt (D)	−15.4	7.6	13.8	12.1
1945	F. Roosevelt (D)**	26.6	−8.1	2.2	−2.1
1949	Truman (D)	12.9	17.6	14.4	8.4
1953*	Eisenhower (R)	−3.8	44.0	20.8	2.3
1957	Eisenhower (R)	−12.8	34.0	16.4	−9.3
1961*	Kennedy (D)**	18.7	−10.8	17.0	14.6
1965	Johnson (D)	10.9	−18.9	15.2	4.3
1969*	Nixon (R)	−15.2	4.8	6.1	14.6
1973	Nixon (R)***	−16.6	−27.6	38.3	17.9
1977*	Carter (D)	−17.3	−3.1	4.2	14.9
1981*	Reagan (R)	−9.2	19.6	20.3	−3.7
1985	Reagan (R)	27.7	22.6	2.3	11.8
1989	G. H. W. Bush (R)	27.0	−4.3	20.3	4.2
1993*	Clinton (D)	13.7	2.1	33.5	26.0
1997	Clinton (D)	22.6	16.1	25.2	−6.2
2001*	G. W. Bush (R)	−7.1	−16.8	25.3	3.1
2005	G. W. Bush (R)	−0.6	16.3	6.4	−33.8
2009*	Obama (D)	18.8	11.0	5.5	7.3
2013	Obama (D)	26.5	7.5	−2.2	13.4
2017*	Trump (R)	25.1	−5.6	22.3	7.2
Total % Gain		137.7	188.9	489.6	282.4
Average % Gain		3.0	4.0	10.4	6.0
# Up		22	28	35	32
# Down		24	19	12	15

*Party in power ousted   **Died in office   ***Resigned   D–Democrat, W–Whig, R–Republican
[1] Based on annual close; prior to 1886 based on Cowles and other indices; 12 Mixed Stocks, 10 Rails, 2 Inds 1886–1889; 20 Mixed Stocks, 18 Rails, 2 Inds 1890–1896; Railroad average 1897 (First industrial average published May 26, 1896).

DOW JONES INDUSTRIALS BULL AND BEAR MARKETS SINCE 1900

Bear markets begin at the end of one bull market and end at the start of the next bull market (10/9/07 to 3/9/09 as an example). The longest bull market on record ended on 7/17/98, and the shortest bear market on record ended on 3/23/2020, when the new bull market began. The greatest bull super cycle in history that began 8/12/82 ended in 2000 after the Dow gained 1409% and NASDAQ climbed 3072%. The Dow gained only 497% in the eight-year super bull from 1921 to the top in 1929. NASDAQ suffered its worst loss ever from the 2000 top to the 2002 bottom, down 77.9%, nearly as much as the 89.2% drop in the Dow from the 1929 top to the 1932 bottom. The third-longest Dow bull since 1900 that began 10/9/02 ended on its fifth anniversary. The ensuing bear market was the second worst bear market since 1900, slashing the Dow 53.8%. At press time, the Dow is currently trading above 34,000 and is within striking distance of its previous all-time high, but inflation concerns are growing which could threaten the current bull market. (See page 134 for S&P 500 and NASDAQ bulls and bears.)

DOW JONES INDUSTRIALS BULL AND BEAR MARKETS SINCE 1900

— Beginning —		— Ending —		Bull		Bear	
Date	DJIA	Date	DJIA	% Gain	Days	% Change	Days
9/24/00	38.80	6/17/01	57.33	47.8%	266	−46.1%	875
11/9/03	30.88	1/19/06	75.45	144.3	802	−48.5	665
11/15/07	38.83	11/19/09	73.64	89.6	735	−27.4	675
9/25/11	53.43	9/30/12	68.97	29.1	371	−24.1	668
7/30/14	52.32	11/21/16	110.15	110.5	845	−40.1	393
12/19/17	65.95	11/3/19	119.62	81.4	684	−46.6	660
8/24/21	63.90	3/20/23	105.38	64.9	573	−18.6	221
10/27/23	85.76	9/3/29	381.17	344.5	2138	−47.9	71
11/13/29	198.69	4/17/30	294.07	48.0	155	−86.0	813
7/8/32	41.22	9/7/32	79.93	93.9	61	−37.2	173
2/27/33	50.16	2/5/34	110.74	120.8	343	−22.8	171
7/26/34	85.51	3/10/37	194.40	127.3	958	−49.1	386
3/31/38	98.95	11/12/38	158.41	60.1	226	−23.3	147
4/8/39	121.44	9/12/39	155.92	28.4	157	−40.4	959
4/28/42	92.92	5/29/46	212.50	128.7	1492	−23.2	353
5/17/47	163.21	6/15/48	193.16	18.4	395	−16.3	363
6/13/49	161.60	1/5/53	293.79	81.8	1302	−13.0	252
9/14/53	255.49	4/6/56	521.05	103.9	935	−19.4	564
10/22/57	419.79	1/5/60	685.47	63.3	805	−17.4	294
10/25/60	566.05	12/13/61	734.91	29.8	414	−27.1	195
6/26/62	535.76	2/9/66	995.15	85.7	1324	−25.2	240
10/7/66	744.32	12/3/68	985.21	32.4	788	−35.9	539
5/26/70	631.16	4/28/71	950.82	50.6	337	−16.1	209
11/23/71	797.97	1/11/73	1051.70	31.8	415	−45.1	694
12/6/74	577.60	9/21/76	1014.79	75.7	655	−26.9	525
2/28/78	742.12	9/8/78	907.74	22.3	192	−16.4	591
4/21/80	759.13	4/27/81	1024.05	34.9	371	−24.1	472
8/12/82	776.92	11/29/83	1287.20	65.7	474	−15.6	238
7/24/84	1086.57	8/25/87	2722.42	150.6	1127	−36.1	55
10/19/87	1738.74	7/17/90	2999.75	72.5	1002	−21.2	86
10/11/90	2365.10	7/17/98	9337.97	294.8	2836	−19.3	45
8/31/98	7539.07	1/14/00	11722.98	55.5	501	−29.7	616
9/21/01	8235.81	3/19/02	10635.25	29.1	179	−31.5	204
10/9/02	7286.27	10/9/07	14164.53	94.4	1826	−53.8	517
3/9/09	6547.05	4/29/11	12810.54	95.7	781	−16.8	157
10/3/11	10655.30	5/19/15	18312.39	71.9	1324	−14.5	268
2/11/16	15660.18	2/12/20	29551.42	88.7	1462	−37.1	40
3/23/20	18591.93	5/7/21	34777.76	87.1*	410*		
				*As of June 4, 2021 — not in averages			
		Average		85.6%	791	−30.8%	389

Based on Dow Jones Industrial Average.
1900–2000 Data: Ned Davis Research
The NYSE was closed from 7/31/1914 to 12/11/1914 due to World War I.
DJIA figures were then adjusted back to reflect the composition change from 12 to 20 stocks in September 1916.

STANDARD & POOR'S 500 BULL AND BEAR MARKETS SINCE 1929
NASDAQ COMPOSITE SINCE 1971

A constant debate of the definition and timing of bull and bear markets permeates Wall Street like the bell that signals the open and close of every trading day. We have relied on the Ned Davis Research parameters for years to track bulls and bears on the Dow (see page 133). Standard & Poor's 500 index has been a stalwart indicator for decades and at times marched to a slightly different beat than the Dow. The moves of the S&P 500 and NASDAQ have been correlated to the bull and bear dates on page 131. Many dates line up for the three indices, but you will notice quite a lag or lead on several occasions, including NASDAQ's independent cadence from 1975 to 1980.

STANDARD & POOR'S 500 BULL AND BEAR MARKETS

— Beginning —		— Ending —		Bull		Bear	
Date	S&P 500	Date	S&P 500	% Gain	Days	% Change	Days
11/13/29	17.66	4/10/30	25.92	46.8%	148	−83.0%	783
6/1/32	4.40	9/7/32	9.31	111.6	98	−40.6	173
2/27/33	5.53	2/6/34	11.82	113.7	344	−31.8	401
3/14/35	8.06	3/6/37	18.68	131.8	723	−49.0	390
3/31/38	8.50	11/9/38	13.79	62.2	223	−26.2	150
4/8/39	10.18	10/25/39	13.21	29.8	200	−43.5	916
4/28/42	7.47	5/29/46	19.25	157.7	1492	−28.8	353
5/17/47	13.71	6/15/48	17.06	24.4	395	−20.6	363
6/13/49	13.55	1/5/53	26.66	96.8	1302	−14.8	252
9/14/53	22.71	8/2/56	49.74	119.0	1053	−21.6	446
10/22/57	38.98	8/3/59	60.71	55.7	650	−13.9	449
10/25/60	52.30	12/12/61	72.64	38.9	413	−28.0	196
6/26/62	52.32	2/9/66	94.06	79.8	1324	−22.2	240
10/7/66	73.20	11/29/68	108.37	48.0	784	−36.1	543
5/26/70	69.29	4/28/71	104.77	51.2	337	−13.9	209
11/23/71	90.16	1/11/73	120.24	33.4	415	−48.2	630
10/3/74	62.28	9/21/76	107.83	73.1	719	−19.4	531
3/6/78	86.90	9/12/78	106.99	23.1	190	−8.2	562
3/27/80	98.22	11/28/80	140.52	43.1	246	−27.1	622
8/12/82	102.42	10/10/83	172.65	68.6	424	−14.4	288
7/24/84	147.82	8/25/87	336.77	127.8	1127	−33.5	101
12/4/87	223.92	7/16/90	368.95	64.8	955	−19.9	87
10/11/90	295.46	7/17/98	1186.75	301.7	2836	−19.3	45
8/31/98	957.28	3/24/00	1527.46	59.6	571	−36.8	546
9/21/01	965.80	1/4/02	1172.51	21.4	105	−33.8	278
10/9/02	776.76	10/9/07	1565.15	101.5	1826	−56.8	517
3/9/09	676.53	4/29/11	1363.61	101.6	781	−19.4	157
10/3/11	1099.23	5/21/15	2130.82	93.8	1326	−14.2	266
2/11/16	1829.08	2/19/20	3386.15	85.1	1469	−33.9	33
3/23/20	2237.40	5/7/21	4232.60	89.2*	410*	*As of June 4, 2021 — not in averages	
		Average		**81.6%**	**775**	**−29.8%**	**363**

NASDAQ COMPOSITE BULL AND BEAR MARKETS

— Beginning —		— Ending —		Bull		Bear	
Date	NASDAQ	Date	NASDAQ	% Gain	Days	% Change	Days
11/23/71	100.31	1/11/73	136.84	36.4%	415	−59.9%	630
10/3/74	54.87	7/15/75	88.00	60.4	285	−16.2	63
9/16/75	73.78	9/13/78	139.25	88.7	1093	−20.4	62
11/14/78	110.88	2/8/80	165.25	49.0	451	−24.9	48
3/27/80	124.09	5/29/81	223.47	80.1	428	−28.8	441
8/13/82	159.14	6/24/83	328.91	106.7	315	−31.5	397
7/25/84	225.30	8/26/87	455.26	102.1	1127	−35.9	63
10/28/87	291.88	10/9/89	485.73	66.4	712	−33.0	372
10/16/90	325.44	7/20/98	2014.25	518.9	2834	−29.5	80
10/8/98	1419.12	3/10/00	5048.62	255.8	519	−71.8	560
9/21/01	1423.19	1/4/02	2059.38	44.7	105	−45.9	278
10/9/02	1114.11	10/31/07	2859.12	156.6	1848	−55.6	495
3/9/09	1268.64	4/29/11	2873.54	126.5	781	−18.7	157
10/3/11	2335.83	7/20/15	5218.86	123.4	1386	−18.2	206
2/11/16	4266.84	2/19/20	9817.18	130.1	1469	−30.1	33
3/23/20	6860.67	4/26/21	14138.78	106.1*	399*	*As of June 4, 2021 — not in averages	
		Average		**129.7%**	**918**	**−34.7%**	**259**

134

JANUARY DAILY POINT CHANGES DOW JONES INDUSTRIALS

Previous Month Close	2012	2013	2014	2015	2016	2017	2018	2019	2020	2021
Close	12217.56	13104.14	16576.66	17823.07	17425.03	19762.60	24719.22	23327.46	28538.44	30606.48
1	S	H	H	H	H	S	H	H	H	H
2	H	308.41	-135.31	9.92	S	H	104.79	18.78	330.36	S
3	179.82	-21.19	28.64	S	S	119.16	98.67	-660.02	-233.92	S
4	21.04	43.85	S	S	-276.09	60.40	152.45	746.94	S	-382.59
5	-2.72	S	S	-331.34	9.72	-42.87	220.74	S	S	167.71
6	-55.78	S	-44.89	-130.01	-252.15	64.51	S	S	68.50	437.80
7	S	-50.92	105.84	212.88	-392.41	S	S	98.19	-119.70	211.73
8	S	-55.44	-68.20	323.35	-167.65	S	-12.87	256.10	161.41	56.84
9	32.77	61.66	-17.98	-170.50	S	-76.42	102.80	91.67	211.81	S
10	69.78	80.71	-7.71	S	S	-31.85	-16.67	122.80	-133.13	S
11	-13.02	17.21	S	S	52.12	98.75	205.60	-5.97	S	-89.28
12	21.57	S	S	-96.53	117.65	-63.28	228.46	S	S	60.00
13	-48.96	S	-179.11	-27.16	-364.81	-5.27	S	S	83.28	-8.22
14	S	18.89	115.92	-186.59	227.64	S	S	-86.11	32.62	-68.95
15	S	27.57	108.08	-106.38	-390.97	S	H	155.75	90.55	-177.26
16	H	-23.66	-64.93	190.86	S	H	-10.33	141.57	267.42	S
17	60.01	84.79	41.55	S	S	-58.96	322.79	162.94	50.46	S
18	96.88	53.68	S	S	H	-22.05	-97.84	336.25	S	H
19	45.03	S	S	H	27.94	-72.32	53.91	S	S	116.26
20	96.50	S	H	3.66	-249.28	94.85	S	S	H	257.86
21	S	H	-44.12	39.05	115.94	S	S	H	-152.06	-12.37
22	S	62.51	-41.10	259.70	210.83	S	142.88	-301.87	-9.77	-179.03
23	-11.66	67.12	-175.99	-141.38	S	-27.40	-3.79	171.14	-26.18	S
24	-33.07	46.00	-318.24	S	S	112.86	41.31	-22.38	-170.36	S
25	81.21	70.65	S	S	-208.29	155.80	140.67	183.96	S	-36.98
26	-22.33	S	S	6.10	282.01	32.40	223.92	S	S	-22.96
27	-74.17	S	-41.23	-291.49	-222.77	-7.13	S	-208.98	-453.93	-633.87
28	S	-14.05	90.68	-195.84	125.18	S	S	51.74	187.05	300.19
29	S	72.49	-189.77	225.48	396.66	S	-177.23	434.90	11.60	-620.74
30	-6.74	-44.00	109.82	-251.90	S	-122.65	-362.59	-15.19	124.99	S
31	-20.81	-49.84	-149.76	S	S	-107.04	72.50	S	-603.41	S
Close	12632.91	13860.58	15698.85	17164.95	16466.30	19864.09	26149.39	24999.67	28256.03	29982.62
Change	415.35	756.44	-877.81	-658.12	-958.73	101.49	1430.17	1672.21	-282.41	-623.86

FEBRUARY DAILY POINT CHANGES DOW JONES INDUSTRIALS

Previous Month Close	2012	2013	2014	2015	2016	2017	2018	2019	2020	2021
Close	12632.91	13860.58	15698.85	17164.95	16466.30	19864.09	26149.39	24999.67	28256.03	29982.62
1	83.55	149.21	S	S	-17.12	26.85	37.32	64.22	S	229.29
2	-11.05	S	S	196.09	-295.64	-6.03	-665.75	S	S	475.57
3	156.82	S	-326.05	305.36	183.12	186.55	S	S	143.78	36.12
4	S	-129.71	72.44	6.62	79.92	S	S	175.48	407.82	332.26
5	S	99.22	-5.01	211.86	-211.61	S	-1175.21	172.15	483.22	92.38
6	-17.10	7.22	188.30	-60.59	S	-19.04	567.02	-21.22	88.92	S
7	33.07	-42.47	165.55	S	S	37.87	-19.42	-220.77	-277.26	S
8	5.75	48.92	S	S	-177.92	-35.95	-1032.89	-63.20	S	237.52
9	6.51	S	S	-95.08	-12.67	118.06	330.44	S	S	-9.93
10	-89.23	S	7.71	139.55	-99.64	96.97	S	S	174.31	61.97
11	S	-21.73	192.98	-6.62	-254.56	S	S	-53.22	-0.48	-7.10
12	S	47.46	-30.83	110.24	313.66	S	410.37	372.65	275.08	27.70
13	72.81	-35.79	63.65	46.97	S	142.79	39.18	117.51	-128.11	S
14	4.24	-9.52	126.80	S	S	92.25	253.04	-103.88	-25.23	S
15	-97.33	8.37	S	S	H	107.45	306.88	443.86	S	H
16	123.13	S	S	H	222.57	7.91	19.01	S	S	64.35
17	45.79	S	H	28.23	257.42	4.28	S	S	H	90.27
18	S	H	-23.99	-17.73	-40.40	S	S	H	-165.89	-119.68
19	S	53.91	-89.84	-44.08	-21.44	S	H	8.07	115.84	0.98
20	H	-108.13	92.67	154.67	S	H	-254.63	63.12	-128.05	S
21	15.82	-46.92	-29.93	S	S	118.95	-166.97	-103.81	-227.57	S
22	-27.02	119.95	S	S	228.67	32.60	164.70	181.18	S	27.37
23	46.02	S	S	-23.60	-188.88	34.72	347.51	S	S	15.66
24	-1.74	S	103.84	92.35	53.21	11.44	S	S	-1031.61	424.51
25	S	-216.40	-27.48	15.38	212.30	S	S	60.14	-879.44	-559.85
26	S	115.96	18.75	-10.15	-57.32	S	399.28	-33.97	-123.77	-469.64
27	-1.44	175.24	74.24	-81.72	S	15.68	-299.24	-72.82	-1190.95	S
28	23.61	-20.88	49.06	S	S	-25.20	-380.83	-69.16	-357.28	S
29	-53.05	—	—	—	-123.47	—	—	—	S	—
Close	12952.07	14054.49	16321.71	18132.70	16516.50	20812.24	25029.20	25916.00	25409.36	30932.37
Change	319.16	193.91	622.86	967.75	50.20	948.15	-1120.19	916.33	-2846.67	949.75

MARCH DAILY POINT CHANGES DOW JONES INDUSTRIALS

Previous Month	2012	2013	2014	2015	2016	2017	2018	2019	2020	2021
Close	12952.07	14054.49	16321.71	18132.70	16516.50	20812.24	25029.20	25916.00	25409.36	30932.37
1	28.23	35.17	S	S	348.58	303.31	-420.22	110.32	S	603.14
2	-2.73	S	S	155.93	34.24	-112.58	-70.92	S	1293.96	-143.99
3	S	S	-153.68	-85.26	44.58	2.74	S	S	-785.91	-121.43
4	S	38.16	227.85	-106.47	62.87	S	S	-206.67	1173.45	-345.95
5	-14.76	125.95	-35.70	38.82	S	S	336.70	-13.02	-969.58	572.16
6	-203.66	42.47	61.71	-278.94	S	-51.37	9.36	-133.17	-256.50	S
7	78.18	33.25	30.83	S	67.18	-29.58	-82.76	-200.23	S	S
8	70.61	67.58	S	S	-109.85	-69.03	93.85	-22.99	S	306.14
9	14.08	S	S	138.94	36.26	2.46	440.53	S	-2013.76	30.30
10	S	S	-34.04	-332.78	-5.23	44.79	S	S	1167.14	464.28
11	S	50.22	-67.43	-27.55	218.18	S	S	200.64	-1464.94	188.57
12	37.69	2.77	-11.17	259.83	S	S	-157.13	-96.22	-2352.60	293.05
13	217.97	5.22	-231.19	-145.91	S	-21.50	-171.58	148.23	1985.00	S
14	16.42	83.86	-43.22	S	15.82	-44.11	-248.91	7.05	S	S
15	58.66	-25.03	S	S	22.40	112.73	115.54	138.93	S	174.82
16	-20.14	S	S	228.11	74.23	-15.55	72.85	S	-2997.10	-127.51
17	S	S	181.55	-128.34	155.73	-19.93	S	S	1048.86	189.42
18	S	-62.05	88.97	227.11	120.81	S	S	65.23	-1338.46	-153.07
19	6.51	3.76	-114.02	-117.16	S	S	-335.60	-26.72	188.27	-234.33
20	-68.94	55.91	108.88	168.62	S	-8.76	116.36	-141.71	-913.21	S
21	-45.57	-90.24	-28.28	S	21.57	-237.85	-44.96	216.84	S	S
22	-78.48	90.54	S	S	-41.30	-6.71	-724.42	-460.19	S	103.23
23	34.59	S	S	-11.61	-79.98	-4.72	-424.69	S	-582.05	-308.05
24	S	S	-26.08	-104.90	13.14	-59.86	S	S	2112.98	-3.09
25	S	-64.28	91.19	-292.60	H	S	S	14.51	495.64	199.42
26	160.90	111.90	-98.89	-40.31	S	S	669.40	140.90	1351.62	453.40
27	-43.90	-33.49	-4.76	34.43	S	-45.74	-344.89	-32.14	-915.39	S
28	-71.52	52.38	58.83	S	19.66	150.52	-9.29	91.87	S	S
29	19.61	H	S	S	97.72	-42.18	254.69	211.22	S	98.49
30	66.22	S	S	263.65	83.55	69.17	H	S	690.70	-104.41
31	S	S	134.60	-200.19	-31.57	-65.27	S	S	-410.32	-85.41
Close	13212.04	14578.54	16457.66	17776.12	17685.09	20663.22	24103.11	25928.68	21917.16	32981.55
Change	259.97	524.05	135.95	-356.58	1168.59	-149.02	-926.09	12.68	-3492.20	2049.18

APRIL DAILY POINT CHANGES DOW JONES INDUSTRIALS

Previous Month	2012	2013	2014	2015	2016	2017	2018	2019	2020	2021
Close	13212.04	14578.54	16457.66	17776.12	17685.09	20663.22	24103.11	25928.68	21917.16	32981.55
1	S	-5.69	74.95	-77.94	107.66	S	S	329.74	-973.65	171.66
2	52.45	89.16	40.39	65.06	S	S	-458.92	-79.29	469.93	H
3	-64.94	-111.66	-0.45	H	S	-13.01	389.17	39.00	-360.91	S
4	-124.80	55.76	-159.84	S	-55.75	39.03	230.94	166.50	S	S
5	-14.61	-40.86	S	S	-133.68	-41.09	240.92	40.36	S	373.98
6	H	S	S	117.61	112.73	14.80	-572.46	S	1627.46	-96.95
7	S	S	-166.84	-5.43	-174.09	-6.85	S	S	-26.13	16.02
8	S	48.23	10.27	27.09	35.00	S	S	-83.97	779.71	57.31
9	-130.55	59.98	181.04	56.22	S	S	46.34	-190.44	285.80	297.03
10	-213.66	128.78	-266.96	98.92	S	1.92	428.90	6.58	H	S
11	89.46	62.90	-143.47	S	-20.55	-6.72	-218.55	-14.11	S	S
12	181.19	-0.08	S	S	164.84	-59.44	293.60	269.25	S	-55.20
13	-136.99	S	S	-80.61	187.03	-138.61	-122.91	S	-328.60	-68.13
14	S	S	146.49	59.66	18.15	H	S	S	558.99	53.62
15	S	-265.86	89.32	75.91	-28.97	S	S	-27.53	-445.41	305.10
16	71.82	157.58	162.29	-6.84	S	S	212.90	67.89	33.33	164.68
17	194.13	-138.19	-16.31	-279.47	S	183.67	213.59	-3.12	704.81	S
18	-82.79	-81.45	H	S	106.70	-113.64	-38.56	110.00	S	S
19	-68.65	10.37	S	S	49.44	-118.79	-83.18	H	S	-123.04
20	65.16	S	S	208.63	42.67	174.22	-201.95	S	-592.05	-256.33
21	S	S	40.71	-85.34	-113.75	-30.95	S	S	-631.56	316.01
22	S	19.66	65.12	88.68	21.23	S	S	-48.49	456.94	-321.41
23	-102.09	152.29	-12.72	20.42	S	S	-14.25	145.34	39.44	227.59
24	74.39	-43.16	0.00	21.45	S	216.13	-424.56	-59.34	260.01	S
25	89.16	24.50	-140.19	S	-26.51	232.23	59.70	-134.97	S	S
26	113.90	11.75	S	S	13.08	-21.03	238.51	81.25	S	-61.92
27	23.69	S	S	-42.17	51.23	6.24	-11.15	S	358.51	3.36
28	S	S	87.28	72.17	-210.79	-40.82	S	S	-32.23	-164.55
29	S	106.20	86.63	-74.61	-57.12	S	S	11.06	532.31	239.98
30	-14.68	21.05	45.47	-195.01	S	S	-148.04	38.52	-288.14	-185.51
Close	13213.63	14839.80	16580.84	17840.52	17773.64	20940.51	24163.15	26592.91	24345.72	33874.85
Change	1.59	261.26	123.18	64.40	88.55	277.29	60.04	664.23	2428.56	893.30

MAY DAILY POINT CHANGES DOW JONES INDUSTRIALS

Previous Month Close	2012	2013	2014	2015	2016	2017	2018	2019	2020	2021
	13213.63	14839.80	16580.84	17840.52	17773.64	20940.51	24163.15	26592.91	24345.72	33874.85
1	65.69	−138.85	−21.97	183.54	S	−27.05	−64.10	−162.77	−622.03	S
2	−10.75	130.63	−45.98	S	117.52	36.43	−174.07	−122.35	S	S
3	−61.98	142.38	S	S	−140.25	8.01	5.17	197.16	S	238.38
4	−168.32	S	S	46.34	−99.65	−6.43	332.36	S	26.07	19.80
5	S	S	17.66	−142.20	9.45	55.47	S	S	133.33	97.31
6	S	−5.07	−129.53	−86.22	79.92	S	S	−66.47	−218.45	318.19
7	−29.74	87.31	117.52	82.08	S	S	94.81	−473.39	211.25	229.23
8	−76.44	48.92	32.43	267.05	S	5.34	2.89	2.24	455.43	S
9	−97.03	−22.50	32.37	S	−34.72	−36.50	182.33	−138.97	S	S
10	19.98	35.87	S	S	222.44	−32.67	196.99	114.01	S	−34.94
11	−34.44	S	S	−85.94	−217.23	−23.69	91.64	S	−109.33	−473.66
12	S	S	112.13	−36.94	9.38	−22.81	S	S	−457.21	−681.50
13	S	−26.81	19.97	−7.74	−185.18	S	S	−617.38	−516.81	433.79
14	−125.25	123.57	−101.47	191.75	S	S	68.24	207.06	377.37	360.68
15	−63.35	60.44	−167.16	20.32	S	85.33	−193.00	115.97	60.08	S
16	−33.45	−42.47	44.50	S	175.39	−2.19	62.52	214.66	S	S
17	−156.06	121.18	S	S	−180.73	−372.82	−54.95	−98.68	S	−54.34
18	−73.11	S	S	26.32	−3.36	56.09	1.11	S	911.95	−267.13
19	S	S	20.55	13.51	−91.22	141.82	S	S	−390.51	−164.62
20	S	−19.12	−137.55	−26.99	65.54	S	S	−84.10	369.04	188.11
21	135.10	52.30	158.75	0.34	S	S	298.20	197.43	−101.78	123.69
22	−1.67	−80.41	10.02	−53.72	S	89.99	−178.88	−100.72	−8.96	S
23	−6.66	−12.67	63.19	S	−8.01	43.08	52.40	−286.14	S	S
24	33.60	8.60	S	S	213.12	74.51	−75.05	95.22	S	186.14
25	−74.92	S	S	H	145.46	70.53	−58.67	S	H	−81.52
26	S	S	H	−190.48	−23.22	−2.67	S	S	529.95	10.59
27	S	H	69.23	121.45	44.93	S	S	H	553.16	141.59
28	H	106.29	−42.63	−36.87	S	S	H	−237.92	−147.63	64.81
29	125.86	−106.59	65.56	−115.44	S	H	−391.64	−221.36	−17.53	S
30	−160.83	21.73	18.43	S	H	−50.81	306.33	43.47	S	S
31	−26.41	−208.96	S	S	−86.02	−20.82	−251.94	−354.84	S	H
Close	12393.45	15115.57	16717.17	18010.68	17787.20	21008.65	24415.84	24815.04	25383.11	34529.45
Change	−820.18	275.77	136.33	170.16	13.56	68.14	252.69	−1777.87	1037.39	654.60

JUNE DAILY POINT CHANGES DOW JONES INDUSTRIALS

Previous Month Close	2011	2012	2013	2014	2015	2016	2017	2018	2019	2020
	12569.79	12393.45	15115.57	16717.17	18010.68	17787.20	21008.65	24415.84	24815.04	25383.11
1	−279.65	−274.88	S	S	29.69	2.47	135.53	219.37	S	91.91
2	−41.59	S	S	26.46	−28.43	48.89	62.11	S	S	267.63
3	−97.29	S	138.46	−21.29	64.33	−31.50	S	S	4.74	527.24
4	S	−17.11	−76.49	15.19	−170.69	S	S	178.48	512.40	11.93
5	S	26.49	−216.95	98.58	−56.12	S	−22.25	−13.71	207.39	829.16
6	−61.30	286.84	80.03	88.17	S	113.27	−47.81	346.41	181.09	S
7	−19.15	46.17	207.50	S	S	17.95	37.46	95.02	263.28	S
8	−21.87	93.24	S	S	−82.91	66.77	8.84	75.12	S	461.46
9	75.42	S	S	18.82	−2.51	−19.86	89.44	S	S	−300.14
10	−172.45	S	−9.53	2.82	236.36	−119.85	S	S	78.74	−282.31
11	S	−142.97	−116.57	−102.04	38.97	S	S	5.78	−14.17	−1861.82
12	S	162.57	−126.79	−109.69	−140.53	S	−36.30	−1.58	−43.68	477.37
13	1.06	−77.42	180.85	41.55	S	−132.86	92.80	−119.53	101.94	S
14	123.14	155.53	−105.90	S	S	−57.66	46.09	−25.89	−17.16	S
15	−178.84	115.26	S	S	−107.67	−34.65	−14.66	−84.83	S	157.62
16	64.25	S	S	5.27	113.31	92.93	24.38	S	S	526.82
17	42.84	S	109.67	27.48	31.26	−57.94	S	S	22.92	−170.37
18	S	−25.35	138.38	98.13	180.10	S	S	−103.01	353.01	−39.51
19	S	95.51	−206.04	14.84	−99.89	S	144.71	−287.26	38.46	−208.64
20	76.02	−12.94	−353.87	25.62	S	129.71	−61.85	−42.41	249.17	S
21	109.63	−250.82	41.08	S	S	24.86	−57.11	−196.10	−34.04	S
22	−80.34	67.21	S	S	103.83	−48.90	−12.74	119.19	S	153.50
23	−59.67	S	S	−9.82	24.29	230.24	−2.53	S	S	131.14
24	−115.42	S	−139.84	−119.13	−178.00	−610.32	S	S	8.41	−710.16
25	S	−138.12	100.75	49.38	−75.71	S	S	−328.09	−179.32	299.66
26	S	32.01	149.83	−21.38	56.32	S	14.79	30.31	−11.40	−730.05
27	108.98	92.34	114.35	5.71	S	−260.51	−98.89	−165.52	−10.24	S
28	145.13	−24.75	−114.89	S	S	269.48	143.95	98.46	73.38	S
29	72.73	277.83	S	S	−350.33	284.96	−167.58	55.36	S	580.25
30	152.92	S	S	−25.24	23.16	235.31	62.60	S	S	217.08
Close	12414.34	12880.09	14909.60	16826.60	17619.51	17929.99	21349.63	24271.41	26599.96	25812.88
Change	−155.45	486.64	−205.97	109.43	−391.17	142.79	340.98	−144.43	1784.92	429.77

JULY DAILY POINT CHANGES DOW JONES INDUSTRIALS

Previous Month Close	2011	2012	2013	2014	2015	2016	2017	2018	2019	2020
	12414.34	12880.09	14909.60	16826.60	17619.51	17929.99	21349.63	24271.41	26599.96	25812.88
1	168.43	S	65.36	129.47	138.40	19.38	S	S	117.47	-77.91
2	S	-8.70	-42.55	20.17	-27.80	S	S	35.77	69.25	92.39
3	S	72.43*	56.14*	92.02	H	S	129.64*	-132.36*	179.32*	H
4	H	H	H	H	S	H	H	H	H	S
5	-12.90	-47.15	147.29	S	S	-108.75	-1.10	181.92	-43.88	S
6	56.15	-124.20	S	S	-46.53	78.00	-158.13	99.74	S	459.67
7	93.47	S	S	-44.05	93.33	-22.74	94.30	S	S	-396.85
8	-62.29	S	88.85	-117.59	-261.49	250.86	S	S	-115.98	177.10
9	S	-36.18	75.65	78.99	33.20	S	S	320.11	-22.65	-361.19
10	S	-83.17	-8.68	-70.54	211.79	S	-5.82	143.07	76.71	369.21
11	-151.44	-48.59	169.26	28.74	S	80.19	0.55	-219.21	227.88	S
12	-58.88	-31.26	3.38	S	S	120.74	123.07	224.44	243.95	S
13	44.73	203.82	S	S	217.27	24.45	20.95	94.52	S	10.50
14	-54.49	S	S	111.61	75.90	134.29	84.65	S	S	556.79
15	42.61	S	19.96	5.26	-3.41	10.14	S	S	27.13	227.51
16	S	-49.88	-32.41	77.52	70.08	S	S	44.95	-23.53	-135.39
17	S	78.33	18.67	-161.39	-33.80	S	-8.02	55.53	-115.78	-62.76
18	-94.57	103.16	78.02	123.37	S	16.50	-54.99	79.40	3.12	S
19	202.26	34.66	-4.80	S	S	25.96	66.02	-134.79	-68.77	S
20	-15.51	-120.79	S	S	13.96	36.02	-28.97	-6.38	S	8.92
21	152.50	S	S	-48.45	-181.12	-77.80	-31.71	S	S	159.53
22	-43.25	S	1.81	61.81	-68.25	53.62	S	S	17.70	165.44
23	S	-101.11	22.19	-26.91	-119.12	S	S	-13.83	177.29	-353.51
24	S	-104.14	-25.50	-2.83	-163.39	S	-66.90	197.65	-79.22	-182.44
25	-88.36	58.73	13.37	-123.23	S	-77.79	100.26	172.16	-128.99	S
26	-91.50	211.88	3.22	S	S	-19.31	97.58	112.97	51.47	S
27	-198.75	187.73	S	S	-127.94	-1.58	85.54	-76.01	S	114.88
28	-62.44	S	S	22.02	189.68	-15.82	33.76	S	S	-205.49
29	-96.87	S	-36.86	-70.48	121.12	-24.11	S	S	28.90	160.29
30	S	-2.65	-1.38	-31.75	-5.41	S	S	-144.23	-23.33	-225.92
31	S	-64.33	-21.05	-317.06	-56.12	S	60.81	108.36	-333.75	114.67
Close	12143.24	13008.68	15499.54	16563.30	17689.86	18432.24	21891.12	25415.19	26864.27	26428.32
Change	-271.10	128.59	589.94	-263.30	70.35	502.25	541.49	1143.78	264.31	615.44

*Shortened trading day

AUGUST DAILY POINT CHANGES DOW JONES INDUSTRIALS

Previous Month Close	2011	2012	2013	2014	2015	2016	2017	2018	2019	2020
	12143.24	13008.68	15499.54	16563.30	17689.86	18432.24	21891.12	25415.19	26864.27	26428.32
1	-10.75	-37.62	128.48	-69.93	S	-27.73	72.80	-81.37	-280.85	S
2	-265.87	-92.18	30.34	S	S	-90.74	52.32	-7.66	-98.41	S
3	29.82	217.29	S	S	-91.66	41.23	9.86	136.42	S	236.08
4	-512.76	S	S	75.91	-47.51	-2.95	66.71	S	S	164.07
5	60.93	S	-46.23	-139.81	-10.22	191.48	S	39.60	-767.27	373.05
6	S	21.34	-93.39	13.87	-120.72	S	25.61	126.73	311.78	185.46
7	S	51.09	-48.07	-75.07	-46.37	S	25.61	126.73	-22.45	46.50
8	-634.76	7.04	27.65	185.66	S	-14.24	-33.08	-45.16	371.12	S
9	429.92	-10.45	-72.81	S	S	3.76	-36.64	-74.52	-90.75	S
10	-519.83	42.76	S	S	241.79	-37.39	-204.69	-196.09	S	357.96
11	423.37	S	S	16.05	-212.33	117.86	14.31	S	S	-104.53
12	125.71	S	-5.83	-9.44	-0.33	-37.05	S	S	-380.07	289.93
13	S	-38.52	31.33	91.26	5.74	S	S	-125.44	372.54	-80.12
14	S	2.71	-113.35	61.78	69.15	S	135.39	112.22	-800.49	34.30
15	213.88	-7.36	-225.47	-50.67	S	59.58	5.28	-137.51	99.97	S
16	-76.97	85.33	-30.72	S	S	-84.03	25.88	396.32	306.62	S
17	4.28	25.09	S	S	67.78	21.92	-274.14	110.59	S	-86.11
18	-419.63	S	-70.73	175.83	-33.84	23.76	-76.22	S	S	-66.84
19	-172.93	S	-7.75	80.85	-162.61	-45.13	S	S	249.78	-85.19
20	S	-3.56	-7.75	59.54	-358.04	S	S	89.37	-173.35	46.85
21	S	-68.06	-105.44	60.36	-530.94	S	29.24	63.60	240.29	190.60
22	37.00	-30.82	66.19	-38.27	S	-23.15	196.14	-88.69	49.51	S
23	322.11	-115.30	46.77	S	S	17.88	-87.80	-76.62	-623.34	S
24	143.95	100.51	S	S	-588.40	-65.82	-28.69	133.37	S	378.13
25	-170.89	S	S	75.65	-204.91	-33.07	30.27	S	S	-60.02
26	134.72	S	-64.05	29.83	619.07	-53.01	S	S	269.93	83.48
27	S	-33.30	-170.33	15.31	369.26	S	S	259.29	-120.93	160.35
28	S	-21.68	48.38	-42.44	-11.76	S	-5.27	14.38	258.20	161.60
29	254.71	4.49	16.44	18.88	S	107.59	56.97	60.55	326.15	S
30	20.70	-106.77	-30.64	S	S	-48.69	27.06	-137.65	41.03	S
31	53.58	90.13	S	S	-114.98	-53.42	55.67	-22.10	S	-223.82
Close	11613.53	13090.84	14810.31	17098.45	16528.03	18400.88	21948.10	25964.82	26403.28	28430.05
Change	-529.71	82.16	-689.23	535.15	-1161.83	-31.36	56.98	549.63	-460.99	2001.73

SEPTEMBER DAILY POINT CHANGES DOW JONES INDUSTRIALS

Previous Month	2011	2012	2013	2014	2015	2016	2017	2018	2019	2020
Close	11613.53	13090.84	14810.31	17098.45	16528.03	18400.88	21948.10	25964.82	26403.28	28430.05
1	−119.96	S	S	H	−469.68	18.42	39.46	S	S	215.61
2	−253.31	S	H	−30.89	293.03	72.66	S	S	H	454.84
3	S	H	23.65	10.72	23.38	S	S	H	−285.26	−807.77
4	S	−54.90	96.91	−8.70	−272.38	S	H	−12.34	237.45	−159.42
5	H	11.54	6.61	67.78	S	H	−234.25	22.51	372.68	S
6	−100.96	244.52	−14.98	S	S	46.16	54.33	20.88	69.31	S
7	275.56	14.64	S	S	H	−11.98	−22.86	−79.33	S	H
8	−119.05	S	S	−25.94	390.30	−46.23	13.01	S	S	−632.42
9	−303.68	S	140.62	−97.55	−239.11	−394.46	S	S	38.05	439.58
10	S	−52.35	127.94	54.84	76.83	S	S	−59.47	73.92	−405.89
11	S	69.07	135.54	−19.71	102.69	S	259.58	113.99	227.61	131.06
12	68.99	9.99	−25.96	−61.49	S	239.62	61.49	27.86	45.41	S
13	44.73	206.51	75.42	S	S	−258.32	39.32	147.07	37.07	S
14	140.88	53.51	S	S	−62.13	−31.98	45.30	8.68	S	327.69
15	186.45	S	S	43.63	228.89	177.71	64.86	S	S	2.27
16	75.91	S	118.72	100.83	140.10	−88.68	S	S	−142.70	36.78
17	S	−40.27	34.95	24.88	−65.21	S	S	−92.55	33.98	−130.40
18	S	11.54	147.21	109.14	−290.16	S	63.01	184.84	36.28	−244.56
19	−108.08	13.32	−40.39	13.75	S	−3.63	39.45	158.80	−52.29	S
20	7.65	18.97	−185.46	S	S	9.79	41.79	251.22	−159.72	S
21	−283.82	−17.46	S	S	125.61	163.74	−53.36	86.52	S	−509.72
22	−391.01	S	S	−107.06	−179.72	98.76	−9.64	S	S	140.48
23	37.65	S	−49.71	−116.81	−50.58	−131.01	S	S	14.92	−525.05
24	S	−20.55	−66.79	154.19	−78.57	S	S	−181.45	−142.22	52.31
25	S	−101.37	−61.33	−264.26	113.35	S	−53.50	−69.84	162.94	358.52
26	272.38	−44.04	55.04	167.35	S	−166.62	−11.77	−106.93	−79.59	S
27	146.83	72.46	−70.06	S	S	133.47	56.39	54.65	−70.87	S
28	−179.79	−48.84	S	S	−312.78	110.94	40.49	18.38	S	410.10
29	143.08	S	S	−41.93	47.24	−195.79	23.89	S	S	−131.40
30	−240.60	S	−128.57	−28.32	234.87	164.70	S	S	96.58	329.04
Close	10913.38	13437.13	15129.67	17042.90	16284.00	18308.15	22405.09	26458.31	26916.83	27781.70
Change	−700.15	346.29	319.36	−55.55	−244.03	−92.73	456.99	493.49	513.55	−648.35

OCTOBER DAILY POINT CHANGES DOW JONES INDUSTRIALS

Previous Month	2011	2012	2013	2014	2015	2016	2017	2018	2019	2020
Close	10913.38	13437.13	15129.67	17042.90	16284.00	18308.15	22405.09	26458.31	26916.83	27781.70
1	S	77.98	62.03	−238.19	−11.99	S	S	192.90	−343.79	35.20
2	S	−32.75	−58.56	−3.66	200.36	S	152.51	122.73	−494.42	−134.09
3	−258.08	12.25	−136.66	208.64	S	−54.30	84.07	54.45	122.42	S
4	153.41	80.75	76.10	S	S	−85.40	19.97	−200.91	372.68	S
5	131.24	34.79	S	S	304.06	112.58	113.75	−180.43	S	465.83
6	183.38	S	S	−17.78	13.76	−12.53	−1.72	S	S	−375.88
7	−20.21	S	−136.34	−272.52	122.10	−28.01	S	S	−95.70	530.70
8	S	−26.50	−159.71	274.83	138.46	S	S	39.73	−313.98	122.05
9	S	−110.12	26.45	−334.97	33.74	S	−12.60	−56.21	181.97	161.39
10	330.06	−128.56	323.09	−115.15	S	88.55	69.61	−831.83	150.66	S
11	−16.88	−18.58	111.04	S	S	−200.38	42.21	−545.91	319.92	S
12	102.55	2.46	S	S	47.37	15.54	−31.88	287.16	S	250.62
13	−40.72	S	S	−223.03	−49.97	−45.26	30.71	S	S	−157.71
14	166.36	S	64.15	−5.88	−157.14	39.44	S	S	−29.23	−165.81
15	S	95.38	−133.25	−173.45	217.00	S	S	−89.44	237.44	−19.80
16	S	127.55	205.82	−24.50	74.22	S	85.24	547.87	−22.82	112.11
17	−247.49	5.22	−2.18	263.17	S	−51.98	40.48	−91.74	23.90	S
18	180.05	−8.06	28.00	S	S	75.54	160.16	−327.23	−255.68	S
19	−72.43	−205.43	S	S	14.57	40.68	5.44	64.89	S	−410.89
20	37.16	S	S	19.26	−13.43	−40.27	165.59	S	S	113.37
21	267.01	S	−7.45	215.14	−48.50	−16.64	S	S	57.44	−97.97
22	S	2.38	75.46	−153.49	320.55	S	S	−126.93	−39.54	152.84
23	S	−243.36	−54.54	216.58	157.54	S	−54.67	−125.98	45.85	−28.09
24	104.83	−25.19	95.88	127.51	S	77.32	167.80	−608.01	−28.42	S
25	−207.00	26.34	61.07	S	S	−53.76	−112.30	401.13	152.53	S
26	162.42	3.53	S	S	−23.65	30.06	71.40	−296.24	S	−650.19
27	339.51	S	S	12.53	−41.62	−29.65	33.33	S	S	−222.19
28	22.56	S	−1.35	187.81	198.09	−8.49	S	S	132.66	−943.24
29	S	H*	111.42	−31.44	−23.72	S	S	−245.39	−19.26	139.16
30	S	H*	−61.59	221.11	−92.26	S	−85.45	431.72	115.23	−157.51
31	−276.10	−10.75	−73.01	195.10	S	−18.77	28.50	241.12	−140.46	S
Close	11955.01	13096.46	15545.75	17390.52	17663.54	18142.42	23377.24	25115.76	27046.23	26501.60
Change	1041.63	−340.67	416.08	347.62	1379.54	−165.73	972.15	−1342.55	129.40	−1280.10

*Hurricane Sandy

NOVEMBER DAILY POINT CHANGES DOW JONES INDUSTRIALS

Previous Month Close	2011	2012	2013	2014	2015	2016	2017	2018	2019	2020
	11955.01	13096.46	15545.75	17390.52	17663.54	18142.42	23377.24	25115.76	27046.23	26501.60
1	−297.05	136.16	69.80	S	S	−105.32	57.77	264.98	301.13	S
2	178.08	−139.46	S	S	165.22	−77.46	81.25	−109.91	S	423.45
3	208.43	S	S	−24.28	89.39	−28.97	22.93	S	S	554.98
4	−61.23	S	23.57	17.60	−50.57	−42.39	S	S	114.75	367.63
5	S	19.28	−20.90	100.69	−4.15	S	S	190.87	30.52	542.52
6	S	133.24	128.66	69.94	46.90	S	9.23	173.31	−0.07	−66.78
7	85.15	−312.95	−152.90	19.46	S	371.32	8.81	545.29	182.24	S
8	101.79	−121.41	167.80	S	S	73.14	6.13	10.92	6.44	S
9	−389.24	4.07	S	S	−179.85	256.95	−101.42	−201.92	S	834.57
10	112.85	S	S	39.81	27.73	218.19	−39.73	S	S	262.95
11	259.89	S	21.32	1.16	−55.99	39.78	S	S	10.25	−23.29
12	S	−0.31	−32.43	−2.70	−254.15	S	S	−602.12	0.00	−317.46
13	S	−58.90	70.96	40.59	−202.83	S	17.49	−100.69	92.10	399.64
14	−74.70	−185.23	54.59	−18.05	S	21.03	−30.23	−205.99	−1.63	S
15	17.18	−28.57	85.48	S	S	54.37	−138.19	208.77	222.93	S
16	−190.57	45.93	S	S	237.77	−54.92	187.08	123.95	S	470.63
17	−134.86	S	S	13.01	6.49	35.68	−100.12	S	S	−167.09
18	25.43	S	14.32	40.07	247.66	−35.89	S	S	31.33	−344.93
19	S	207.65	−8.99	−2.09	−4.41	S	S	−395.78	−102.20	44.81
20	S	−7.45	−66.21	33.27	91.06	S	72.09	−551.80	−112.93	−219.75
21	−248.85	48.38	109.17	91.06	S	88.76	160.50	−0.95	−54.80	S
22	−53.59	H	54.78	S	S	67.18	−64.65	H	109.33	S
23	−236.17	172.79*	S	S	−31.13	59.31	H	−178.74*	S	327.79
24	H	S	S	7.84	19.51	H	31.81*	S	S	454.97
25	−25.77*	S	7.77	−2.96	1.20	68.96*	S	S	190.85	−173.77
26	S	−42.31	0.26	−2.69	H	S	S	354.29	55.21	H
27	S	−89.24	24.53	H	−14.90*	S	22.79	108.49	42.32	37.90*
28	291.23	106.98	H	15.99*	S	−54.24	255.93	617.70	H	S
29	32.62	36.71	−10.92*	S	S	23.70	103.97	−27.59	−112.59*	S
30	490.05	3.76	S	S	−78.57	1.98	331.67	199.62	S	−271.73
Close	12045.68	13025.58	16086.41	17828.24	17719.92	19123.58	24272.35	25538.46	28051.41	29638.64
Change	90.67	−70.88	540.66	437.72	56.38	981.16	895.11	422.70	1005.18	3137.04

*Shortened trading day

DECEMBER DAILY POINT CHANGES DOW JONES INDUSTRIALS

Previous Month Close	2011	2012	2013	2014	2015	2016	2017	2018	2019	2020
	12045.68	13025.58	16086.41	17828.24	17719.92	19123.58	24272.35	25538.46	28051.41	29638.64
1	−25.65	S	S	−51.44	168.43	68.35	−40.76	S	S	185.28
2	−0.61	S	−77.64	102.75	−158.67	−21.51	S	S	−268.37	59.87
3	S	−59.98	−94.15	33.07	−252.01	S	S	287.97	−280.23	85.73
4	S	−13.82	−24.85	−12.52	369.96	S	58.46	−799.36	146.97	248.74
5	78.41	82.71	−68.26	58.69	S	45.82	−109.41	H**	28.01	S
6	52.30	39.55	198.69	S	S	35.54	−39.73	−79.40	337.27	S
7	46.24	81.09	S	S	−117.12	297.84	70.57	−558.72	S	−148.47
8	−198.67	S	S	−106.31	−162.51	65.19	117.68	S	S	104.09
9	186.56	S	5.33	−51.28	−75.70	142.04	S	S	−105.46	−105.07
10	S	14.75	−52.40	−268.05	82.45	S	S	34.31	−27.88	−69.55
11	S	78.56	−129.60	63.19	−309.54	S	56.87	−53.02	29.58	47.11
12	−162.87	−2.99	−104.10	−315.51	S	39.58	118.77	157.03	220.75	S
13	−66.45	−74.73	15.93	S	S	114.78	80.63	70.11	3.33	S
14	−131.46	−35.71	S	S	103.29	−118.68	−76.77	−496.87	S	−184.82
15	45.33	S	S	−99.99	156.41	59.71	143.08	S	100.51	337.76
16	−2.42	S	129.21	−111.97	224.18	−8.83	S	S	100.51	−44.77
17	S	100.38	−9.31	288.00	−253.25	S	S	−507.53	31.27	148.83
18	S	115.57	292.71	421.28	−367.29	S	140.46	82.66	−27.88	−124.32
19	−100.13	−98.99	11.11	26.65	S	39.65	−37.45	−351.98	137.68	S
20	337.32	59.75	42.06	S	S	91.56	−28.10	−464.06	78.13	S
21	4.16	−120.88	S	S	123.07	−32.66	55.64	−414.23	S	37.40
22	61.91	S	S	154.64	165.65	−23.08	−28.23	S	S	−200.94
23	124.35	S	73.47	64.73	185.34	14.93	S	S	96.44	114.32
24	S	−51.76*	62.94*	6.04*	−50.44*	S	S	−653.17*	−36.08*	70.04*
25	S	H	H	H	H	S	H	H	H	H
26	H	−24.49	122.33	23.50	S	H	−7.85	1086.25	105.94	S
27	−2.65	−18.28	−1.47	S	−23.90	S	11.23	28.09	23.87	S
28	−139.94	−158.20	S	S	−111.36	63.21	−76.42	S	204.10	
29	135.63	S	S	−15.48	192.71	−13.90	−118.29	S	S	−68.30
30	−69.48	S	25.88	−55.16	−117.11	−57.18	S	S	−183.12	73.89
31	S	166.03	72.37	−160.00	−178.84	S	S	265.06	76.30	196.92
Close	12217.56	13104.14	16576.66	17823.07	17425.03	19762.60	24719.22	23327.46	28538.44	30606.48
Change	171.88	78.56	490.25	−5.17	−294.89	639.02	446.87	−2211.00	487.03	967.84

* Shortened trading day,   ** President H.W. Bush Funeral

A TYPICAL DAY IN THE MARKET

Half-hourly data became available for the Dow Jones Industrial Average starting in January 1987. The NYSE switched 10:00 a.m. openings to 9:30 a.m. in October 1985. Below is the comparison between half-hourly performance from January 1987 to June 4, 2021, and hourly performance from November 1963 to June 1985. Stronger closings in a more bullish climate are evident. Morning and afternoon weaknesses appear an hour earlier.

MARKET % PERFORMANCE EACH HALF-HOUR OF THE DAY
(January 1987–June 4, 2021)

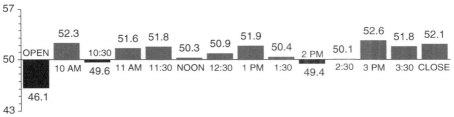

Based on the number of times the Dow Jones Industrial Average increased over the previous half-hour

MARKET % PERFORMANCE EACH HOUR OF THE DAY
(November 1963–June 1985)

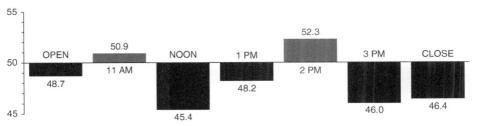

Based on the number of times the Dow Jones Industrial Average increased over the previous hour

On the next page, half-hourly movements since January 1987 are separated by day of the week. From 1953 to 1989, Monday was the worst day of the week, especially during long bear markets, but times changed. Monday reversed positions and became the best day of the week and on the plus side eleven years in a row from 1990 to 2000.

During the last 20 years (2001–June 4, 2021) Monday is the weakest day of the week. Tuesday is the best (page 72). On all days, stocks do tend to firm up near the close with weakness in the early morning and from 1:30 to 2:30 frequently.

THROUGH THE WEEK ON A HALF-HOURLY BASIS

From the chart showing the percentage of times the Dow Jones Industrial Average rose over the preceding half-hour (January 1987 to June 4, 2021*), the typical week unfolds.

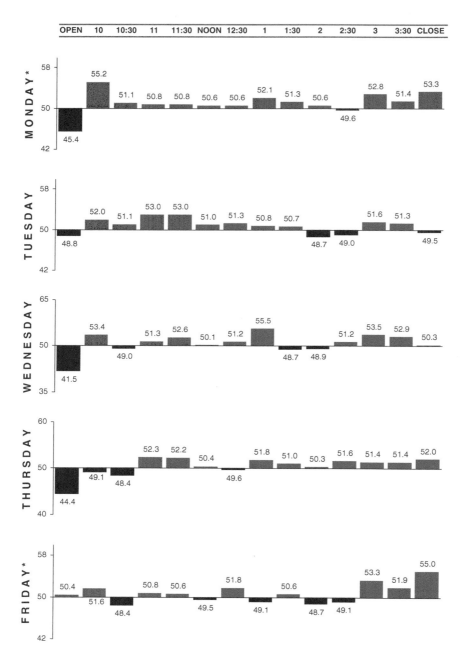

* Monday denotes first trading day of week, Friday denotes last trading day of week

TUESDAY MOST PROFITABLE DAY OF WEEK

Between 1952 and 1989, Monday was the worst trading day of the week. The first trading day of the week (including Tuesday when Monday is a holiday) rose only 44.3% of the time, while the other trading days closed higher 54.8% of the time. (NYSE Saturday trading was discontinued in June 1952.)

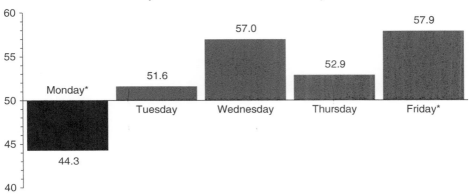

MARKET % PERFORMANCE EACH DAY OF THE WEEK
(June 1952–December 1989)

A dramatic reversal occurred in 1990—Monday became the most powerful day of the week. However, during the last 20 years, Tuesday has produced the most Dow point gains. Since the top in 2000, traders have not been inclined to stay long over the weekend nor buy up equities at the outset of the week. This is not uncommon during uncertain market times. Monday was the worst day during the 2007–2009 bear, and only Tuesday was a net gainer. Since the March 2009 bottom, Tuesday is best. See pages 72 and 145.

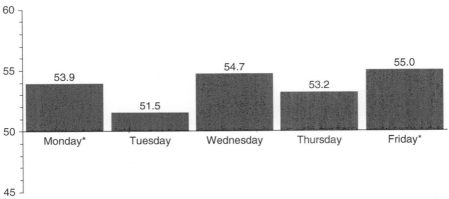

MARKET % PERFORMANCE EACH DAY OF THE WEEK
(January 1990–June 4, 2021)

Charts based on the number of times S&P 500 closed higher than previous day
* Monday denotes first trading day of week, Friday denotes last trading day of week

NASDAQ STRONGEST LAST 3 DAYS OF WEEK

Despite 20 years less data, daily trading patterns on NASDAQ through 1989 appear to be fairly similar to the S&P on page 143, except for more bullishness on Thursdays. During the mostly flat markets of the 1970s and early 1980s, it would appear that apprehensive investors decided to throw in the towel over weekends and sell on Mondays and Tuesdays.

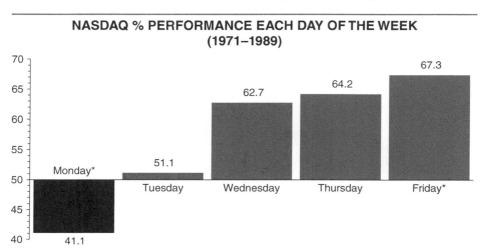

NASDAQ % PERFORMANCE EACH DAY OF THE WEEK
(1971–1989)

Notice the modest difference in the daily trading pattern between NASDAQ and S&P from January 1, 1990, to recent times. NASDAQ's weekly patterns are beginning to move in step with the rest of the market as technology continues to take an ever-increasing role throughout the economy. Notice the similarities to the S&P since 2001 on pages 145 and 146—Monday and Friday weakness, midweek strength during periods of uncertainty like 2015 to 2016.

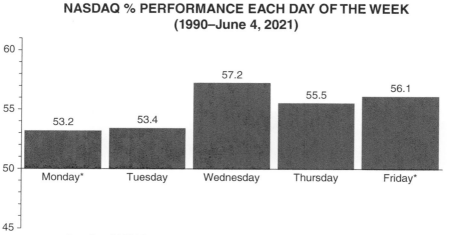

NASDAQ % PERFORMANCE EACH DAY OF THE WEEK
(1990–June 4, 2021)

Based on NASDAQ composite, prior to Feb. 5, 1971 based on National Quotation Bureau indices
* Monday denotes first trading day of week, Friday denotes last trading day of week

S&P DAILY PERFORMANCE EACH YEAR SINCE 1952

To determine if market trend alters performance of different days of the week, we separated 23 bear years—1953, '56, '57, '60, '62, '66, '69, '70, '73, '74, '77, '78, '81, '84, '87, '90, '94, 2000, 2001, 2002, 2008, 2011 and 2015—from 46 bull market years. While Tuesdays and Thursdays did not vary much between bull and bear years, Mondays and Fridays were sharply affected. There was a swing of 10.4 percentage points in Monday's performance and 9.4 in Friday's. Tuesday is the best day of the week based on total points gained. See page 72.

PERCENTAGE OF TIMES MARKET CLOSED HIGHER THAN PREVIOUS DAY
(JUNE 1952 - JUNE 4, 2021)

	Monday*	Tuesday	Wednesday	Thursday	Friday**
1952	48.4%	55.6%	58.1%	51.9%	66.7%
1953	32.7	50.0	54.9	57.5	56.6
1954	50.0	57.5	63.5	59.2	73.1
1955	50.0	45.7	63.5	60.0	78.9
1956	36.5	39.6	46.9	50.0	59.6
1957	25.0	54.0	66.7	48.9	44.2
1958	59.6	52.0	59.6	68.1	72.6
1959	42.3	53.1	55.8	48.9	69.8
1960	34.6	50.0	44.2	54.0	59.6
1961	52.9	54.4	64.7	56.0	67.3
1962	28.3	52.1	54.0	51.0	50.0
1963	46.2	63.3	51.0	57.5	69.2
1964	40.4	48.0	61.5	58.7	77.4
1965	44.2	57.5	55.8	51.0	71.2
1966	36.5	47.8	53.9	42.0	57.7
1967	38.5	50.0	60.8	64.0	69.2
1968†	49.1	57.5	64.3	42.6	54.9
1969	30.8	45.8	50.0	67.4	50.0
1970	38.5	46.0	63.5	48.9	52.8
1971	44.2	64.6	57.7	55.1	51.9
1972	38.5	60.9	57.7	51.0	67.3
1973	32.1	51.1	52.9	44.9	44.2
1974	32.7	57.1	51.0	36.7	30.8
1975	53.9	38.8	61.5	56.3	55.8
1976	55.8	55.3	55.8	40.8	58.5
1977	40.4	40.4	46.2	53.1	53.9
1978	51.9	43.5	59.6	54.0	48.1
1979	54.7	53.2	58.8	66.0	44.2
1980	55.8	54.2	71.7	35.4	59.6
1981	44.2	38.8	55.8	53.2	47.2
1982	46.2	39.6	44.2	44.9	50.0
1983	55.8	46.8	61.5	52.0	55.8
1984	39.6	63.8	31.4	46.0	44.2
1985	44.2	61.2	54.9	56.3	53.9
1986	51.9	44.9	67.3	58.3	55.8
1987	51.9	57.1	63.5	61.7	49.1
1988	51.9	61.7	51.9	48.0	59.6
1989	51.9	47.8	69.2	58.0	69.2
1990	67.9	53.2	52.9	40.0	51.9
1991	44.2	46.9	52.9	49.0	51.9
1992	51.9	49.0	53.9	56.3	45.3
1993	65.4	41.7	55.8	44.9	48.1
1994	55.8	46.8	52.9	48.0	59.6
1995	63.5	56.5	63.5	62.0	63.5
1996	54.7	44.9	51.0	57.1	63.5
1997	67.3	67.4	42.3	41.7	57.7
1998	57.7	62.5	57.7	38.3	60.4
1999	46.2	29.8	67.3	53.1	57.7
2000	51.9	43.5	40.4	56.0	46.2
2001	45.3	51.1	44.0	59.2	43.1
2002	40.4	37.5	56.9	38.8	48.1
2003	59.6	62.5	42.3	58.3	50.0
2004	51.9	61.7	59.6	52.1	52.8
2005	59.6	47.8	59.6	56.0	55.8
2006	55.8	55.6	67.3	52.0	48.1
2007	47.2	50.0	64.0	50.0	61.5
2008	42.3	50.0	41.5	60.4	55.8
2009	53.9	50.0	57.7	63.8	52.8
2010	61.5	57.5	55.8	53.1	57.7
2011	48.1	56.5	55.8	56.0	57.7
2012	52.8	48.9	50.0	58.0	53.9
2013	51.9	60.4	54.9	59.2	65.4
2014	53.9	56.3	57.7	56.3	61.5
2015	51.9	43.8	44.2	53.2	43.4
2016	50.0	58.7	55.8	50.0	46.2
2017	55.8	55.6	61.5	50.0	61.5
2018	52.8	60.9	50.0	46.0	53.9
2019	50.0	54.2	60.8	65.3	67.3
2020	63.5	54.2	61.5	52.1	54.7
2021‡	50.0	31.6	59.1	66.7	63.6
Average	**48.6%**	**51.8%**	**55.9%**	**52.8%**	**56.5%**
46 Bull Years	**52.1%**	**53.4%**	**58.1%**	**53.6%**	**59.6%**
23 Bear Years	**41.7%**	**48.7%**	**51.4%**	**51.3%**	**50.2%**

Based on S&P 500

† Most Wednesdays closed last 7 months of 1968   ‡ Through 6/4/2021 only, not included in averages
*Monday denotes first trading day of week, Friday denotes last trading day of week.

NASDAQ DAILY PERFORMANCE EACH YEAR SINCE 1971

After dropping a hefty 77.9% from its 2000 high (versus −37.8% on the Dow and −49.1% on the S&P 500), NASDAQ tech stocks still outpace the blue chips and big caps—but not nearly by as much as they did. From January 1, 1971, through June 4, 2021, NASDAQ moved up an impressive 15316%. The Dow (up 4043%) and the S&P (up 4490%) gained less than a third as much.

Monday's performance on NASDAQ was lackluster during the three-year bear market of 2000–2002. As NASDAQ rebounded (up 50% in 2003), strength returned to Monday during 2003–2006. During the bear market from late 2007 to early 2009, weakness was most consistent on Monday and Friday. At press time, Mondays, Tuesdays and Wednesdays have been challenging.

PERCENTAGE OF TIMES NASDAQ CLOSED HIGHER THAN PREVIOUS DAY
(1971 - JUNE 4, 2021)

	Monday*	Tuesday	Wednesday	Thursday	Friday**
1971	51.9%	52.1%	59.6%	65.3%	71.2%
1972	30.8	60.9	63.5	57.1	78.9
1973	34.0	48.9	52.9	53.1	48.1
1974	30.8	44.9	52.9	51.0	42.3
1975	44.2	42.9	63.5	64.6	63.5
1976	50.0	63.8	67.3	59.2	58.5
1977	51.9	40.4	53.9	63.3	73.1
1978	48.1	47.8	73.1	72.0	84.6
1979	45.3	53.2	64.7	86.0	82.7
1980	46.2	64.6	84.9	52.1	73.1
1981	42.3	32.7	67.3	76.6	69.8
1982	34.6	47.9	59.6	51.0	63.5
1983	42.3	44.7	67.3	68.0	73.1
1984	22.6	53.2	35.3	52.0	51.9
1985	36.5	59.2	62.8	68.8	66.0
1986	38.5	55.1	65.4	72.9	75.0
1987	42.3	49.0	65.4	68.1	66.0
1988	50.0	55.3	61.5	66.0	63.5
1989	38.5	54.4	71.2	72.0	75.0
1990	54.7	42.6	60.8	46.0	55.8
1991	51.9	59.2	66.7	65.3	51.9
1992	44.2	53.1	59.6	60.4	45.3
1993	55.8	56.3	69.2	57.1	67.3
1994	51.9	46.8	54.9	52.0	55.8
1995	50.0	52.2	63.5	64.0	63.5
1996	50.9	57.1	64.7	61.2	63.5
1997	65.4	59.2	53.9	52.1	55.8
1998	59.6	58.3	65.4	44.7	58.5
1999	61.5	40.4	63.5	57.1	65.4
2000	40.4	41.3	42.3	60.0	57.7
2001	41.5	57.8	52.0	55.1	47.1
2002	44.2	37.5	56.9	46.9	46.2
2003	57.7	60.4	40.4	60.4	46.2
2004	57.7	59.6	53.9	50.0	50.9
2005	61.5	47.8	51.9	48.0	59.6
2006	55.8	51.1	65.4	50.0	44.2
2007	47.2	63.0	66.0	56.0	57.7
2008	34.6	52.1	49.1	54.2	42.3
2009	51.9	54.2	63.5	63.8	50.9
2010	61.5	53.2	61.5	55.1	61.5
2011	50.0	56.5	50.0	64.0	53.9
2012	49.1	53.3	50.0	54.0	51.9
2013	57.7	60.4	52.9	59.2	67.3
2014	57.7	58.3	57.7	52.1	59.6
2015	55.8	39.6	53.9	59.6	49.1
2016	51.9	52.2	55.8	50.0	57.7
2017	59.6	62.2	67.3	50.0	67.3
2018	54.7	69.6	50.0	46.0	50.0
2019	50.0	58.3	62.8	59.2	59.6
2020	69.2	58.3	67.3	60.4	54.7
2021†	45.5	36.8	36.4	61.9	77.3
Average	**48.7%**	**52.9%**	**59.7%**	**58.7%**	**59.9%**
37 Bull Years	**51.1%**	**55.1%**	**61.9%**	**59.3%**	**62.5%**
13 Bear Years	**41.9%**	**46.4%**	**53.4%**	**56.8%**	**52.8%**

Based on NASDAQ composite; prior to Feb. 5, 1971 based on National Quotation Bureau indices
† Through 6/4/2021 only, not included in averages
*Monday denotes first trading day of week, Friday denotes last trading day of week

MONTHLY CASH INFLOWS INTO S&P STOCKS

For many years, the last trading day of the month, plus the first four of the following month, were the best market days of the month. This pattern is quite clear in the first chart, showing these five consecutive trading days towering above the other 16 trading days of the average month in the 1953–1981 period. The rationale was that individuals and institutions tended to operate similarly, causing a massive flow of cash into stocks near beginnings of months.

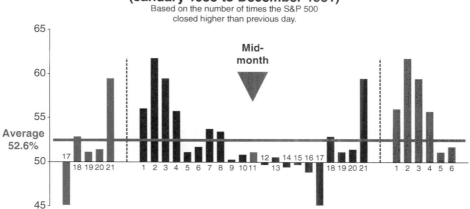

MARKET % PERFORMANCE EACH DAY OF THE MONTH
(January 1953 to December 1981)
Based on the number of times the S&P 500 closed higher than previous day.

Clearly, "front-running" traders took advantage of this phenomenon, drastically altering the previous pattern. The second chart from 1982 onward shows the trading shift caused by these "anticipators" to the last three trading days of the month, plus the first two. Another astonishing development shows the ninth, tenth and eleventh trading days rising strongly as well. Growth of 401(k) retirement plans, IRAs, and similar plans (participants' salaries are usually paid twice monthly) is responsible for this midmonth bulge. First trading days of the month have produced the greatest gains in recent years (see page 90).

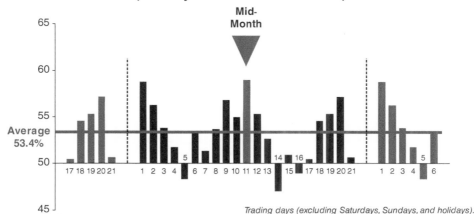

MARKET % PERFORMANCE EACH DAY OF THE MONTH
(January 1982 to December 2020)

Trading days (excluding Saturdays, Sundays, and holidays).

MONTHLY CASH INFLOWS INTO NASDAQ STOCKS

NASDAQ stocks moved up 58.1% of the time through 1981 compared to 52.6% for the S&P on page 147. Ends and beginnings of the month are fairly similar, specifically the last plus the first four trading days. But notice how investors piled into NASDAQ stocks until midmonth. NASDAQ rose 118.6% from January 1, 1971, to December 31, 1981, compared to 33.0% for the S&P.

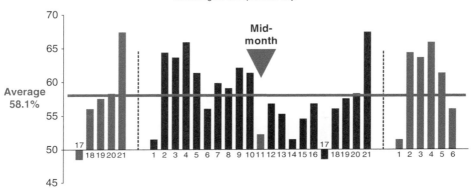

NASDAQ % PERFORMANCE EACH DAY OF THE MONTH
(January 1971 to December 1981)
Based on the number of times the NASDAQ composite
closed higher than previous day.

After the air was let out of the tech market in 2000–2002, S&P's 3965% gain over the last 39 years is more evenly matched with NASDAQ's 6481% gain. Last three, first four, and middle ninth, tenth, eleventh and twelfth days rose the most. Where the S&P has three days of the month that go down more often than up, NASDAQ has one. NASDAQ exhibits the most strength on the first trading day of the month. Over the past 20 years, last days have weakened considerably, down more frequently than not.

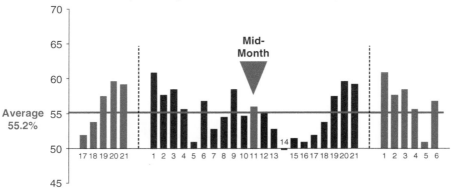

NASDAQ % PERFORMANCE EACH DAY OF THE MONTH
(January 1982 to December 2020)

Trading days (excluding Saturdays, Sundays, and holidays).
Based on NASDAQ composite, prior to February 5, 1971, based on National Quotation Bureau indices.

NOVEMBER, DECEMBER AND JANUARY: YEAR'S BEST THREE-MONTH SPAN

The most important observation to be made from a chart showing the average monthly percent change in market prices since 1950 is that institutions (mutual funds, pension funds, banks, etc.) determine the trading patterns in today's market.

The "investment calendar" reflects the annual, semiannual, and quarterly operations of institutions during January, April, and July. October, besides being the last campaign month before elections, is also the time when most bear markets seem to end, as in 1946, 1957, 1960, 1966, 1974, 1987, 1990, 1998 and 2002. (August and September tend to combine to make the worst consecutive two-month period.)

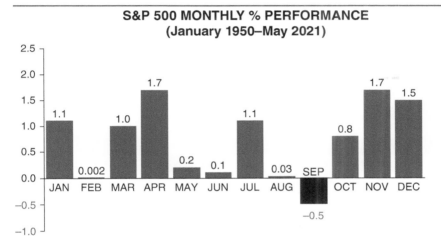

S&P 500 MONTHLY % PERFORMANCE
(January 1950–May 2021)

Average month-to-month % change in S&P 500.
(Based on monthly closing prices.)

Unusual year-end strength comes from corporate and private pension funds, producing a 4.3% gain on average between November 1 and January 31. In 2007–2008, these three months were all down for the fourth time since 1930; previously in 1931–1932, 1940–1941 and 1969–1970, also bear markets. September's dismal performance makes it the worst month of the year. However, in the last 17 years, it has been up 11 times after being down 5 in a row 1999–2003.

In midterm-election years since 1950, October is the best month +2.7% (13–5). November is second best with an average 2.6% gain. February, March, April and July are also positive. June is the worst month, –1.8%. January, May, August and September are also net decliners.

See page 52 for monthly performance tables for the S&P 500 and the Dow Jones industrials. See pages 54, 56, 62 and 64 for unique switching strategies.

On page 66, you can see how the first month of the first three quarters far outperforms the second and third months since 1950, and note the improvement in May's and October's performance since 1991.

NOVEMBER THROUGH JUNE:
NASDAQ'S EIGHT-MONTH RUN

The two-and-a-half-year plunge of 77.9% in NASDAQ stocks, between March 10, 2000, and October 9, 2002, brought several horrendous monthly losses (the two greatest were November 2000, −22.9% and February 2001, −22.4%), which trimmed average monthly performance over the $49^1/_3$-year period. Ample Octobers in 15 of the last 23 years, including three huge turnarounds in 2001 (+12.8%), 2002 (+13.5%) and 2011 (+11.1%) have put bear-killing October in the number one spot since 1998. January's 2.8% average gain is still awesome, and more than twice S&P's 1.2% January average since 1971.

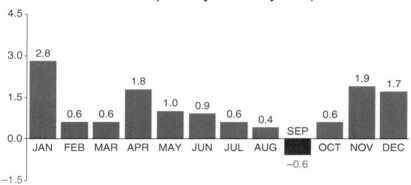

Average month-to-month % change in NASDAQ composite, prior to February 5, 1971, based on National Quotation Bureau indices. (Based on monthly closing prices.)

Bear in mind, when comparing NASDAQ to the S&P on page 149, that there are 23 fewer years of data here. During this $50^1/_3$-year (1971–May 2021) period, NASDAQ gained 15243%, while the S&P and the Dow rose only 4462% and 4016%, respectively. On page 60, you can see a statistical monthly comparison between NASDAQ and the Dow.

Year-end strength is even more pronounced in NASDAQ, producing a 6.4% gain on average between November 1 and January 31—nearly 1.5 times greater than that of the S&P 500 on page 149. September is the worst month of the year for the over-the-counter index as well, posting an average loss of −0.6%. These extremes underscore NASDAQ's higher volatility—and moves of greater magnitude.

In midterm-election years since 1971, November is best with an average gain of 3.5% (8–4). January, February, March and October are all also positive. April, May, June, August, September and December are all losers. July is the worst, −1.9% (4–8).

DOW JONES INDUSTRIALS ANNUAL HIGHS, LOWS & CLOSES SINCE 1901

YEAR	HIGH DATE	HIGH CLOSE	LOW DATE	LOW CLOSE	YEAR CLOSE	YEAR	HIGH DATE	HIGH CLOSE	LOW DATE	LOW CLOSE	YEAR CLOSE
1901	6/17	57.33	12/24	45.07	47.29	1933	7/18	108.67	2/27	50.16	99.90
1902	4/24	50.14	12/15	43.64	47.10	1934	2/5	110.74	7/26	85.51	104.04
1903	2/16	49.59	11/9	30.88	35.98	1935	11/19	148.44	3/14	96.71	144.13
1904	12/5	53.65	3/12	34.00	50.99	1936	11/17	184.90	1/6	143.11	179.90
1905	12/29	70.74	1/25	50.37	70.47	1937	3/10	194.40	11/24	113.64	120.85
1906	1/19	75.45	7/13	62.40	69.12	1938	11/12	158.41	3/31	98.95	154.76
1907	1/7	70.60	11/15	38.83	43.04	1939	9/12	155.92	4/8	121.44	150.24
1908	11/13	64.74	2/13	42.94	63.11	1940	1/3	152.80	6/10	111.84	131.13
1909	11/19	73.64	2/23	58.54	72.56	1941	1/10	133.59	12/23	106.34	110.96
1910	1/3	72.04	7/26	53.93	59.60	1942	12/26	119.71	4/28	92.92	119.40
1911	6/19	63.78	9/25	53.43	59.84	1943	7/14	145.82	1/8	119.26	135.89
1912	9/30	68.97	2/10	58.72	64.37	1944	12/16	152.53	2/7	134.22	152.32
1913	1/9	64.88	6/11	52.83	57.71	1945	12/11	195.82	1/24	151.35	192.91
1914	3/20	61.12	7/30	52.32	54.58	1946	5/29	212.50	10/9	163.12	177.20
1915	12/27	99.21	2/24	54.22	99.15	1947	7/24	186.85	5/17	163.21	181.16
1916	11/21	110.15	4/22	84.96	95.00	1948	6/15	193.16	3/16	165.39	177.30
1917	1/3	99.18	12/19	65.95	74.38	1949	12/30	200.52	6/13	161.60	200.13
1918	10/18	89.07	1/15	73.38	82.20	1950	11/24	235.47	1/13	196.81	235.41
1919	11/3	119.62	2/8	79.15	107.23	1951	9/13	276.37	1/3	238.99	269.23
1920	1/3	109.88	12/21	66.75	71.95	1952	12/30	292.00	5/1	256.35	291.90
1921	12/15	81.50	8/24	63.90	81.10	1953	1/5	293.79	9/14	255.49	280.90
1922	10/14	103.43	1/10	78.59	98.73	1954	12/31	404.39	1/11	279.87	404.39
1923	3/20	105.38	10/27	85.76	95.52	1955	12/30	488.40	1/17	388.20	488.40
1924	12/31	120.51	5/20	88.33	120.51	1956	4/6	521.05	1/23	462.35	499.47
1925	11/6	159.39	3/30	115.00	156.66	1957	7/12	520.77	10/22	419.79	435.69
1926	8/14	166.64	3/30	135.20	157.20	1958	12/31	583.65	2/25	436.89	583.65
1927	12/31	202.40	1/25	152.73	202.40	1959	12/31	679.36	2/9	574.46	679.36
1928	12/31	300.00	2/20	191.33	300.00	1960	1/5	685.47	10/25	566.05	615.89
1929	9/3	381.17	11/13	198.69	248.48	1961	12/13	734.91	1/3	610.25	731.14
1930	4/17	294.07	12/16	157.51	164.58	1962	1/3	726.01	6/26	535.76	652.10
1931	2/24	194.36	12/17	73.79	77.90	1963	12/18	767.21	1/2	646.79	762.95
1932	3/8	88.78	7/8	41.22	59.93	1964	11/18	891.71	1/2	766.08	874.13

continued

DOW JONES INDUSTRIALS ANNUAL HIGHS, LOWS & CLOSES SINCE 1901 (continued)

YEAR	HIGH DATE	HIGH CLOSE	LOW DATE	LOW CLOSE	YEAR CLOSE	YEAR	HIGH DATE	HIGH CLOSE	LOW DATE	LOW CLOSE	YEAR CLOSE
1965	12/31	969.26	6/28	840.59	969.26	1994	1/31	3978.36	4/4	3593.35	3834.44
1966	2/9	995.15	10/7	744.32	785.69	1995	12/13	5216.47	1/30	3832.08	5117.12
1967	9/25	943.08	1/3	786.41	905.11	1996	12/27	6560.91	1/10	5032.94	6448.27
1968	12/3	985.21	3/21	825.13	943.75	1997	8/6	8259.31	4/11	6391.69	7908.25
1969	5/14	968.85	12/17	769.93	800.36	1998	11/23	9374.27	8/31	7539.07	9181.43
1970	12/29	842.00	5/26	631.16	838.92	1999	12/31	11497.12	1/22	9120.67	11497.12
1971	4/28	950.82	11/23	797.97	890.20	2000	1/14	11722.98	3/7	9796.03	10786.85
1972	12/11	1036.27	1/26	889.15	1020.02	2001	5/21	11337.92	9/21	8235.81	10021.50
1973	1/11	1051.70	12/5	788.31	850.86	2002	3/19	10635.25	10/9	7286.27	8341.63
1974	3/13	891.66	12/6	577.60	616.24	2003	12/31	10453.92	3/11	7524.06	10453.92
1975	7/15	881.81	1/2	632.04	852.41	2004	12/28	10854.54	10/25	9749.99	10783.01
1976	9/21	1014.79	1/2	858.71	1004.65	2005	3/4	10940.55	4/20	10012.36	10717.50
1977	1/3	999.75	11/2	800.85	831.17	2006	12/27	12510.57	1/20	10667.39	12463.15
1978	9/8	907.74	2/28	742.12	805.01	2007	10/9	14164.53	3/5	12050.41	13264.82
1979	10/5	897.61	11/7	796.67	838.74	2008	5/2	13058.20	11/20	7552.29	8776.39
1980	11/20	1000.17	4/21	759.13	963.99	2009	12/30	10548.51	3/9	6547.05	10428.05
1981	4/27	1024.05	9/25	824.01	875.00	2010	12/29	11585.38	7/2	9686.48	11577.51
1982	12/27	1070.55	8/12	776.92	1046.54	2011	4/29	12810.54	10/3	10655.30	12217.56
1983	11/29	1287.20	1/3	1027.04	1258.64	2012	10/5	13610.15	6/4	12101.46	13104.14
1984	1/6	1286.64	7/24	1086.57	1211.57	2013	12/31	16576.66	1/8	13328.85	16576.66
1985	12/16	1553.10	1/4	1184.96	1546.67	2014	12/26	18053.71	2/3	15372.80	17823.07
1986	12/2	1955.57	1/22	1502.29	1895.95	2015	5/19	18312.39	8/25	15666.44	17425.03
1987	8/25	2722.42	10/19	1738.74	1938.83	2016	12/20	19974.62	2/11	15660.18	19762.60
1988	10/21	2183.50	1/20	1879.14	2168.57	2017	12/28	24837.51	1/19	19732.40	24719.22
1989	10/9	2791.41	1/3	2144.64	2753.20	2018	10/3	26828.39	12/24	21792.20	23327.46
1990	7/17	2999.75	10/11	2365.10	2633.66	2019	12/27	28645.26	1/3	22686.22	28538.44
1991	12/31	3168.83	1/9	2470.30	3168.83	2020	12/31	30606.48	3/23	18591.93	30606.48
1992	6/1	3413.21	10/9	3136.58	3301.11	2021*	5/7	34777.76	1/29	29982.62	*At press time*
1993	12/29	3794.33	1/20	3241.95	3754.09						

*Through June 4, 2021

152

S&P 500 ANNUAL HIGHS, LOWS & CLOSES SINCE 1930

YEAR	HIGH DATE	HIGH CLOSE	LOW DATE	LOW CLOSE	YEAR CLOSE	YEAR	HIGH DATE	HIGH CLOSE	LOW DATE	LOW CLOSE	YEAR CLOSE
1930	4/10	25.92	12/16	14.44	15.34	1976	9/21	107.83	1/2	90.90	107.46
1931	2/24	18.17	12/17	7.72	8.12	1977	1/3	107.00	11/2	90.71	95.10
1932	9/7	9.31	6/1	4.40	6.89	1978	9/12	106.99	3/6	86.90	96.11
1933	7/18	12.20	2/27	5.53	10.10	1979	10/5	111.27	2/27	96.13	107.94
1934	2/6	11.82	7/26	8.36	9.50	1980	11/28	140.52	3/27	98.22	135.76
1935	11/19	13.46	3/14	8.06	13.43	1981	1/6	138.12	9/25	112.77	122.55
1936	11/9	17.69	1/2	13.40	17.18	1982	11/9	143.02	8/12	102.42	140.64
1937	3/6	18.68	11/24	10.17	10.55	1983	10/10	172.65	1/3	138.34	164.93
1938	11/9	13.79	3/31	8.50	13.21	1984	11/6	170.41	7/24	147.82	167.24
1939	1/4	13.23	4/8	10.18	12.49	1985	12/16	212.02	1/4	163.68	211.28
1940	1/3	12.77	6/10	8.99	10.58	1986	12/2	254.00	1/22	203.49	242.17
1941	1/10	10.86	12/29	8.37	8.69	1987	8/25	336.77	12/4	223.92	247.08
1942	12/31	9.77	4/28	7.47	9.77	1988	10/21	283.66	1/20	242.63	277.72
1943	7/14	12.64	1/2	9.84	11.67	1989	10/9	359.80	1/3	275.31	353.40
1944	12/16	13.29	2/7	11.56	13.28	1990	7/16	368.95	10/11	295.46	330.22
1945	12/10	17.68	1/23	13.21	17.36	1991	12/31	417.09	1/9	311.49	417.09
1946	5/29	19.25	10/9	14.12	15.30	1992	12/18	441.28	4/8	394.50	435.71
1947	2/8	16.20	5/17	13.71	15.30	1993	12/28	470.94	1/8	429.05	466.45
1948	6/15	17.06	2/14	13.84	15.20	1994	2/2	482.00	4/4	438.92	459.27
1949	12/30	16.79	6/13	13.55	16.76	1995	12/13	621.69	1/3	459.11	615.93
1950	12/29	20.43	1/14	16.65	20.41	1996	11/25	757.03	1/10	598.48	740.74
1951	10/15	23.85	1/3	20.69	23.77	1997	12/5	983.79	1/2	737.01	970.43
1952	12/30	26.59	2/20	23.09	26.57	1998	12/29	1241.81	1/9	927.69	1229.23
1953	1/5	26.66	9/14	22.71	24.81	1999	12/31	1469.25	1/14	1212.19	1469.25
1954	12/31	35.98	1/11	24.80	35.98	2000	3/24	1527.46	12/20	1264.74	1320.28
1955	11/14	46.41	1/17	34.58	45.48	2001	2/1	1373.47	9/21	965.80	1148.08
1956	8/2	49.74	1/23	43.11	46.67	2002	1/4	1172.51	10/9	776.76	879.82
1957	7/15	49.13	10/22	38.98	39.99	2003	12/31	1111.92	3/11	800.73	1111.92
1958	12/31	55.21	1/2	40.33	55.21	2004	12/30	1213.55	8/12	1063.23	1211.92
1959	8/3	60.71	2/9	53.58	59.89	2005	12/14	1272.74	4/20	1137.50	1248.29
1960	1/5	60.39	10/25	52.30	58.11	2006	12/15	1427.09	6/13	1223.69	1418.30
1961	12/12	72.64	1/3	57.57	71.55	2007	10/9	1565.15	3/5	1374.12	1468.36
1962	1/3	71.13	6/26	52.32	63.10	2008	1/2	1447.16	11/20	752.44	903.25
1963	12/31	75.02	1/2	62.69	75.02	2009	12/28	1127.78	3/9	676.53	1115.10
1964	11/20	86.28	1/2	75.43	84.75	2010	12/29	1259.78	7/2	1022.58	1257.64
1965	11/15	92.63	6/28	81.60	92.43	2011	4/29	1363.61	10/3	1099.23	1257.60
1966	2/9	94.06	10/7	73.20	80.33	2012	9/14	1465.77	1/3	1277.06	1426.19
1967	9/25	97.59	1/3	80.38	96.47	2013	12/31	1848.36	1/8	1457.15	1848.36
1968	11/29	108.37	3/5	87.72	103.86	2014	12/29	2090.57	2/3	1741.89	2058.90
1969	5/14	106.16	12/17	89.20	92.06	2015	5/21	2130.82	8/25	1867.61	2043.94
1970	1/5	93.46	5/26	69.29	92.15	2016	12/13	2271.72	2/11	1829.08	2238.83
1971	4/28	104.77	11/23	90.16	102.09	2017	12/18	2690.16	1/3	2257.83	2673.61
1972	12/11	119.12	1/3	101.67	118.05	2018	9/20	2930.75	12/24	2351.10	2506.85
1973	1/11	120.24	12/5	92.16	97.55	2019	12/27	3240.02	1/3	2447.89	3230.78
1974	1/3	99.80	10/3	62.68	68.56	2020	12/31	3756.07	3/23	2237.40	3756.07
1975	7/15	95.61	1/8	70.04	90.19	2021*	5/7	4232.60	1/4	3700.65	At press time

*Through June 4, 2021

NASDAQ ANNUAL HIGHS, LOWS & CLOSES SINCE 1971

YEAR	HIGH DATE	HIGH CLOSE	LOW DATE	LOW CLOSE	YEAR CLOSE
1971	12/31	114.12	1/5	89.06	114.12
1972	12/8	135.15	1/3	113.65	133.73
1973	1/11	136.84	12/24	88.67	92.19
1974	3/15	96.53	10/3	54.87	59.82
1975	7/15	88.00	1/2	60.70	77.62
1976	12/31	97.88	1/2	78.06	97.88
1977	12/30	105.05	4/5	93.66	105.05
1978	9/13	139.25	1/11	99.09	117.98
1979	10/5	152.29	1/2	117.84	151.14
1980	11/28	208.15	3/27	124.09	202.34
1981	5/29	223.47	9/28	175.03	195.84
1982	12/8	240.70	8/13	159.14	232.41
1983	6/24	328.91	1/3	230.59	278.60
1984	1/6	287.90	7/25	225.30	247.35
1985	12/16	325.16	1/2	245.91	324.93
1986	7/3	411.16	1/9	323.01	349.33
1987	8/26	455.26	10/28	291.88	330.47
1988	7/5	396.11	1/12	331.97	381.38
1989	10/9	485.73	1/3	378.56	454.82
1990	7/16	469.60	10/16	325.44	373.84
1991	12/31	586.34	1/14	355.75	586.34
1992	12/31	676.95	6/26	547.84	676.95
1993	10/15	787.42	4/26	645.87	776.80
1994	3/18	803.93	6/24	693.79	751.96
1995	12/4	1069.79	1/3	743.58	1052.13
1996	12/9	1316.27	1/15	988.57	1291.03
1997	10/9	1745.85	4/2	1201.00	1570.35
1998	12/31	2192.69	10/8	1419.12	2192.69
1999	12/31	4069.31	1/4	2208.05	4069.31
2000	3/10	5048.62	12/20	2332.78	2470.52
2001	1/24	2859.15	9/21	1423.19	1950.40
2002	1/4	2059.38	10/9	1114.11	1335.51
2003	12/30	2009.88	3/11	1271.47	2003.37
2004	12/30	2178.34	8/12	1752.49	2175.44
2005	12/2	2273.37	4/28	1904.18	2205.32
2006	11/22	2465.98	7/21	2020.39	2415.29
2007	10/31	2859.12	3/5	2340.68	2652.28
2008	1/2	2609.63	11/20	1316.12	1577.03
2009	12/30	2291.28	3/9	1268.64	2269.15
2010	12/22	2671.48	7/2	2091.79	2652.87
2011	4/29	2873.54	10/3	2335.83	2605.15
2012	9/14	3183.95	1/4	2648.36	3019.51
2013	12/31	4176.59	1/8	3091.81	4176.59
2014	12/29	4806.91	2/3	3996.96	4736.05
2015	7/20	5218.86	8/25	4506.49	5007.41
2016	12/27	5487.44	2/11	4266.84	5383.12
2017	12/18	6994.76	1/3	5429.08	6903.39
2018	8/29	8109.69	12/24	6192.92	6635.28
2019	12/26	9022.39	1/3	6463.50	8972.60
2020	12/28	12899.42	3/23	6860.67	12888.28
2021*	4/26	14138.78	3/8	12609.16	*At press time*

RUSSELL 1000 ANNUAL HIGHS, LOWS & CLOSES SINCE 1979

YEAR	HIGH DATE	HIGH CLOSE	LOW DATE	LOW CLOSE	YEAR CLOSE	YEAR	HIGH DATE	HIGH CLOSE	LOW DATE	LOW CLOSE	YEAR CLOSE
1979	10/5	61.18	2/27	51.83	59.87	2001	1/30	727.35	9/21	507.98	604.94
1980	11/28	78.26	3/27	53.68	75.20	2002	3/19	618.74	10/9	410.52	466.18
1981	1/6	76.34	9/25	62.03	67.93	2003	12/31	594.56	3/11	425.31	594.56
1982	11/9	78.47	8/12	55.98	77.24	2004	12/30	651.76	8/13	566.06	650.99
1983	10/10	95.07	1/3	76.04	90.38	2005	12/14	692.09	4/20	613.37	679.42
1984	1/6	92.80	7/24	79.49	90.31	2006	12/15	775.08	6/13	665.81	770.08
1985	12/16	114.97	1/4	88.61	114.39	2007	10/9	852.32	3/5	749.85	799.82
1986	7/2	137.87	1/22	111.14	130.00	2008	1/2	788.62	11/20	402.91	487.77
1987	8/25	176.22	12/4	117.65	130.02	2009	12/28	619.22	3/9	367.55	612.01
1988	10/21	149.94	1/20	128.35	146.99	2010	12/29	698.11	7/2	562.58	696.90
1989	10/9	189.93	1/3	145.78	185.11	2011	4/29	758.45	10/3	604.42	693.36
1990	7/16	191.56	10/11	152.36	171.22	2012	9/14	809.01	1/4	703.72	789.90
1991	12/31	220.61	1/9	161.94	220.61	2013	12/31	1030.36	1/8	807.95	1030.36
1992	12/18	235.06	4/8	208.87	233.59	2014	12/29	1161.45	2/3	972.95	1144.37
1993	10/15	252.77	1/8	229.91	250.71	2015	5/21	1189.55	8/25	1042.77	1131.88
1994	2/1	258.31	4/4	235.38	244.65	2016	12/13	1260.06	2/11	1005.89	1241.66
1995	12/13	331.18	1/3	244.41	328.89	2017	12/18	1490.06	1/3	1252.11	1481.81
1996	12/2	401.21	1/10	318.24	393.75	2018	9/20	1624.28	12/24	1298.02	1384.26
1997	12/5	519.72	4/11	389.03	513.79	2019	12/26	1789.56	1/3	1351.87	1784.21
1998	12/29	645.36	1/9	490.26	642.87	2020	12/31	2120.87	3/23	1224.45	2120.87
1999	12/31	767.97	2/9	632.53	767.97	2021*	6/4	2376.97	1/4	2089.72	*At press time*
2000	9/1	813.71	12/20	668.75	700.09						

RUSSELL 2000 ANNUAL HIGHS, LOWS & CLOSES SINCE 1979

YEAR	HIGH DATE	HIGH CLOSE	LOW DATE	LOW CLOSE	YEAR CLOSE	YEAR	HIGH DATE	HIGH CLOSE	LOW DATE	LOW CLOSE	YEAR CLOSE
1979	12/31	55.91	1/2	40.81	55.91	2001	5/22	517.23	9/21	378.89	488.50
1980	11/28	77.70	3/27	45.36	74.80	2002	4/16	522.95	10/9	327.04	383.09
1981	6/15	85.16	9/25	65.37	73.67	2003	12/30	565.47	3/12	345.94	556.91
1982	12/8	91.01	8/12	60.33	88.90	2004	12/28	654.57	8/12	517.10	651.57
1983	6/24	126.99	1/3	88.29	112.27	2005	12/2	690.57	4/28	575.02	673.22
1984	1/12	116.69	7/25	93.95	101.49	2006	12/27	797.73	7/21	671.94	787.66
1985	12/31	129.87	1/2	101.21	129.87	2007	7/13	855.77	11/26	735.07	766.03
1986	7/3	155.30	1/9	128.23	135.00	2008	6/5	763.27	11/20	385.31	499.45
1987	8/25	174.44	10/28	106.08	120.42	2009	12/24	634.07	3/9	343.26	625.39
1988	7/15	151.42	1/12	121.23	147.37	2010	12/27	792.35	2/8	586.49	783.65
1989	10/9	180.78	1/3	146.79	168.30	2011	4/29	865.29	10/3	609.49	740.92
1990	6/15	170.90	10/30	118.82	132.16	2012	9/14	864.70	6/4	737.24	849.35
1991	12/31	189.94	1/15	125.25	189.94	2013	12/31	1163.64	1/3	872.60	1163.64
1992	12/31	221.01	7/8	185.81	221.01	2014	12/29	1219.11	10/13	1049.30	1204.70
1993	11/2	260.17	2/23	217.55	258.59	2015	6/23	1295.80	9/29	1083.91	1135.89
1994	3/18	271.08	12/9	235.16	250.36	2016	12/9	1388.07	2/11	953.72	1357.13
1995	9/14	316.12	1/30	246.56	315.97	2017	12/28	1548.93	4/13	1345.24	1535.51
1996	5/22	364.61	1/16	301.75	362.61	2018	8/31	1740.75	12/24	1266.92	1348.56
1997	10/13	465.21	4/25	335.85	437.02	2019	12/24	1678.01	1/3	1330.83	1668.47
1998	4/21	491.41	10/8	310.28	421.96	2020	12/23	2007.10	3/18	991.16	1974.86
1999	12/31	504.75	3/23	383.37	504.75	2021*	3/15	2360.17	1/4	1945.91	*At press time*
2000	3/9	606.05	12/20	443.80	483.53						

*Through June 4, 2021

155

DOW JONES INDUSTRIALS MONTHLY PERCENT CHANGES SINCE 1950

	Jan	Feb	Mar	Apr	May	Jun	Jul	Aug	Sep	Oct	Nov	Dec	Year
1950	0.8	0.8	1.3	4.0	4.2	−6.4	0.1	3.6	4.4	−0.6	1.2	3.4	17.6
1951	5.7	1.3	−1.6	4.5	−3.7	−2.8	6.3	4.8	0.3	−3.2	−0.4	3.0	14.4
1952	0.5	−3.9	3.6	−4.4	2.1	4.3	1.9	−1.6	−1.6	−0.5	5.4	2.9	8.4
1953	−0.7	−1.9	−1.5	−1.8	−0.9	−1.5	2.7	−5.1	1.1	4.5	2.0	−0.2	−3.8
1954	4.1	0.7	3.0	5.2	2.6	1.8	4.3	−3.5	7.3	−2.3	9.8	4.6	44.0
1955	1.1	0.7	−0.5	3.9	−0.2	6.2	3.2	0.5	−0.3	−2.5	6.2	1.1	20.8
1956	−3.6	2.7	5.8	0.8	−7.4	3.1	5.1	−3.0	−5.3	1.0	−1.5	5.6	2.3
1957	−4.1	−3.0	2.2	4.1	2.1	−0.3	1.0	−4.8	−5.8	−3.3	2.0	−3.2	−12.8
1958	3.3	−2.2	1.6	2.0	1.5	3.3	5.2	1.1	4.6	2.1	2.6	4.7	34.0
1959	1.8	1.6	−0.3	3.7	3.2	−0.03	4.9	−1.6	−4.9	2.4	1.9	3.1	16.4
1960	−8.4	1.2	−2.1	−2.4	4.0	2.4	−3.7	1.5	−7.3	0.04	2.9	3.1	−9.3
1961	5.2	2.1	2.2	0.3	2.7	−1.8	3.1	2.1	−2.6	0.4	2.5	1.3	18.7
1962	−4.3	1.1	−0.2	−5.9	−7.8	−8.5	6.5	1.9	−5.0	1.9	10.1	0.4	−10.8
1963	4.7	−2.9	3.0	5.2	1.3	−2.8	−1.6	4.9	0.5	3.1	−0.6	1.7	17.0
1964	2.9	1.9	1.6	−0.3	1.2	1.3	1.2	−0.3	4.4	−0.3	0.3	−0.1	14.6
1965	3.3	0.1	−1.6	3.7	−0.5	−5.4	1.6	1.3	4.2	3.2	−1.5	2.4	10.9
1966	1.5	−3.2	−2.8	1.0	−5.3	−1.6	−2.6	−7.0	−1.8	4.2	−1.9	−0.7	−18.9
1967	8.2	−1.2	3.2	3.6	−5.0	0.9	5.1	−0.3	2.8	−5.1	−0.4	3.3	15.2
1968	−5.5	−1.7	0.02	8.5	−1.4	−0.1	−1.6	1.5	4.4	1.8	3.4	−4.2	4.3
1969	0.2	−4.3	3.3	1.6	−1.3	−6.9	−6.6	2.6	−2.8	5.3	−5.1	−1.5	−15.2
1970	−7.0	4.5	1.0	−6.3	−4.8	−2.4	7.4	4.1	−0.5	−0.7	5.1	5.6	4.8
1971	3.5	1.2	2.9	4.1	−3.6	−1.8	−3.7	4.6	−1.2	−5.4	−0.9	7.1	6.1
1972	1.3	2.9	1.4	1.4	0.7	−3.3	−0.5	4.2	−1.1	0.2	6.6	0.2	14.6
1973	−2.1	−4.4	−0.4	−3.1	−2.2	−1.1	3.9	−4.2	6.7	1.0	−14.0	3.5	−16.6
1974	0.6	0.6	−1.6	−1.2	−4.1	0.03	−5.6	−10.4	−10.4	9.5	−7.0	−0.4	−27.6
1975	14.2	5.0	3.9	6.9	1.3	5.6	−5.4	0.5	−5.0	5.3	2.9	−1.0	38.3
1976	14.4	−0.3	2.8	−0.3	−2.2	2.8	−1.8	−1.1	1.7	−2.6	−1.8	6.1	17.9
1977	−5.0	−1.9	−1.8	0.8	−3.0	2.0	−2.9	−3.2	−1.7	−3.4	1.4	0.2	−17.3
1978	−7.4	−3.6	2.1	10.6	0.4	−2.6	5.3	1.7	−1.3	−8.5	0.8	0.7	−3.1
1979	4.2	−3.6	6.6	−0.8	−3.8	2.4	0.5	4.9	−1.0	−7.2	0.8	2.0	4.2
1980	4.4	−1.5	−9.0	4.0	4.1	2.0	7.8	−0.3	−0.02	−0.9	7.4	−3.0	14.9
1981	−1.7	2.9	3.0	−0.6	−0.6	−1.5	−2.5	−7.4	−3.6	0.3	4.3	−1.6	−9.2
1982	−0.4	−5.4	−0.2	3.1	−3.4	−0.9	−0.4	11.5	−0.6	10.7	4.8	0.7	19.6
1983	2.8	3.4	1.6	8.5	−2.1	1.8	−1.9	1.4	1.4	−0.6	4.1	−1.4	20.3
1984	−3.0	−5.4	0.9	0.5	−5.6	2.5	−1.5	9.8	−1.4	0.1	−1.5	1.9	−3.7
1985	6.2	−0.2	−1.3	−0.7	4.6	1.5	0.9	−1.0	−0.4	3.4	7.1	5.1	27.7
1986	1.6	8.8	6.4	−1.9	5.2	0.9	−6.2	6.9	−6.9	6.2	1.9	−1.0	22.6
1987	13.8	3.1	3.6	−0.8	0.2	5.5	6.3	3.5	−2.5	−23.2	−8.0	5.7	2.3

continued

156

	Jan	Feb	Mar	Apr	May	Jun	Jul	Aug	Sep	Oct	Nov	Dec	Year
1988	1.0	5.8	−4.0	2.2	−0.1	5.4	−0.6	−4.6	4.0	1.7	−1.6	2.6	11.8
1989	8.0	−3.6	1.6	5.5	2.5	−1.6	9.0	2.9	−1.6	−1.8	2.3	1.7	27.0
1990	−5.9	1.4	3.0	−1.9	8.3	0.1	0.9	−10.0	−6.2	−0.4	4.8	2.9	−4.3
1991	3.9	5.3	1.1	−0.9	4.8	−4.0	4.1	0.6	−0.9	1.7	−5.7	9.5	20.3
1992	1.7	1.4	−1.0	3.8	1.1	−2.3	2.3	−4.0	0.4	−1.4	2.4	−0.1	4.2
1993	0.3	1.8	1.9	−0.2	2.9	−0.3	0.7	3.2	−2.6	3.5	0.1	1.9	13.7
1994	6.0	−3.7	−5.1	1.3	2.1	−3.5	3.8	4.0	−1.8	1.7	−4.3	2.5	2.1
1995	0.2	4.3	3.7	3.9	3.3	2.0	3.3	−2.1	3.9	−0.7	6.7	0.8	33.5
1996	5.4	1.7	1.9	−0.3	1.3	0.2	−2.2	1.6	4.7	2.5	8.2	−1.1	26.0
1997	5.7	0.9	−4.3	6.5	4.6	4.7	7.2	−7.3	4.2	−6.3	5.1	1.1	22.6
1998	−0.02	8.1	3.0	3.0	−1.8	0.6	−0.8	−15.1	4.0	9.6	6.1	0.7	16.1
1999	1.9	−0.6	5.2	10.2	−2.1	3.9	−2.9	1.6	−4.5	3.8	1.4	5.7	25.2
2000	−4.8	−7.4	7.8	−1.7	−2.0	−0.7	0.7	6.6	−5.0	3.0	−5.1	3.6	−6.2
2001	0.9	−3.6	−5.9	8.7	1.6	−3.8	0.2	−5.4	−11.1	2.6	8.6	1.7	−7.1
2002	−1.0	1.9	2.9	−4.4	−0.2	−6.9	−5.5	−0.8	−12.4	10.6	5.9	−6.2	−16.8
2003	−3.5	−2.0	1.3	6.1	4.4	1.5	2.8	2.0	−1.5	5.7	−0.2	6.9	25.3
2004	0.3	0.9	−2.1	−1.3	−0.4	2.4	−2.8	0.3	−0.9	−0.5	4.0	3.4	3.1
2005	−2.7	2.6	−2.4	−3.0	2.7	−1.8	3.6	−1.5	0.8	−1.2	3.5	−0.8	−0.6
2006	1.4	1.2	1.1	2.3	−1.7	−0.2	0.3	1.7	2.6	3.4	1.2	2.0	16.3
2007	1.3	−2.8	0.7	5.7	4.3	−1.6	−1.5	1.1	4.0	0.2	−4.0	−0.8	6.4
2008	−4.6	−3.0	−0.03	4.5	−1.4	−10.2	0.2	1.5	−6.0	−14.1	−5.3	−0.6	−33.8
2009	−8.8	−11.7	7.7	7.3	4.1	−0.6	8.6	3.5	2.3	0.005	6.5	0.8	18.8
2010	−3.5	2.6	5.1	1.4	−7.9	−3.6	7.1	−4.3	7.7	3.1	−1.0	5.2	11.0
2011	2.7	2.8	0.8	4.0	−1.9	−1.2	−2.2	−4.4	−6.0	9.5	0.8	1.4	5.5
2012	3.4	2.5	2.0	0.01	−6.2	3.9	1.0	0.6	2.6	−2.5	−0.5	0.6	7.3
2013	5.8	1.4	3.7	1.8	1.9	−1.4	4.0	−4.4	2.2	2.8	3.5	3.0	26.5
2014	−5.3	4.0	0.8	0.7	0.8	0.7	−1.6	3.2	−0.3	2.0	2.5	−0.03	7.5
2015	−3.7	5.6	−2.0	0.4	1.0	−2.2	0.4	−6.6	−1.5	8.5	0.3	−1.7	−2.2
2016	−5.5	0.3	7.1	0.5	0.1	0.8	2.8	−0.2	−0.5	−0.9	5.4	3.3	13.4
2017	0.5	4.8	−0.7	1.3	0.3	1.6	2.5	0.3	2.1	4.3	3.8	1.8	25.1
2018	5.8	−4.3	−3.7	0.2	1.0	−0.6	4.7	2.2	1.9	−5.1	1.7	−8.7	−5.6
2019	7.2	3.7	0.1	2.6	−6.7	7.2	1.0	−1.7	1.9	0.5	3.7	1.7	22.3
2020	−1.0	−10.1	−13.7	11.1	4.3	1.7	2.4	7.6	−2.3	−4.6	11.8	3.3	7.2
2021	−2.0	3.2	6.6	2.7	1.9								
TOTALS	68.2	11.4	66.2	145.5	−0.6	−11.2	89.3	−3.8	−47.0	37.5	125.5	109.2	
AVG.	0.9	0.2	0.9	2.0	−0.01	−0.2	1.3	−0.1	−0.7	0.5	1.8	1.5	
# Up	45	43	46	50	39	34	46	40	29	42	49	50	
# Down	27	29	26	22	33	37	25	31	42	29	22	21	

DOW JONES INDUSTRIALS MONTHLY POINT CHANGES SINCE 1950

	Jan	Feb	Mar	Apr	May	Jun	Jul	Aug	Sep	Oct	Nov	Dec	Close
1950	1.66	1.65	2.61	8.28	9.09	−14.31	0.29	7.47	9.49	−1.35	2.59	7.81	235.41
1951	13.42	3.22	−4.11	11.19	−9.48	−7.01	15.22	12.39	0.91	−8.81	−1.08	7.96	269.23
1952	1.46	−10.61	9.38	−11.83	5.31	11.32	5.30	−4.52	−4.43	−1.38	14.43	8.24	291.90
1953	−2.13	−5.50	−4.40	−5.12	−2.47	−4.02	7.12	−14.16	2.82	11.77	5.56	−0.47	280.90
1954	11.49	2.15	8.97	15.82	8.16	6.04	14.39	−12.12	24.66	−8.32	34.63	17.62	404.39
1955	4.44	3.04	−2.17	15.95	−0.79	26.52	14.47	2.33	−1.56	−11.75	28.39	5.14	488.40
1956	−17.66	12.91	28.14	4.33	−38.07	14.73	25.03	−15.77	−26.79	4.60	−7.07	26.69	499.47
1957	−20.31	−14.54	10.19	19.55	10.57	−1.64	5.23	−24.17	−28.05	−15.26	8.83	−14.18	435.69
1958	14.33	−10.10	6.84	9.10	6.84	15.48	24.81	5.64	23.46	11.13	14.24	26.19	583.65
1959	10.31	9.54	−1.79	22.04	20.04	−0.19	31.28	−10.47	−32.73	14.92	12.58	20.18	679.36
1960	−56.74	7.50	−13.53	−14.89	23.80	15.12	−23.89	9.26	−45.85	0.22	16.86	18.67	615.89
1961	32.31	13.88	14.55	2.08	18.01	−12.76	21.41	14.57	−18.73	2.71	17.68	9.54	731.14
1962	−31.14	8.05	−1.10	−41.62	−51.97	−52.08	36.65	11.25	−30.20	10.79	59.53	2.80	652.10
1963	30.75	−19.91	19.58	35.18	9.26	−20.08	−11.45	33.89	3.47	22.44	−4.71	12.43	762.95
1964	22.39	14.80	13.15	−2.52	9.79	10.94	9.60	−2.62	36.89	−2.29	2.35	−1.30	874.13
1965	28.73	0.62	−14.43	33.26	−4.27	−50.01	13.71	11.36	37.48	30.24	−14.11	22.55	969.26
1966	14.25	−31.62	−27.12	8.91	−49.61	−13.97	−22.72	−58.97	−14.19	32.85	−15.48	−5.90	785.69
1967	64.20	−10.52	26.61	31.07	−44.49	7.70	43.98	−2.95	25.37	−46.92	−3.93	29.30	905.11
1968	−49.64	−14.97	0.17	71.55	−13.22	−1.20	−14.80	13.01	39.78	16.60	32.69	−41.33	943.75
1969	2.30	−40.84	30.27	14.70	−12.62	−64.37	−57.72	21.25	−23.63	42.90	−43.69	−11.94	800.36
1970	−56.30	33.53	7.98	−49.50	−35.63	−16.91	50.59	30.46	−3.90	−5.07	38.48	44.83	838.92
1971	29.58	10.33	25.54	37.38	−33.94	−16.67	−32.71	39.64	−10.88	−48.19	−7.66	58.86	890.20
1972	11.97	25.96	12.57	13.47	6.55	−31.69	−4.29	38.99	−10.46	2.25	62.69	1.81	1020.02
1973	−21.00	−43.95	−4.06	−29.58	−20.02	−9.70	34.69	−38.83	59.53	9.48	−134.33	28.61	850.86
1974	4.69	4.98	−13.85	−9.93	−34.58	0.24	−44.98	−78.85	−70.71	57.65	−46.86	−2.42	616.24
1975	87.45	35.36	29.10	53.19	10.95	46.70	−47.48	3.83	−41.46	42.16	24.63	−8.26	852.41
1976	122.87	−2.67	26.84	−2.60	−21.62	27.55	−18.14	−10.90	16.45	−25.26	−17.71	57.43	1004.65
1977	−50.28	−17.95	−17.29	7.77	−28.24	17.64	−26.23	−28.58	−14.38	−28.76	11.35	1.47	831.17
1978	−61.25	−27.80	15.24	79.96	3.29	−21.66	43.32	14.55	−11.00	−73.37	6.58	5.98	805.01
1979	34.21	−30.40	53.36	−7.28	−32.57	19.65	4.44	41.21	−9.05	−62.88	6.65	16.39	838.74
1980	37.11	−12.71	−77.39	31.31	33.79	17.07	67.40	−2.73	−0.17	−7.93	68.85	−29.35	963.99
1981	−16.72	27.31	29.29	−6.12	−6.00	−14.87	−24.54	−70.87	−31.49	2.57	36.43	−13.98	875.00
1982	−3.90	−46.71	−1.62	25.59	−28.82	−7.61	−3.33	92.71	−5.06	95.47	47.56	7.26	1046.54
1983	29.16	36.92	17.41	96.17	−26.22	21.98	−22.74	16.94	16.97	−7.93	50.82	−17.38	1258.64
1984	−38.06	−65.95	10.26	5.86	−65.90	27.55	−17.12	109.10	−17.67	0.67	−18.44	22.63	1211.57
1985	75.20	−2.76	−17.23	−8.72	57.35	20.05	11.99	−13.44	−5.38	45.68	97.82	74.54	1546.67
1986	24.32	138.07	109.55	−34.63	92.73	16.01	−117.41	123.03	−130.76	110.23	36.42	−18.28	1895.95
1987	262.09	65.95	80.70	−18.33	5.21	126.96	153.54	90.88	−66.67	−602.75	−159.98	105.28	1938.83

continued

	Jan	Feb	Mar	Apr	May	Jun	Jul	Aug	Sep	Oct	Nov	Dec	Close
1988	19.39	113.40	−83.56	44.27	−1.21	110.59	−12.98	−97.08	81.26	35.74	−34.14	54.06	2168.57
1989	173.75	−83.93	35.23	125.18	61.35	−40.09	220.60	76.61	−44.45	−47.74	61.19	46.93	2753.20
1990	−162.66	36.71	79.96	−50.45	219.90	4.03	24.51	−290.84	−161.88	−10.15	117.32	74.01	2633.66
1991	102.73	145.79	31.68	−25.99	139.63	−120.75	118.07	18.78	−26.83	52.33	−174.42	274.15	3168.83
1992	54.56	44.28	−32.20	123.65	37.76	−78.36	75.26	−136.43	14.31	−45.38	78.88	−4.05	3301.11
1993	8.92	60.78	64.30	−7.56	99.88	−11.35	23.39	111.78	−96.13	125.47	3.36	70.14	3754.09
1994	224.27	−146.34	−196.06	45.73	76.68	−133.41	139.54	148.92	−70.23	64.93	−168.89	95.21	3834.44
1995	9.42	167.19	146.64	163.58	143.87	90.96	152.37	−97.91	178.52	−33.60	319.01	42.63	5117.12
1996	278.18	90.32	101.52	−18.06	74.10	11.45	−125.72	87.30	265.96	147.21	492.32	−73.43	6448.27
1997	364.82	64.65	−294.26	425.51	322.05	341.75	549.82	−600.19	322.84	−503.18	381.05	85.12	7908.25
1998	−1.75	639.22	254.09	263.56	−163.42	52.07	−68.73	−1344.22	303.55	749.48	524.45	64.88	9181.43
1999	177.40	−52.25	479.58	1002.88	−229.30	411.06	−315.65	174.13	−492.33	392.91	147.95	619.31	11497.12
2000	−556.59	−812.22	793.61	−188.01	−211.58	−74.44	74.09	693.12	−564.18	320.22	−556.65	372.36	10786.85
2001	100.51	−392.08	−616.50	856.19	176.97	−409.54	20.41	−573.06	−1102.19	227.58	776.42	169.94	10021.50
2002	−101.50	186.13	297.81	−457.72	−20.97	−681.99	−506.67	−73.09	−1071.57	805.10	499.06	−554.46	8341.63
2003	−287.82	−162.73	101.05	487.96	370.17	135.18	248.36	182.02	−140.76	526.06	−18.66	671.46	10453.92
2004	34.15	95.85	−226.22	−132.13	−37.12	247.03	−295.77	34.21	−93.65	−52.80	400.55	354.99	10783.01
2005	−293.07	276.29	−262.47	−311.25	274.97	−192.51	365.94	−159.31	87.10	−128.63	365.80	−88.37	10717.50
2006	147.36	128.55	115.91	257.82	−198.83	−18.09	35.46	195.47	297.92	401.66	141.20	241.22	12463.15
2007	158.54	−353.06	85.72	708.56	564.73	−219.02	−196.63	145.75	537.89	34.38	−558.29	−106.90	13264.82
2008	−614.46	−383.97	−3.50	557.24	−181.81	−1288.31	28.01	165.53	−692.89	−1525.65	−495.97	−52.65	8776.39
2009	−775.53	−937.93	545.99	559.20	332.21	−53.33	724.61	324.67	216.00	0.45	632.11	83.21	10428.05
2010	−360.72	257.93	531.37	151.98	−871.98	−362.61	691.92	−451.22	773.33	330.44	−112.47	571.49	11577.51
2011	314.42	334.41	93.39	490.81	−240.75	−155.45	−271.10	−529.71	−700.15	1041.63	90.67	171.88	12217.56
2012	415.35	319.16	259.97	1.59	−820.18	486.64	128.59	82.16	346.29	−340.67	−70.88	78.56	13104.14
2013	756.44	193.91	524.05	261.26	275.77	−205.97	589.94	−689.23	319.36	416.08	540.66	490.25	16576.66
2014	−877.81	622.86	135.95	123.18	136.33	109.43	−263.30	535.15	−55.55	347.62	437.72	−5.17	17823.07
2015	−658.12	967.75	−356.58	64.40	170.16	−391.17	70.35	−1161.83	−244.03	1379.54	56.38	−294.89	17425.03
2016	−958.73	50.20	1168.59	88.55	13.56	142.79	502.25	−31.36	−92.73	−165.73	981.16	639.02	19762.60
2017	101.49	948.15	−149.02	277.29	68.14	340.98	541.49	56.98	456.99	972.15	895.11	446.87	24719.22
2018	1430.17	−1120.19	−926.09	60.04	252.69	−144.43	1143.78	549.63	493.49	−1342.55	422.70	−2211.00	23327.46
2019	1672.21	916.33	12.68	664.23	−1777.87	1784.92	264.31	−460.99	513.55	129.40	1005.18	487.03	28538.44
2020	−282.41	−2846.67	−3492.20	2428.56	1037.39	429.77	615.44	2001.73	−648.35	−1280.10	3137.04	967.84	30606.48
2021	−623.86	949.75	2049.18	893.30	654.60								
TOTALS	534.61	364.50	1657.82	10346.39	518.10	206.33	5436.87	−758.72	−1447.46	2633.31	10580.51	4257.06	
# Up	45	43	46	50	39	34	46	40	29	42	49	50	
# Down	27	29	26	22	33	37	25	31	42	29	22	21	

DOW JONES INDUSTRIALS MONTHLY CLOSING PRICES SINCE 1950

	Jan	Feb	Mar	Apr	May	Jun	Jul	Aug	Sep	Oct	Nov	Dec
1950	201.79	203.44	206.05	214.33	223.42	209.11	209.40	216.87	226.36	225.01	227.60	235.41
1951	248.83	252.05	247.94	259.13	249.65	242.64	257.86	270.25	271.16	262.35	261.27	269.23
1952	270.69	260.08	269.46	257.63	262.94	274.26	279.56	275.04	270.61	269.23	283.66	291.90
1953	289.77	284.27	279.87	274.75	272.28	268.26	275.38	261.22	264.04	275.81	281.37	280.90
1954	292.39	294.54	303.51	319.33	327.49	333.53	347.92	335.80	360.46	352.14	386.77	404.39
1955	408.83	411.87	409.70	425.65	424.86	451.38	465.85	468.18	466.62	454.87	483.26	488.40
1956	470.74	483.65	511.79	516.12	478.05	492.78	517.81	502.04	475.25	479.85	472.78	499.47
1957	479.16	464.62	474.81	494.36	504.93	503.29	508.52	484.35	456.30	441.04	449.87	435.69
1958	450.02	439.92	446.76	455.86	462.70	478.18	502.99	508.63	532.09	543.22	557.46	583.65
1959	593.96	603.50	601.71	623.75	643.79	643.60	674.88	664.41	631.68	646.60	659.18	679.36
1960	622.62	630.12	616.59	601.70	625.50	640.62	616.73	625.99	580.14	580.36	597.22	615.89
1961	648.20	662.08	676.63	678.71	696.72	683.96	705.37	719.94	701.21	703.92	721.60	731.14
1962	700.00	708.05	706.95	665.33	613.36	561.28	597.93	609.18	578.98	589.77	649.30	652.10
1963	682.85	662.94	682.52	717.70	726.96	706.88	695.43	729.32	732.79	755.23	750.52	762.95
1964	785.34	800.14	813.29	810.77	820.56	831.50	841.10	838.48	875.37	873.08	875.43	874.13
1965	902.86	903.48	889.05	922.31	918.04	868.03	881.74	893.10	930.58	960.82	946.71	969.26
1966	983.51	951.89	924.77	933.68	884.07	870.10	847.38	788.41	774.22	807.07	791.59	785.69
1967	849.89	839.37	865.98	897.05	852.56	860.26	904.24	901.29	926.66	879.74	875.81	905.11
1968	855.47	840.50	840.67	912.22	899.00	897.80	883.00	896.01	935.79	952.39	985.08	943.75
1969	946.05	905.21	935.48	950.18	937.56	873.19	815.47	836.72	813.09	855.99	812.30	800.36
1970	744.06	777.59	785.57	736.07	700.44	683.53	734.12	764.58	760.68	755.61	794.09	838.92
1971	868.50	878.83	904.37	941.75	907.81	891.14	858.43	898.07	887.19	839.00	831.34	890.20
1972	902.17	928.13	940.70	954.17	960.72	929.03	924.74	963.73	953.27	955.52	1018.21	1020.02
1973	999.02	955.07	951.01	921.43	901.41	891.71	926.40	887.57	947.10	956.58	822.25	850.86
1974	855.55	860.53	846.68	836.75	802.17	802.41	757.43	678.58	607.87	665.52	618.66	616.24
1975	703.69	739.05	768.15	821.34	832.29	878.99	831.51	835.34	793.88	836.04	860.67	852.41
1976	975.28	972.61	999.45	996.85	975.23	1002.78	984.64	973.74	990.19	964.93	947.22	1004.65
1977	954.37	936.42	919.13	926.90	898.66	916.30	890.07	861.49	847.11	818.35	829.70	831.17
1978	769.92	742.12	757.36	837.32	840.61	818.95	862.27	876.82	865.82	792.45	799.03	805.01
1979	839.22	808.82	862.18	854.90	822.33	841.98	846.42	887.63	878.58	815.70	822.35	838.74
1980	875.85	863.14	785.75	817.06	850.85	867.92	935.32	932.59	932.42	924.49	993.34	963.99
1981	947.27	974.58	1003.87	997.75	991.75	976.88	952.34	881.47	849.98	852.55	888.98	875.00
1982	871.10	824.39	822.77	848.36	819.54	811.93	808.60	901.31	896.25	991.72	1039.28	1046.54
1983	1075.70	1112.62	1130.03	1226.20	1199.98	1221.96	1199.22	1216.16	1233.13	1225.20	1276.02	1258.64
1984	1220.58	1154.63	1164.89	1170.75	1104.85	1132.40	1115.28	1224.38	1206.71	1207.38	1188.94	1211.57
1985	1286.77	1284.01	1266.78	1258.06	1315.41	1335.46	1347.45	1334.01	1328.63	1374.31	1472.13	1546.67

continued

160

	Jan	Feb	Mar	Apr	May	Jun	Jul	Aug	Sep	Oct	Nov	Dec
1986	1570.99	1709.06	1818.61	1783.98	1876.71	1892.72	1775.31	1898.34	1767.58	1877.81	1914.23	1895.95
1987	2158.04	2223.99	2304.69	2286.36	2291.57	2418.53	2572.07	2662.95	2596.28	1993.53	1833.55	1938.83
1988	1958.22	2071.62	1988.06	2032.33	2031.12	2141.71	2128.73	2031.65	2112.91	2148.65	2114.51	2168.57
1989	2342.32	2258.39	2293.62	2418.80	2480.15	2440.06	2660.66	2737.27	2692.82	2645.08	2706.27	2753.20
1990	2590.54	2627.25	2707.21	2656.76	2876.66	2880.69	2905.20	2614.36	2452.48	2442.33	2559.65	2633.66
1991	2736.39	2882.18	2913.86	2887.87	3027.50	2906.75	3024.82	3043.60	3016.77	3069.10	2894.68	3168.83
1992	3223.39	3267.67	3235.47	3359.12	3396.88	3318.52	3393.78	3257.35	3271.66	3226.28	3305.16	3301.11
1993	3310.03	3370.81	3435.11	3427.55	3527.43	3516.08	3539.47	3651.25	3555.12	3680.59	3683.95	3754.09
1994	3978.36	3832.02	3635.96	3681.69	3758.37	3624.96	3764.50	3913.42	3843.19	3908.12	3739.23	3834.44
1995	3843.86	4011.05	4157.69	4321.27	4465.14	4556.10	4708.47	4610.56	4789.08	4755.48	5074.49	5117.12
1996	5395.30	5485.62	5587.14	5569.08	5643.18	5654.63	5528.91	5616.21	5882.17	6029.38	6521.70	6448.27
1997	6813.09	6877.74	6583.48	7008.99	7331.04	7672.79	8222.61	7622.42	7945.26	7442.08	7823.13	7908.25
1998	7906.50	8545.72	8799.81	9063.37	8899.95	8952.02	8883.29	7539.07	7842.62	8592.10	9116.55	9181.43
1999	9358.83	9306.58	9786.16	10789.04	10559.74	10970.80	10655.15	10829.28	10336.95	10729.86	10877.81	11497.12
2000	10940.53	10128.31	10921.92	10733.91	10522.33	10447.89	10521.98	11215.10	10650.92	10971.14	10414.49	10786.85
2001	10887.36	10495.28	9878.78	10734.97	10911.94	10502.40	10522.81	9949.75	8847.56	9075.14	9851.56	10021.50
2002	9920.00	10106.13	10403.94	9946.22	9925.25	9243.26	8736.59	8663.50	7591.93	8397.03	8896.09	8341.63
2003	8053.81	7891.08	7992.13	8480.09	8850.26	8985.44	9233.80	9415.82	9275.06	9801.12	9782.46	10453.92
2004	10488.07	10583.92	10357.70	10225.57	10188.45	10435.48	10139.71	10173.92	10080.27	10027.47	10428.02	10783.01
2005	10489.94	10766.23	10503.76	10192.51	10467.48	10274.97	10640.91	10481.60	10568.70	10440.07	10805.87	10717.50
2006	10864.86	10993.41	11109.32	11367.14	11168.31	11150.22	11185.68	11381.15	11679.07	12080.73	12221.93	12463.15
2007	12621.69	12268.63	12354.35	13062.91	13627.64	13408.62	13211.99	13357.74	13895.63	13930.01	13371.72	13264.82
2008	12650.36	12266.39	12262.89	12820.13	12638.32	11350.01	11378.02	11543.55	10850.66	9325.01	8829.04	8776.39
2009	8000.86	7062.93	7608.92	8168.12	8500.33	8447.00	9171.61	9496.28	9712.28	9712.73	10344.84	10428.05
2010	10067.33	10325.26	10856.63	11008.61	10136.63	9774.02	10465.94	10014.72	10788.05	11118.49	11006.02	11577.51
2011	11891.93	12226.34	12319.73	12810.54	12569.79	12414.34	12143.24	11613.53	10913.38	11955.01	12045.68	12217.56
2012	12632.91	12952.07	13212.04	13213.63	12393.45	12880.09	13008.68	13090.84	13437.13	13096.46	13025.58	13104.14
2013	13860.58	14054.49	14578.54	14839.80	15115.57	14909.60	15499.54	14810.31	15129.67	15545.75	16086.41	16576.66
2014	15698.85	16321.71	16457.66	16580.84	16717.17	16826.60	16563.30	17098.45	17042.90	17390.52	17828.24	17823.07
2015	17164.95	18132.70	17776.12	17840.52	18010.68	17619.51	17689.86	16528.03	16284.00	17663.54	17719.92	17425.03
2016	16466.30	16516.50	17685.09	17773.64	17787.20	17929.99	18432.24	18400.88	18308.15	18142.42	19123.58	19762.60
2017	19864.09	20812.24	20663.22	20940.51	21008.65	21349.63	21891.12	21948.10	22405.09	23377.24	24272.35	24719.22
2018	26149.39	25029.20	24103.11	24163.15	24415.84	24271.41	25415.19	25964.82	26458.31	25115.76	25538.46	23327.46
2019	24999.67	25916.00	25928.68	26592.91	24815.04	26599.96	26864.27	26403.28	26916.83	27046.23	28051.41	28538.44
2020	28256.03	25409.36	21917.16	24345.72	25383.11	25812.88	26428.32	28430.05	27781.70	26501.60	29638.64	30606.48
2021	29982.62	30932.37	32981.55	33874.85	34529.45							

	Jan	Feb	Mar	Apr	May	Jun	Jul	Aug	Sep	Oct	Nov	Dec	Year
1950	1.7	1.0	0.4	4.5	3.9	−5.8	0.8	3.3	5.6	0.4	−0.1	4.6	21.8
1951	6.1	0.6	−1.8	4.8	−4.1	−2.6	6.9	3.9	−0.1	−1.4	−0.3	3.9	16.5
1952	1.6	−3.6	4.8	−4.3	2.3	4.6	1.8	−1.5	−2.0	−0.1	4.6	3.5	11.8
1953	−0.7	−1.8	−2.4	−2.6	−0.3	−1.6	2.5	−5.8	0.1	5.1	0.9	0.2	−6.6
1954	5.1	0.3	3.0	4.9	3.3	0.1	5.7	−3.4	8.3	−1.9	8.1	5.1	45.0
1955	1.8	0.4	−0.5	3.8	−0.1	8.2	6.1	−0.8	1.1	−3.0	7.5	−0.1	26.4
1956	−3.6	3.5	6.9	−0.2	−6.6	3.9	5.2	−3.8	−4.5	0.5	−1.1	3.5	2.6
1957	−4.2	−3.3	2.0	3.7	3.7	−0.1	1.1	−5.6	−6.2	−3.2	1.6	−4.1	−14.3
1958	4.3	−2.1	3.1	3.2	1.5	2.6	4.3	1.2	4.8	2.5	2.2	5.2	38.1
1959	0.4	−0.02	0.1	3.9	1.9	−0.4	3.5	−1.5	−4.6	1.1	1.3	2.8	8.5
1960	−7.1	0.9	−1.4	−1.8	2.7	2.0	−2.5	2.6	−6.0	−0.2	4.0	4.6	−3.0
1961	6.3	2.7	2.6	0.4	1.9	−2.9	3.3	2.0	−2.0	2.8	3.9	0.3	23.1
1962	−3.8	1.6	−0.6	−6.2	−8.6	−8.2	6.4	1.5	−4.8	0.4	10.2	1.3	−11.8
1963	4.9	−2.9	3.5	4.9	1.4	−2.0	−0.3	4.9	−1.1	3.2	−1.1	2.4	18.9
1964	2.7	1.0	1.5	0.6	1.1	1.6	1.8	−1.6	2.9	0.8	−0.5	0.4	13.0
1965	3.3	−0.1	−1.5	3.4	−0.8	−4.9	1.3	2.3	3.2	2.7	−0.9	0.9	9.1
1966	0.5	−1.8	−2.2	2.1	−5.4	−1.6	−1.3	−7.8	−0.7	4.8	0.3	−0.1	−13.1
1967	7.8	0.2	3.9	4.2	−5.2	1.8	4.5	−1.2	3.3	−2.9	0.1	2.6	20.1
1968	−4.4	−3.1	0.9	8.2	1.1	0.9	−1.8	1.1	3.9	0.7	4.8	−4.2	7.7
1969	−0.8	−4.7	3.4	2.1	−0.2	−5.6	−6.0	4.0	−2.5	4.4	−3.5	−1.9	−11.4
1970	−7.6	5.3	0.1	−9.0	−6.1	−5.0	7.3	4.4	3.3	−1.1	4.7	5.7	0.1
1971	4.0	0.9	3.7	3.6	−4.2	0.1	−4.1	3.6	−0.7	−4.2	−0.3	8.6	10.8
1972	1.8	2.5	0.6	0.4	1.7	−2.2	0.2	3.4	−0.5	0.9	4.6	1.2	15.6
1973	−1.7	−3.7	−0.1	−4.1	−1.9	−0.7	3.8	−3.7	4.0	−0.1	−11.4	1.7	−17.4
1974	−1.0	−0.4	−2.3	−3.9	−3.4	−1.5	−7.8	−9.0	−11.9	16.3	−5.3	−2.0	−29.7
1975	12.3	6.0	2.2	4.7	4.4	4.4	−6.8	−2.1	−3.5	6.2	2.5	−1.2	31.5
1976	11.8	−1.1	3.1	−1.1	−1.4	4.1	−0.8	−0.5	2.3	−2.2	−0.8	5.2	19.1
1977	−5.1	−2.2	−1.4	0.02	−2.4	4.5	−1.6	−2.1	−0.2	−4.3	2.7	0.3	−11.5
1978	−6.2	−2.5	2.5	8.5	0.4	−1.8	5.4	2.6	−0.7	−9.2	1.7	1.5	1.1
1979	4.0	−3.7	5.5	0.2	−2.6	3.9	0.9	5.3	N/C	−6.9	4.3	1.7	12.3
1980	5.8	−0.4	−10.2	4.1	4.7	2.7	6.5	0.6	2.5	1.6	10.2	−3.4	25.8
1981	−4.6	1.3	3.6	−2.3	−0.2	−1.0	−0.2	−6.2	−5.4	4.9	3.7	−3.0	−9.7
1982	−1.8	−6.1	−1.0	4.0	−3.9	−2.0	−2.3	11.6	0.8	11.0	3.6	1.5	14.8
1983	3.3	1.9	3.3	7.5	−1.2	3.5	−3.3	1.1	1.0	−1.5	1.7	−0.9	17.3
1984	−0.9	−3.9	1.3	0.5	−5.9	1.7	−1.6	10.6	−0.3	−0.01	−1.5	2.2	1.4
1985	7.4	0.9	−0.3	−0.5	5.4	1.2	−0.5	−1.2	−3.5	4.3	6.5	4.5	26.3
1986	0.2	7.1	5.3	−1.4	5.0	1.4	−5.9	7.1	−8.5	5.5	2.1	−2.8	14.6
1987	13.2	3.7	2.6	−1.1	0.6	4.8	4.8	3.5	−2.4	−21.8	−8.5	7.3	2.0

continued

	Jan	Feb	Mar	Apr	May	Jun	Jul	Aug	Sep	Oct	Nov	Dec	Year
1988	4.0	4.2	−3.3	0.9	0.3	4.3	−0.5	−3.9	4.0	2.6	−1.9	1.5	12.4
1989	7.1	−2.9	2.1	5.0	3.5	−0.8	8.8	1.6	−0.7	−2.5	1.7	2.1	27.3
1990	−6.9	0.9	2.4	−2.7	9.2	−0.9	−0.5	−9.4	−5.1	−0.7	6.0	2.5	−6.6
1991	4.2	6.7	2.2	0.03	3.9	−4.8	4.5	2.0	−1.9	1.2	−4.4	11.2	26.3
1992	−2.0	1.0	−2.2	2.8	0.1	−1.7	3.9	−2.4	0.9	0.2	3.0	1.0	4.5
1993	0.7	1.0	1.9	−2.5	2.3	0.1	−0.5	3.4	−1.0	1.9	−1.3	1.0	7.1
1994	3.3	−3.0	−4.6	1.2	1.2	−2.7	3.1	3.8	−2.7	2.1	−4.0	1.2	−1.5
1995	2.4	3.6	2.7	2.8	3.6	2.1	3.2	−0.03	4.0	−0.5	4.1	1.7	34.1
1996	3.3	0.7	0.8	1.3	2.3	0.2	−4.6	1.9	5.4	2.6	7.3	−2.2	20.3
1997	6.1	0.6	−4.3	5.8	5.9	4.3	7.8	−5.7	5.3	−3.4	4.5	1.6	31.0
1998	1.0	7.0	5.0	0.9	−1.9	3.9	−1.2	−14.6	6.2	8.0	5.9	5.6	26.7
1999	4.1	−3.2	3.9	3.8	−2.5	5.4	−3.2	−0.6	−2.9	6.3	1.9	5.8	19.5
2000	−5.1	−2.0	9.7	−3.1	−2.2	2.4	−1.6	6.1	−5.3	−0.5	−8.0	0.4	−10.1
2001	3.5	−9.2	−6.4	7.7	0.5	−2.5	−1.1	−6.4	−8.2	1.8	7.5	0.8	−13.0
2002	−1.6	−2.1	3.7	−6.1	−0.9	−7.2	−7.9	0.5	−11.0	8.6	5.7	−6.0	−23.4
2003	−2.7	−1.7	1.0	8.0	5.1	1.1	1.6	1.8	−1.2	5.5	0.7	5.1	26.4
2004	1.7	1.2	−1.6	−1.7	1.2	1.8	−3.4	0.2	0.9	1.4	3.9	3.2	9.0
2005	−2.5	1.9	−1.9	−2.0	3.0	−0.01	3.6	−1.1	0.7	−1.8	3.5	−0.1	3.0
2006	2.5	0.05	1.1	1.2	−3.1	0.01	0.5	2.1	2.5	3.2	1.6	1.3	13.6
2007	1.4	−2.2	1.0	4.3	3.3	−1.8	−3.2	1.3	3.6	1.5	−4.4	−0.9	3.5
2008	−6.1	−3.5	−0.6	4.8	1.1	−8.6	−1.0	1.2	−9.1	−16.9	−7.5	0.8	−38.5
2009	−8.6	−11.0	8.5	9.4	5.3	0.02	7.4	3.4	3.6	−2.0	5.7	1.8	23.5
2010	−3.7	2.9	5.9	1.5	−8.2	−5.4	6.9	−4.7	8.8	3.7	−0.2	6.5	12.8
2011	2.3	3.2	−0.1	2.8	−1.4	−1.8	−2.1	−5.7	−7.2	10.8	−0.5	0.9	−0.003
2012	4.4	4.1	3.1	−0.7	−6.3	4.0	1.3	2.0	2.4	−2.0	0.3	0.7	13.4
2013	5.0	1.1	3.6	1.8	2.1	−1.5	4.9	−3.1	3.0	4.5	2.8	2.4	29.6
2014	−3.6	4.3	0.7	0.6	2.1	1.9	−1.5	3.8	−1.6	2.3	2.5	−0.4	11.4
2015	−3.1	5.5	−1.7	0.9	1.0	−2.1	2.0	−6.3	−2.6	8.3	0.1	−1.8	−0.7
2016	−5.1	−0.4	6.6	0.3	1.5	0.1	3.6	−0.1	−0.1	−1.9	3.4	1.8	9.5
2017	1.8	3.7	−0.04	0.9	1.2	0.5	1.9	0.1	1.9	2.2	2.8	1.0	19.4
2018	5.6	−3.9	−2.7	0.3	2.2	0.5	3.6	3.0	0.4	−6.9	1.8	−9.2	−6.2
2019	7.9	3.0	1.8	3.9	−6.6	6.9	1.3	−1.8	1.7	2.0	3.4	2.9	28.9
2020	−0.2	−8.4	−12.5	12.7	4.5	1.8	5.5	7.0	−3.9	−2.8	10.8	3.7	16.3
2021	−1.1	2.6	4.2	5.2	0.5								
TOTALS	76.8	0.1	74.2	121.8	16.3	7.6	80.4	2.2	−34.2	54.9	121.2	106.9	
AVG.	1.1	0.002	1.0	1.7	0.2	0.1	1.1	0.03	−0.5	0.8	1.7	1.5	
# Up	43	40	46	52	43	39	41	39	32	42	49	53	
# Down	29	32	26	20	29	32	30	32	38	29	22	18	

163

	Jan	Feb	Mar	Apr	May	Jun	Jul	Aug	Sep	Oct	Nov	Dec
1950	17.05	17.22	17.29	18.07	18.78	17.69	17.84	18.42	19.45	19.53	19.51	20.41
1951	21.66	21.80	21.40	22.43	21.52	20.96	22.40	23.28	23.26	22.94	22.88	23.77
1952	24.14	23.26	24.37	23.32	23.86	24.96	25.40	25.03	24.54	24.52	25.66	26.57
1953	26.38	25.90	25.29	24.62	24.54	24.14	24.75	23.32	23.35	24.54	24.76	24.81
1954	26.08	26.15	26.94	28.26	29.19	29.21	30.88	29.83	32.31	31.68	34.24	35.98
1955	36.63	36.76	36.58	37.96	37.91	41.03	43.52	43.18	43.67	42.34	45.51	45.48
1956	43.82	45.34	48.48	48.38	45.20	46.97	49.39	47.51	45.35	45.58	45.08	46.67
1957	44.72	43.26	44.11	45.74	47.43	47.37	47.91	45.22	42.42	41.06	41.72	39.99
1958	41.70	40.84	42.10	43.44	44.09	45.24	47.19	47.75	50.06	51.33	52.48	55.21
1959	55.42	55.41	55.44	57.59	58.68	58.47	60.51	59.60	56.88	57.52	58.28	59.89
1960	55.61	56.12	55.34	54.37	55.83	56.92	55.51	56.96	53.52	53.39	55.54	58.11
1961	61.78	63.44	65.06	65.31	66.56	64.64	66.76	68.07	66.73	68.62	71.32	71.55
1962	68.84	69.96	69.55	65.24	59.63	54.75	58.23	59.12	56.27	56.52	62.26	63.10
1963	66.20	64.29	66.57	69.80	70.80	69.37	69.13	72.50	71.70	74.01	73.23	75.02
1964	77.04	77.80	78.98	79.46	80.37	81.69	83.18	81.83	84.18	84.86	84.42	84.75
1965	87.56	87.43	86.16	89.11	88.42	84.12	85.25	87.17	89.96	92.42	91.61	92.43
1966	92.88	91.22	89.23	91.06	86.13	84.74	83.60	77.10	76.56	80.20	80.45	80.33
1967	86.61	86.78	90.20	94.01	89.08	90.64	94.75	93.64	96.71	93.90	94.00	96.47
1968	92.24	89.36	90.20	97.59	98.68	99.58	97.74	98.86	102.67	103.41	108.37	103.86
1969	103.01	98.13	101.51	103.69	103.46	97.71	91.83	95.51	93.12	97.24	93.81	92.06
1970	85.02	89.50	89.63	81.52	76.55	72.72	78.05	81.52	84.21	83.25	87.20	92.15
1971	95.88	96.75	100.31	103.95	99.63	99.70	95.58	99.03	98.34	94.23	93.99	102.09
1972	103.94	106.57	107.20	107.67	109.53	107.14	107.39	111.09	110.55	111.58	116.67	118.05
1973	116.03	111.68	111.52	106.97	104.95	104.26	108.22	104.25	108.43	108.29	95.96	97.55
1974	96.57	96.22	93.98	90.31	87.28	86.00	79.31	72.15	63.54	73.90	69.97	68.56
1975	76.98	81.59	83.36	87.30	91.15	95.19	88.75	86.88	83.87	89.04	91.24	90.19
1976	100.86	99.71	102.77	101.64	100.18	104.28	103.44	102.91	105.24	102.90	102.10	107.46
1977	102.03	99.82	98.42	98.44	96.12	100.48	98.85	96.77	96.53	92.34	94.83	95.10
1978	89.25	87.04	89.21	96.83	97.24	95.53	100.68	103.29	102.54	93.15	94.70	96.11
1979	99.93	96.28	101.59	101.76	99.08	102.91	103.81	109.32	109.32	101.82	106.16	107.94
1980	114.16	113.66	102.09	106.29	111.24	114.24	121.67	122.38	125.46	127.47	140.52	135.76
1981	129.55	131.27	136.00	132.81	132.59	131.21	130.92	122.79	116.18	121.89	126.35	122.55
1982	120.40	113.11	111.96	116.44	111.88	109.61	107.09	119.51	120.42	133.71	138.54	140.64
1983	145.30	148.06	152.96	164.42	162.39	168.11	162.56	164.40	166.07	163.55	166.40	164.93
1984	163.41	157.06	159.18	160.05	150.55	153.18	150.66	166.68	166.10	166.09	163.58	167.24
1985	179.63	181.18	180.66	179.83	189.55	191.85	190.92	188.63	182.08	189.82	202.17	211.28

continued

164

	Jan	Feb	Mar	Apr	May	Jun	Jul	Aug	Sep	Oct	Nov	Dec
1986	211.78	226.92	238.90	235.52	247.35	250.84	236.12	252.93	231.32	243.98	249.22	242.17
1987	274.08	284.20	291.70	288.36	290.10	304.00	318.66	329.80	321.83	251.79	230.30	247.08
1988	257.07	267.82	258.89	261.33	262.16	273.50	272.02	261.52	271.91	278.97	273.70	277.72
1989	297.47	288.86	294.87	309.64	320.52	317.98	346.08	351.45	349.15	340.36	345.99	353.40
1990	329.08	331.89	339.94	330.80	361.23	358.02	356.15	322.56	306.05	304.00	322.22	330.22
1991	343.93	367.07	375.22	375.35	389.83	371.16	387.81	395.43	387.86	392.46	375.22	417.09
1992	408.79	412.70	403.69	414.95	415.35	408.14	424.21	414.03	417.80	418.68	431.35	435.71
1993	438.78	443.38	451.67	440.19	450.19	450.53	448.13	463.56	458.93	467.83	461.79	466.45
1994	481.61	467.14	445.77	450.91	456.50	444.27	458.26	475.49	462.69	472.35	453.69	459.27
1995	470.42	487.39	500.71	514.71	533.40	544.75	562.06	561.88	584.41	581.50	605.37	615.93
1996	636.02	640.43	645.50	654.17	669.12	670.63	639.95	651.99	687.31	705.27	757.02	740.74
1997	786.16	790.82	757.12	801.34	848.28	885.14	954.29	899.47	947.28	914.62	955.40	970.43
1998	980.28	1049.34	1101.75	1111.75	1090.82	1133.84	1120.67	957.28	1017.01	1098.67	1163.63	1229.23
1999	1279.64	1238.33	1286.37	1335.18	1301.84	1372.71	1328.72	1320.41	1282.71	1362.93	1388.91	1469.25
2000	1394.46	1366.42	1498.58	1452.43	1420.60	1454.60	1430.83	1517.68	1436.51	1429.40	1314.95	1320.28
2001	1366.01	1239.94	1160.33	1249.46	1255.82	1224.42	1211.23	1133.58	1040.94	1059.78	1139.45	1148.08
2002	1130.20	1106.73	1147.39	1076.92	1067.14	989.82	911.62	916.07	815.28	885.76	936.31	879.82
2003	855.70	841.15	849.18	916.92	963.59	974.50	990.31	1008.01	995.97	1050.71	1058.20	1111.92
2004	1131.13	1144.94	1126.21	1107.30	1120.68	1140.84	1101.72	1104.24	1114.58	1130.20	1173.82	1211.92
2005	1181.27	1203.60	1180.59	1156.85	1191.50	1191.33	1234.18	1220.33	1228.81	1207.01	1249.48	1248.29
2006	1280.08	1280.66	1294.83	1310.61	1270.09	1270.20	1276.66	1303.82	1335.85	1377.94	1400.63	1418.30
2007	1438.24	1406.82	1420.86	1482.37	1530.62	1503.35	1455.27	1473.99	1526.75	1549.38	1481.14	1468.36
2008	1378.55	1330.63	1322.70	1385.59	1400.38	1280.00	1267.38	1282.83	1166.36	968.75	896.24	903.25
2009	825.88	735.09	797.87	872.81	919.14	919.32	987.48	1020.62	1057.08	1036.19	1095.63	1115.10
2010	1073.87	1104.49	1169.43	1186.69	1089.41	1030.71	1101.60	1049.33	1141.20	1183.26	1180.55	1257.64
2011	1286.12	1327.22	1325.83	1363.61	1345.20	1320.64	1292.28	1218.89	1131.42	1253.30	1246.96	1257.60
2012	1312.41	1365.68	1408.47	1397.91	1310.33	1362.16	1379.32	1406.58	1440.67	1412.16	1416.18	1426.19
2013	1498.11	1514.68	1569.19	1597.57	1630.74	1606.28	1685.73	1632.97	1681.55	1756.54	1805.81	1848.36
2014	1782.59	1859.45	1872.34	1883.95	1923.57	1960.23	1930.67	2003.37	1972.29	2018.05	2067.56	2058.90
2015	1994.99	2104.50	2067.89	2085.51	2107.39	2063.11	2103.84	1972.18	1920.03	2079.36	2080.41	2043.94
2016	1940.24	1932.23	2059.74	2065.30	2096.96	2098.86	2173.60	2170.95	2168.27	2126.15	2198.81	2238.83
2017	2278.87	2363.64	2362.72	2384.20	2411.80	2423.41	2470.30	2471.65	2519.36	2575.26	2647.58	2673.61
2018	2823.81	2713.83	2640.87	2648.05	2705.27	2718.37	2816.29	2901.52	2913.98	2711.74	2760.16	2506.85
2019	2704.10	2784.49	2834.40	2945.83	2752.06	2941.76	2980.38	2926.46	2976.74	3037.56	3140.98	3230.78
2020	3225.52	2954.22	2584.59	2912.43	3044.31	3100.29	3271.12	3500.31	3363.00	3269.96	3621.63	3756.07
2021	3714.24	3811.15	3972.89	4181.17	4204.11							

	Jan	Feb	Mar	Apr	May	Jun	Jul	Aug	Sep	Oct	Nov	Dec	Year
1971	10.2	2.6	4.6	6.0	-3.6	-0.4	-2.3	3.0	0.6	-3.6	-1.1	9.8	27.4
1972	4.2	5.5	2.2	2.5	0.9	-1.8	-1.8	1.7	-0.3	0.5	2.1	0.6	17.2
1973	-4.0	-6.2	-2.4	-8.2	-4.8	-1.6	7.6	-3.5	6.0	-0.9	-15.1	-1.4	-31.1
1974	3.0	-0.6	-2.2	-5.9	-7.7	-5.3	-7.9	-10.9	-10.7	17.2	-3.5	-5.0	-35.1
1975	16.6	4.6	3.6	3.8	5.8	4.7	-4.4	-5.0	-5.9	3.6	2.4	-1.5	29.8
1976	12.1	3.7	0.4	-0.6	-2.3	2.6	1.1	-1.7	1.7	-1.0	0.9	7.4	26.1
1977	-2.4	-1.0	-0.5	1.4	0.1	4.3	0.9	-0.5	0.7	-3.3	5.8	1.8	7.3
1978	-4.0	0.6	4.7	8.5	4.4	0.05	5.0	6.9	-1.6	-16.4	3.2	2.9	12.3
1979	6.6	-2.6	7.5	1.6	-1.8	5.1	2.3	6.4	-0.3	-9.6	6.4	4.8	28.1
1980	7.0	-2.3	-17.1	6.9	7.5	4.9	8.9	5.7	3.4	2.7	8.0	-2.8	33.9
1981	-2.2	0.1	6.1	3.1	3.1	-3.5	-1.9	-7.5	-8.0	8.4	3.1	-2.7	-3.2
1982	-3.8	-4.8	-2.1	5.2	-3.3	-4.1	-2.3	6.2	5.6	13.3	9.3	0.04	18.7
1983	6.9	5.0	3.9	8.2	5.3	3.2	-4.6	-3.8	1.4	-7.4	4.1	-2.5	19.9
1984	-3.7	-5.9	-0.7	-1.3	-5.9	2.9	-4.2	10.9	-1.8	-1.2	-1.8	2.0	-11.2
1985	12.7	2.0	-1.7	0.5	3.6	1.9	1.7	-1.2	-5.8	4.4	7.3	3.5	31.4
1986	3.3	7.1	4.2	2.3	4.4	1.3	-8.4	3.1	-8.4	2.9	-0.3	-2.8	7.5
1987	12.2	8.4	1.2	-2.8	-0.3	2.0	2.4	4.6	-2.3	-27.2	-5.6	8.3	-5.4
1988	4.3	6.5	2.1	1.2	-2.3	6.6	-1.9	-2.8	3.0	-1.4	-2.9	2.7	15.4
1989	5.2	-0.4	1.8	5.1	4.4	-2.4	4.3	3.4	0.8	-3.7	0.1	-0.3	19.3
1990	-8.6	2.4	2.3	-3.6	9.3	0.7	-5.2	-13.0	-9.6	-4.3	8.9	4.1	-178
1991	10.8	9.4	6.5	0.5	4.4	-6.0	5.5	4.7	0.2	3.1	-3.5	11.9	56.8
1992	5.8	2.1	-4.7	-4.2	1.1	-3.7	3.1	-3.0	3.6	3.8	7.9	3.7	15.5
1993	2.9	-3.7	2.9	-4.2	5.9	0.5	0.1	5.4	2.7	2.2	-3.2	3.0	14.7
1994	3.0	-1.0	-6.2	-1.3	0.2	-4.0	2.3	6.0	-0.2	1.7	-3.5	0.2	-3.2
1995	0.4	5.1	3.0	3.3	2.4	8.0	7.3	1.9	2.3	-0.7	2.2	-0.7	39.9
1996	0.7	3.8	0.1	8.1	4.4	-4.7	-8.8	5.6	7.5	-0.4	5.8	-0.1	22.7
1997	6.9	-5.1	-6.7	3.2	11.1	3.0	10.5	-0.4	6.2	-5.5	0.4	-1.9	21.6
1998	3.1	9.3	3.7	1.8	-4.8	6.5	-1.2	-19.9	13.0	4.6	10.1	12.5	39.6
1999	14.3	-8.7	7.6	3.3	-2.8	8.7	-1.8	3.8	0.2	8.0	12.5	22.0	85.6
2000	-3.2	19.2	-2.6	-15.6	-11.9	16.6	-5.0	11.7	-12.7	-8.3	-22.9	-4.9	-39.3
2001	12.2	-22.4	-14.5	15.0	-0.3	2.4	-6.2	-10.9	-17.0	12.8	14.2	1.0	-21.1
2002	-0.8	-10.5	6.6	-8.5	-4.3	-9.4	-9.2	-1.0	-10.9	13.5	11.2	-9.7	-31.5
2003	-1.1	1.3	0.3	9.2	9.0	1.7	6.9	4.3	-1.3	8.1	1.5	2.2	50.0
2004	3.1	-1.8	-1.8	-3.7	3.5	3.1	-7.8	-2.6	3.2	4.1	6.2	3.7	8.6
2005	-5.2	-0.5	-2.6	-3.9	7.6	-0.5	6.2	-1.5	-0.02	-1.5	5.3	-1.2	1.4
2006	4.6	-1.1	2.6	-0.7	-6.2	-0.3	-3.7	4.4	3.4	4.8	2.7	-0.7	9.5
2007	2.0	-1.9	0.2	4.3	3.1	-0.05	-2.2	2.0	4.0	5.8	-6.9	-0.3	9.8
2008	-9.9	-5.0	0.3	5.9	4.6	-9.1	1.4	1.8	-11.6	-17.7	-10.8	2.7	-40.5
2009	-6.4	-6.7	10.9	12.3	3.3	3.4	7.8	1.5	5.6	-3.6	4.9	5.8	43.9
2010	-5.4	4.2	7.1	2.6	-8.3	-6.5	6.9	-6.2	12.0	5.9	-0.4	6.2	16.9
2011	1.8	3.0	-0.04	3.3	-1.3	-2.2	-0.6	-6.4	-6.4	11.1	-2.4	-0.6	-1.8
2012	8.0	5.4	4.2	-1.5	-7.2	3.8	0.2	4.3	1.6	-4.5	1.1	0.3	15.9
2013	4.1	0.6	3.4	1.9	3.8	-1.5	6.6	-1.0	5.1	3.9	3.6	2.9	38.3
2014	-1.7	5.0	-2.5	-2.0	3.1	3.9	-0.9	4.8	-1.9	3.1	3.5	-1.2	13.4
2015	-2.1	7.1	-1.3	0.8	2.6	-1.6	2.8	-6.9	-3.3	9.4	1.1	-2.0	5.7
2016	-7.9	-1.2	6.8	-1.9	3.6	-2.1	6.6	1.0	1.9	-2.3	2.6	1.1	7.5
2017	4.3	3.8	1.5	2.3	2.5	-0.9	3.4	1.3	1.0	3.6	2.2	0.4	28.2
2018	7.4	-1.9	-2.9	0.04	5.3	0.9	2.2	5.7	-0.8	-9.2	0.3	-9.5	-3.9
2019	9.7	3.4	2.6	4.7	-7.9	7.4	2.1	-2.6	0.5	3.7	4.5	3.5	35.2
2020	2.0	-6.4	-10.1	15.4	6.8	6.0	6.8	9.6	-5.2	-2.3	11.8	5.7	43.6
2021	1.4	0.9	0.4	5.4	-1.5								
TOTALS	140.4	30.4	32.7	89.7	48.6	44.5	30.6	19.4	-28.8	30.2	93.3	84.9	
AVG.	2.8	0.6	0.6	1.8	1.0	0.9	0.6	0.4	-0.6	0.6	1.9	1.7	
# Up	34	28	32	34	31	28	28	28	27	27	35	30	
# Down	17	23	19	17	20	22	22	22	23	23	15	20	

Based on NASDAQ composite, prior to Feb. 5, 1971, based on National Quotation Bureau indices

NASDAQ COMPOSITE MONTHLY CLOSING PRICES SINCE 1971

	Jan	Feb	Mar	Apr	May	Jun	Jul	Aug	Sep	Oct	Nov	Dec
1971	98.77	101.34	105.97	112.30	108.25	107.80	105.27	108.42	109.03	105.10	103.97	114.12
1972	118.87	125.38	128.14	131.33	132.53	130.08	127.75	129.95	129.61	130.24	132.96	133.73
1973	128.40	120.41	117.46	107.85	102.64	100.98	108.64	104.87	111.20	110.17	93.51	92.19
1974	94.93	94.35	92.27	86.86	80.20	75.96	69.99	62.37	55.67	65.23	62.95	59.82
1975	69.78	73.00	75.66	78.54	83.10	87.02	83.19	79.01	74.33	76.99	78.80	77.62
1976	87.05	90.26	90.62	90.08	88.04	90.32	91.29	89.70	91.26	90.35	91.12	97.88
1977	95.54	94.57	94.13	95.48	95.59	99.73	100.65	100.10	100.85	97.52	103.15	105.05
1978	100.84	101.47	106.20	115.18	120.24	120.30	126.32	135.01	132.89	111.12	114.69	117.98
1979	125.82	122.56	131.76	133.82	131.42	138.13	141.33	150.44	149.98	135.53	144.26	151.14
1980	161.75	158.03	131.00	139.99	150.45	157.78	171.81	181.52	187.76	192.78	208.15	202.34
1981	197.81	198.01	210.18	216.74	223.47	215.75	211.63	195.75	180.03	195.24	201.37	195.84
1982	188.39	179.43	175.65	184.70	178.54	171.30	167.35	177.71	187.65	212.63	232.31	232.41
1983	248.35	260.67	270.80	293.06	308.73	318.70	303.96	292.42	296.65	274.55	285.67	278.60
1984	268.43	252.57	250.78	247.44	232.82	239.65	229.70	254.64	249.94	247.03	242.53	247.35
1985	278.70	284.17	279.20	280.56	290.80	296.20	301.29	297.71	280.33	292.54	313.95	324.93
1986	335.77	359.53	374.72	383.24	400.16	405.51	371.37	382.86	350.67	360.77	359.57	349.33
1987	392.06	424.97	430.05	417.81	416.54	424.67	434.93	454.97	444.29	323.30	305.16	330.47
1988	344.66	366.95	374.64	379.23	370.34	394.66	387.33	376.55	387.71	382.46	371.45	381.38
1989	401.30	399.71	406.73	427.55	446.17	435.29	453.84	469.33	472.92	455.63	456.09	454.82
1990	415.81	425.83	435.54	420.07	458.97	462.29	438.24	381.21	344.51	329.84	359.06	373.84
1991	414.20	453.05	482.30	484.72	506.11	475.92	502.04	525.68	526.88	542.98	523.90	586.34
1992	620.21	633.47	603.77	578.68	585.31	563.60	580.83	563.12	583.27	605.17	652.73	676.95
1993	696.34	670.77	690.13	661.42	700.53	703.95	704.70	742.84	762.78	779.26	754.39	776.80
1994	800.47	792.50	743.46	733.84	735.19	705.96	722.16	765.62	764.29	777.49	750.32	751.96
1995	755.20	793.73	817.21	843.98	864.58	933.45	1001.21	1020.11	1043.54	1036.06	1059.20	1052.13
1996	1059.79	1100.05	1101.40	1190.52	1243.43	1185.02	1080.59	1141.50	1226.92	1221.51	1292.61	1291.03
1997	1379.85	1309.00	1221.70	1260.76	1400.32	1442.07	1593.81	1587.32	1685.69	1593.61	1600.55	1570.35
1998	1619.36	1770.51	1835.68	1868.41	1778.87	1894.74	1872.39	1499.25	1693.84	1771.39	1949.54	2192.69
1999	2505.89	2288.03	2461.40	2542.85	2470.52	2686.12	2638.49	2739.35	2746.16	2966.43	3336.16	4069.31
2000	3940.35	4696.69	4572.83	3860.66	3400.91	3966.11	3766.99	4206.35	3672.82	3369.63	2597.93	2470.52
2001	2772.73	2151.83	1840.26	2116.24	2110.49	2160.54	2027.13	1805.43	1498.80	1690.20	1930.58	1950.40
2002	1934.03	1731.49	1845.35	1688.23	1615.73	1463.21	1328.26	1314.85	1172.06	1329.75	1478.78	1335.51
2003	1320.91	1337.52	1341.17	1464.31	1595.91	1622.80	1735.02	1810.45	1786.94	1932.21	1960.26	2003.37
2004	2066.15	2029.82	1994.22	1920.15	1986.74	2047.79	1887.36	1838.10	1896.84	1974.99	2096.81	2175.44
2005	2062.41	2051.72	1999.23	1921.65	2068.22	2056.96	2184.83	2152.09	2151.69	2120.30	2232.82	2205.32
2006	2305.82	2281.39	2339.79	2322.57	2178.88	2172.09	2091.47	2183.75	2258.43	2366.71	2431.77	2415.29
2007	2463.93	2416.15	2421.64	2525.09	2604.52	2603.23	2545.57	2596.36	2701.50	2859.12	2660.96	2652.28
2008	2389.86	2271.48	2279.10	2412.80	2522.66	2292.98	2325.55	2367.52	2091.88	1720.95	1535.57	1577.03
2009	1476.42	1377.84	1528.59	1717.30	1774.33	1835.04	1978.50	2009.06	2122.42	2045.11	2144.60	2269.15
2010	2147.35	2238.26	2397.96	2461.19	2257.04	2109.24	2254.70	2114.03	2368.62	2507.41	2498.23	2652.87
2011	2700.08	2782.27	2781.07	2873.54	2835.30	2773.52	2756.38	2579.46	2415.40	2684.41	2620.34	2605.15
2012	2813.84	2966.89	3091.57	3046.36	2827.34	2935.05	2939.52	3066.96	3116.23	2977.23	3010.24	3019.51
2013	3142.13	3160.19	3267.52	3328.79	3455.91	3403.25	3626.37	3589.87	3771.48	3919.71	4059.89	4176.59
2014	4103.88	4308.12	4198.99	4114.56	4242.62	4408.18	4369.77	4580.27	4493.39	4630.74	4791.63	4736.05
2015	4635.24	4963.53	4900.88	4941.42	5070.03	4986.87	5128.28	4776.51	4620.16	5053.75	5108.67	5007.41
2016	4613.95	4557.95	4869.85	4775.36	4948.05	4842.67	5162.13	5213.22	5312.00	5189.13	5323.68	5383.12
2017	5614.79	5825.44	5911.74	6047.61	6198.52	6140.42	6348.12	6428.66	6495.96	6727.67	6873.97	6903.39
2018	7411.48	7273.01	7063.44	7066.27	7442.12	7510.30	7671.79	8109.54	8046.35	7305.90	7330.54	6635.28
2019	7281.74	7532.53	7729.32	8095.39	7453.15	8006.24	8175.42	7962.88	7999.34	8292.36	8665.47	8972.60
2020	9150.94	8567.37	7700.10	8889.55	9489.87	10058.77	10745.27	11775.46	11167.51	10911.59	12198.74	12888.28
2021	13070.69	13192.35	13246.87	13962.68	13748.74							

Based on NASDAQ composite, prior to Feb. 5, 1971, based on National Quotation Bureau indices

RUSSELL 1000 INDEX MONTHLY PERCENT CHANGES SINCE 1979

	Jan	Feb	Mar	Apr	May	Jun	Jul	Aug	Sep	Oct	Nov	Dec	Year
1979	4.2	-3.5	6.0	0.3	-2.2	4.3	1.1	5.6	0.02	-7.1	5.1	2.1	16.1
1980	5.9	-0.5	-11.5	4.6	5.0	3.2	6.4	1.1	2.6	1.8	10.1	-3.9	25.6
1981	-4.6	1.0	3.8	-1.9	0.2	-1.2	-0.1	-6.2	-6.4	5.4	4.0	-3.3	-9.7
1982	-2.7	-5.9	-1.3	3.9	-3.6	-2.6	-2.3	11.3	1.2	11.3	4.0	1.3	13.7
1983	3.2	2.1	3.2	7.1	-0.2	3.7	-3.2	0.5	1.3	-2.4	2.0	-1.2	17.0
1984	-1.9	-4.4	1.1	0.3	-5.9	2.1	-1.8	10.8	-0.2	-0.1	-1.4	2.2	-0.1
1985	7.8	1.1	-0.4	-0.3	5.4	1.6	-0.8	-1.0	-3.9	4.5	6.5	4.1	26.7
1986	0.9	7.2	5.1	-1.3	5.0	1.4	-5.9	6.8	-8.5	5.1	1.4	-3.0	13.6
1987	12.7	4.0	1.9	-1.8	0.4	4.5	4.2	3.8	-2.4	-21.9	-8.0	7.2	0.02
1988	4.3	4.4	-2.9	0.7	0.2	4.8	-0.9	-3.3	3.9	2.0	-2.0	1.7	13.1
1989	6.8	-2.5	2.0	4.9	3.8	-0.8	8.2	1.7	-0.5	-2.8	1.5	1.8	25.9
1990	-7.4	1.2	2.2	-2.8	8.9	-0.7	-1.1	-9.6	-5.3	-0.8	6.4	2.7	-7.5
1991	4.5	6.9	2.5	-0.1	3.8	-4.7	4.6	2.2	-1.5	1.4	-4.1	11.2	28.8
1992	-1.4	0.9	-2.4	2.3	0.3	-1.9	4.1	-2.5	1.0	0.7	3.5	1.4	5.9
1993	0.7	0.6	2.2	-2.8	2.4	0.4	-0.4	3.5	-0.5	1.2	-1.7	1.6	7.3
1994	2.9	-2.9	-4.5	1.1	1.0	-2.9	3.1	3.9	-2.6	1.7	-3.9	1.2	-2.4
1995	2.4	3.8	2.3	2.5	3.5	2.4	3.7	0.5	3.9	-0.6	4.2	1.4	34.4
1996	3.1	1.1	0.7	1.4	2.1	-0.1	-4.9	2.5	5.5	2.1	7.1	-1.8	19.7
1997	5.8	0.2	-4.6	5.3	6.2	4.0	8.0	-4.9	5.4	-3.4	4.2	1.9	30.5
1998	0.6	7.0	4.9	0.9	-2.3	3.6	-1.3	-15.1	6.5	7.8	6.1	6.2	25.1
1999	3.5	-3.3	3.7	4.2	-2.3	5.1	-3.2	-1.0	-2.8	6.5	2.5	6.0	19.5
2000	-4.2	-0.4	8.9	-3.3	-2.7	2.5	-1.8	7.4	-4.8	-1.2	-9.3	1.1	-8.8
2001	3.2	-9.5	-6.7	8.0	0.5	-2.4	-1.4	-6.2	-8.6	2.0	7.5	0.9	-13.6
2002	-1.4	-2.1	4.0	-5.8	-1.0	-7.5	-7.5	0.3	-10.9	8.1	5.7	-5.8	-22.9
2003	-2.5	-1.7	0.9	7.9	5.5	1.2	1.8	1.9	-1.2	5.7	1.0	4.6	27.5
2004	1.8	1.2	-1.5	-1.9	1.3	1.7	-3.6	0.3	1.1	1.5	4.1	3.5	9.5
2005	-2.6	2.0	-1.7	-2.0	3.4	0.3	3.8	-1.1	0.8	-1.9	3.5	0.01	4.4
2006	2.7	0.01	1.3	1.1	-3.2	0.003	0.1	2.2	2.3	3.3	1.9	1.1	13.3
2007	1.8	-1.9	0.9	4.1	3.4	-2.0	-3.2	1.2	3.7	1.6	-4.5	-0.8	3.9
2008	-6.1	-3.3	-0.8	5.0	1.6	-8.5	-1.3	1.2	-9.7	-17.6	-7.9	1.3	-39.0
2009	-8.3	-10.7	8.5	10.0	5.3	0.1	7.5	3.4	3.9	-2.3	5.6	2.3	25.5
2010	-3.7	3.1	6.0	1.8	-8.1	-5.7	6.8	-4.7	9.0	3.8	0.1	6.5	13.9
2011	2.3	3.3	0.1	2.9	-1.3	-1.9	-2.3	-6.0	-7.6	11.1	-0.5	0.7	-0.5
2012	4.8	4.1	3.0	-0.7	-6.4	3.7	1.1	2.2	2.4	-1.8	0.5	0.8	13.9
2013	5.3	1.1	3.7	1.7	2.0	-1.5	5.2	-3.0	3.3	4.3	2.6	2.5	30.4
2014	-3.3	4.5	0.5	0.4	2.1	2.1	-1.7	3.9	-1.9	2.3	2.4	-0.4	11.1
2015	-2.8	5.5	-1.4	0.6	1.1	-2.0	1.8	-6.2	-2.9	8.0	0.1	-2.0	-1.1
2016	-5.5	-0.3	6.8	0.4	1.5	0.1	3.7	-0.1	-0.1	-2.1	3.7	1.7	9.7
2017	1.9	3.6	-0.1	0.9	1.0	0.5	1.9	0.1	2.0	2.2	2.8	1.0	19.3
2018	5.4	-3.9	-2.4	0.2	2.3	0.5	3.3	3.2	0.2	-7.2	1.8	-9.3	-6.6
2019	8.2	3.2	1.6	3.9	-6.6	6.9	1.4	-2.0	1.6	2.0	3.6	2.7	28.9
2020	-0.01	-8.3	-13.4	13.1	5.1	2.1	5.7	7.2	-3.8	-2.5	11.6	4.1	18.9
2021	-0.9	2.8	3.7	5.3	0.3								
TOTALS	47.4	10.8	35.9	82.1	38.8	16.4	38.8	15.8	-24.5	31.7	83.8	57.3	
AVG.	1.1	0.3	0.8	1.9	0.9	0.4	0.9	0.4	-0.6	0.8	2.0	1.4	
# Up	26	26	28	31	30	26	22	26	21	26	32	32	
# Down	17	17	15	12	13	16	20	16	21	16	10	10	

	Jan	Feb	Mar	Apr	May	Jun	Jul	Aug	Sep	Oct	Nov	Dec
1979	53.76	51.88	54.97	55.15	53.92	56.25	56.86	60.04	60.05	55.78	58.65	59.87
1980	63.40	63.07	55.79	58.38	61.31	63.27	67.30	68.05	69.84	71.08	78.26	75.20
1981	71.75	72.49	75.21	73.77	73.90	73.01	72.92	68.42	64.06	67.54	70.23	67.93
1982	66.12	62.21	61.43	63.85	61.53	59.92	58.54	65.14	65.89	73.34	76.28	77.24
1983	79.75	81.45	84.06	90.04	89.89	93.18	90.18	90.65	91.85	89.69	91.50	90.38
1984	88.69	84.76	85.73	86.00	80.94	82.61	81.13	89.87	89.67	89.62	88.36	90.31
1985	97.31	98.38	98.03	97.72	103.02	104.65	103.78	102.76	98.75	103.16	109.91	114.39
1986	115.39	123.71	130.07	128.44	134.82	136.75	128.74	137.43	125.70	132.11	133.97	130.00
1987	146.48	152.29	155.20	152.39	152.94	159.84	166.57	172.95	168.83	131.89	121.28	130.02
1988	135.55	141.54	137.45	138.37	138.66	145.31	143.99	139.26	144.68	147.55	144.59	146.99
1989	156.93	152.98	155.99	163.63	169.85	168.49	182.27	185.33	184.40	179.17	181.85	185.11
1990	171.44	173.43	177.28	172.32	187.66	186.29	184.32	166.69	157.83	156.62	166.69	171.22
1991	179.00	191.34	196.15	195.94	203.32	193.78	202.67	207.18	204.02	206.96	198.46	220.61
1992	217.52	219.50	214.29	219.13	219.71	215.60	224.37	218.86	221.15	222.65	230.44	233.59
1993	235.25	236.67	241.80	235.13	240.80	241.78	240.78	249.20	247.95	250.97	246.70	250.71
1994	258.08	250.52	239.19	241.71	244.13	237.11	244.44	254.04	247.49	251.62	241.82	244.65
1995	250.52	260.08	266.11	272.81	282.48	289.29	299.98	301.40	313.28	311.37	324.36	328.89
1996	338.97	342.56	345.01	349.84	357.35	357.10	339.44	347.79	366.77	374.38	401.05	393.75
1997	416.77	417.46	398.19	419.15	445.06	462.95	499.89	475.33	500.78	483.86	504.25	513.79
1998	517.02	553.14	580.31	585.46	572.16	592.57	584.97	496.66	529.11	570.63	605.31	642.87
1999	665.64	643.67	667.49	695.25	679.10	713.61	690.51	683.27	663.83	707.19	724.66	767.97
2000	736.08	733.04	797.99	771.58	750.98	769.68	755.57	811.17	772.60	763.06	692.40	700.09
2001	722.55	654.25	610.36	658.90	662.39	646.64	637.43	597.67	546.46	557.29	599.32	604.94
2002	596.66	583.88	607.35	572.04	566.18	523.72	484.39	486.08	433.22	468.51	495.00	466.18
2003	454.30	446.37	450.35	486.09	512.92	518.94	528.53	538.40	532.15	562.51	568.32	594.56
2004	605.21	612.58	603.42	591.83	599.40	609.31	587.21	589.09	595.66	604.51	629.26	650.99
2005	633.99	646.93	635.78	623.32	644.28	645.92	670.26	663.13	668.53	656.09	679.35	679.42
2006	697.79	697.83	706.74	714.37	691.78	691.80	692.59	707.55	723.48	747.30	761.43	770.08
2007	784.11	768.92	775.97	807.82	835.14	818.17	792.11	801.22	830.59	844.20	806.44	799.82
2008	750.97	726.42	720.32	756.03	768.28	703.22	694.07	702.17	634.08	522.47	481.43	487.77
2009	447.32	399.61	433.67	476.84	501.95	502.27	539.88	558.21	579.97	566.50	598.41	612.01
2010	589.41	607.45	643.79	655.06	601.79	567.37	606.09	577.68	629.78	653.57	654.24	696.90
2011	712.97	736.24	737.07	758.45	748.75	734.48	717.77	674.79	623.45	692.41	688.77	693.36
2012	726.33	756.42	778.92	773.50	724.12	750.61	758.60	775.07	793.74	779.35	783.37	789.90
2013	831.74	840.97	872.11	886.89	904.44	890.67	937.16	909.28	939.50	979.68	1004.97	1030.36
2014	996.48	1041.36	1046.42	1050.20	1071.96	1094.59	1075.60	1117.71	1096.43	1121.98	1148.90	1144.37
2015	1111.85	1173.46	1156.95	1164.03	1176.67	1152.64	1173.55	1100.51	1068.46	1153.55	1154.66	1131.88
2016	1069.78	1066.58	1138.84	1143.76	1160.95	1161.57	1204.43	1203.05	1202.25	1177.22	1220.68	1241.66
2017	1265.35	1311.34	1310.06	1322.44	1336.18	1343.52	1368.57	1369.61	1396.90	1427.43	1467.42	1481.81
2018	1561.66	1501.23	1464.87	1468.28	1502.31	1509.96	1560.36	1610.70	1614.54	1498.65	1525.56	1384.26
2019	1498.36	1545.73	1570.23	1631.87	1524.42	1629.02	1652.40	1618.61	1644.18	1677.08	1736.85	1784.21
2020	1784.03	1635.21	1416.49	1601.82	1682.75	1717.47	1815.99	1946.15	1872.70	1825.67	2037.36	2120.87
2021	2101.36	2159.32	2238.17	2356.67	2364.53							

	Jan	Feb	Mar	Apr	May	Jun	Jul	Aug	Sep	Oct	Nov	Dec	Year
1979	9.0	−3.2	9.7	2.3	−1.8	5.3	2.9	7.8	−0.7	−11.3	8.1	6.6	38.0
1980	8.2	−2.1	−18.5	6.0	8.0	4.0	11.0	6.5	2.9	3.9	7.0	−3.7	33.8
1981	−0.6	0.3	7.7	2.5	3.0	−2.5	−2.6	−8.0	−8.6	8.2	2.8	−2.0	−1.5
1982	−3.7	−5.3	−1.5	5.1	−3.2	−4.0	−1.7	7.5	3.6	14.1	8.8	1.1	20.7
1983	7.5	6.0	2.5	7.2	7.0	4.4	−3.0	−4.0	1.6	−7.0	5.0	−2.1	26.3
1984	−1.8	−5.9	0.4	−0.7	−5.4	2.6	−5.0	11.5	−1.0	−2.0	−2.9	1.4	−9.6
1985	13.1	2.4	−2.2	−1.4	3.4	1.0	2.7	−1.2	−6.2	3.6	6.8	4.2	28.0
1986	1.5	7.0	4.7	1.4	3.3	−0.2	−9.5	3.0	−6.3	3.9	−0.5	−3.1	4.0
1987	11.5	8.2	2.4	−3.0	−0.5	2.3	2.8	2.9	−2.0	−30.8	−5.5	7.8	−10.8
1988	4.0	8.7	4.4	2.0	−2.5	7.0	−0.9	−2.8	2.3	−1.2	−3.6	3.8	22.4
1989	4.4	0.5	2.2	4.3	4.2	−2.4	4.2	2.1	0.01	−6.0	0.4	0.1	14.2
1990	−8.9	2.9	3.7	−3.4	6.8	0.1	−4.5	−13.6	−9.2	−6.2	7.3	3.7	−21.5
1991	9.1	11.0	6.9	−0.2	4.5	−6.0	3.1	3.7	0.6	2.7	−4.7	7.7	43.7
1992	8.0	2.9	−3.5	−3.7	1.2	−5.0	3.2	−3.1	2.2	3.1	7.5	3.4	16.4
1993	3.2	−2.5	3.1	−2.8	4.3	0.5	1.3	4.1	2.7	2.5	−3.4	3.3	17.0
1994	3.1	−0.4	−5.4	0.6	−1.3	−3.6	1.6	5.4	−0.5	−0.4	−4.2	2.5	−3.2
1995	−1.4	3.9	1.6	2.1	1.5	5.0	5.7	1.9	1.7	−4.6	4.2	2.4	26.2
1996	−0.2	3.0	1.8	5.3	3.9	−4.2	−8.8	5.7	3.7	−1.7	4.0	2.4	14.8
1997	1.9	−2.5	−4.9	0.1	11.0	4.1	4.6	2.2	7.2	−4.5	−0.8	1.7	20.5
1998	−1.6	7.4	4.1	0.5	−5.4	0.2	−8.2	−19.5	7.6	4.0	5.2	6.1	−3.4
1999	1.2	−8.2	1.4	8.8	1.4	4.3	−2.8	−3.8	−0.1	0.3	5.9	11.2	19.6
2000	−1.7	16.4	−6.7	−6.1	−5.9	8.6	−3.2	7.4	−3.1	−4.5	−10.4	8.4	−4.2
2001	5.1	−6.7	−5.0	7.7	2.3	3.3	−5.4	−3.3	−13.6	5.8	7.6	6.0	1.0
2002	−1.1	−2.8	7.9	0.8	−4.5	−5.1	−15.2	−0.4	−7.3	3.1	8.8	−5.7	−21.6
2003	−2.9	−3.1	1.1	9.4	10.6	1.7	6.2	4.5	−2.0	8.3	3.5	1.9	45.4
2004	4.3	0.8	0.8	−5.2	1.5	4.1	−6.8	−0.6	4.6	1.9	8.6	2.8	17.0
2005	−4.2	1.6	−3.0	−5.8	6.4	3.7	6.3	−1.9	0.2	−3.2	4.7	−0.6	3.3
2006	8.9	−0.3	4.7	−0.1	−5.7	0.5	−3.3	2.9	0.7	5.7	2.5	0.2	17.0
2007	1.6	−0.9	0.9	1.7	4.0	−1.6	−6.9	2.2	1.6	2.8	−7.3	−0.2	−2.7
2008	−6.9	−3.8	0.3	4.1	4.5	−7.8	3.6	3.5	−8.1	−20.9	−12.0	5.6	−34.8
2009	−11.2	−12.3	8.7	15.3	2.9	1.3	9.5	2.8	5.6	−6.9	3.0	7.9	25.2
2010	−3.7	4.4	8.0	5.6	−7.7	−7.9	6.8	−7.5	12.3	4.0	3.4	7.8	25.3
2011	−0.3	5.4	2.4	2.6	−2.0	−2.5	−3.7	−8.8	−11.4	15.0	−0.5	0.5	−5.5
2012	7.0	2.3	2.4	−1.6	−6.7	4.8	−1.4	3.2	3.1	−2.2	0.4	3.3	14.6
2013	6.2	1.0	4.4	−0.4	3.9	−0.7	6.9	−3.3	6.2	2.5	3.9	1.8	37.0
2014	−2.8	4.6	−0.8	−3.9	0.7	5.2	−6.1	4.8	−6.2	6.5	−0.02	2.7	3.5
2015	−3.3	5.8	1.6	−2.6	2.2	0.6	−1.2	−6.4	−5.1	5.6	3.1	−5.2	−5.7
2016	−8.8	−0.1	7.8	1.5	2.1	−0.2	5.9	1.6	0.9	−4.8	11.0	2.6	19.5
2017	0.3	1.8	−0.1	1.0	−2.2	3.3	0.7	−1.4	6.1	0.8	2.8	−0.6	13.1
2018	2.6	−4.0	1.1	0.8	5.9	0.6	1.7	4.2	−2.5	−10.9	1.4	−12.0	−12.2
2019	11.2	5.1	−2.3	3.3	−7.9	6.9	0.5	−5.1	1.9	2.6	4.0	2.7	23.7
2020	−3.3	−8.5	−21.9	13.7	6.4	3.4	2.7	5.5	−3.5	2.0	18.3	8.5	18.4
2021	5.0	6.1	0.9	2.1	0.1								
TOTALS	69.5	46.9	33.8	76.9	54.3	35.1	−6.3	12.2	−18.1	−16.2	104.2	96.9	
AVG.	1.6	1.1	0.8	1.8	1.3	0.8	−0.2	0.3	−0.4	−0.4	2.5	2.3	
# Up	24	25	30	28	28	27	22	24	23	24	29	32	
# Down	19	18	13	15	15	15	20	18	19	18	13	10	

RUSSELL 2000 INDEX MONTHLY CLOSING PRICES SINCE 1979

	Jan	Feb	Mar	Apr	May	Jun	Jul	Aug	Sep	Oct	Nov	Dec
1979	44.18	42.78	46.94	48.00	47.13	49.62	51.08	55.05	54.68	48.51	52.43	55.91
1980	60.50	59.22	48.27	51.18	55.26	57.47	63.81	67.97	69.94	72.64	77.70	74.80
1981	74.33	74.52	80.25	82.25	84.72	82.56	80.41	73.94	67.55	73.06	75.14	73.67
1982	70.96	67.21	66.21	69.59	67.39	64.67	63.59	68.38	70.84	80.86	87.96	88.90
1983	95.53	101.23	103.77	111.20	118.94	124.17	120.43	115.60	117.43	109.17	114.66	112.27
1984	110.21	103.72	104.10	103.34	97.75	100.30	95.25	106.21	105.17	103.07	100.11	101.49
1985	114.77	117.54	114.92	113.35	117.26	118.38	121.56	120.10	112.65	116.73	124.62	129.87
1986	131.78	141.00	147.63	149.66	154.61	154.23	139.65	143.83	134.73	139.95	139.26	135.00
1987	150.48	162.84	166.79	161.82	161.02	164.75	169.42	174.25	170.81	118.26	111.70	120.42
1988	125.24	136.10	142.15	145.01	141.37	151.30	149.89	145.74	149.08	147.25	142.01	147.37
1989	153.84	154.56	157.89	164.68	171.53	167.42	174.50	178.20	178.21	167.47	168.17	168.30
1990	153.27	157.72	163.63	158.09	168.91	169.04	161.51	139.52	126.70	118.83	127.50	132.16
1991	144.17	160.00	171.01	170.61	178.34	167.61	172.76	179.11	180.16	185.00	176.37	189.94
1992	205.16	211.15	203.69	196.25	198.52	188.64	194.74	188.79	192.92	198.90	213.81	221.01
1993	228.10	222.41	229.21	222.68	232.19	233.35	236.46	246.19	252.95	259.18	250.41	258.59
1994	266.52	265.53	251.06	252.55	249.28	240.29	244.06	257.32	256.12	255.02	244.25	250.36
1995	246.85	256.57	260.77	266.17	270.25	283.63	299.72	305.31	310.38	296.25	308.58	315.97
1996	315.38	324.93	330.77	348.28	361.85	346.61	316.00	333.88	346.39	340.57	354.11	362.61
1997	369.45	360.05	342.56	343.00	380.76	396.37	414.48	423.43	453.82	433.26	429.92	437.02
1998	430.05	461.83	480.68	482.89	456.62	457.39	419.75	337.95	363.59	378.16	397.75	421.96
1999	427.22	392.26	397.63	432.81	438.68	457.68	444.77	427.83	427.30	428.64	454.08	504.75
2000	496.23	577.71	539.09	506.25	476.18	517.23	500.64	537.89	521.37	497.68	445.94	483.53
2001	508.34	474.37	450.53	485.32	496.50	512.64	484.78	468.56	404.87	428.17	460.78	488.50
2002	483.10	469.36	506.46	510.67	487.47	462.64	392.42	390.96	362.27	373.50	406.35	383.09
2003	372.17	360.52	364.54	398.68	441.00	448.37	476.02	497.42	487.68	528.22	546.51	556.91
2004	580.76	585.56	590.31	559.80	568.28	591.52	551.29	547.93	572.94	583.79	633.77	651.57
2005	624.02	634.06	615.07	579.38	616.71	639.66	679.75	666.51	667.80	646.61	677.29	673.22
2006	733.20	730.64	765.14	764.54	721.01	724.67	700.56	720.53	725.59	766.84	786.12	787.66
2007	800.34	793.30	800.71	814.57	847.19	833.69	776.13	792.86	805.45	828.02	767.77	766.03
2008	713.30	686.18	687.97	716.18	748.28	689.66	714.52	739.50	679.58	537.52	473.14	499.45
2009	443.53	389.02	422.75	487.56	501.58	508.28	556.71	572.07	604.28	562.77	579.73	625.39
2010	602.04	628.56	678.64	716.60	661.61	609.49	650.89	602.06	676.14	703.35	727.01	783.65
2011	781.25	823.45	843.55	865.29	848.30	827.43	797.03	726.81	644.16	741.06	737.42	740.92
2012	792.82	810.94	830.30	816.88	761.82	798.49	786.94	812.09	837.45	818.73	821.92	849.35
2013	902.09	911.11	951.54	947.46	984.14	977.48	1045.26	1010.90	1073.79	1100.15	1142.89	1163.64
2014	1130.88	1183.03	1173.04	1126.86	1134.50	1192.96	1120.07	1174.35	1101.68	1173.51	1173.23	1204.70
2015	1165.39	1233.37	1252.77	1220.13	1246.53	1253.95	1238.68	1159.45	1100.69	1161.86	1198.11	1135.89
2016	1035.38	1033.90	1114.03	1130.84	1154.79	1151.92	1219.94	1239.91	1251.65	1191.39	1322.34	1357.13
2017	1361.82	1386.68	1385.92	1400.43	1370.21	1415.36	1425.14	1405.28	1490.86	1502.77	1544.14	1535.51
2018	1574.98	1512.45	1529.43	1541.88	1633.61	1643.07	1670.80	1740.75	1696.57	1511.41	1533.27	1348.56
2019	1499.42	1575.55	1539.74	1591.21	1465.49	1566.57	1574.61	1494.84	1523.37	1562.45	1624.50	1668.47
2020	1614.06	1476.43	1153.10	1310.66	1394.04	1441.37	1480.43	1561.88	1507.69	1538.48	1819.82	1974.86
2021	2073.64	2201.05	2220.52	2266.45	2268.97							

171

10 BEST DAYS BY PERCENT AND POINT

	BY PERCENT CHANGE				BY POINT CHANGE		
DAY	CLOSE	PNT CHANGE	% CHANGE	DAY	CLOSE	PNT CHANGE	% CHANGE
DJIA 1901 to 1949							
3/15/33	62.10	8.26	15.3	10/30/29	258.47	28.40	12.3
10/6/31	99.34	12.86	14.9	11/14/29	217.28	18.59	9.4
10/30/29	258.47	28.40	12.3	10/5/29	341.36	16.19	5.0
9/21/32	75.16	7.67	11.4	10/31/29	273.51	15.04	5.8
8/3/32	58.22	5.06	9.5	10/6/31	99.34	12.86	14.9
2/11/32	78.60	6.80	9.5	11/15/29	228.73	11.45	5.3
11/14/29	217.28	18.59	9.4	6/19/30	228.97	10.13	4.6
12/18/31	80.69	6.90	9.4	9/5/39	148.12	10.03	7.3
2/13/32	85.82	7.22	9.2	11/22/28	290.34	9.81	3.5
5/6/32	59.01	4.91	9.1	10/1/30	214.14	9.24	4.5
DJIA 1950 to JUNE 4, 2021							
3/24/2020	20704.91	2112.98	11.4	3/24/2020	20704.91	2112.98	11.4
10/13/2008	9387.61	936.42	11.1	3/13/2020	23185.62	1985.00	9.4
10/28/2008	9065.12	889.35	10.9	4/6/2020	22679.99	1627.46	7.7
10/21/1987	2027.85	186.84	10.2	3/26/2020	22552.17	1351.62	6.4
3/13/2020	23185.62	1985.00	9.4	3/2/2020	26703.32	1293.96	5.1
4/6/2020	22679.99	1627.46	7.7	3/4/2020	27090.86	1173.45	4.5
3/23/2009	7775.86	497.48	6.8	3/10/2020	25018.16	1167.14	4.9
11/13/2008	8835.25	552.59	6.7	12/26/2018	22878.45	1086.25	5.0
11/21/2008	8046.42	494.13	6.5	3/17/2020	21237.38	1048.86	5.2
3/26/2020	22552.17	1351.62	6.4	10/13/2008	9387.61	936.42	11.1
S&P 500 1930 to JUNE 4, 2021							
3/15/1933	6.81	0.97	16.6	3/13/2020	2711.02	230.38	9.3
10/6/1931	9.91	1.09	12.4	3/24/2020	2447.33	209.93	9.4
9/21/1932	8.52	0.90	11.8	4/6/2020	2663.68	175.03	7.0
10/13/2008	1003.35	104.13	11.6	3/26/2020	2630.07	154.51	6.2
10/28/2008	940.51	91.59	10.8	3/17/2020	2529.19	143.06	6.0
2/16/1935	10.00	0.94	10.4	3/2/2020	3090.23	136.01	4.6
8/17/1935	11.70	1.08	10.2	3/10/2020	2882.23	135.67	4.9
3/16/1935	9.05	0.82	10.0	3/4/2020	3130.12	126.75	4.2
9/12/1938	12.06	1.06	9.6	12/26/2018	2467.70	116.60	5.0
9/5/1939	12.64	1.11	9.6	10/13/2008	1003.35	104.13	11.6
NASDAQ 1971 to JUNE 4, 2021							
1/3/2001	2616.69	324.83	14.2	3/13/2020	7874.88	673.08	9.4
10/13/2008	1844.25	194.74	11.8	3/24/2020	7417.86	557.19	8.1
12/5/2000	2889.80	274.05	10.5	4/6/2020	7913.24	540.16	7.3
10/28/2008	1649.47	143.57	9.5	3/9/2021	13073.82	464.66	3.7
3/13/2020	7874.88	673.08	9.4	11/4/2020	11590.78	430.21	3.9
4/5/2001	1785.00	146.20	8.9	3/17/2020	7334.78	430.19	6.2
3/24/2020	7417.86	557.19	8.1	3/26/2020	7797.54	413.24	5.6
4/18/2001	2079.44	156.22	8.1	3/1/2021	13588.83	396.48	3.0
5/30/2000	3459.48	254.37	7.9	3/10/2020	8344.25	393.57	5.0
10/13/2000	3316.77	242.09	7.9	3/2/2020	8952.17	384.80	4.5
RUSSELL 1000 1979 to JUNE 4, 2021							
10/13/2008	542.98	56.75	11.7	3/13/2020	1488.04	123.38	9.0
10/28/2008	503.74	47.68	10.5	3/24/2020	1340.32	115.87	9.5
3/24/2020	1340.32	115.87	9.5	4/6/2020	1455.56	96.55	7.1
3/13/2020	1488.04	123.38	9.0	3/26/2020	1442.70	83.87	6.2
10/21/1987	135.85	11.15	8.9	3/17/2020	1381.49	74.98	5.7
4/6/2020	1455.56	96.55	7.1	3/10/2020	1588.36	73.59	4.9
3/23/2009	446.90	29.36	7.0	3/2/2020	1708.13	72.92	4.5
11/13/2008	489.83	31.99	7.0	3/4/2020	1729.80	68.44	4.1
11/24/2008	456.14	28.26	6.6	12/26/2018	1362.48	64.46	5.0
3/10/2009	391.01	23.46	6.4	10/13/2008	542.98	56.75	11.7
RUSSELL 2000 1979 to JUNE 4, 2021							
3/24/2020	1096.54	94.14	9.4	3/24/2020	1096.54	94.14	9.4
10/13/2008	570.89	48.41	9.3	3/13/2020	1210.13	87.20	7.8
11/13/2008	491.23	38.43	8.5	4/6/2020	1138.78	86.73	8.2
3/23/2009	433.72	33.61	8.4	1/6/2021	2057.92	78.81	4.0
4/6/2020	1138.78	86.73	8.2	5/18/2020	1333.69	76.70	6.1
3/13/2020	1210.13	87.20	7.8	3/1/2021	2275.32	74.27	3.4
10/21/1987	130.65	9.26	7.6	3/26/2020	1180.32	69.95	6.3
10/28/2008	482.55	34.15	7.6	3/17/2020	1106.51	69.09	6.7
11/24/2008	436.80	30.26	7.4	3/19/2020	1058.75	67.59	6.8
3/10/2009	367.75	24.49	7.1	12/26/2018	1329.81	62.89	5.0

10 <u>WORST</u> DAYS BY PERCENT AND POINT

	BY PERCENT CHANGE				BY POINT CHANGE		
DAY	CLOSE	PNT CHANGE	% CHANGE	DAY	CLOSE	PNT CHANGE	% CHANGE
DJIA 1901 to 1949							
10/28/1929	260.64	−38.33	−12.8	10/28/1929	260.64	−38.33	−12.8
10/29/1929	230.07	−30.57	−11.7	10/29/1929	230.07	−30.57	−11.7
11/6/1929	232.13	−25.55	−9.9	11/6/1929	232.13	−25.55	−9.9
8/12/1932	63.11	−5.79	−8.4	10/23/1929	305.85	−20.66	−6.3
3/14/1907	55.84	−5.05	−8.3	11/11/1929	220.39	−16.14	−6.8
7/21/1933	88.71	−7.55	−7.8	11/4/1929	257.68	−15.83	−5.8
10/18/1937	125.73	−10.57	−7.8	12/12/1929	243.14	−15.30	−5.9
2/1/1917	88.52	−6.91	−7.2	10/3/1929	329.95	−14.55	−4.2
10/5/1932	66.07	−5.09	−7.2	6/16/1930	230.05	−14.20	−5.8
9/24/1931	107.79	−8.20	−7.1	8/9/1929	337.99	−14.11	−4.0
DJIA 1950 to JUNE 4, 2021							
10/19/1987	1738.74	−508.00	−22.6	3/16/2020	20188.52	−2997.10	−12.9
3/16/2020	20188.52	−2997.10	−12.9	3/12/2020	21200.62	−2352.60	−10.0
3/12/2020	21200.62	−2352.60	−10.0	3/9/2020	23851.02	−2013.76	−7.8
10/26/1987	1793.93	−156.83	−8.0	6/11/2020	25128.17	−1861.82	−6.9
10/15/2008	8577.91	−733.08	−7.9	3/11/2020	23553.22	−1464.94	−5.9
3/9/2020	23851.02	−2013.76	−7.8	3/18/2020	19898.92	−1338.46	−6.3
12/1/2008	8149.09	−679.95	−7.7	2/27/2020	25766.64	−1190.95	−4.4
10/9/2008	8579.19	−678.91	−7.3	2/5/2018	24345.75	−1175.21	−4.6
10/27/1997	7161.15	−554.26	−7.2	2/8/2018	23860.46	−1032.89	−4.2
9/17/2001	8920.70	−684.81	−7.1	2/24/2020	27960.80	−1031.61	−3.6
S&P 500 1930 to JUNE 4, 2021							
10/19/1987	224.84	−57.86	−20.5	3/16/2020	2386.13	−324.89	−12.0
3/16/2020	2386.13	−324.89	−12.0	3/12/2020	2480.64	−260.74	−9.5
3/18/1935	8.14	−0.91	−10.1	3/9/2020	2746.56	−225.81	−7.6
4/16/1935	8.22	−0.91	−10.0	6/11/2020	3002.10	−188.04	−5.9
9/3/1946	15.00	−1.65	−9.9	3/11/2020	2741.38	−140.85	−4.9
3/12/2020	2480.64	−260.74	−9.5	2/27/2020	2978.76	−137.63	−4.4
10/18/1937	10.76	−1.10	−9.3	3/18/2020	2398.10	−131.09	−5.2
10/15/2008	907.84	−90.17	−9.0	9/3/2020	3455.06	−125.78	−3.5
12/1/2008	816.21	−80.03	−8.9	10/28/2020	3271.03	−119.65	−3.5
7/20/1933	10.57	−1.03	−8.9	4/1/2020	2470.50	−114.09	−4.4
NASDAQ 1971 to JUNE 4, 2021							
3/16/2020	6904.59	−970.29	−12.3	3/16/2020	6904.59	−970.29	−12.3
10/19/1987	360.21	−46.12	−11.4	3/12/2020	7201.80	−750.25	−9.4
4/14/2000	3321.29	−355.49	−9.7	3/9/2020	7950.68	−624.94	−7.3
3/12/2020	7201.80	−750.25	−9.4	9/3/2020	11458.10	−598.34	−5.0
9/29/2008	1983.73	−199.61	−9.1	6/11/2020	9492.73	−527.62	−5.3
10/26/1987	298.90	−29.55	−9.0	2/25/2021	13119.43	−478.54	−3.5
10/20/1987	327.79	−32.42	−9.0	9/8/2020	10847.69	−465.44	−4.1
12/1/2008	1398.07	−137.50	−9.0	10/28/2020	11004.87	−426.48	−3.7
8/31/1998	1499.25	−140.43	−8.6	2/27/2020	8566.48	−414.29	−4.6
10/15/2008	1628.33	−150.68	−8.5	3/18/2021	13116.17	−409.03	−3.0
RUSSELL 1000 1979 to JUNE 4, 2021							
10/19/1987	121.04	−28.40	−19.0	3/16/2020	1306.51	−181.53	−12.2
3/16/2020	1306.51	−181.53	−12.2	3/12/2020	1364.66	−144.34	−9.6
3/12/2020	1364.66	−144.34	−9.6	3/9/2020	1514.77	−127.21	−7.8
10/15/2008	489.71	−49.11	−9.1	6/11/2020	1660.70	−104.50	−5.9
12/1/2008	437.75	−43.68	−9.1	3/11/2020	1509.00	−79.36	−5.0
9/29/2008	602.34	−57.35	−8.7	3/18/2020	1304.56	−76.93	−5.6
10/26/1987	119.45	−10.74	−8.3	2/27/2020	1649.14	−75.62	−4.4
3/9/2020	1514.77	−127.21	−7.8	9/3/2020	1917.03	−72.05	−3.6
10/9/2008	492.13	−40.05	−7.5	10/28/2020	1829.66	−65.00	−3.4
8/8/2011	617.28	−45.56	−6.9	4/1/2020	1352.66	−63.83	−4.5
RUSSELL 2000 1979 to JUNE 4, 2021							
3/16/2020	1037.42	−172.71	−14.3	3/16/2020	1037.42	−172.71	−14.3
10/19/1987	133.60	−19.14	−12.5	3/12/2020	1122.93	−141.37	−11.2
12/1/2008	417.07	−56.07	−11.9	3/9/2020	1313.44	−135.78	−9.4
3/12/2020	1122.93	−141.37	−11.2	3/18/2020	991.16	−115.35	−10.4
3/18/2020	991.16	−115.35	−10.4	6/11/2020	1356.22	−111.17	−7.6
10/15/2008	502.11	−52.54	−9.5	3/11/2020	1264.30	−86.60	−6.4
3/9/2020	1313.44	−135.78	−9.4	2/25/2021	2200.17	−84.21	−3.7
10/26/1987	110.33	−11.26	−9.3	3/23/2021	2185.69	−81.15	−3.6
10/20/1987	121.39	−12.21	−9.1	4/1/2020	1071.99	−81.11	−7.0
8/8/2011	650.96	−63.67	−8.9	5/12/2021	2135.14	−71.85	−3.3

10 BEST WEEKS BY PERCENT AND POINT

	BY PERCENT CHANGE				BY POINT CHANGE		
WEEK ENDS	CLOSE	PNT CHANGE	% CHANGE	WEEK ENDS	CLOSE	PNT CHANGE	% CHANGE
DJIA 1901 to 1949							
8/6/1932	66.56	12.30	22.7	12/7/1929	263.46	24.51	10.3
6/25/1938	131.94	18.71	16.5	6/25/1938	131.94	18.71	16.5
2/13/1932	85.82	11.37	15.3	6/27/1931	156.93	17.97	12.9
4/22/1933	72.24	9.36	14.9	11/22/1929	245.74	17.01	7.4
10/10/1931	105.61	12.84	13.8	8/17/1929	360.70	15.86	4.6
7/30/1932	54.26	6.42	13.4	12/22/1928	285.94	15.22	5.6
6/27/1931	156.93	17.97	12.9	8/24/1929	375.44	14.74	4.1
9/24/1932	74.83	8.39	12.6	2/21/1929	310.06	14.21	4.8
8/27/1932	75.61	8.43	12.6	5/10/1930	272.01	13.70	5.3
3/18/1933	60.56	6.72	12.5	11/15/1930	186.68	13.54	7.8
DJIA 1950 to JUNE 4, 2021							
3/27/2020	21636.78	2462.80	12.8	4/9/2020	23719.37	2666.84	12.7
4/9/2020	23719.37	2666.84	12.7	3/27/2020	21636.78	2462.80	12.8
10/11/1974	658.17	73.61	12.6	11/6/2020	28323.40	1821.80	6.9
10/31/2008	9325.01	946.06	11.3	6/5/2020	27110.98	1727.87	6.8
8/20/1982	869.29	81.24	10.3	3/12/2021	32778.64	1282.34	4.1
11/28/2008	8829.04	782.62	9.7	11/30/2018	25538.46	1252.51	5.2
3/13/2009	7223.98	597.04	9.0	6/7/2019	25983.94	1168.90	4.7
10/8/1982	986.85	79.11	8.7	2/5/2021	31148.24	1165.62	3.9
3/21/2003	8521.97	662.26	8.4	11/13/2020	29479.81	1156.41	4.1
8/3/1984	1202.08	87.46	7.9	2/16/2018	25219.38	1028.48	4.3
S&P 500 1930 to JUNE 4, 2021							
8/6/1932	7.22	1.12	18.4	4/9/2020	2789.82	301.17	12.1
6/25/1938	11.39	1.72	17.8	11/6/2020	3509.44	239.48	7.3
7/30/1932	6.10	0.89	17.1	3/27/2020	2541.47	236.55	10.3
4/22/1933	7.75	1.09	16.4	2/5/2021	3886.83	172.59	4.7
10/11/1974	71.14	8.80	14.1	6/5/2020	3193.93	149.62	4.9
2/13/1932	8.80	1.08	14.0	10/9/2020	3477.13	128.69	3.8
9/24/1932	8.52	1.02	13.6	11/30/2018	2760.16	127.60	4.9
10/10/1931	10.64	1.27	13.6	6/7/2019	2873.34	121.28	4.4
8/27/1932	8.57	1.01	13.4	7/2/2020	3130.01	120.96	4.0
3/18/1933	6.61	0.77	13.2	2/16/2018	2732.22	112.67	4.3
NASDAQ 1971 to JUNE 4, 2021							
6/2/2000	3813.38	608.27	19.0	11/6/2020	11895.23	983.64	9.0
4/12/2001	1961.43	241.07	14.0	2/5/2021	13856.30	785.61	6.0
11/28/2008	1535.57	151.22	10.9	4/9/2020	8153.58	780.50	10.6
10/31/2008	1720.95	168.92	10.9	3/27/2020	7502.38	622.86	9.1
3/13/2009	1431.50	137.65	10.6	6/2/2000	3813.38	608.27	19.0
4/9/2020	8153.58	780.50	10.6	1/22/2021	13543.06	544.56	4.2
4/20/2001	2163.41	201.98	10.3	5/8/2020	9121.32	516.37	6.0
12/8/2000	2917.43	272.14	10.3	10/9/2020	11579.94	504.92	4.6
4/20/2000	3643.88	322.59	9.7	4/17/2020	8650.14	496.56	6.1
10/11/1974	60.42	5.26	9.5	7/2/2020	10207.63	450.41	4.6
RUSSELL 1000 1979 to JUNE 4, 2021							
4/9/2020	1530.05	171.04	12.6	4/9/2020	1530.05	171.04	12.6
11/28/2008	481.43	53.55	12.5	11/6/2020	1962.60	136.93	7.5
10/31/2008	522.47	50.94	10.8	3/27/2020	1394.65	133.96	10.6
3/13/2009	411.10	39.88	10.7	2/5/2021	2204.27	102.91	4.9
3/27/2020	1394.65	133.96	10.6	6/5/2020	1767.94	85.19	5.1
8/20/1982	61.51	4.83	8.5	10/9/2020	1943.01	74.39	4.0
6/2/2000	785.02	57.93	8.0	11/30/2018	1525.56	69.33	4.8
9/28/2001	546.46	38.48	7.6	7/2/2020	1735.01	67.76	4.1
10/16/1998	546.09	38.45	7.6	6/7/2019	1591.13	66.71	4.4
8/3/1984	87.43	6.13	7.5	2/16/2018	1512.36	62.68	4.3
RUSSELL 2000 1979 to JUNE 4, 2021							
4/9/2020	1246.73	194.68	18.5	4/9/2020	1246.73	194.68	18.5
11/28/2008	473.14	66.60	16.4	3/12/2021	2352.79	160.58	7.3
10/31/2008	537.52	66.40	14.1	2/5/2021	2233.33	159.69	7.7
6/2/2000	513.03	55.66	12.2	11/11/2016	1282.38	118.94	10.2
3/13/2009	393.09	42.04	12.0	3/27/2020	1131.99	118.10	11.7
3/27/2020	1131.99	118.10	11.7	1/8/2021	2091.66	116.80	5.9
12/2/2011	735.02	68.86	10.3	6/5/2020	1507.15	113.11	8.1
11/11/2016	1282.38	118.94	10.2	11/6/2020	1644.16	105.68	6.9
10/14/2011	712.46	56.25	8.6	11/13/2020	1744.04	99.88	6.1
6/5/2020	1507.15	113.11	8.1	5/22/2020	1355.53	98.54	7.8

10 WORST WEEKS BY PERCENT AND POINT

	BY PERCENT CHANGE				BY POINT CHANGE		
WEEK ENDS	CLOSE	PNT CHANGE	% CHANGE	WEEK ENDS	CLOSE	PNT CHANGE	% CHANGE
DJIA 1901 to 1949							
7/22/1933	88.42	−17.68	−16.7	11/8/1929	236.53	−36.98	−13.5
5/18/1940	122.43	−22.42	−15.5	12/8/1928	257.33	−33.47	−11.5
10/8/1932	61.17	−10.92	−15.2	6/21/1930	215.30	−28.95	−11.9
10/3/1931	92.77	−14.59	−13.6	10/19/1929	323.87	−28.82	−8.2
11/8/1929	236.53	−36.98	−13.5	5/3/1930	258.31	−27.15	−9.5
9/17/1932	66.44	−10.10	−13.2	10/31/1929	273.51	−25.46	−8.5
10/21/1933	83.64	−11.95	−12.5	10/26/1929	298.97	−24.90	−7.7
12/12/1931	78.93	−11.21	−12.4	5/18/1940	122.43	−22.42	−15.5
5/8/1915	62.77	−8.74	−12.2	2/8/1929	301.53	−18.23	−5.7
6/21/1930	215.30	−28.95	−11.9	10/11/1930	193.05	−18.05	−8.6
DJIA 1950 to JUNE 4, 2021							
10/10/2008	8451.19	−1874.19	−18.2	3/20/2020	19173.98	−4011.64	−17.3
3/20/2020	19173.98	−4011.64	−17.3	2/28/2020	25409.36	−3583.05	−12.4
9/21/2001	8235.81	−1369.70	−14.3	3/13/2020	23185.62	−2679.16	−10.4
10/23/1987	1950.76	−295.98	−13.2	10/10/2008	8451.19	−1874.19	−18.2
2/28/2020	25409.36	−3583.05	−12.4	10/30/2020	26501.60	−1833.97	−6.5
3/13/2020	23185.62	−2679.16	−10.4	12/21/2018	22445.37	−1655.14	−6.9
10/16/1987	2246.74	−235.47	−9.5	6/12/2020	25605.54	−1505.44	−5.6
10/13/1989	2569.26	−216.26	−7.8	3/23/2018	23533.20	−1413.31	−5.7
3/16/2001	9823.41	−821.21	−7.7	9/21/2001	8235.81	−1369.70	−14.3
7/19/2002	8019.26	−665.27	−7.7	2/9/2018	24190.90	−1330.06	−5.2
S&P 500 1930 to JUNE 4, 2021							
7/22/1933	9.71	−2.20	−18.5	3/20/2020	2304.92	−406.10	−15.0
10/10/2008	899.22	−200.01	−18.2	2/28/2020	2954.22	−383.53	−11.5
5/18/1940	9.75	−2.05	−17.4	3/13/2020	2711.02	−261.35	−8.8
10/8/1932	6.77	−1.38	−16.9	10/10/2008	899.22	−200.01	−18.2
3/20/2020	2304.92	−406.10	−15.0	10/30/2020	3269.96	−195.43	−5.6
9/17/1932	7.50	−1.28	−14.6	12/21/2018	2416.62	−183.33	−7.1
10/21/1933	8.57	−1.31	−13.3	3/23/2018	2588.26	−163.75	−6.0
10/3/1931	9.37	−1.36	−12.7	4/14/2000	1356.56	−159.79	−10.5
10/23/1987	248.22	−34.48	−12.2	6/12/2020	3041.31	−152.62	−4.8
12/12/1931	8.20	−1.13	−12.1	2/9/2018	2619.55	−142.58	−5.2
NASDAQ 1971 to JUNE 4, 2021							
4/14/2000	3321.29	−1125.16	−25.3	4/14/2000	3321.29	−1125.16	−25.3
10/23/1987	328.45	−77.88	−19.2	2/28/2020	8567.37	−1009.22	−10.5
9/21/2001	1423.19	−272.19	−16.1	3/20/2020	6879.52	−995.36	−12.6
10/10/2008	1649.51	−297.88	−15.3	3/13/2020	7874.88	−700.74	−8.2
3/20/2020	6879.52	−995.36	−12.6	2/26/2021	13192.35	−682.11	−4.9
11/10/2000	3028.99	−422.59	−12.2	10/30/2020	10911.59	−636.69	−5.5
10/3/2008	1947.39	−235.95	−10.8	12/21/2018	6332.99	−577.67	−8.4
7/28/2000	3663.00	−431.45	−10.5	3/23/2018	6992.67	−489.32	−6.5
2/28/2020	8567.37	−1009.22	−10.5	1/29/2021	13070.69	−472.37	−3.5
10/24/2008	1552.03	−159.26	−9.3	9/11/2020	10853.55	−459.58	−4.1
RUSSELL 1000 1979 to JUNE 4, 2021							
10/10/2008	486.23	−108.31	−18.2	3/20/2020	1260.69	−227.35	−15.3
3/20/2020	1260.69	−227.35	−15.3	2/28/2020	1635.21	−214.22	−11.6
10/23/1987	130.19	−19.25	−12.9	3/13/2020	1488.04	−153.94	−9.4
9/21/2001	507.98	−67.59	−11.7	10/30/2020	1825.67	−110.60	−5.7
2/28/2020	1635.21	−214.22	−11.6	10/10/2008	486.23	−108.31	−18.2
4/14/2000	715.20	−90.39	−11.2	12/21/2018	1333.95	−102.36	−7.1
10/3/2008	594.54	−65.15	−9.9	4/14/2000	715.20	−90.39	−11.2
3/13/2020	1488.04	−153.94	−9.4	3/23/2018	1436.72	−88.62	−5.8
10/16/1987	149.44	−14.42	−8.8	6/12/2020	1682.92	−85.02	−4.8
11/21/2008	427.88	−41.15	−8.8	2/9/2018	1449.68	−78.59	−5.1
RUSSELL 2000 1979 to JUNE 4, 2021							
10/23/1987	121.59	−31.15	−20.4	3/13/2020	1210.13	−239.09	−16.5
3/13/2020	1210.13	−239.09	−16.5	2/28/2020	1476.43	−202.18	−12.0
4/14/2000	453.72	−89.27	−16.4	3/20/2020	1013.89	−196.24	−16.2
3/20/2020	1013.89	−196.24	−16.2	6/12/2020	1387.68	−119.47	−7.9
10/10/2008	522.48	−96.92	−15.7	12/21/2018	1292.09	−118.72	−8.4
9/21/2001	378.89	−61.84	−14.0	10/30/2020	1538.48	−102.02	−6.2
10/3/2008	619.40	−85.39	−12.1	10/10/2008	522.48	−96.92	−15.7
2/28/2020	1476.43	−202.18	−12.0	1/29/2021	2073.64	−95.12	−4.4
11/21/2008	406.54	−49.98	−11.0	1/8/2016	1046.20	−89.69	−7.9
10/24/2008	471.12	−55.31	−10.5	4/14/2000	453.72	−89.27	−16.4

10 **BEST** MONTHS BY PERCENT AND POINT

	BY PERCENT CHANGE				BY POINT CHANGE		
MONTH	CLOSE	PNT CHANGE	% CHANGE	MONTH	CLOSE	PNT CHANGE	% CHANGE
			DJIA 1901 to 1949				
Apr-1933	77.66	22.26	40.2	Nov-1928	293.38	41.22	16.3
Aug-1932	73.16	18.90	34.8	Jun-1929	333.79	36.38	12.2
Jul-1932	54.26	11.42	26.7	Aug-1929	380.33	32.63	9.4
Jun-1938	133.88	26.14	24.3	Jun-1938	133.88	26.14	24.3
Apr-1915	71.78	10.95	18.0	Aug-1928	240.41	24.41	11.3
Jun-1931	150.18	21.72	16.9	Apr-1933	77.66	22.26	40.2
Nov-1928	293.38	41.22	16.3	Feb-1931	189.66	22.11	13.2
Nov-1904	52.76	6.59	14.3	Jun-1931	150.18	21.72	16.9
May-1919	105.50	12.62	13.6	Aug-1932	73.16	18.90	34.8
Sep-1939	152.54	18.13	13.5	Jan-1930	267.14	18.66	7.5
			DJIA 1950 to MAY 2021				
Jan-1976	975.28	122.87	14.4	Nov-2020	29638.64	3137.04	11.8
Jan-1975	703.69	87.45	14.2	Apr-2020	24345.72	2428.56	11.1
Jan-1987	2158.04	262.09	13.8	Mar-2021	32981.55	2049.18	6.6
Nov-2020	29638.64	3137.04	11.8	Aug-2020	28430.05	2001.73	7.6
Aug-1982	901.31	92.71	11.5	Jun-2019	26599.96	1784.92	7.2
Apr-2020	24345.72	2428.56	11.1	Jan-2019	24999.67	1672.21	7.2
Oct-1982	991.72	95.47	10.7	Jan-2018	26149.39	1430.17	5.8
Oct-2002	8397.03	805.10	10.6	Oct-2015	17663.54	1379.54	8.5
Apr-1978	837.32	79.96	10.6	Mar-2016	17685.09	1168.59	7.1
Apr-1999	10789.04	1002.88	10.3	Jul-2018	25415.19	1143.78	4.7
			S&P 500 1930 to MAY 2021				
Apr-1933	8.32	2.47	42.2	Nov-2020	3621.63	351.67	10.8
Jul-1932	6.10	1.67	37.7	Apr-2020	2912.43	327.84	12.7
Aug-1932	8.39	2.29	37.5	Aug-2020	3500.31	229.19	7.0
Jun-1938	11.56	2.29	24.7	Apr-2021	4181.17	208.28	5.2
Sep-1939	13.02	1.84	16.5	Jan-2019	2704.10	197.25	7.9
Oct-1974	73.90	10.36	16.3	Jun-2019	2941.76	189.70	6.9
May-1933	9.64	1.32	15.9	Jul-2020	3271.12	170.83	5.5
Apr-1938	9.70	1.20	14.1	Mar-2021	3972.89	161.74	4.2
Jun-1931	14.83	1.81	13.9	Oct-2015	2079.36	159.33	8.3
Jan-1987	274.08	31.91	13.2	Jan-2018	2823.81	150.20	5.6
			NASDAQ 1971 to MAY 2021				
Dec-1999	4069.31	733.15	22.0	Nov-2020	12198.74	1287.15	11.8
Feb-2000	4696.69	756.34	19.2	Apr-2020	8889.55	1189.45	15.5
Oct-1974	65.23	9.56	17.2	Aug-2020	11775.46	1030.19	9.6
Jan-1975	69.78	9.96	16.7	Feb-2000	4696.69	756.34	19.2
Jun-2000	3966.11	565.20	16.6	Dec-1999	4069.31	733.15	22.0
Apr-2020	8889.55	1189.45	15.5	Apr-2021	13962.68	715.81	5.4
Apr-2001	2116.24	275.98	15.0	Dec-2020	12888.28	689.54	5.7
Jan-1999	2505.89	313.20	14.3	Jul-2020	10745.27	686.50	6.8
Nov-2001	1930.58	240.38	14.2	Jan-2019	7281.74	646.46	9.7
Oct-2002	1329.75	157.69	13.5	May-2020	9489.87	600.32	6.8
			RUSSELL 1000 1979 to MAY 2021				
Apr-2020	1601.82	185.33	13.1	Nov-2020	2037.36	211.69	11.6
Jan-1987	146.48	16.48	12.7	Apr-2020	1601.82	185.33	13.1
Nov-2020	2037.36	211.69	11.6	Aug-2020	1946.15	130.16	7.2
Oct-1982	73.34	7.45	11.3	Apr-2021	2356.67	118.50	5.3
Aug-1982	65.14	6.60	11.3	Jan-2019	1498.36	114.10	8.2
Dec-1991	220.61	22.15	11.2	Jun-2019	1629.02	104.60	6.9
Oct-2011	692.41	68.96	11.1	Jul-2020	1815.99	98.52	5.7
Aug-1984	89.87	8.74	10.8	Oct-2015	1153.55	85.09	8.0
Nov-1980	78.26	7.18	10.1	Dec-2020	2120.87	83.51	4.1
Apr-2009	476.84	43.17	10.0	May-2020	1682.75	80.93	5.1
			RUSSELL 2000 1979 to MAY 2021				
Nov-2020	1819.82	281.34	18.3	Nov-2020	1819.82	281.34	18.3
Feb-2000	577.71	81.48	16.4	Apr-2020	1310.66	157.56	13.7
Apr-2009	487.56	64.81	15.3	Dec-2020	1974.86	155.04	8.5
Oct-2011	741.06	96.90	15.0	Jan-2019	1499.42	150.86	11.2
Oct-1982	80.86	10.02	14.1	Nov-2016	1322.34	130.95	11.0
Apr-2020	1310.66	157.56	13.7	Feb-2021	2201.05	127.41	6.1
Jan-1985	114.77	13.28	13.1	Jun-2019	1566.57	101.08	6.9
Sep-2010	676.14	74.08	12.3	Jan-2021	2073.64	98.78	5.0
Aug-1984	106.21	10.96	11.5	Oct-2011	741.06	96.90	15.0
Jan-1987	150.48	15.48	11.5	May-2018	1633.61	91.73	6.0

10 <u>WORST</u> MONTHS BY PERCENT AND POINT

	BY PERCENT CHANGE				BY POINT CHANGE		
MONTH	CLOSE	PNT CHANGE	% CHANGE	MONTH	CLOSE	PNT CHANGE	% CHANGE
DJIA 1901 to 1949							
Sep-1931	96.61	−42.80	−30.7	Oct-1929	273.51	−69.94	−20.4
Mar-1938	98.95	−30.69	−23.7	Jun-1930	226.34	−48.73	−17.7
Apr-1932	56.11	−17.17	−23.4	Sep-1931	96.61	−42.80	−30.7
May-1940	116.22	−32.21	−21.7	Sep-1929	343.45	−36.88	−9.7
Oct-1929	273.51	−69.94	−20.4	Sep-1930	204.90	−35.52	−14.8
May-1932	44.74	−11.37	−20.3	Nov-1929	238.95	−34.56	−12.6
Jun-1930	226.34	−48.73	−17.7	May-1940	116.22	−32.21	−21.7
Dec-1931	77.90	−15.97	−17.0	Mar-1938	98.95	−30.69	−23.7
Feb-1933	51.39	−9.51	−15.6	Sep-1937	154.57	−22.84	−12.9
May-1931	128.46	−22.73	−15.0	May-1931	128.46	−22.73	−15.0
DJIA 1950 to MAY 2021							
Oct-1987	1993.53	−602.75	−23.2	Mar-2020	21917.16	−3492.20	−13.7
Aug-1998	7539.07	−1344.22	−15.1	Feb-2020	25409.36	−2846.67	−10.1
Oct-2008	9325.01	−1525.65	−14.1	Dec-2018	23327.46	−2211.00	−8.7
Nov-1973	822.25	−134.33	−14.0	May-2019	24815.04	−1777.87	−6.7
Mar-2020	21917.16	−3492.20	−13.7	Oct-2008	9325.01	−1525.65	−14.1
Sep-2002	7591.93	−1071.57	−12.4	Aug-1998	7539.07	−1344.22	−15.1
Feb-2009	7062.93	−937.93	−11.7	Oct-2018	25115.76	−1342.55	−5.1
Sep-2001	8847.56	−1102.19	−11.1	Jun-2008	11350.01	−1288.31	−10.2
Sep-1974	607.87	−70.71	−10.4	Oct-2015	26501.60	−1280.10	−4.6
Aug-1974	678.58	−78.85	−10.4	Aug-2015	16528.03	−1161.83	−6.6
S&P 500 1930 to MAY 2021							
Sep-1931	9.71	−4.15	−29.9	Mar-2020	2584.59	−369.63	−12.5
Mar-1938	8.50	−2.84	−25.0	Feb-2020	2954.22	−271.30	−8.4
May-1940	9.27	−2.92	−24.0	Dec-2018	2506.85	−253.31	−9.2
May-1932	4.47	−1.36	−23.3	Oct-2018	2711.74	−202.24	−6.9
Oct-1987	251.79	−70.04	−21.8	Oct-2008	968.75	−197.61	−16.9
Apr-1932	5.83	−1.48	−20.2	May-2019	2752.06	−193.77	−6.6
Feb-1933	5.66	−1.28	−18.4	Aug-1998	957.28	−163.39	−14.6
Oct-2008	968.75	−197.61	−16.9	Sep-2020	3363.00	−137.31	−3.9
Jun-1930	20.46	−4.03	−16.5	Aug-2015	1972.18	−131.66	−6.3
Aug-1998	957.28	−163.39	−14.6	Feb-2001	1239.94	−126.07	−9.2
NASDAQ 1971 to MAY 2021							
Oct-1987	323.30	−120.99	−27.2	Mar-2020	7700.10	−867.27	−10.1
Nov-2000	2597.93	−771.70	−22.9	Nov-2000	2597.93	−771.70	−22.9
Feb-2001	2151.83	−620.90	−22.4	Oct-2018	7305.90	−740.45	−9.2
Aug-1998	1499.25	−373.14	−19.9	Apr-2000	3860.66	−712.17	−15.6
Oct-2008	1720.95	−370.93	−17.7	Dec-2018	6635.28	−695.26	−9.5
Mar-1980	131.00	−27.03	−17.1	May-2019	7453.15	−642.24	−7.9
Sep-2001	1498.80	−306.63	−17.0	Feb-2001	2151.83	−620.90	−22.4
Oct-1978	111.12	−21.77	−16.4	Sep-2020	11167.51	−607.95	−5.2
Apr-2000	3860.66	−712.17	−15.6	Feb-2000	8567.37	−583.57	−6.4
Nov-1973	93.51	−16.66	−15.1	Sep-2000	3672.82	−533.53	−12.7
RUSSELL 1000 1979 to MAY 2021							
Oct-1987	131.89	−36.94	−21.9	Mar-2020	1416.49	−218.72	−13.4
Oct-2008	522.47	−111.61	−17.6	Feb-2020	1635.21	−148.82	−8.3
Aug-1998	496.66	−88.31	−15.1	Dec-2018	1384.26	−141.30	−9.3
Mar-2020	1416.49	−218.72	−13.4	Oct-2018	1498.65	−115.89	−7.2
Mar-1980	55.79	−7.28	−11.5	Oct-2008	522.47	−111.61	−17.6
Sep-2002	433.22	−52.86	−10.9	May-2019	1524.42	−107.45	−6.6
Feb-2009	399.61	−47.71	−10.7	Aug-1998	496.66	−88.31	−15.1
Sep-2008	634.08	−68.09	−9.7	Sep-2020	1872.70	−73.45	−3.8
Aug-1990	166.69	−17.63	−9.6	Aug-2015	1100.51	−73.04	−6.2
Feb-2001	654.25	−68.30	−9.5	Nov-2000	692.40	−70.66	−9.3
RUSSELL 2000 1979 to MAY 2021							
Oct-1987	118.26	−52.05	−30.8	Mar-2020	1153.10	−323.33	−21.9
Mar-2020	1153.10	−323.33	−21.9	Oct-2018	1511.41	−185.16	−10.9
Oct-2008	537.52	−142.06	−20.9	Dec-2018	1348.56	−184.71	−12.0
Aug-1998	337.95	−81.80	−19.5	Oct-2008	537.52	−142.06	−20.9
Mar-1980	48.27	−10.95	−18.5	Feb-2020	1476.43	−137.63	−8.5
Jul-2002	392.42	−70.22	−15.2	May-2019	1465.49	−125.72	−7.9
Aug-1990	139.52	−21.99	−13.6	Jan-2016	1035.38	−100.51	−8.8
Sep-2001	404.87	−63.69	−13.6	Sep-2011	644.16	−82.65	−11.4
Feb-2009	389.02	−54.51	−12.3	Aug-1998	337.95	−81.80	−19.5
Dec-2018	1348.56	−184.71	−12.0	Aug-2019	1494.84	−79.77	−5.1

10 BEST QUARTERS BY PERCENT AND POINT

	BY PERCENT CHANGE				BY POINT CHANGE		
QUARTER	CLOSE	PNT CHANGE	% CHANGE	QUARTER	CLOSE	PNT CHANGE	% CHANGE
			DJIA 1901 to 1949				
Jun-1933	98.14	42.74	77.1	Dec-1928	300.00	60.57	25.3
Sep-1932	71.56	28.72	67.0	Jun-1933	98.14	42.74	77.1
Jun-1938	133.88	34.93	35.3	Mar-1930	286.10	37.62	15.1
Sep-1915	90.58	20.52	29.3	Jun-1938	133.88	34.93	35.3
Dec-1928	300.00	60.57	25.3	Sep-1927	197.59	31.36	18.9
Dec-1904	50.99	8.80	20.9	Sep-1928	239.43	28.88	13.7
Jun-1919	106.98	18.13	20.4	Sep-1932	71.56	28.72	67.0
Sep-1927	197.59	31.36	18.9	Jun-1929	333.79	24.94	8.1
Dec-1905	70.47	10.47	17.4	Sep-1939	152.54	21.91	16.8
Jun-1935	118.21	17.40	17.3	Sep-1915	90.58	20.52	29.3
			DJIA 1950 to MARCH 2021				
Mar-1975	768.15	151.91	24.7	Jun-2020	25812.88	3895.72	17.8
Mar-1987	2304.69	408.74	21.6	Dec-2020	30606.48	2824.78	10.2
Jun-2020	25812.88	3895.72	17.8	Mar-2019	25928.68	2601.22	11.2
Mar-1986	1818.61	271.94	17.6	Mar-2021	32981.55	2375.07	7.8
Mar-1976	999.45	147.04	17.3	Dec-2017	24719.22	2314.13	10.3
Dec-1998	9181.43	1338.81	17.1	Sep-2018	26458.31	2186.90	9.0
Dec-1982	1046.54	150.29	16.8	Sep-2020	27781.70	1968.82	7.6
Jun-1997	7672.79	1089.31	16.6	Dec-2019	28538.44	1621.61	6.0
Dec-1985	1546.67	218.04	16.4	Mar-2013	14578.54	1474.40	11.3
Sep-2009	9712.28	1265.28	15.0	Dec-2016	19762.60	1454.45	7.9
			S&P 500 1930 to MARCH 2021				
Jun-1933	10.91	5.06	86.5	Jun-2020	3100.29	515.70	20.0
Sep-1932	8.08	3.65	82.4	Dec-2020	3756.07	393.07	11.7
Jun-1938	11.56	3.06	36.0	Mar-2019	2834.40	327.55	13.1
Mar-1975	83.36	14.80	21.6	Sep-2020	3363.00	262.71	8.5
Dec-1998	1229.23	212.22	20.9	Dec-2019	3230.78	254.04	8.5
Jun-1935	10.23	1.76	20.8	Mar-2021	3972.89	216.82	5.8
Mar-1987	291.70	49.53	20.5	Dec-1998	1229.23	212.22	20.9
Jun-2020	3100.29	515.70	20.0	Sep-2018	2913.98	195.61	7.2
Sep-1939	13.02	2.16	19.9	Dec-1999	1469.25	186.54	14.5
Mar-1943	11.58	1.81	18.5	Dec-2013	1848.36	166.81	9.9
			NASDAQ 1971 to MARCH 2021				
Dec-1999	4069.31	1323.15	48.2	Jun-2020	10058.77	2358.67	30.6
Jun-2020	10058.77	2358.67	30.6	Dec-2020	12888.28	1720.77	15.4
Dec-2001	1950.40	451.60	30.1	Dec-1999	4069.31	1323.15	48.2
Dec-1998	2192.69	498.85	29.5	Sep-2020	11167.51	1108.74	11.0
Mar-1991	482.30	108.46	29.0	Mar-2019	7729.32	1094.04	16.5
Mar-1975	75.66	15.84	26.5	Dec-2019	8972.60	973.26	12.2
Dec-1982	232.41	44.76	23.9	Sep-2018	8046.35	536.05	7.1
Mar-1987	430.05	80.72	23.1	Mar-2017	5911.74	528.62	9.8
Jun-2003	1622.80	281.63	21.0	Mar-2020	4572.83	503.52	12.4
Jun-1980	157.78	26.78	20.4	Dec-1998	2192.69	498.85	29.5
			RUSSELL 1000 1979 to MARCH 2021				
Dec-1998	642.87	113.76	21.5	Jun-2020	1717.47	300.98	21.3
Jun-2020	1717.47	300.98	21.3	Dec-2020	2120.87	248.17	13.3
Mar-1987	155.20	25.20	19.4	Mar-2019	1570.23	185.97	13.4
Dec-1982	77.24	11.35	17.2	Sep-2020	1872.70	155.23	9.0
Jun-1997	462.95	64.76	16.3	Dec-2019	1784.21	140.03	8.5
Dec-1985	114.39	15.64	15.8	Mar-2021	2238.17	117.30	5.5
Jun-2009	502.27	68.60	15.8	Dec-1998	642.87	113.76	21.5
Dec-1999	767.97	104.14	15.7	Sep-2018	1614.54	104.58	6.9
Sep-2009	579.97	77.70	15.5	Dec-1999	767.97	104.14	15.7
Jun-2003	518.94	68.59	15.2	Dec-2013	1030.36	90.86	9.7
			RUSSELL 2000 1979 to MARCH 2021				
Dec-2020	1974.86	467.17	31.0	Dec-2020	1974.86	467.17	31.0
Mar-1991	171.01	38.85	29.4	Jun-2020	1441.37	288.27	25.0
Dec-1982	88.90	18.06	25.5	Mar-2021	2220.52	245.66	12.4
Jun-2020	1441.37	288.27	25.0	Mar-2019	1539.74	191.18	14.2
Mar-1987	166.79	31.79	23.6	Dec-2019	1668.47	145.10	9.5
Jun-2003	448.37	83.83	23.0	Jun-2018	1643.07	113.64	7.4
Sep-1980	69.94	12.47	21.7	Dec-2010	783.65	107.51	15.9
Dec-2001	488.50	83.63	20.7	Dec-2016	1357.13	105.48	8.4
Jun-2009	508.28	85.53	20.2	Dec-2014	1204.70	103.02	9.4
Jun-1983	124.17	20.40	19.7	Mar-2013	951.54	102.19	12.0

10 <u>WORST</u> QUARTERS BY PERCENT AND POINT

	BY PERCENT CHANGE				BY POINT CHANGE		
QUARTER	CLOSE	PNT CHANGE	% CHANGE	QUARTER	CLOSE	PNT CHANGE	% CHANGE
DJIA 1901 to 1949							
Jun-1932	42.84	−30.44	−41.5	Dec-1929	248.48	−94.97	−27.7
Sep-1931	96.61	−53.57	−35.7	Jun-1930	226.34	−59.76	−20.9
Dec-1929	248.48	−94.97	−27.7	Sep-1931	96.61	−53.57	−35.7
Sep-1903	33.55	−9.73	−22.5	Dec-1930	164.58	−40.32	−19.7
Dec-1937	120.85	−33.72	−21.8	Dec-1937	120.85	−33.72	−21.8
Jun-1930	226.34	−59.76	−20.9	Sep-1946	172.42	−33.20	−16.1
Dec-1930	164.58	−40.32	−19.7	Jun-1932	42.84	−30.44	−41.5
Dec-1931	77.90	−18.71	−19.4	Jun-1940	121.87	−26.08	−17.6
Mar-1938	98.95	−21.90	−18.1	Mar-1939	131.84	−22.92	−14.8
Jun-1940	121.87	−26.08	−17.6	Jun-1931	150.18	−22.18	−12.9
DJIA 1950 to MARCH 2021							
Dec-1987	1938.83	−657.45	−25.3	Mar-2020	21917.16	−6621.28	−23.2
Sep-1974	607.87	−194.54	−24.2	Dec-2018	23327.46	−3130.85	−11.8
Mar-2020	21917.16	−6621.28	−23.2	Dec-2008	8776.39	−2074.27	−19.1
Jun-1962	561.28	−145.67	−20.6	Sep-2001	8847.56	−1654.84	−15.8
Dec-2008	8776.39	−2074.27	−19.1	Sep-2002	7591.93	−1651.33	−17.9
Sep-2002	7591.93	−1651.33	−17.9	Sep-2011	10913.38	−1500.96	−12.1
Sep-2001	8847.56	−1654.84	−15.8	Sep-2015	16284.00	−1335.51	−7.6
Sep-1990	2452.48	−428.21	−14.9	Mar-2009	7608.92	−1167.47	−13.3
Mar-2009	7608.92	−1167.47	−13.3	Jun-2002	9243.26	−1160.68	−11.2
Sep-1981	849.98	−126.90	−13.0	Sep-1998	7842.62	−1109.40	−12.4
S&P 500 1930 to MARCH 2021							
Jun-1932	4.43	−2.88	−39.4	Mar-2020	2584.59	−646.19	−20.0
Sep-1931	9.71	−5.12	−34.5	Dec-2018	2506.85	−407.13	−14.0
Sep-1974	63.54	−22.46	−26.1	Dec-2008	903.25	−263.11	−22.6
Dec-1937	10.55	−3.21	−23.3	Sep-2011	1131.42	−189.22	−14.3
Dec-1987	247.08	−74.75	−23.2	Sep-2001	1040.94	−183.48	−15.0
Dec-2008	903.25	−263.11	−22.6	Sep-2002	815.28	−174.54	−17.6
Jun-1962	54.75	−14.80	−21.3	Mar-2001	1160.33	−159.95	−12.1
Mar-2020	2584.59	−646.19	−20.0	Jun-2002	989.82	−157.57	−13.7
Mar-1938	8.50	−2.05	−19.4	Mar-2008	1322.70	−145.66	−9.9
Jun-1970	72.72	−16.91	−18.9	Sep-2015	1920.03	−143.08	−6.9
NASDAQ 1971 to MARCH 2021							
Dec-2000	2470.52	−1202.30	−32.7	Dec-2018	6635.28	−1411.07	−17.5
Sep-2001	1498.80	−661.74	−30.6	Mar-2020	7700.10	−1272.50	−14.2
Sep-1974	55.67	−20.29	−26.7	Dec-2000	2470.52	−1202.30	−32.7
Dec-1987	330.47	−113.82	−25.6	Sep-2001	1498.80	−661.74	−30.6
Mar-2001	1840.26	−630.26	−25.5	Mar-2001	1840.26	−630.26	−25.5
Sep-1990	344.51	−117.78	−25.5	Jun-2000	3966.11	−606.72	−13.3
Dec-2008	1577.03	−514.85	−24.6	Dec-2008	1577.03	−514.85	−24.6
Jun-2002	1463.21	−382.14	−20.7	Jun-2002	1463.21	−382.14	−20.7
Sep-2002	1172.06	−291.15	−19.9	Mar-2008	2279.10	−373.18	−14.1
Jun-1974	75.96	−16.31	−17.7	Sep-2015	4620.16	−366.71	−7.4
RUSSELL 1000 1979 to MARCH 2021							
Dec-2008	487.77	−146.31	−23.1	Mar-2020	1416.49	−367.72	−20.6
Dec-1987	130.02	−38.81	−23.0	Dec-2018	1384.26	−230.28	−14.3
Mar-2020	1416.49	−367.72	−20.6	Dec-2008	487.77	−146.31	−23.1
Sep-2002	433.22	−90.50	−17.3	Sep-2011	623.45	−111.03	−15.1
Sep-2001	546.46	−100.18	−15.5	Sep-2001	546.46	−100.18	−15.5
Sep-1990	157.83	−28.46	−15.3	Sep-2002	433.22	−90.50	−17.3
Sep-2011	623.45	−111.03	−15.1	Mar-2001	610.36	−89.73	−12.8
Dec-2018	1384.26	−230.28	−14.3	Sep-2015	1068.46	−84.18	−7.3
Jun-2002	523.72	−83.63	−13.8	Jun-2002	523.72	−83.63	−13.8
Mar-2001	610.36	−89.73	−12.8	Mar-2008	720.32	−79.50	−9.9
RUSSELL 2000 1979 to MARCH 2021							
Mar-2020	1153.10	−515.37	−30.9	Mar-2020	1153.10	−515.37	−30.9
Dec-1987	120.42	−50.39	−29.5	Dec-2018	1348.56	−348.01	−20.5
Dec-2008	499.45	−180.13	−26.5	Sep-2011	644.16	−183.27	−22.1
Sep-1990	126.70	−42.34	−25.0	Dec-2008	499.45	−180.13	−26.5
Sep-2011	644.16	−183.27	−22.1	Sep-2015	1100.69	−153.26	−12.2
Sep-2002	362.27	−100.37	−21.7	Sep-2001	404.87	−107.77	−21.0
Sep-2001	404.87	−107.77	−21.0	Sep-2002	362.27	−100.37	−21.7
Dec-2018	1348.56	−348.01	−20.5	Sep-1998	363.59	−93.80	−20.5
Sep-1998	363.59	−93.80	−20.5	Sep-2014	1101.68	−91.28	−7.7
Sep-1981	67.55	−15.01	−18.2	Mar-2008	687.97	−78.06	−10.2

10 BEST YEARS BY PERCENT AND POINT

	BY PERCENT CHANGE				BY POINT CHANGE		
YEAR	CLOSE	PNT CHANGE	% CHANGE	YEAR	CLOSE	PNT CHANGE	% CHANGE
			DJIA 1901 to 1949				
1915	99.15	44.57	81.7	1928	300.00	97.60	48.2
1933	99.90	39.97	66.7	1927	202.40	45.20	28.8
1928	300.00	97.60	48.2	1915	99.15	44.57	81.7
1908	63.11	20.07	46.6	1945	192.91	40.59	26.6
1904	50.99	15.01	41.7	1935	144.13	40.09	38.5
1935	144.13	40.09	38.5	1933	99.90	39.97	66.7
1905	70.47	19.48	38.2	1925	156.66	36.15	30.0
1919	107.23	25.03	30.5	1936	179.90	35.77	24.8
1925	156.66	36.15	30.0	1938	154.76	33.91	28.1
1927	202.40	45.20	28.8	1919	107.23	25.03	30.5
			DJIA 1950 TO 2020				
1954	404.39	123.49	44.0	2019	28538.44	5210.98	22.3
1975	852.41	236.17	38.3	2017	24719.22	4956.62	25.1
1958	583.65	147.96	34.0	2013	16576.66	3472.52	26.5
1995	5117.12	1282.68	33.5	2016	19762.60	2337.57	13.4
1985	1546.67	335.10	27.7	1999	11497.12	2315.69	25.2
1989	2753.20	584.63	27.0	2003	10453.92	2112.29	25.3
2013	16576.66	3472.52	26.5	2020	30606.48	2068.04	7.3
1996	6448.27	1331.15	26.0	2006	12463.15	1745.65	16.3
2003	10453.92	2112.29	25.3	2009	10428.05	1651.66	18.8
1999	11497.12	2315.69	25.2	1997	7908.25	1459.98	22.6
			S&P 500 1930 TO 2020				
1933	10.10	3.21	46.6	2019	3230.78	723.93	28.9
1954	35.98	11.17	45.0	2020	3756.07	525.29	16.3
1935	13.43	3.93	41.4	2017	2673.61	434.78	19.4
1958	55.21	15.22	38.1	2013	1848.36	422.17	29.6
1995	615.93	156.66	34.1	1998	1229.23	258.80	26.7
1975	90.19	21.63	31.5	1999	1469.25	240.02	19.5
1997	970.43	229.69	31.0	2003	1111.92	232.10	26.4
1945	17.36	4.08	30.7	1997	970.43	229.69	31.0
2013	1848.36	422.17	29.6	2009	1115.10	211.85	23.5
2019	3230.78	723.93	28.9	2014	2058.90	210.54	11.4
			NASDAQ 1971 TO 2020				
1999	4069.31	1876.62	85.6	2020	12888.28	3915.68	43.6
1991	586.34	212.50	56.8	2019	8972.60	2337.32	35.2
2003	2003.37	667.86	50.0	1999	4069.31	1876.62	85.6
2009	2269.15	692.12	43.9	2017	6903.39	1520.27	28.2
2020	12888.28	3915.68	43.6	2013	4176.59	1157.08	38.3
1995	1052.13	300.17	39.9	2009	2269.15	692.12	43.9
1998	2192.69	622.34	39.6	2003	2003.37	667.86	50.0
2013	4176.59	1157.08	38.3	1998	2192.69	622.34	39.6
2019	8972.60	2337.32	35.2	2014	4736.05	559.46	13.4
1980	202.34	51.20	33.9	2012	3019.51	414.36	15.9
			RUSSELL 1000 1979 TO 2020				
1995	328.89	84.24	34.4	2019	1784.21	399.95	28.9
1997	513.79	120.04	30.5	2020	2120.87	336.66	18.9
2013	1030.36	240.46	30.4	2013	1030.36	240.46	30.4
2019	1784.21	399.95	28.9	2017	1481.81	240.15	19.3
1991	220.61	49.39	28.9	1998	642.87	129.08	25.1
2003	594.56	128.38	27.5	2003	594.56	128.38	27.5
1985	114.39	24.08	26.7	1999	767.97	125.10	19.5
1989	185.11	38.12	25.9	2009	612.01	124.24	25.5
1980	75.20	15.33	25.6	1997	513.79	120.04	30.5
2009	612.01	124.24	25.5	2014	1144.37	114.01	11.1
			RUSSELL 2000 1979 TO 2020				
2003	556.91	173.82	45.4	2019	1668.47	319.91	23.7
1991	189.94	57.78	43.7	2013	1163.64	314.29	37.0
1979	55.91	15.39	38.0	2020	1974.86	306.39	18.4
2013	1163.64	314.29	37.0	2016	1357.13	221.24	19.5
1980	74.80	18.89	33.8	2017	1535.51	178.38	13.1
1985	129.87	28.38	28.0	2003	556.91	173.82	45.4
1983	112.27	23.37	26.3	2010	783.65	158.26	25.3
1995	315.97	65.61	26.2	2009	625.39	125.94	25.2
2010	783.65	158.26	25.3	2006	787.66	114.44	17.0
2009	625.39	125.94	25.2	2012	849.35	108.43	14.6

10 <u>WORST</u> YEARS BY PERCENT AND POINT

	BY PERCENT CHANGE				BY POINT CHANGE		
YEAR	CLOSE	PNT CHANGE	% CHANGE	YEAR	CLOSE	PNT CHANGE	% CHANGE
DJIA 1901 to 1949							
1931	77.90	−86.68	−52.7	1931	77.90	−86.68	−52.7
1907	43.04	−26.08	−37.7	1930	164.58	−83.90	−33.8
1930	164.58	−83.90	−33.8	1937	120.85	−59.05	−32.8
1920	71.95	−35.28	−32.9	1929	248.48	−51.52	−17.2
1937	120.85	−59.05	−32.8	1920	71.95	−35.28	−32.9
1903	35.98	−11.12	−23.6	1907	43.04	−26.08	−37.7
1932	59.93	−17.97	−23.1	1917	74.38	−20.62	−21.7
1917	74.38	−20.62	−21.7	1941	110.96	−20.17	−15.4
1910	59.60	−12.96	−17.9	1940	131.13	−19.11	−12.7
1929	248.48	−51.52	−17.2	1932	59.93	−17.97	−23.1
DJIA 1950 TO 2020							
2008	8776.39	−4488.43	−33.8	2008	8776.39	−4488.43	−33.8
1974	616.24	−234.62	−27.6	2002	8341.63	−1679.87	−16.8
1966	785.69	−183.57	−18.9	2018	23327.46	−1391.76	−5.6
1977	831.17	−173.48	−17.3	2001	10021.50	−765.35	−7.1
2002	8341.63	−1679.87	−16.8	2000	10786.85	−710.27	−6.2
1973	850.86	−169.16	−16.6	2015	17425.03	−398.04	−2.2
1969	800.36	−143.39	−15.2	1974	616.24	−234.62	−27.6
1957	435.69	−63.78	−12.8	1966	785.69	−183.57	−18.9
1962	652.10	−79.04	−10.8	1977	831.17	−173.48	−17.3
1960	615.89	−63.47	−9.3	1973	850.86	−169.16	−16.6
S&P 500 1930 TO 2020							
1931	8.12	−7.22	−47.1	2008	903.25	−565.11	−38.5
1937	10.55	−6.63	−38.6	2002	879.82	−268.26	−23.4
2008	903.25	−565.11	−38.5	2001	1148.08	−172.20	−13.0
1974	68.56	−28.99	−29.7	2018	2506.85	−166.76	−6.2
1930	15.34	−6.11	−28.5	2000	1320.28	−148.97	−10.1
2002	879.82	−268.26	−23.4	1974	68.56	−28.99	−29.7
1941	8.69	−1.89	−17.9	1990	330.22	−23.18	−6.6
1973	97.55	−20.50	−17.4	1973	97.55	−20.50	−17.4
1940	10.58	−1.91	−15.3	2015	2043.94	−14.96	−0.7
1932	6.89	−1.23	−15.1	1981	122.55	−13.21	−9.7
NASDAQ 1971 TO 2020							
2008	1577.03	−1075.25	−40.5	2000	2470.52	−1598.79	−39.3
2000	2470.52	−1598.79	−39.3	2008	1577.03	−1075.25	−40.5
1974	59.82	−32.37	−35.1	2002	1335.51	−614.89	−31.5
2002	1335.51	−614.89	−31.5	2001	1950.40	−520.12	−21.1
1973	92.19	−41.54	−31.1	2018	6635.28	−268.11	−3.9
2001	1950.40	−520.12	−21.1	1990	373.84	−80.98	−17.8
1990	373.84	−80.98	−17.8	2011	2605.15	−47.72	−1.8
1984	247.35	−31.25	−11.2	1973	92.19	−41.54	−31.1
1987	330.47	−18.86	−5.4	1974	59.82	−32.37	−35.1
2018	6635.28	−268.11	−3.9	1984	247.35	−31.25	−11.2
RUSSELL 1000 1979 TO 2020							
2008	487.77	−312.05	−39.0	2008	487.77	−312.05	−39.0
2002	466.18	−138.76	−22.9	2002	466.18	−138.76	−22.9
2001	604.94	−95.15	−13.6	2018	1384.26	−97.55	−6.6
1981	67.93	−7.27	−9.7	2001	604.94	−95.15	−13.6
2000	700.09	−67.88	−8.8	2000	700.09	−67.88	−8.8
1990	171.22	−13.89	−7.5	1990	171.22	−13.89	−7.5
2018	1384.26	−97.55	−6.6	2015	1131.88	−12.49	−1.1
1994	244.65	−6.06	−2.4	1981	67.93	−7.27	−9.7
2015	1131.88	−12.49	−1.1	1994	244.65	−6.06	−2.4
2011	693.36	−3.54	−0.5	2011	693.36	−3.54	−0.5
RUSSELL 2000 1979 TO 2020							
2008	499.45	−266.58	−34.8	2008	499.45	−266.58	−34.8
2002	383.09	−105.41	−21.6	2018	1348.56	−186.95	−12.2
1990	132.16	−36.14	−21.5	2002	383.09	−105.41	−21.6
2018	1348.56	−186.95	−12.2	2015	1135.89	−68.81	−5.7
1987	120.42	−14.58	−10.8	2011	740.92	−42.73	−5.5
1984	101.49	−10.78	−9.6	1990	132.16	−36.14	−21.5
2015	1135.89	−68.81	−5.7	2007	766.03	−21.63	−2.7
2011	740.92	−42.73	−5.5	2000	483.53	−21.22	−4.2
2000	483.53	−21.22	−4.2	1998	421.96	−15.06	−3.4
1998	421.96	−15.06	−3.4	1987	120.42	−14.58	−10.8

181

STRATEGY
PLANNING
AND RECORD
SECTION

CONTENTS

*These forms are available at our website, www.stocktradersalmanac.com under "Forms"
located at the bottom of the homepage.*

PORTFOLIO AT START OF 2022

DATE ACQUIRED	NO. OF SHARES	SECURITY	PRICE	TOTAL COST	PAPER PROFITS	PAPER LOSSES

ADDITIONAL PURCHASES

DATE ACQUIRED	NO. OF SHARES	SECURITY	PRICE	TOTAL COST	REASON FOR PURCHASE PRIME OBJECTIVE, ETC.

ADDITIONAL PURCHASES

DATE ACQUIRED	NO. OF SHARES	SECURITY	PRICE	TOTAL COST	REASON FOR PURCHASE PRIME OBJECTIVE, ETC.

SHORT-TERM TRANSACTIONS

Pages 186–189 can accompany next year's income tax return (Schedule D). Enter transactions as completed to avoid last-minute pressures.

NO. OF SHARES	SECURITY	DATE ACQUIRED	DATE SOLD	SALE PRICE	COST	LOSS	GAIN

TOTALS:
Carry over to next page

SHORT-TERM TRANSACTIONS *(continued)*

NO. OF SHARES	SECURITY	DATE ACQUIRED	DATE SOLD	SALE PRICE	COST	LOSS	GAIN

TOTALS:

187

LONG-TERM TRANSACTIONS

Pages 186–189 can accompany next year's income tax return (Schedule D). Enter transactions as completed to avoid last-minute pressures.

NO. OF SHARES	SECURITY	DATE ACQUIRED	DATE SOLD	SALE PRICE	COST	LOSS	GAIN

TOTALS: Carry over to next page

LONG-TERM TRANSACTIONS *(continued)*

NO. OF SHARES	SECURITY	DATE ACQUIRED	DATE SOLD	SALE PRICE	COST	LOSS	GAIN

TOTALS:

INTEREST/DIVIDENDS RECEIVED DURING 2022

SHARES	STOCK/BOND	FIRST QUARTER		SECOND QUARTER		THIRD QUARTER		FOURTH QUARTER	
		$		$		$		$	

BROKERAGE ACCOUNT DATA 2022

	MARGIN INTEREST	TRANSFER TAXES	CAPITAL ADDED	CAPITAL WITHDRAWN
JAN				
FEB				
MAR				
APR				
MAY				
JUN				
JUL				
AUG				
SEP				
OCT				
NOV				
DEC				

WEEKLY PORTFOLIO PRICE RECORD 2022 (FIRST HALF)

Place purchase price above stock name and weekly closes below.

STOCKS Week Ending	1	2	3	4	5	6	7	8	9	10
JANUARY 7										
14										
21										
28										
FEBRUARY 4										
11										
18										
25										
MARCH 4										
11										
18										
25										
APRIL 1										
8										
15										
22										
29										
MAY 6										
13										
20										
27										
JUNE 3										
10										
17										
24										

WEEKLY PORTFOLIO PRICE RECORD 2022 (SECOND HALF)

Place purchase price above stock name and weekly closes below.

STOCKS										
Week Ending	1	2	3	4	5	6	7	8	9	10
JULY 1										
8										
15										
22										
29										
AUGUST 5										
12										
19										
26										
SEPTEMBER 2										
9										
16										
23										
30										
OCTOBER 7										
14										
21										
28										
NOVEMBER 4										
11										
18										
25										
DECEMBER 2										
9										
16										
23										
30										

WEEKLY INDICATOR DATA 2022 (FIRST HALF)

	Week Ending	Dow Jones Industrial Average	Net Change for Week	Net Change on Friday	Net Change Next Monday	S&P or NASDAQ	NYSE Ad-vances	NYSE De-clines	New Highs	New Lows	CBOE Put/Call Ratio	90-Day Treas. Rate	Moody's AAA Rate
JANUARY	7												
	14												
	21												
	28												
FEBRUARY	4												
	11												
	18												
	25												
MARCH	4												
	11												
	18												
	25												
APRIL	1												
	8												
	15												
	22												
	29												
MAY	6												
	13												
	20												
	27												
JUNE	3												
	10												
	17												
	24												

WEEKLY INDICATOR DATA 2022 (SECOND HALF)

	Week Ending	Dow Jones Industrial Average	Net Change for Week	Net Change on Friday	Net Change Next Monday	S&P or NASDAQ	NYSE Advances	NYSE Declines	New Highs	New Lows	CBOE Put/Call Ratio	90-Day Treas. Rate	Moody's AAA Rate
JULY	1												
	8												
	15												
	22												
	29												
AUGUST	5												
	12												
	19												
	26												
SEPTEMBER	2												
	9												
	16												
	23												
	30												
OCTOBER	7												
	14												
	21												
	28												
NOVEMBER	4												
	11												
	18												
	25												
DECEMBER	2												
	9												
	16												
	23												
	30												

MONTHLY INDICATOR DATA 2022

	DJIA% Last 3 + 1st 2 Days	DJIA% 9th to 11th Trading Days	DJIA% Change Rest of Month	DJIA% Change Whole Month	% Change Your Stocks	Gross Domestic Product	Prime Rate	Trade Deficit $ Billion	CPI % Change	% Unem- ployment Rate
JAN										
FEB										
MAR										
APR										
MAY										
JUN										
JUL										
AUG										
SEP										
OCT										
NOV										
DEC										

INSTRUCTIONS:

Weekly Indicator Data (pages 187–188). Keeping data on several indicators may give you a better feel of the market. In addition to the closing DJIA and its net change for the week, post the net change for Friday's Dow and also the following Monday's. A series of "down Fridays" followed by "down Mondays" often precedes a downswing (see page 76). Tracking either the S&P or NASDAQ composite, and advances and declines, will help prevent the Dow from misleading you. New highs and lows and put/call ratios (www.cboe. com) are also useful indicators. Many of these weekly figures appear in weekend papers or *Barron's* (https://www.barrons.com/market-data/market-lab). Data for the 90-day Treasury Rate and Moody's AAA Bond Rate are quite important for tracking short- and long-term interest rates. These figures are available from:

Weekly U.S. Financial Data
Federal Reserve Bank of St. Louis
P.O. Box 442
St. Louis, MO 63166
https://fred.stlouisfed.org/

Monthly Indicator Data. The purpose of the first three columns is to enable you to track the market's bullish bias near the end, beginning and middle of the month, which has been shifting lately (see pages 86, 147 and 148). Market direction, performance of your stocks, gross domestic product, prime rate, trade deficit, Consumer Price Index, and unemployment rate are worthwhile indicators to follow. Or, readers may wish to gauge other data.

PORTFOLIO AT END OF 2022

DATE ACQUIRED	NO. OF SHARES	SECURITY	PRICE	TOTAL COST	PAPER PROFITS	PAPER LOSSES

IF YOU DON'T PROFIT FROM YOUR INVESTMENT MISTAKES, SOMEONE ELSE WILL

No matter how much we may deny it, almost every successful person on Wall Street pays a great deal of attention to trading suggestions—especially when they come from "the right sources."

One of the hardest things to learn is to distinguish between good tips and bad ones. Usually, the best tips have a logical reason behind them, which accompanies the tip. Poor tips usually have no reason to support them.

The important thing to remember is that the market discounts. It does not review, it does not reflect. The Street's real interest in "tips," inside information, buying and selling suggestions and everything else of this kind emanates from a desire to find out just what the market has on hand to discount. The process of finding out involves separating the wheat from the chaff—and there is plenty of chaff.

HOW TO MAKE USE OF STOCK "TIPS"

- The source should be **reliable**. (By listing all "tips" and suggestions on a Performance Record of Recommendations, such as the form below, and then periodically evaluating the outcomes, you will soon know the "batting average" of your sources.)

- The story should make sense. Would the merger violate antitrust laws? Are there too many computers on the market already? How many years will it take to become profitable?

- The stock should not have had a recent sharp run-up. Otherwise, the story may already be discounted, and confirmation or denial in the press would most likely be accompanied by a sell-off in the stock.

PERFORMANCE RECORD OF RECOMMENDATIONS

STOCK RECOMMENDED	BY WHOM	DATE	PRICE	REASON FOR RECOMMENDATION	SUBSEQUENT ACTION OF STOCK

INDIVIDUAL RETIREMENT ACCOUNT (IRA): MOST AWESOME MASS INVESTMENT INCENTIVE EVER DEVISED

MAX IRA INVESTMENTS OF $6,000* A YEAR COMPOUNDED AT VARIOUS INTEREST RATES OF RETURN FOR DIFFERENT PERIODS

Annual Rate	5 Yrs	10 Yrs	15 Yrs	20 Yrs	25 Yrs	30 Yrs	35 Yrs	40 Yrs	45 Yrs	50 Yrs
1%	$30,912	$63,401	$97,547	$133,435	$171,154	$210,796	$252,461	$296,251	$342,275	$390,647
2%	31,849	67,012	105,836	148,700	196,025	248,277	305,966	369,660	439,983	517,626
3%	32,810	70,847	114,941	166,059	225,318	294,016	373,656	465,980	573,009	697,085
4%	33,798	74,918	124,947	185,815	259,870	349,970	459,590	592,959	755,223	952,643
5%	34,811	79,241	135,945	208,316	300,681	418,565	569,018	761,039	1,006,111	1,318,892
6%	35,852	83,830	148,035	233,956	348,938	502,810	708,725	984,286	1,353,049	1,846,536
7%	36,920	88,702	161,328	263,191	406,059	606,438	887,481	1,281,657	1,834,511	2,609,916
8%	38,016	93,873	175,946	296,538	473,726	734,075	1,116,613	1,678,686	2,504,556	3,718,031
9%	39,140	99,362	192,020	334,587	553,944	891,451	1,410,748	2,209,751	3,439,116	5,330,646
10%	40,294	105,187	209,698	378,015	649,091	1,085,661	1,788,761	2,921,111	4,744,772	7,681,796
11%	41,477	111,369	229,140	427,591	761,993	1,325,479	2,274,986	3,874,962	6,571,013	11,114,016
12%	42,691	117,927	250,520	484,192	896,004	1,621,756	2,900,779	5,154,854	9,127,306	16,128,123
13%	43,936	124,886	274,030	548,820	1,055,101	1,987,891	3,706,496	6,872,915	12,706,836	23,455,458
14%	45,213	132,267	299,882	622,611	1,243,996	2,440,422	4,744,037	9,179,452	17,719,463	34,162,526
15%	46,522	140,096	328,305	706,861	1,468,272	2,999,742	6,080,074	12,275,723	24,737,386	49,802,242
16%	47,865	148,397	359,550	803,043	1,734,530	3,690,970	7,800,162	16,430,870	34,558,306	72,632,115
17%	49,241	157,200	393,893	912,831	2,050,576	4,545,023	10,013,967	22,004,343	48,292,620	105,928,302
18%	50,652	166,531	431,634	1,038,126	2,425,633	5,599,912	12,861,893	29,475,548	67,483,566	154,436,703
19%	52,098	176,421	473,101	1,181,085	2,870,583	6,902,325	16,523,486	39,482,979	94,272,449	225,019,501
20%	53,580	186,903	518,653	1,344,154	3,398,264	8,509,547	21,228,056	52,875,776	131,625,432	327,579,773

* At press time—2021 contribution limit will be indexed to inflation.

G. M. LOEB'S "BATTLE PLAN" FOR INVESTMENT SURVIVAL

LIFE IS CHANGE: Nothing can ever be the same a minute from now as it was a minute ago. Everything you own is changing in price and value. You can find that last price of an active security on the stock ticker, but you cannot find the next price anywhere. The value of your money is changing. Even the value of your home is changing, though no one walks in front of it with a sandwich board consistently posting the changes.

RECOGNIZE CHANGE: Your basic objective should be to profit from change. The art of investing is being able to recognize change and to adjust investment goals accordingly.

WRITE THINGS DOWN: You will score more investment success and avoid more investment failures if you write things down. Very few investors have the drive and inclination to do this.

KEEP A CHECKLIST: If you aim to improve your investment results, get into the habit of keeping a checklist on every issue you consider buying. Before making a commitment, it will pay you to write down the answers to at least some of the basic questions—How much am I investing in this company? How much do I think I can make? How much do I have to risk? How long do I expect to take to reach my goal?

HAVE A SINGLE RULING REASON: Above all, writing things down is the best way to find "the ruling reason." When all is said and done, there is invariably a single reason that stands out above all others, why a particular security transaction can be expected to show a profit. All too often, many relatively unimportant statistics are allowed to obscure this single important point.

Any one of a dozen factors may be the point of a particular purchase or sale. It could be a technical reason—an increase in earnings or dividend not yet discounted in the market price—a change of management—a promising new product—an expected improvement in the market's valuation of earnings—or many others. But, in any given case, one of these factors will almost certainly be more important than all the rest put together.

CLOSING OUT A COMMITMENT: If you have a loss, the solution is automatic, provided you decide what to do at the time you buy. Otherwise, the question divides itself into two parts. Are we in a bull or bear market? Few of us really know until it is too late. For the sake of the record, if you think it is a bear market, just put that consideration first and sell as much as your conviction suggests and your nature allows.

If you think it is a bull market, or at least a market where some stocks move up, some mark time and only a few decline, do not sell unless:

- ✓ You see a bear market ahead.
- ✓ You see trouble for a particular company in which you own shares.
- ✓ Time and circumstances have turned up a new and seemingly far better buy than the issue you like least in your list.
- ✓ Your shares stop going up and start going down.

A subsidiary question is, which stock to sell first? Two further observations may help:

- ✓ Do not sell solely because you think a stock is "overvalued."
- ✓ If you want to sell some of your stocks and not all, in most cases it is better to go against your emotional inclinations and sell first the issues with losses, small profits or none at all, the weakest, the most disappointing and so on.

Mr. Loeb is the author of *The Battle for Investment Survival*, John Wiley & Sons.

G. M. LOEB'S INVESTMENT SURVIVAL CHECKLIST

OBJECTIVES AND RISKS

Security			Price	Shares	Date

"Ruling reason" for commitment	Amount of commitment
	$_____
	% of my investment capital
	_____ %

Price objective	Est. time to achieve it	I will risk	Which would be
		_____ points	$_____

TECHNICAL POSITION

Price action of stock:	Dow Jones Industrial Average
❏ Hitting new highs ❏ In a trading range	
❏ Pausing in an uptrend ❏ Moving up from low ground	Trend of market
❏ Acting stronger than market ❏ _____	

SELECTED YARDSTICKS

	Price Range		Earnings Per Share Actual or Projected	Price/Earnings Ratio Actual or Projected
	High	Low		
Current year				
Previous year				
Merger possibilities			Years for earnings to double in past	
Comment on future			Years for market price to double in past	

PERIODIC RECHECKS

Date	Stock Price	DJIA	Comment	Action taken, if any

COMPLETED TRANSACTIONS

Date closed	Period of time held	Profit or loss

Reason for profit or loss

NOTES

NOTES

NOTES

NOTES